Discovering the American Past

SIXTH EDITION

Discovering the American Past

A Look at the Evidence

VOLUME I: TO 1877

William Bruce Wheeler
University of Tennessee

Susan D. Becker
University of Tennessee, Emerita

Houghton Mifflin Company   Boston   New York

Publisher: Charles Hartford
Senior Sponsoring Editor: Sally Constable
Development Editor: Lisa Kalner Williams
Senior Project Editor: Christina Horn
Editorial Assistant: Kristen Truncellito
Senior Art and Design Coordinator: Jill Haber
Senior Photo Editor: Jennifer Meyer Dare
Composition Buyer: Chuck Dutton
Associate Strategic Buyer: Brian Pieragostini
Senior Marketing Manager: Sandra McGuire
Market Specialist: Molly Parke

Cover image: The logbook of an American whaling captain, recording the incredible catch of eleven whales in a single day. The two tails are the ones that got away. On top rests a carved whale's tooth, or scrimshaw, dated 1835. At the National Museum of American History, Washington, D.C.

Cover photograph: © Michael Freeman.

Printed in the U.S.A.

Library of Congress Control Number: 2005935018

Instructor's exam copy:
ISBN 13: 978-0-618-73254-8
ISBN 10: 0-618-73254-3

For orders, use student text ISBNs:
ISBN 13: 978-0-618-52259-0
ISBN 10: 0-618-52259-X

5 6 7 8 9-CRS-09 08

Contents

Contents

CHAPTER **6**

Land, Growth, and Justice: The Removal of the Cherokees

Contents

Preface

During the July 4 weekend of 2005, motion picture studios, investors, and producers were frantic. For almost two years attendance at movie theaters had been in a noticeable decline. By mid-2005 the slump was the worst in almost twenty years. At the same time, television executives were in a panic. In spite of the enormous number of choices via network, cable, and satellite dish offerings, television viewership too was down.

In the midst of these disturbing statistics (disturbing at least for motion picture and television executives), more Americans than ever before were *reading*—reading everything from Harry Potter novels to books about America's past. Anticipating the three hundredth anniversary of the birth of Benjamin Franklin in 2006, readers gobbled up first-rate biographies penned by Edmund Morgan, Walter Isaacson, and Gordon Wood. David McCullough and the late Shelby Foote became celebrities for their historical studies. In fact, McCullough's latest book, *1776* (Simon & Schuster, 2005), was the cover story in the May 23, 2005, issue of *Newsweek;* the newsmagazine claimed that McCullough's books "have become the most widely ready nonfiction of the age."[1] And McCullough's work is not alone: Edmund Morgan's *Benjamin Franklin* (Yale University Press, 2002), a more traditionally scholarly work, sold over 170,000 copies as of September 2005.[2]

In all, those cynical men and women who a few years ago accused Americans of no longer being readers joyously retracted their warnings of reading's demise. The American public was reading again, and history books were being purchased and consumed by more people than ever.

How can we account for this welcome phenomenon? It is possible that, in the midst of a tangled and confusing era fraught with both domestic and foreign challenges and dangers, Americans were seeking in their collective past the origins of their own contemporary greatness—and difficulties. As educator Diane Ravitch put it in a 2001 address to the New Jersey Council for History Education, "we study history because it provides us with knowledge, vocabulary, idioms, and language in which to make connections between the

1. *Newsweek,* May 23, 2005. The newsmagazine also published a short excerpt of *1776,* thus making it immediately available even before the book's publication to its readers.
2. Figures given to authors by Yale University Press, September 2005.

past, the present and the future."[3] Putting Ravitch's theory into practice, many readers have returned to the dark and uncertain days of America's own struggle for independence and survival or to its agonizing Civil War, to snatch the kernels of their past vision and strength that they surely need to navigate the treacherous road ahead. Others have returned to their own past to see how Americans dealt with civil rights, imperialism, government propaganda, diversity, gender issues, and so forth. In short, American readers were coming to see history as not only entertaining but also important in their efforts to understand themselves—where they had come from, where they were at present, and where they might be going.

As with previous editions, we began this book with an urgent desire to tap into the interest students have in the past and a firm belief that the study of American history can contribute to an understanding of the contemporary world. *Discovering the American Past* does this in two important ways: (1) putting the present in perspective by giving us an appreciation of the trends, forces, and people who served to shape present-day American life; and (2) teaching us the skills we need to examine and analyze our present environment and culture. Our goals, therefore, are to increase students' interest in historical issues and to help them develop and sharpen the critical skills they will need to live in today's world.

In order to truly appreciate both the writings about the past as well as the people, events, and epochs of the past itself, these students of history have to go to the evidence—the "raw material" of history that historians like McCullough, Morgan, Isaacson, Wood, and others use to attempt to reconstruct the past. *Discovering the American Past* is intended to help those interested in history to find, assess, arrange, and use such historical evidence. We aim to provide an engaging mixture of types of primary sources, ranging from the more traditional sources such as letters, newspapers, public documents, speeches, and oral reminiscences to the less traditional sources such as photographs, architecture, statistics, art, films, and cartoons. We also establish a healthy balance among political, social, diplomatic, intellectual, economic, and cultural history. As much as possible, we have tried "to let the evidence speak for itself" and have avoided (we hope) leading students toward one particular interpretation or another. In this book, then, we have created a kind of historical sampler that we believe will help students learn the methods and skills all educated people must be able to use, as well as help them learn the historical content. Over the years, we have found this approach to be effective

3. See Diane Ravitch, "Obstacles to Teaching History Today," excerpts from a speech delivered to the New Jersey Council for History Education on March 15, 2001, and published in *History Matters!* 13 (June 2001), pp. 1, 6–7.

in many different classroom situations, including seminars, small classes, and large lecture classes.

Format of the Book

Each chapter is divided into six parts: The Problem, Background, The Method, The Evidence, Questions to Consider, and Epilogue. Each of these parts builds upon the others, creating a uniquely integrated chapter structure that helps guide the reader through the analytical process. "The Problem" section begins with a brief discussion of the central issues of the chapter and then states the questions students will explore. A "Background" section follows, designed to help students understand the historical context of the problem. The section called "The Method" gives students suggestions for studying and analyzing the evidence. "The Evidence" section is the heart of the chapter, providing a variety of primary source material on the particular historical event or issue described in the chapter's "Problem" section. "Questions to Consider," the section that follows, focuses students' attention on specific evidence and on linkages among different evidence material. The "Epilogue" section gives the aftermath or the historical outcome of the evidence—what happened to the people involved, who won an election, how a debate ended, and so on.

Changes in the Sixth Edition

Each chapter in this edition has had to pass three important screening groups: (1) the authors (and some of our graduate students) who used the chapters to teach our students, (2) student evaluators who used *Discovering the American Past* in class, and (3) instructors who either used the book or read and assessed the new and revised chapters. With advice from our screeners, we have made the following alterations that we believe will make *Discovering the American Past* even more useful and contemporary: For example, Volume I contains three entirely new chapters: Chapter 9, "The Diplomacy, Politics, and Intrigue of 'Manifest Destiny': The Annexation of Texas"; Chapter 10, "'No More Pint o' Salt for Me': The Port Royal Experiment, 1861–1865"; and Chapter 11, "The Reconstruction Era: Farmers and Workers in the West and North, 1866–1877." Chapter 3 now focuses entirely on the Chesapeake Bay colonies and on the evolution of the slave-based plantation system. Chapters 1 and 6 both have incorporated more Native American voices. Chapter 4 includes more evidence from the 1770 trial of Captain Thomas Preston. Chapters 2, 5, 7, and 8 have been revised to reflect the most recent scholarship.

Volume II offers two completely new chapters—Chapter 4, "Progressives and the Family: The Redefinition of Childhood, 1880–1920," and Chapter 8, "Going to War with Japan: A Problem in Diplomacy and Causation"—in addition to "The Reconstruction Era: Farmers and Workers in the West and North, 1866–1877." Chapter 2 has added an additional focus on African American manhood. Chapter 3 offers a more precise selection of material artifacts. Chapter 5 has sharpened its treatment of government-initiated propaganda. Chapter 10 connects Vietnam with more recent U.S. military operations in Bosnia, Somalia, Afghanistan, and Iraq. Finally, significant new material has been provided in Chapters 6, 7, 9, and 11, the last one addressing the issue of post-9/11 immigration.

Instructor's Resource Manual

Because we value the teaching of American history and yet fully understand how difficult it is to do well, we have written our own Instructor's Resource Manual to accompany *Discovering the American Past*. In this manual, we explain our specific content and skills objectives for each chapter. In addition, we include an expanded discussion of the method and evidence sections. We also answer some of students' frequently asked questions about the material in each problem. Our suggestions for teaching and evaluating student learning draw not only upon our own experiences but also upon the experiences of those of you who have shared your classroom ideas with us. Finally, we wrote updated bibliographic essays for each problem.

Acknowledgments

We would like to thank all the students and instructors who have helped us in developing and refining our ideas for this edition. We are also appreciative of Ms. Mary Ann Bright, who assisted in the preparation of the manuscript. At Houghton Mifflin, we are especially grateful for the hard work and encouragement of Lisa Kalner Williams and Christina Horn, professional in every sense of the word. Finally we are indebted to colleagues at both our own and at other institutions who reviewed the manuscript and made significant contributions to this edition: Stephen V. Ash, University of Tennessee; Thomas J. Brown, University of South Carolina; John Davies, University of Delaware; Matthew Dennis, University of Oregon; Todd M. Kerstetter, Texas Christian University; Michael L. Krenn, Appalachian State University; Lorraine M. Lees, Old Dominion University; Margaret A. Lowe, Bridgewater State College; Pamela Riney-Kehrberg, Iowa State University; and Matthew C. Whitaker, Arizona State University.

Over the years, former students have written to us to express their appreciation for the knowledge and skills they learned from this book. It is we, however, who have learned at least as much from them: that most students do not want to be just silent note-takers but rather *active participants* in their own educations and their own world. We dedicate this edition to them, as well as to students of the present and future who will learn that lesson.

W. B. W.
S. D. B.

1

First Encounters: The Confrontation Between Cortés and Montezuma (1519–1521)

The Problem

Within a few years of Christopher Columbus's claim that he had reached the Indies, most Europeans came to realize that he had been mistaken. Instead of reaching the Indies as he claimed, Columbus had stumbled across what to Europeans was a new land populated by strange, new people.[1] And although the discovery, exploration, exploitation, and ultimately colonization of the "New World" was but one aspect of European expansion in the fifteenth–seventeenth centuries, in the end it was that aspect that would have the most significant effect on world history.

Europeans became increasingly fascinated with the New World and its inhabitants. Explorers' accounts were published and widely circulated, as were artistic renderings of the Indians by European artists, many of whom had never traveled to the New World or met a single Indian.

In turn, Native Americans doubtless recorded their own impressions of Europeans. Because most Indian cultures had not developed forms of writing, these impressions were preserved orally, largely through stories and songs. In central Mexico, however, the Aztecs and other peoples did record their observations of Europeans in writing and art. And although the Spanish *conquistadores* (conquerors) attempted to destroy all such records, a few of the written and artistic renderings have survived to tell the Indians' side of the story of the first encounters.

There is little doubt that the impressions created by these written and artistic works fostered perceptions that made Indian-white relations confusing, difficult, and ultimately tragic. The European hunger for land and treasure as well as for a forced labor supply may

---

1. Although Europeans quickly realized that the name Columbus conferred on Native Americans was inaccurate, the word *Indian* continued to be used. Alternative names have never replaced it.

✦ CHAPTER 1

First Encounters:
The Confrontation
Between Cortés
and Montezuma
(1519–1521)

have made the tragedies that followed almost inevitable, and yet Europeans' early perceptions of Indians were an important factor in how explorers and early colonists dealt with Native American peoples and, in the end, subdued them. At the same time, the early impressions that Indians gained of Europeans (whether passed down orally or by other means) offered to many Native Americans a clear message concerning how they should respond to white encroachment.

In this chapter, you will be concentrating on the conquest of Mexico by Hernando Cortés, which took place between 1519 and 1521. In many ways, that confrontation was typical of the first encounters between Europeans and Native Americans. You will be examining and analyzing two separate sets of evidence: (1) selections written by Cortés to King Charles I of Spain, together with some artistic representations of Native Americans by European artists, and (2) selected written and artistic impressions of Cortés and his *conquistadores* by Aztecs and other Native Americans of central Mexico, created within a few years of the events they described. Your task is twofold. First, you must use written and artistic accounts to determine the impressions that each side formed of the other. Second, you must reach some conclusions about how those impressions (whether totally accurate or inaccurate) might have influenced how Europeans and

early colonists dealt with Native Americans and how Native Americans dealt with them.

Before you begin, we would like to issue a note of caution. When dealing with the evidence provided by European conquerors such as Cortés or by European artists, you will *not* be trying to determine what the Native Americans the Europeans encountered were really like but only what Cortés and selected European artists perceived them to be like. To find out what the diverse peoples collectively known as Indians were really like, you would have to consult the works of archaeologists, cultural anthropologists, and cultural geographers. And yet, if we want to determine how Europeans perceived Indians, Cortés's letters and selected European works of art can provide excellent clues.

This chapter also will give you a revealing look at how historical evidence is created and how the availability—and unavailability—of that evidence influences the ways in which a past event or person is depicted by historians. For example, Cortés and his soldiers attempted to destroy as many of the Native American historical records as they could, for obvious reasons. But some pieces of that evidence survived. Without those pieces of evidence, historians' accounts of the first encounters very likely would be dramatically different.

Background

By the time Europeans first encountered the various peoples they collectively called Indians, Native Americans had inhabited the Western Hemisphere for approximately 20,000 to 40,000 years.[2] Although there is considerable disagreement about when these people first appeared in the Americas, it is reasonable to assume that they first migrated to the Western Hemisphere sometime in the middle of the Pleistocene Age. During that period, roughly from 75,000 to 8000 B.C.E., huge glaciers covered a large portion of North America, the ice cap extending southward to the approximate present border of the United States and Canada. These glaciers, which in some places were more than 9,000 feet thick, interrupted the water cycle because moisture falling as rain or snow was caught by the glaciers and frozen and was thus prevented from draining back into the seas or evaporating into the atmosphere.

This process lowered ocean levels 250 to 300 feet, exposing a natural land bridge spanning the Bering Strait (between present-day Alaska and the former Soviet Union) across which people from Asia could easily migrate, probably in search of game. It is probable that various peoples from Asia did exactly that and then followed an ice-free corridor along the base of the Rocky Mountains southward into the more temperate areas of the American Southwest and then either eastward into other areas of North America or even farther southward into Central and South America. Recent discoveries suggest that other migrants may have arrived by a sea route. These migrations took thousands of years, and some Indian peoples were still moving when Europeans first encountered them.

About 8000 B.C.E., the glacial cap began to retreat fairly rapidly, raising ocean levels to approximately their present-day levels and cutting off further migration from Asia, thus isolating America's first human inhabitants from other peoples for thousands of years. This isolation was almost surely the cause of the inhabitants' extraordinarily high susceptibility to the diseases that Europeans later brought with them, such as measles, tuberculosis, and smallpox, to which the peoples of other continents had built up natural resistance. The glacial retreat also caused large portions of the American Southwest to become hot and arid, thus scattering Indian peoples in almost all directions. Nevertheless, for thousands of years a strong oral tradition enabled Indians to preserve stories of their origins and subsequent isolation. Almost all Indian peoples retained accounts of a long migration from the west and of a flood.

The original inhabitants of the Western Hemisphere obtained their food principally by hunting and gathering, killing mammoths, huge bison, deer, elk, antelope, camels, horses, and other

2. Other estimates run as high as 70,000 years. Whatever the case, it is almost certain that Indians were not native to the Western Hemisphere because no subhuman remains have ever been found.

✦ CHAPTER 1

First Encounters:
The Confrontation
Between Cortés
and Montezuma
(1519–1521)

game with stone weapons and picking wild fruits and grasses. Beginning about 5000 B.C.E., however, Indians in present-day Mexico began practicing agriculture. By the time Europeans arrived, most Indians were domesticating plants and raising crops, although their levels of agricultural sophistication were extremely diverse.

The development of agriculture, which occurred about the same time in Europe and in the Americas, profoundly affected Indian life. Those peoples who adopted agriculture abandoned their nomadic ways and lived in settled villages (some of the Central American ones became magnificent cities). This more sedentary life permitted them to erect permanent housing, create and preserve pottery and art, and establish more complex political and social institutions. Agriculture also led to a sexual division of labor, with women planting, raising, and harvesting crops and men hunting to supplement their villages' diets with game. With more and better food, it is likely that Indian populations grew more rapidly, thus furthering the need for more complex political and social structures. The development of agriculture also affected these peoples' religious beliefs and ceremonies, increasing the homage to sun and rain gods who could bring forth good harvests. Contact with other Indian peoples led to trading, a practice with which Indians were quite familiar by the time of European intrusion.

Those Indian cultures that made the transition from food gathering to food producing often attained an impressive degree of economic, political, social, and technological sophistication. In Central America, the Mayas of present-day Mexico and Guatemala built great cities, fashioned elaborate gold and silver jewelry, devised a form of writing, were proficient in mathematics and astronomy, and constructed a calendar that could predict solar eclipses and was more accurate than any system in use in Europe at the time.

Around the year 1200 C.E., several Nahuatl-speaking tribes from the north began to drift into central Mexico. Collectively known to modern scholars as Aztecs (a designation these people never used), these tribesmen ultimately overthrew the Mayas, built on Mayan achievements, and extended their political and economic power either by assimilating other groups or by conquering and subjugating them. by 1428 it was possible to refer to an Aztec empire in central Mexico that by the time of Cortés's arrival contained approximately one million people.

In 1325 the growing empire's capital, Tenochtitlán (pronounced tay-NAWCH-teet LAHN), was founded. At its height the city contained magnificent pyramids and public buildings, a fresh water supply brought to the capital by complex engineering, causeways that connected the island city to other islands and the mainland, a complex economy with a vast trading network, and even a compulsory education system for both boys and girls (no state in the United States would have such a system for more than three hundred years). Raw materials and treasure flowed into Tenochtitlán from all over the Aztec empire, which stretched from the Pacific Ocean to the Gulf of Mexico and from central Mexico to present-day Guatemala. Little wonder that the *conquistadores* with Hernando Cortés were awed and enchanted when they saw this city of approximately three hundred thousand people.

In many ways, Cortés was the typical Spanish *conquistador*. Born in 1485 to a respected but poor family (his father had been a career military officer but never rose above the rank of captain), Cortés spent two unsuccessful years studying for the law. Abandoning that goal, he became a soldier and was determined to gain fame and fortune through a military career. In 1504, when he was only nineteen years old, he boarded a ship bound for the Spanish possessions in the New World. After fourteen years of military service, Cortés finally got his big break in 1518, when he was chosen to command a new armada, the purpose of which was to conquer Mexico. Earlier, unsuccessful expeditions had given some indications of gold in Mexico, and Cortés was sent to find it as well as to try to locate members of the earlier expeditions who might still be alive. Because Cortés himself financed a good portion of the new armada (he had to borrow money to do so), he had the opportunity to realize his dreams of wealth if his men found treasure. When Cortés landed at Vera Cruz, he was thirty-four years old.

◆

The Method

In this chapter, you will be working with two distinct types of evidence: (1) written accounts and (2) artistic representations. In addition, the evidence has been divided into two sets: (1) Hernando Cortés's and European artists' perceptions of Indians and (2) Indians' written and artistic accounts of Cortés's invasion of the Aztec capital, Tenochtitlán (1519–1521). As noted previously, Cortés's account comes from letters he wrote to the Spanish king soon after the events he described took place. As for the European artists, some of them undoubtedly used their active imaginations to construct their images of Indians, whereas others relied on explorers' accounts or word-of-mouth reports from those who had seen Native Americans whom the explorers had brought to Europe.

The Indians' accounts of Europeans pose something of a problem. To begin with, only twelve documents (songs, codices,[3] paintings) and approximately eighty pictographs[4] survive, some of them produced decades after the events they describe and almost surely not by eyewitnesses. For example, the Florentine Codex is unquestionably the most complete account of the Spanish conquest. Yet that document was not prepared until 1585, and then by Franciscan friar Bernardino de Sahagun, who produced the codex from memory after the 1555 original (in the Nahuatl language) and a Spanish translation by Sahagun both were lost. The Aztec accounts in the Evidence section of this chapter are from the Florentine Codex,

3. Codex (pl. codices): manuscript.
4. Pictures made using hieroglyphic symbols.

✦ CHAPTER 1

First Encounters:
The Confrontation
Between Cortés
and Montezuma
(1519–1521)

some other written fragments, and a song that was composed around 1523.

And yet, even though the writers (like Bernardino de Sahagun) and artists might not have been eyewitnesses themselves, it is highly possible that they knew of eyewitnesses who could have reported to them what they experienced or saw. Thanks to Roman Catholic missionaries who preserved these accounts, we have what we can assume are firsthand reactions by Native Americans to European intruders.

Even so, the Native American accounts of Cortés's conquest pose some problems for historians. In addition to the difficulty that Native American place and people names present to non-Indians who attempt to pronounce them, it is not always clear in these accounts precisely what is being described. For example, the Native Americans at first believed that Cortés and his party were some form of god ("As for their food, it is like human food."), which explains their sacrifices before Cortés, their offering of gifts, and their preparations to "celebrate their god's fiesta." Precisely when they abandoned this notion is unclear, for at the same time that they were conducting their celebration, they simultaneously posted guards at the Eagle Gate. It will take some care and thought to determine exactly what was taking place.

Also, occasionally historical evidence can be contradictory. For instance, Cortés claimed that he attacked the Aztecs only after learning that they were plotting to kill him and his men. Yet the Native American account suggests that no such plot existed and that Cortés's attack was unprovoked. Can you determine from the accounts which explanation is the more nearly correct? Read carefully through both Cortés's and the Native American accounts, and you will see that determining what actually happened is not so difficult as it first appears to be. Also, you will see that both Cortés and the Native American chroniclers occasionally describe the same events, which can make for some fascinating comparisons.

The two types of evidence in this chapter (written accounts and artistic representations) must be dealt with differently. As you read the written accounts, think of some adjectives that Europeans who read Cortés's letters, some of which were published and widely distributed, might have used to describe Indians. For the Native American written accounts, imagine what adjectives Native Americans who shared the accounts might have used to describe Europeans. How do those adjectives present a collective image of Indians? Of Europeans? How do the stories each author tells reinforce that image? As you read each written account, make a list of adjectives for each set of evidence, then combine them to form a collective image. Be willing to read between the lines. Sometimes, for example, Cortés may simply have been trying to explain a specific incident or practice of the Indians. Yet, intentionally or unintentionally, he was creating an image in the minds of readers. Be equally cautious and sensitive when reading the Indians' written accounts.

The second type of evidence, artistic representations, is quite different from the first. If you think of art as words made into pictures, you will see that you can approach this type of evidence as you did the written accounts. Study each picture carefully, looking especially for how Native Americans or Europeans are portrayed. How are they portrayed physically? How is their supposed nature or character portrayed in their behavior in the works of art? Again, as with the written accounts, create a list of adjectives and deduce the images Europeans would have had of Indians and the images Indians would have had of Europeans. As you analyze the evidence in this chapter, keep two central questions in mind: (1) What images do the written and artistic accounts create of Native Americans and of Europeans? (2) In what ways might those images or impressions have influenced how European explorers and early colonists dealt with Native Americans and how Native Americans dealt with them?

The Evidence

EUROPEAN ACCOUNTS

Source 1 from Francis Augustus MacNutt, *Fernando Cortés: His Five Letters of Relation to the Emperor Charles V* (Cleveland: Arthur H. Clark Co., 1908), Vol. I, pp. 161–166, 211–216.

1. Selections from Cortés's First Letter to King Charles I of Spain, July 10, 1519.

According to our judgment, it is credible that there is everything in this country which existed in that from whence Solomon is said to have brought the gold for the Temple, but, as we have been here so short a time, we have not been able to see more than the distance of five leagues inland, and about ten or twelve leagues of the coast length on each side, which we have explored since we landed; although from the sea it must be more, and we saw much more while sailing.

The people who inhabit this country, from the Island of Cozumel, and the Cape of Yucatan to the place where we now are, are a people of middle size, with bodies and features well proportioned, except that in each province their customs differ, some piercing the ears, and putting large and ugly objects in them, and others piercing the nostrils down to the mouth, and putting in large round stones like mirrors, and others piercing their under lips down as far as their gums, and hanging from them large round stones, or pieces of gold, so weighty that they pull down the nether lip, and make it appear very

[7]

◆ CHAPTER 1

First Encounters:
The Confrontation
Between Cortés
and Montezuma
(1519–1521)

deformed. The clothing which they wear is like long veils, very curiously worked. The men wear breech-cloths about their bodies, and large mantles, very thin, and painted in the style of Moorish draperies. The women of the ordinary people wear, from their waists to their feet, clothes also very much painted, some covering their breasts and leaving the rest of the body uncovered. The superior women, however, wear very thin shirts of cotton, worked and made in the style of *rochets* [blouses with long, straight sleeves]. Their food is maize and grain, as in the other Islands, and *potuyuca,* as they eat it in the Island of Cuba, and they eat it broiled, since they do not make bread of it; and they have their fishing, and hunting, and they roast many chickens, like those of the Tierra Firma, which are as large as peacocks.[5]

There are some large towns well laid out, the houses being of stone, and mortar when they have it. The apartments are small, low, and in the Moorish style, and, when they cannot find stone, they make them of adobes, whitewashing them, and the roof is of straw. Some of the houses of the principal people are very cool, and have many apartments, for we have seen more than five courts in one house, and the apartments very well distributed, each principal department of service being separate. Within them they have their wells and reservoirs for water, and rooms for the slaves and dependents, of whom they have many. Each of these chiefs has at the entrance of his house, but outside of it, a large court-yard, and in some there are two and three and four very high buildings, with steps leading up to them, and they are very well built; and in them they have their mosques[6] and prayer places, and very broad galleries on all sides, and there they keep the idols which they worship, some being of stone, some of gold, and some of wood, and they honour and serve them in such wise, and with so many ceremonies, that much paper would be required to give Your Royal Highnesses an entire and exact description of all of them. These houses and mosques, wherever they exist, are the largest and best built in the town, and they keep them very well adorned, decorated with feather-work and well-woven stuffs, and with all manner of ornaments. Every day, before they undertake any work, they burn incense in the said mosques, and sometimes they sacrifice their own persons, some cutting their tongues and others their ears, and some hacking the body with knives; and they offer up to their idols all the blood which flows, sprinkling it on all sides of those mosques, at other times throwing it up towards the heavens, and practising many other kinds of ceremonies, so that they undertake nothing without first offering sacrifice there.

5. These were turkeys, which were unknown in Europe.
6. Temples.

They have another custom, horrible, and abominable, and deserving punishment, and which we have never before seen in any other place, and it is this, that, as often as they have anything to ask of their idols, in order that their petition may be more acceptable, they take many boys or girls, and even grown men and women, and in the presence of those idols they open their breasts, while they are alive, and take out the hearts and entrails, and burn the said entrails and hearts before the idols, offering that smoke in sacrifice to them. Some of us who have seen this say that it is the most terrible and frightful thing to behold that has ever been seen. So frequently, and so often do these Indians do this, according to our information, and partly by what we have seen in the short time we are in this country, that no year passes in which they do not kill and sacrifice fifty souls in each mosque; and this is practised, and held as customary, from the Isle of Cozumel to the country in which we are now settled. Your Majesties may rest assured that, according to the size of the land, which to us seems very considerable, and the many mosques which they have, there is no year, as far as we have until now discovered and seen, when they do not kill and sacrifice in this manner some three or four thousand souls. Now let Your Royal Highnesses consider if they ought not to prevent so great an evil and crime, and certainly God, Our Lord, will be well pleased, if, through the command of Your Royal Highnesses, these peoples should be initiated and instructed in our Very Holy Catholic Faith, and the devotion, faith, and hope, which they have in their idols, be transferred to the Divine Omnipotence of God; because it is certain, that, if they served God with the same faith, and fervour, and diligence, they would surely work miracles.

It should be believed, that it is not without cause that God, Our Lord, has permitted that these parts should be discovered in the name of Your Royal Highnesses, so that this fruit and merit before God should be enjoyed by Your Majesties, of having instructed these barbarian people, and brought them through your commands to the True Faith. As far as we are able to know them, we believe that, if there were interpreters and persons who could make them understand the truth of the Faith, and their error, many, and perhaps all, would shortly quit the errors which they hold, and come to the true knowledge; because they live civilly and reasonably, better than any of the other peoples found in these parts.

To endeavour to give to Your Majesties all the particulars about this country and its people, might occasion some errors in the account, because much of it we have not seen, and only know it through information given us by the natives; therefore we do not undertake to give more than what may be accepted by Your Highnesses as true. Your Majesties may, if you deem proper,

◆ CHAPTER 1

First Encounters:
The Confrontation
Between Cortés
and Montezuma
(1519–1521)

give this account as true to Our Very Holy Father, in order that diligence and good system may be used in effecting the conversion of these people, because it is hoped that great fruit and much good may be obtained; also that His Holiness may approve and allow that the wicked and rebellious, being first admonished, may be punished and chastised as enemies of Our Holy Catholic Faith, which will be an occasion of punishment and fear to those who may be reluctant in receiving knowledge of the Truth; thereby, that the great evils and injuries they practise in the service of the Devil, will be forsaken. Because, besides what we have just related to Your Majesties about the men, and women, and children, whom they kill and offer in their sacrifices, we have learned, and been positively informed, that they are all sodomites,[7] and given to that abominable sin. In all this, we beseech Your Majesties to order such measures taken as are most profitable to the service of God, and to that of Your Royal Highnesses, and so that we who are here in your service may also be favoured and recompensed. . . .

. . . Along the road we encountered many signs, such as the natives of this province had foretold us, for we found the high road blocked up, and another opened, and some pits, although not many, and some of the city streets were closed, and many stones were piled on the house tops. They thus obliged us to be cautious, and on our guard.

I found there certain messengers from Montezuma, who came to speak with those others who were with me, but to me they said nothing, because, in order to inform their master, they had come to learn what those who were with me had done and agreed with me. These latter messengers departed, therefore, as soon as they had spoken with the first, and even the chief of those who had formerly been with me also left.

During the three days which I remained there I was ill provided for, and every day was worse, and the lords and chiefs of the city came rarely to see and speak to me. I was somewhat perplexed by this, but the interpreter whom I have, an Indian woman of this country whom I obtained in Putunchan, the great river I have already mentioned in the first letter to Your Majesty, was told by another woman native of this city, that many of Montezuma's people had gathered close by, and that those of the city had sent away their wives, and children, and all their goods, intending to fall upon us and kill us all; and that, if she wished to escape, she should go with her, as she would hide her. The female interpreter told it to that Geronimo de Aguilar, the interpreter whom I obtained in Yucatan, and of whom I have written to Your Highness, who reported it to me. I captured one of the natives of the said city, who was

7. People who practice anal or oral copulation with members of the opposite (or same) gender or who have sex with animals.

walking about there, and took him secretly apart so that no one saw it, and questioned him; and he confirmed all that the Indian woman and the natives of Tascaltecal had told me. As well on account of this information as from the signs I had observed, I determined to anticipate them, rather than be surprised, so I had some of the lords of the city called, saying that I wished to speak with them, and I shut them in a chamber by themselves. In the meantime I had our people prepared, so that, at the firing of a musket, they should fall on a crowd of Indians who were near to our quarters, and many others who were inside them. It was done in this wise, that, after I had taken these lords, and left them bound in the chamber, I mounted a horse, and ordered the musket to be fired, and we did such execution that, in two hours, more than three thousand persons had perished.

In order that Your Majesty may see how well prepared they were, before I went out of our quarters, they had occupied all the streets, and stationed all their men, but, as we took them by surprise, they were easily overcome, especially as the chiefs were wanting, for I had already taken them prisoners. I ordered fire to be set to some towers and strong houses, where they defended themselves, and assaulted us; and thus I scoured the city fighting during five hours, leaving our dwelling place which was very strong, well guarded, until I had forced all the people out of the city at various points, in which those five thousand natives of Tascaltecal and the four hundred of Cempoal gave me good assistance.

◆ CHAPTER 1

First Encounters:
The Confrontation
Between Cortés
and Montezuma
(1519–1521)

Sources 2 through 5 from Hugh Honor, *The European Vision of America* (Cleveland: Cleveland Museum of Art, 1975), plates 3, 8, 64, 65. Source 2 photo: The British Library.

2. German Woodcut, 1509.

Source 3: Museo National de Arte Antiga, Lisbon.

3. Portuguese Oil on Panel, 1550.

Source 4: Library of Congress/Rare Book Division.

4. German Engraving, 1590.

✦ CHAPTER 1

First Encounters:
The Confrontation
Between Cortés
and Montezuma
(1519–1521)

Source 5: Library of Congress/Rare Book Division.

5. German Engraving, 1591.

Source 6 from Stefan Lorant, ed., *The New World: The First Pictures of America* (New York: Duell, Sloan & Pearce, 1946), p. 51. Photo: Metropolitan Museum of Art.

6. German Engraving, 1591.

Source 7 from Honor, *The European Vision of America*, plate 91. Photo: New-York Historical Society.

7. French Engraving, 1579–1600.

AMERICA,

◆ CHAPTER 1

First Encounters:
The Confrontation
Between Cortés
and Montezuma
(1519–1521)

NATIVE AMERICAN ACCOUNTS

Sources 8 and 9 from Miguel Leon-Portilla, ed., *The Broken Spears*. Copyright © 1962, 1990 by Miguel Leon-Portilla. Expanded and Updated Edition © 1992 by Miguel Leon-Portilla. Reprinted by permission of Beacon Press, Boston.

8. Cortés's Conquest of Tenochtitlán.

[*The account begins by reciting the eight omens and the eight "wonders" (unique natural occurrences) that foretold the arrival of the Spaniards. Learning of their arrival, Montezuma*[8] *ordered that envoys be sent to greet the Spaniards and bring them gifts.*]

One by one they did reverence to Cortés by touching the ground before him with their lips. They said to him: "If the god will deign to hear us, your deputy Motecuhzoma has sent us to render you homage. He has the City of Mexico in his care. He says: 'The god is weary.'"

Then they arrayed the Captain in the finery they had brought him as presents. With great care they fastened the turquoise mask in place, the mask of the god with its crossband of quetzal[9] feathers. A golden earring hung down on either side of this mask. They dressed him in the decorated vest and the collar woven in the *petatillo* style—the collar of *chalchihuites,* with a disk of gold in the center.

Next they fastened the mirror to his hips, dressed him in the cloak known as "the ringing bell" and adorned his feet with the greaves used by the Huastecas, which were set with *chalchihuites* and hung with little gold bells. In his hand they placed the shield with its fringe and pendant of quetzal feathers, its ornaments of gold and mother-of-pearl. Finally they set before him the pair of black sandals. As for the other objects of divine finery, they only laid them out for him to see.

The Captain asked them: "And is this all? Is this your gift of welcome? Is this how you greet people?"

They replied: "This is all, our lord. This is what we have brought you."

[*When the envoys returned to Tenochtitlán, Montezuma ordered that two prisoners be sacrificed and that their blood be sprinkled onto the envoys, as "they had seen the gods, their eyes had looked on their faces."*]

When the sacrifice was finished, the messengers reported to the king. They told him how they had made the journey, what they had seen, and what food the strangers ate. Motecuhzoma was astonished and terrified by their report, and the description of the strangers' food astonished him above all else.

8. *Montezuma* is the Spanish spelling. Probably closer to the Aztecs' pronunciation would be *Motecuhzoma*. He ascended to the throne in 1502.
9. A type of bird native to Central America. The male has feathers up to two feet in length.

He was also terrified to learn how the cannon roared, how its noise resounded, how it caused one to faint and grow deaf. The messengers told him: "A thing like a ball of stone comes out of its entrails: it comes out shooting sparks and raining fire. The smoke that comes out with it has a pestilent odor, like that of rotten mud. This odor penetrates even to the brain and causes the greatest discomfort. If the cannon is aimed against a mountain, the mountain splits and cracks open. If it is aimed against a tree, it shatters the tree into splinters. This is a most unnatural sight, as if the tree had exploded from within."

The messengers also said: "Their trappings and arms are all made of iron. They dress in iron and wear iron casques[10] on their heads. Their swords are iron; their bows are iron; their shields are iron; their spears are iron. Their deer[11] carry them on their backs wherever they wish to go. These deer, our lord, are as tall as the roof of a house.

"The strangers' bodies are completely covered, so that only their faces can be seen. Their skin is white, as if it were made of lime. They have yellow hair, though some of them have black. Their beards are long and yellow, and their moustaches are also yellow. Their hair is curly, with very fine strands.

"As for their food, it is like human food. It is large and white, and not heavy.[12] It is something like straw, but with the taste of a cornstalk, of the pith of a cornstalk. It is a little sweet, as if it were flavored with honey; it tastes of honey, it is sweet-tasting food.

"Their dogs are enormous, with flat ears and long, dangling tongues. The color of their eyes is a burning yellow; their eyes flash fire and shoot off sparks. Their bellies are hollow, their flanks long and narrow. They are tireless and very powerful. They bound here and there, panting, with their tongues hanging out. And they are spotted like an ocelot."

When Motecuhzoma heard this report, he was filled with terror. It was as if his heart had fainted, as if it had shriveled. It was as if he were conquered by despair. . . .

[*Montezuma then sent a group of magicians to the Spanish, along with more captives to be sacrificed "because the strangers might wish to drink their blood." But the Spanish, predictably, were disgusted. The Spanish then marched toward Tenochtitlán, recruiting allies against Montezuma and destroying those Indians loyal to the emperor. Some Indians brought gifts of gold to appease the Spanish, whose bodies "swelled with greed. . . . They hungered like pigs for the gold." The Spanish finally arrived at the Aztec capital.*]

10. Helmets.
11. Horses.
12. Probably pasta.

✦ CHAPTER 1

First Encounters:
The Confrontation
Between Cortés
and Montezuma
(1519–1521)

When the Spaniards were installed in the palace, they asked Motecuhzoma about the city's resources and reserves and about the warriors' ensigns and shields. They questioned him closely and then demanded gold.

Motecuhzoma guided them to it. They surrounded him and crowded close with their weapons. He walked in the center, while they formed a circle around him.

When they arrived at the treasure house called Teucalco, the riches of gold and feathers were brought out to them: ornaments made of quetzal feathers, richly worked shields, disks of gold, the necklaces of the idols, gold nose plugs, gold greaves[13] and bracelets and crowns.

The Spaniards immediately stripped the feathers from the gold shields and ensigns.[14] They gathered all the gold into a great mound and set fire to everything else, regardless of its value. Then they melted down the gold into ingots. As for the precious green stones, they took only the best of them. . . .

[*As the Spanish arrived in Tenochtitlán, the people were preparing for a festival to honor Huitzilopochtli, the mythical founder of the Aztecs and their principal god.*]

At this moment in the fiesta, when the dance was loveliest and when song was linked to song, the Spaniards were seized with an urge to kill the celebrants. They all ran forward, armed as if for battle. They closed the entrances and passageways, all the gates of the patio: the Eagle Gate in the lesser palace, the Gate of the Canestalk and the Gate of the Serpent of Mirrors. They posted guards so that no one could escape, and then rushed into the Sacred Patio to slaughter the celebrants. They came on foot, carrying their swords and their wooden or metal shields.

They ran in among the dancers, forcing their way to the place where the drums were played. They attacked the man who was drumming and cut off his arms. Then they cut off his head, and it rolled across the floor.

They attacked the celebrants, stabbing them, spearing them, striking them with their swords. They attacked some of them from behind, and these fell instantly to the ground with their entrails hanging out. Others they beheaded: they cut off their heads, or split their heads to pieces.

They struck others in the shoulders, and their arms were torn from their bodies. They wounded some in the thigh and some in the calf. They slashed others in the abdomen, and their entrails all spilled to the ground. Some attempted to run away, but their intestines dragged as they ran; they seemed to tangle their feet in their own entrails. No matter how they tried to save themselves, they could find no escape.

13. Leg armor worn below the knee.
14. Flags or banners.

Some attempted to force their way out, but the Spaniards murdered them at the gates. Others climbed the walls, but they could not save themselves. Those who ran into the communal houses were safe there for a while; so were those who lay down among the victims and pretended to be dead. But if they stood up again, the Spaniards saw them and killed them.

The blood of the warriors flowed like water and gathered into pools. The pools widened, and the stench of blood and entrails filled the air. The Spaniards ran into the communal houses to kill those who were hiding. They ran everywhere and searched everywhere; they invaded every room, hunting and killing.

When the news of this massacre was heard outside the Sacred Patio, a great cry went up: "Mexicanos, come running! Bring your spears and shields! The strangers have murdered our warriors!"

This cry was answered with a roar of grief and anger: the people shouted and wailed and beat their palms against their mouths. The captains assembled at once, as if the hour had been determined in advance. They all carried their spears and shields.

Then the battle began. The Aztecs attacked with javelins and arrows, even with the light spears that are used for hunting birds. They hurled their javelins with all their strength, and the cloud of missiles spread out over the Spaniards like a yellow cloak.

The Spaniards immediately took refuge in the palace. They began to shoot at the Mexicans with their iron arrows and to fire their cannons and arquebuses. And they shackled Motecuhzoma in chains. . . .

Soon after, an epidemic broke out in Tenochtitlán. . . . It began to spread during the thirteenth month and lasted for seventy days, striking everywhere in the city and killing a vast number of our people. Sores erupted on our faces, our breasts, our bellies; we were covered with agonizing sores from head to foot.

The illness was so dreadful that no one could walk or move. The sick were so utterly helpless that they could only lie on their beds like corpses, unable to move their limbs or even their heads. They could not lie face down or roll from one side to the other. If they did move their bodies, they screamed with pain.

A great many died from this plague, and many others died of hunger. They could not get up to search for food, and everyone else was too sick to care for them, so they starved to death in their beds.[15]

Some people came down with a milder form of the disease; they suffered less than the others and made a good recovery. But they could not escape en-

15. The epidemic probably was smallpox.

[19]

✦ CHAPTER 1

First Encounters:
The Confrontation
Between Cortés
and Montezuma
(1519–1521)

tirely. Their looks were ravaged, for wherever a sore broke out, it gouged an ugly pockmark in the skin. And a few of the survivors were left completely blind. . . .

Cuauhtemoc was taken to Cortes along with three other princes. The Captain was accompanied by Pedro de Alvarado and La Malinche.

When the princes were made captives, the people began to leave, searching for a place to stay. Everyone was in tatters, and the women's thighs were almost naked. The Christians searched all the refugees. They even opened the women's skirts and blouses and felt everywhere: their ears, their breasts, their hair. Our people scattered in all directions. They went to neighboring villages and huddled in corners in the houses of strangers.

The city was conquered in the year 3-House. The date on which we departed was the day 1-Serpent in the ninth month. . . .

[The account next describes Cortés's torture of the remaining Aztec leaders in an attempt to find where the Aztecs' treasures were hidden.]

When the envoys from Tlatelolco had departed, the leaders of Tenochtitlán were brought before the Captain, who wished to make them talk. This was when Cuauhtemoc's feet were burned. They brought him in at daybreak and tied him to a stake.

They found the gold in Cuitlahuactonco, in the house of a chief named Itzpotonqui. As soon as they had seized it, they brought our princes—all of them bound—to Coyoacan.

About this same time, the priest in charge of the temple of Huitzilopochtli was put to death. The Spaniards had tried to learn from him where the god's finery and that of the high priests was kept. Later they were informed that it was being guarded by certain chiefs in Cuauhchichilco and Xaltocan. They seized it and then hanged two of the chiefs in the middle of the Mazatlan road. . . .

They hanged Macuilxochitl, the king of Huitzilopochco, in Coyoacan. They also hanged Pizotzin, the king of Culhuacan. And they fed the Keeper of the Black House, along with several others, to their dogs.

And three wise men of Ehecatl, from Tezcoco, were devoured by the dogs. They had come only to surrender; no one brought them or sent them there. They arrived bearing their painted sheets of paper. There were four of them, and only one escaped; the other three were overtaken, there in Coyoacan. . . .

[Here the account describes Cortés's siege of Tenochtitlán, a siege that was successful due in part to bickering among the Aztecs themselves (in which several leaders were put to death), in part to the panic caused by Cortés's cannon, and in part to a number of nearby Indian peoples whom the Aztecs had dominated turning on their former masters and supporting the Spanish. Of course, the devastating smallpox epidemic and general starvation due to the siege also played important roles.]

Broken spears lie in the roads;
We have torn our hair in our grief.
The houses are roofless now, and their walls
are red with blood.

Worms are swarming in the streets and plazas,
and the walls are splattered with gore.
The water has turned red, as if it were dyed,
and when we drink it,
it has the taste of brine.

We have pounded our hands in despair
against the adobe walls,
for our inheritance, our city, is lost and dead.
The shields of our warriors were its defense,
but they could not save it.

We have chewed dry twigs and salt grasses;
we have filled our mouths with dust and bits of adobe;
we have eaten lizards, rats and worms.

9. Song, "Flowers and Songs of Sorrow," c. 1523

Nothing but flowers and songs of sorrow
are left in Mexico and Tlatelolco,
where once we saw warriors and wise men.

We know it is true
that we must perish,
for we are mortal men.
You, the Giver of Life,
you have ordained it.

We wander here and there
in our desolate poverty.
We are mortal men.
We have seen bloodshed and pain
where once we saw beauty and valor.

We are crushed to the ground;
we lie in ruins.
There is nothing but grief and suffering
in Mexico and Tlatelolco,
where once we saw beauty and valor.

Have you grown weary of your servants?
Are you angry with your servants,
O Giver of Life?

Sources 10 through 12 are present-day adaptations of Aztec artistic works that were created not long after the events they depict took place. The modern adaptations can be found in Leon-Portilla, *The Broken Spears*, pp. 21, 82, 143. Illustrations by Alberto Beltran.

10. Native Americans Greet Cortés and His Men.

11. Spanish Response to Native American Greeting.

✦ CHAPTER 1

First Encounters:
The Confrontation
Between Cortés
and Montezuma
(1519–1521)

12. Fate of the Wise Men of Ehecatl.

Questions to Consider

As you read Cortés's account (Source 1), it helps to look for five factors:

1. Physical appearance (bodies, hair, clothing, jewelry, and so on). This description can provide important clues about Cortés's attitude toward the Indians he confronted.
2. Nature or character (childlike, bellicose, cunning, honest, intellectual, lazy, and so on). Be sure to note the examples Cortés used to provide his analysis of the Indians' nature or character.
3. Political, social, and religious practices (behavior of women, ceremonies, eating habits, government, and so on). Descriptions of these practices can provide excellent insight into the explorer's general perception of the Indians he encountered. Be especially sensitive to Cortés's use of descriptive adjectives.
4. Overall impression of the Indians. What was Cortés's collective image or impression?
5. What did Cortés think should be done with the Indians?

Once you have analyzed Cortés's account using points 1 through 4, you should be able to explain how, based on his overall impression of the Indians, he thought the Indians should be dealt with (point 5). Sometimes Cortés comes right out and tells you, but in other cases you will have to use a little imagination. Ask yourself the following question: If I had been living in Spain in 1522 and read Cortés's account, what would my perception of Native Americans have been? Based on that perception, how would I have thought those peoples should be dealt with?

You can handle the artistic representations (Sources 2 through 7) in the same way. Each artist tried to convey his notion of the Indians' nature or character. Some of these impressions are obvious, but others are less so. Think of the art as words made into pictures. How are the Indians portrayed? What are they doing? How are they dealing with Europeans? On the basis of these artistic representations, decide how the various artists believed Indians should be dealt with. For example, Source 4 shows two views of an Indian woman with her child. How are Native Americans depicted in this painting by John White? What ideas or feelings is the painting attempting to elicit in those who saw it? Moreover, how would that perception have affected the artist's—and viewer's—opinion of how Indians should be treated? Follow these steps for all the artistic representations (Sources 2 through 7).

Finally, put together the two types of evidence. Is there more than one "image" of Native Americans? How might each perception have affected the ways Europeans and early colonists dealt with Indians?

On the surface, the Native Americans' perception of Europeans was one-dimensional and is easily discovered: the Aztec writers and artists portrayed Cortés and his men as brutal and sadistic murderers who were driven mad by their lust for gold. Closer examination

✦ CHAPTER 1

First Encounters:
The Confrontation
Between Cortés
and Montezuma
(1519–1521)

of the early section of the written account (Source 8) and of one of the artistic representations (Source 10), however, reveals other perceptions as well. In the written account, when Montezuma's envoys reported back to him, how did they describe the Europeans (you may use points 1 through 4 above)? What was Montezuma's reaction to the report? The other artistic accounts (Sources 11–12) are quite direct, and you should have no difficulty discovering the Indians' overall perception of Europeans. You will, however, have to infer from the accounts how Indians believed Europeans should be dealt with in the future, since none of the written or artistic accounts deals with that question.

✦

Epilogue

In many respects, the encounter between Cortés and the native peoples of Mexico was typical of many first encounters between Europeans and Native Americans. For one thing, the Indian peoples were terribly vulnerable to the numerous diseases that Europeans unwittingly brought with them. Whether warlike or peaceful, millions of Native Americans fell victim to smallpox, measles, and other diseases against which they had no resistance. Whole villages were wiped out and whole nations decimated as (in the words of one Roman Catholic priest who traveled with Cortés) "they died in heaps."

In addition, although the Indians had brave warriors who fought fiercely in hand-to-hand combat, their swords and other weapons were no match for European muskets and cannons. Battles between Indian peoples were often fought to gain captives, most of whom were later sacrificed to the gods. The Spanish, sometimes greatly outnumbered, tried to kill their enemies in battle rather than take captives. By no means passive peoples in what ultimately would become a contest for a hemisphere, Indians nevertheless had not developed the military technology and tactics to hold Europeans permanently at bay.

Nor were the Indians themselves united against their European intruders. All the explorers and early settlers were able to pit one Indian people against another, thus dividing the opposition and in the end conquering them all. In this practice Cortés was particularly adept; he found a number of villages ready to revolt against Montezuma and used those schisms to his advantage. Brief attempts at Indian unity against European intruders generally proved temporary and therefore unsuccessful.

Sometimes the Native Americans' initial misperceptions of Europeans worked to their own disadvantage. As we have seen, some Central American Indians, including the mighty Aztecs, thought Cortés's men were the "white gods" from the east whom prophets predicted would appear. Cortés's actions quickly disabused them of this notion, but by then much damage had been done. In a somewhat similar vein, Indians of the Powhatan Confederacy in Virginia at first thought the Europeans were indolent because they could not grow their own food. Like the Aztecs' misperception, this mistaken image was soon shattered. In sum, Native Americans' perceptions of Europeans often worked against any notions that they were a threat—until it was too late.

Finally, once Europeans had established footholds in the New World, the Indians often undercut their own positions. For one thing, they rarely were able to unite against the Europeans, fractured as they so often were by intertribal conflicts and jealousies. Therefore, Europeans often were able to enlist Indian allies to fight against those Native Americans who opposed them. Also, after the Indians in North America came to recognize the value of European manufactured goods, they increasingly engaged in wholesale hunting and trapping of animals with the skins and furs Europeans wanted in exchange for those goods. Before the arrival of Europeans, Native Americans saw themselves as part of a complete ecosystem that could sustain all life so long as it was kept in balance. In contrast, Europeans saw the environment as a series of commodities to be exploited, a perception that Indians who desired European goods were quickly forced to adopt. Thus not only did the Indians lose their economic and cultural independence, but they also nearly eliminated certain animal species that had sustained them for so

long. An ecological disaster was in the making, driven by the European view of the environment as something to conquer and exploit.

For a number of reasons, Native Americans were extremely vulnerable to the European "invasion" of America. At the same time, however, a major biological "event" was in process that would change life in both the Old World and the New. Called by historians the Columbian Exchange, the process involved the transplantation to the New World (sometimes accidentally) of various plants (cabbages, radishes, bananas, wheat, onions, sugar cane), animals (horses, pigs, cattle, sheep, cats), and diseases. At the same time, Europeans returned home with maize, peanuts, squash, sweet potatoes, pumpkins, pineapples, tomatoes, and cocoa. Less beneficial was the possible transportation from the New World to the Old of venereal syphilis. Indeed, some five hundred years later, the Columbian Exchange is still going on. In the Great Smoky Mountains of North Carolina and Tennessee, wild boars, imported from Germany in the nineteenth century for sportsmen, threaten the plants, grasses, and small animals of the region. The zebra mussel, released by accident into the Great Lakes in ballast water from Eastern Europe, has spread into rivers in Illinois, Mississippi, Ohio, and Tennessee. An Asian variety of the gypsy moth is chewing its way through the forests of the Pacific Northwest. A recent survey in Olympic National Park has identified 169 species of plants and animals not indigenous to the Western Hemisphere. In the South, the kudzu

◆ CHAPTER 1

First Encounters:
The Confrontation
Between Cortés
and Montezuma
(1519–1521)

vine, imported from Japan to combat erosion, was dubbed by the *Los Angeles Times* (July 21, 1992) "the national plant of Dixie." Whether purposeful or by accident, whether beneficial or detrimental, the Columbian Exchange continues.

Because Europeans ultimately were victorious in their "invasion" of the Western Hemisphere, it is their images of Native Americans that for the most part have survived. Christopher Columbus, who recorded the Europeans' first encounter, depicted Native Americans as innocent, naive children. But he also wrote, "I could conquer the whole of them with fifty men, and govern them as I pleased." For his part, Amerigo Vespucci was less kind, depicting Native Americans as barbarous because "they have no regular time for their meals . . . [and] in making water they are dirty and without shame, for while talking with us they do such things." By placing this badge of inferiority on Indian peoples, most Europeans could justify a number of ways Indians could be dealt with (avoidance, conquest, "civilizing," trading, removal, extermination). Ultimately for the Indian peoples, all methods proved disastrous. Although different European peoples (Spanish, French, English) often treated Indians differently, in the end the results were the same.

Hernando Cortés returned to Spain in 1528 a fabulously wealthy man. But the ultimate *conquistador* lost most of his fortune in ill-fated expeditions and died in modest circumstances in 1547. In his will, he recognized the four children he had fathered by Native American women while in Mexico (Cortés was married at the time) and worried about the morality of what he had done. In 1562, his body was taken to Mexico to be reburied, but for Hernando Cortés's remains, there would be no rest. In 1794, they were moved again, this time to the chapel of a Mexican hospital that he had endowed. In 1823, Cortés's remains disappeared for good, perhaps as the result of an effort to protect them from politically oriented grave robbers after Mexico declared its independence from Spain. Rumors abound that they were secretly carried back across the Atlantic, this time to Italy. The ultimate *conquistador* has vanished, but his legacy lives on.

2

The Threat of Anne Hutchinson

The Problem

In the cold, early spring of 1638, Anne Hutchinson and her children left Massachusetts to join her husband and their many friends who had moved to an island in Narragansett Bay near what is now Rhode Island. Just a year before, in 1637, Hutchinson and her family had been highly respected, prominent members of a Puritan church in Boston. But then she was put on trial and sentenced to banishment from the Massachusetts Bay colony and excommunication from her church—next to death, the worst punishment that could befall a Puritan in the New World.

What had Anne Hutchinson done? Why was she such a threat to the Massachusetts Bay colony? You will be reading the transcript of her trial in 1637 to find the answers to these questions.

Background

The English men and women who came to the New World in the seventeenth and early eighteenth centuries did so for a variety of reasons. Many who arrived at Jamestown colony were motivated by the promise of wealth; at one point, Virginians grew tobacco in the streets and even threatened their own existence by favoring tobacco (a crop they could sell) over food crops. In contrast, the majority of the early settlers of Pennsylvania were Friends (Quakers) in search of religious freedom. In short, the American colonies represented for thousands of English men and women a chance to make significant changes in their lives.

Such was the case with the Puritans who settled and dominated the colony of Massachusetts Bay, founded in 1630. Although still members of the Church of England, the Puritans were convinced that many of that church's beliefs and practices were wrong and that the Church of England needed to be thoroughly purified (hence their name). Puritans were convinced that the Church of England, which had broken away from the Roman Catholic Church and the pope during the reign of Henry VIII, was still encumbered with unnecessary ceremony, rituals, and hierarchy—things they called "popery." Popery, the Puritans believed, actually obstructed the ties between God and human beings, and therefore should be eliminated.

Believing it impossible to effect their reforms in England, many Puritans sought "voluntary banishment," as one of them called it, to the New World. Fired by the sense that God was using them to revolutionize human history, more than one thousand men, women, and children arrived during the first decades of the founding of New England to form their model community based on the laws of God and his commandments. "We shall be as a city upon a hill," exulted Puritan leader and colonial governor John Winthrop, "the eyes of all people are upon us."

There were at least five central characteristics of American Puritanism. First, the idea that Massachusetts Bay should be a "city upon a hill" implied that the New World experiment was a kind of holy mission. Its success could be a very important stimulus to religious reformers back home in England. Failure of the mission, however, would be a disaster. The Massachusetts settlers thus carried with them a double responsibility: to create a successful, orderly, godly community in the New World and to serve as a perfect, shining example to the rest of the Protestant world, especially to England.

Belief in a "covenant of grace" was a second important aspect of the New England Way. American Puritans did not believe that human salvation could be earned by individual effort, such as

going to church, leading a good life, or helping one's neighbors. The Puritans called the idea that one could *earn* salvation a "covenant of works," a notion they believed was absolutely wrong. They insisted that salvation came only as a free gift from God (a "covenant of grace"), and those few who received it were the true "saints," full members of the church.

There was a paradox at the heart of this distinction between the covenant of grace and the covenant of works, however. Puritans believed that God expected everyone to lead a good life and behave themselves. Those who were not yet saved would be preparing for the possibility of God's grace, while those who were already saints would naturally live according to God's laws. Some ministers, like John Cotton, deemphasized the idea of preparation, maintaining that God's grace could be granted instantaneously to anyone. Other ministers put more emphasis on preparing to receive God's grace.

The third significant characteristic of Puritanism was the belief that the community, as well as the individual, entered into a contract, or covenant, with God. Seeing themselves as the modern version of the ancient Israelites, Puritans believed that God had made a specific contract with the Puritans of New England. As Winthrop explained, "Thus stands the cause between God and us: we are entered into covenant with Him. . . . The God of Israel is among us." To Puritans, the covenant meant that the entire community must follow God's laws as interpreted by Puritan leaders. If they did, God would reward them; if not, the community would be punished. Therefore, community solidarity was essential, and individual desires and thoughts had to be subjugated to those of the community.

Thus, although Puritans sought religious freedom for themselves, they were not really willing to grant it to others. Dissent and discord, they reasoned, would lead to the breakdown of community cohesion, the inevitable violation of the covenant, and the punishment of the community in the same way God had punished the ancient Israelites when they had broken their covenant. Non-Puritans who migrated to the Massachusetts Bay colony were required to attend the Puritan church, although they could not become members and hence could not vote in either church or civil elections. Those who refused to abide by these rules were banished from the colony. Moreover, those Puritans who were not saints also had to obey these regulations and similarly could not be church members or vote.

Thus, there was a hierarchy of authority in Massachusetts that controlled both the colony's church and the government. Within this hierarchy, the ministers played a very important role. Expected to be highly educated and articulate, the ministers of each Puritan church were to be the teachers and leaders of their respective congregations. Of course, the civil officials of Massachusetts Bay, such as the governor and his council, were good Puritans and full members of their churches. Their job was to ensure that the laws and practices of civil government were in accord with the requirements of living in a godly community. Civil authorities, then, were expected to support the religious authorities, and vice versa.

Finally, New England Puritans placed more emphasis than English Puritans on the importance of having a conversion experience—an experience when you knew that you had been "saved." Young people and adults prayed, tried to live according to biblical precepts, and often kept diaries in which they reflected on their shortcomings and "sinfulness." Only a conversion experience would admit a person into full church membership. To become a saint, one had to be examined by a church committee and demonstrate that he or she had experienced the presence of God and the Holy Spirit. There was no agreement among the ministers about the exact nature of this revelation, although people sometimes reported a physical sensation. For most it simply meant that individuals would recognize the Holy Spirit moving within themselves. Some ministers urged their congregations not to fear, and even to seek out, more direct contact with God. This was far more controversial, as you will see in Anne Hutchinson's trial.

In fact, there was a good deal of dissension in Massachusetts Bay colony. Religious squabbles were common, often arising between saints over biblical interpretation, the theological correctness of one minister or another, or the behavior of certain fellow colonists. Indeed, to a limited extent, Puritans actually welcomed these disputes because they seemed to demonstrate that religion was still a vital part of the colonists' lives. As John Winthrop said, "The business of religion is the business of the Puritans." Participants of weeknight gatherings at various church members' homes often engaged in these religious debates, tolerated by both the ministers and the colony's civil leaders as long as the squabbles did not get out of control.

By the mid-1630s, however, one of the disputes had grown to such an extent that it threatened the religious and secular unity of the colony. Some Puritans in both England and Massachusetts Bay had begun to espouse an extreme version of the covenant of grace: they believed that, having been assured of salvation, an individual was virtually freed from the man-made laws of both church and state, taking commands only from God, who communicated his wishes to the saints. Called Antinomians (from *anti,* "against," and *nomos,* "law"), these Puritan extremists attacked what one of them called the "deadness" of religious services and charged that several ministers were preaching the covenant of works. This charge was extremely offensive to these ministers, who did not at all believe they were teaching salvation through good behavior but rather preparation for the possibility of God's grace. Carried to its logical extension, of course, Antinomianism threatened to overthrow the authority of the ministers and even the power of the colonial government itself. Growing in number and intensity, the Antinomians in 1636 were able to elect one of their followers to replace Winthrop as colonial governor, although Winthrop managed to return to office the next year.

Into this highly charged atmosphere stepped Anne Hutchinson, age forty-three, who arrived in Massachusetts Bay in 1634 and soon became embroiled in the Antinomian controversy, or, as other Puritans called it, the "Antinomian heresy." The daughter of a clergyman who had been imprisoned

twice for his religious unorthodoxy, Anne had married prosperous businessman William Hutchinson in 1612, when she was twenty-one years old. Before arriving in Massachusetts Bay, she had given birth to fourteen children, eleven of whom were alive in 1634.

In a society that emphasized the greater good of the community rather than the concept of individual happiness, relationships between men and women were complementary and complex. New England "goodwives," as married women were called, performed a variety of tasks essential to their families and communities. Spiritually, they were equal to their husbands in the eyes of God, but economically and politically, wives were expected to help with and supplement their husbands' public activities. In other words, both men and women had rights and responsibilities with respect to each other, their children, their neighbors, their communities, and their church. In carrying out these responsibilities, male and female roles sometimes overlapped, but more often they were divided into public (male) and private (female) spheres.

As in any other society, there were some unhappy marriages, cases of domestic violence and desertion, and even what we would call divorce. But the shared ideals and sense of mission of so many of the immigrants ensured that such dysfunctional relationships were relatively uncommon. Although building a new society in a wilderness was a difficult and dangerous undertaking, most women fulfilled their roles willingly and competently.

Anne Hutchinson's many duties at home did not prevent her from remaining very active in the church. Extremely interested in religion and theological questions, she was particularly influenced by John Cotton, a Puritan minister who had been forced to flee from England to Massachusetts Bay in 1633 because of his religious ideas. Cotton, who was Cambridge-educated, and very influential, preached at a Boston church. Upon arrival in the colony, Cotton said he was shocked by the extent to which colonists had been "lulled into security" by their growing belief that they could earn salvation through good works. Attacking this in sermons and in letters to other clergymen, Cotton helped fuel the Antinomian cause as well as Anne Hutchinson's religious ardor.

At first the Hutchinsons were seen as welcome additions to the community, largely because of William's prosperity and Anne's expertise in herbal medicines, nursing the sick, and midwifery. Soon, however, Anne Hutchinson began to drift into religious issues. She began to hold weeknight meetings in her home, at first to expand upon the previous Sunday's sermons and later to expound her own religious notions—ideas very close to those of the Antinomians. In November 1637, Anne's brother-in-law (John Wheelwright, another Puritan minister) was

banished from the colony because of his radical sermons, and Anne was brought to trial before the General Court of Massachusetts Bay. With Governor Winthrop presiding, the court met to decide the fate of Anne Hutchinson. Privately, Winthrop called Hutchinson a person of "nimble wit and active spirit and a very voluble [fluent] tongue." Winthrop himself, however, believed that women should be submissive and supportive, like his wife and sister, and there was ample support for his position in the Bible.[1] No matter what he thought of Hutchinson's abilities, publicly the governor was determined to be rid of her.

Why were Winthrop and other orthodox Puritans so opposed to Hutchinson? What crime had she committed? Some of Wheelwright's followers had been punished for having signed a petition supporting him, but Hutchinson had not signed the petition. Many other Puritans had held religious discussions in their homes, and more than a few had opposed the views of their ministers. Technically, Hutchinson had broken no law. Why, then, was she considered such a threat that she was brought to trial and ultimately banished from the colony?

The Method

For two days, Anne Hutchinson stood before the General Court, presided over by the unsympathetic Governor John Winthrop. Fortunately, a fairly complete transcript of the proceedings has been preserved. In that transcript are the clues that you as the historian-

detective will need to answer the questions previously posed. Although spelling and punctuation have been modernized in most cases, the portions

1. Genesis 1:28–3:24; the First Letter of Paul to the Corinthians 11:1–16; the Letter of Paul to the Ephesians, Chapters 5 and 6, all verses.

of the transcript you are about to read are reproduced verbatim. At first, some of the seventeenth-century phraseology might seem a bit strange. As are most spoken languages, English is constantly changing (think of how much English has changed since Chaucer's day). Yet if you read slowly and carefully, the transcript should give you no problem.

Before you begin studying the transcript, keep in mind two additional instructions:

1. Be careful not to lose sight of the central question: Why was Anne Hutchinson such a threat to Massachusetts Bay colony? The transcript raises several other questions, some of them so interesting that they might pull you off the main track. As you read through the transcript, make a list of the various ways you think Hutchinson might have threatened Massachusetts Bay.

2. Be willing to read between the lines. As you read each statement, ask yourself what is being said. Then try to deduce what is actually meant by what is being said in the context of the early 1600s. Sometimes people say exactly what they mean, but often they do not. They might intentionally or unintentionally disguise the real meaning of what they are saying, but the real meaning can usually be found. In conversation with a person face to face, voice inflection, body language, and other visual clues often provide the real meaning to what is being said. In this case, where personal observation is impossible, you must use both logic and imagination to read between the lines.

◆

The Evidence

Source 1 from an excerpt of the examination from Thomas Hutchinson (Anne's great-grandson), in Lawrence Shaw Mayo, ed., *The History of the Colony and Province of Massachusetts-Bay* (Cambridge, Mass.: Harvard University Press, 1936), Vol. II, pp. 366–391. Copyright © 1936 by the President and Fellows of Harvard College. Reprinted by permission of the publisher.

1. The Examination of Mrs. Anne Hutchinson at the Court of Newton, November 1637.[2]

CHARACTERS

Mrs. Anne Hutchinson, the accused

---

2. Normally the trial would have been held in Boston, but Anne Hutchinson had numerous supporters in that city, so the proceedings were moved to the small town of Newton, where she had few allies.

General Court, consisting of the governor, deputy governor, assistants, and
   deputies
Governor, John Winthrop, chair of the court
Deputy Governor, Thomas Dudley
Assistants, Mr. Bradstreet, Mr. Nowel, Mr. Endicott, Mr. Harlakenden, Mr.
   Stoughton
Deputies, Mr. Coggeshall, Mr. Bartholomew, Mr. Jennison, Mr. Coddington,
   Mr. Colborn
Clergymen and Ruling Elders:
Mr. Peters, minister in Salem
Mr. Leveret, a ruling elder in a Boston church
Mr. Cotton, minister in Boston
Mr. Wilson, minister in Boston, who supposedly made notes of a previous
   meeting between Anne Hutchinson, Cotton, and the other ministers
Mr. Sims, minister in Charlestown

MR. WINTHROP, GOVERNOR. Mrs. Hutchinson, you are called here as one of those
   that have troubled the peace of the commonwealth and the churches
   here; you are known to be a woman that hath had a great share in the
   promoting and divulging of those opinions that are causes of this <u>trouble</u>,
   and to be nearly joined not only in <u>affinity</u> and <u>affection</u> with some of
   those the court had taken notice of and passed censure upon, but you
   have spoken divers things as we have been informed very prejudicial to
   the honour of the churches and ministers thereof, and you have maintained a meeting and an assembly in your house that hath been condemned by the general assembly as a thing not tolerable nor comely in
   the sight of God nor fitting for your sex, and notwithstanding that was
   cried down you have continued the same. Therefore we have thought
   good to send for you to understand how things are, that if you be in an erroneous way we may reduce you so that you may become a profitable
   member here among us. Otherwise if you be obstinate in your course that
   then the court may take such course that you may trouble us no further.
   Therefore I would intreat you to express whether you do assent and hold
   in practice to those opinions and factions that have been handled in court
   already, that is to say, whether you do not justify Mr. Wheelwright's sermon and the petition.
MRS. HUTCHINSON. I am called here to answer before you but I hear no things
   laid to my charge.
GOV. I have told you some already and more I can tell you.
MRS. H. Name one, Sir.

GOV. Have I not named some already?

MRS. H. What have I said or done?

[*Here, in a portion of the transcript not reproduced, Winthrop accused Hutchinson of harboring and giving comfort to a faction that was dangerous to the colony.*]

MRS. H. Must not I then entertain the saints because I must keep my conscience?

GOV. Say that one brother should commit felony or treason and come to his brother's house. If he knows him guilty and conceals him he is guilty of the same. It is his conscience to entertain him, but if his conscience comes into act in giving countenance and entertainment to him that hath broken the law he is guilty too. So if you do countenance those that are transgressors of the law you are in the same fact.

MRS. H. What law do they transgress?

GOV. The law of God and of the state.

MRS. H. In what particular?

GOV. Why in this among the rest, whereas the Lord doth say honour thy father and thy mother.[3]

MRS. H. Ey, Sir, in the Lord.

GOV. This honour you have broke in giving countenance to them.

MRS. H. In entertaining those did I entertain them against any act (for there is the thing) or what God hath appointed?

GOV. You knew that Mr. Wheelwright did preach this sermon and those that countenance him in this do break a law?

MRS. H. What law have I broken?

GOV. Why the fifth commandment.[4]

MRS. H. I deny that for he [Wheelwright] saith in the Lord.

GOV. You have joined with them in the faction.

MRS. H. In what faction have I joined with them?

GOV. In presenting the petition.

MRS. H. Suppose I had set my hand to the petition. What then?

GOV. You saw that case tried before.

MRS. H. But I had not my hand to the petition.

GOV. You have councelled them.

MRS. H. Wherein?

GOV. Why in entertaining them.

3. Exodus 20:12. Anne Hutchinson's natural father was in England and her natural mother was dead. To what, then, was Winthrop referring?
4. "Honour thy father and thy mother: that thy days may be long upon the land which the Lord thy God giveth thee." Exodus 20:12.

MRS. H. What breach of law is that, Sir?

GOV. Why dishonouring of parents.

MRS. H. But put the case, Sir, that I do fear the Lord and my parents. May not I entertain them that fear the Lord because my parents will not give me leave?

GOV. If they be the fathers of the commonwealth, and they of another religion, if you entertain them then you dishonour your parents and are justly punishable.

MRS. H. If I entertain them, as they have dishonoured their parents I do.

GOV. No but you by countenancing them above others put honour upon them.

MRS. H. I may put honour upon them as the children of God and as they do honour the Lord.

GOV. We do not mean to discourse with those of your sex but only this: you do adhere unto them and do endeavour to set forward this faction and so you do dishonour us.

MRS. H. I do acknowledge no such thing. Neither do I think that I ever put any dishonour upon you.

GOV. Why do you keep such a meeting at your house as you do every week upon a set day? . . .

MRS. H. It is lawful for me so to do, as it is all your practices, and can you find a warrant for yourself and condemn me for the same thing? The ground of my taking it up was, when I first came to this land because I did not go to such meetings as those were, it was presently reported that I did not allow of such meetings but held them unlawful and therefore in that regard they said I was proud and did despise all ordinances. Upon that a friend came unto me and told me of it and I to prevent such aspersions took it up, but it was in practice before I came. Therefore I was not the first.

GOV. For this, that you appeal to our practice you need no confutation. If your meeting had answered to the former it had not been offensive, but I will say that there was no meeting of women alone, but your meeting is of another sort for there are sometimes men among you.

MRS. H. There was never any man with us.

GOV. Well, admit there was no man at your meeting and that you was sorry for it, there is no warrant for your doings, and by what warrant do you continue such a course?

MRS. H. I conceive there lies a clear rule in Titus[5] that the elder women should instruct the younger and then I must have a time wherein I must do it.

---

5. A reference to The Epistle of Paul to Titus in the Bible, probably the section stating that older women "may teach the young women to be sober, to love their husbands, to love their children," etc.

GOV. All this I grant you, I grant you a time for it, but what is this to the purpose that you Mrs. Hutchinson must call a company together from their callings to come to be taught of you?

MRS. H. Will it please you to answer me this and to give me a rule for then I will willingly submit to any truth. If any come to my house to be instructed in the ways of God what rule have I to put them away?

GOV. But suppose that a hundred men come unto you to be instructed. Will you forbear to instruct them?

MRS. H. As far as I conceive I cross a rule in it.

GOV. Very well and do you not so here?

MRS. H. No, Sir, for my ground is they are men.

GOV. Men and women all is one for that, but suppose that a man should come and say, "Mrs. Hutchinson, I hear that you are a woman that God hath given his grace unto and you have knowledge in the word of God. I pray instruct me a little." Ought you not to instruct this man?

MRS. H. I think I may. Do you think it is not lawful for me to teach women and why do you call me to teach the court?

GOV. We do not call you to teach the court but to lay open yourself.

[*In this portion of the transcript not reproduced, Hutchinson and Winthrop continued to wrangle over specifically what law she had broken.*]

GOV. Your course is not to be suffered for. Besides that we find such a course as this to be greatly prejudicial to the state. Besides the occasion that it is to seduce many honest persons that are called to those meetings and your opinions being known to be different from the word of God may seduce many simple souls that resort unto you. Besides that the occasion which hath come of late hath come from none but such as have frequented your meetings, so that now they are flown off from magistrates and ministers and since they have come to you. And besides that it will not well stand with the commonwealth that families should be neglected for so many neighbours and dames and so much time spent. We see no rule of God for this. We see not that any should have authority to set up any other exercises besides what authority hath already set up and so what hurt comes of this you will be guilty of and we for suffering you.

MRS. H. Sir, I do not believe that to be so.

GOV. Well, we see how it is. We must therefore put it away from you or restrain you from maintaining this course.

MRS. H. If you have a rule for it from God's word you may.

GOV. We are your judges, and not you ours and we must compel you to it.

[Here followed a discussion of whether men as well as women attended Hutchinson's meetings. In response to one question, Hutchinson denied that women ever taught at men's meetings.]

DEPUTY GOVERNOR. I would go a little higher with Mrs. Hutchinson. About three years ago we were all in peace. Mrs. Hutchinson from that time she came hath made a disturbance, and some that came over with her in the ship did inform me what she was as soon as she was landed. I being then in place dealt with the pastor and teacher of Boston and desired them to enquire of her, and then I was satisfied that she held nothing different from us. But within half a year after, she had vented divers of her strange opinions and had made parties in the country, and at length it comes that Mr. Cotton and Mr. Vane[6] were of her judgment, but Mr. Cotton had cleared himself that he was not of that mind. But now it appears by this woman's meeting that Mrs. Hutchinson hath so forestalled the minds of many by their resort to her meeting that now she hath a potent party in the country. Now if all these things have endangered us as from that foundation and if she in particular hath disparaged all our ministers in the land that they have preached a covenant of works,[7] and only Mr. Cotton a covenant of grace,[8] why this is not to be suffered, and therefore being driven to the foundation and it being found that Mrs. Hutchinson is she that hath depraved all the ministers and hath been the cause of what is falled out, why we must take away the foundation and the building will fall.

MRS. H. I pray, Sir, prove it that I said they preached nothing but a covenant of works.

DEP. GOV. Nothing but a covenant of works. Why a Jesuit[9] may preach truth sometimes.

MRS. H. Did I ever say they preached a covenant of works then?

DEP. GOV. If they do not preach a covenant of grace clearly, then they preach a covenant of works.

MRS. H. No, Sir. One may preach a covenant of grace more clearly than another, so I said.

DEP. GOV. We are not upon that now but upon position.

MRS. H. Prove this then Sir that you say I said.

---

6. Henry Vane, supported by the Antinomians and merchant allies, was elected governor of Massachusetts Bay colony in 1636 and lost that office to Winthrop in 1637.
7. For an explanation of the covenant of works, see the "Background" section.
8. For an explanation of the covenant of grace, see the "Background" section.
9. The Society of Jesus (Jesuits) is a Roman Catholic order that places special emphasis on missionary work. The Jesuits were known at this time for combating Protestantism and were particularly detested by many Protestants, including the Puritans.

DEP. GOV. When they do preach a covenant of works do they preach truth?

MRS. H. Yes, Sir. But when they preach a covenant of works for salvation, that is not truth.

DEP. GOV. I do but ask you this: when the ministers do preach a covenant of works do they preach a way of salvation?

MRS. H. I did not come hither to answer to questions of that sort.

DEP. GOV. Because you will deny the thing.

MRS. H. Ey, but that is to be proved first.

DEP. GOV. I will make it plain that you did say that the ministers did preach a covenant of works.

MRS. H. I deny that.

DEP. GOV. And that you said they were not able ministers of the New Testament, but Mr. Cotton only.

MRS. H. If ever I spake that I proved it by God's word.

COURT. Very well, very well.

MRS. H. If one shall come unto me in private, and desire me seriously to tell then what I thought of such an one, I must either speak false or true in my answer.

[*In this lengthy section, Hutchinson was accused of having gone to a meeting of ministers and accusing them all—except John Cotton—of preaching a covenant of works rather than a covenant of grace. The accusation, if proved, would have been an extremely serious one. Several of the ministers testified that Hutchinson had made this accusation.*]

DEP. GOV. I called these witnesses and you deny them. You see they have proved this and you deny this, but it is clear. You said they preached a covenant of works and that they were not able ministers of the New Testament; now there are two other things that you did affirm which were that the scriptures in the letter of them held forth nothing but a covenant of works and likewise that those that were under a covenant of works cannot be saved.

MRS. H. Prove that I said so.

GOV. Did you say so?

MRS. H. No, Sir. It is your conclusion.

DEP. GOV. What do I do charging of you if you deny what is so fully proved?

GOV. Here are six undeniable ministers who say it is true and yet you deny that you did say that they did preach a covenant of works and that they were not able ministers of the gospel, and it appears plainly that you have spoken it, and whereas you say that it was drawn from you in a way of friendship, you did profess then that it was out of conscience that you spake and said, "The fear of man is a snare. Wherefore shall I be afraid, I will speak plainly and freely."

MRS. H. That I absolutely deny, for the first question was thus answered by me to them: They thought that I did conceive there was a difference between them and Mr. Cotton. At the first I was somewhat reserved. Then said Mr. Peters, "I pray answer the question directly as fully and as plainly as you desire we should tell you our minds. Mrs. Hutchinson we come for plain dealing and telling you our hearts." Then I said I would deal as plainly as I could, and whereas they say I said they were under a covenant of works and in the state of the apostles why these two speeches cross one another. I might say they might preach a covenant of works as did the apostles, but to preach a covenant of works and to be under a covenant of works is another business.

DEP. GOV. There have been six witnesses to prove this and yet you deny it.

MRS. H. I deny that these were the first words that were spoken.

GOV. You make the case worse, for you clearly shew that the ground of your opening your mind was not to satisfy them but to satisfy your own conscience.

[*There was a brief argument here about what Hutchinson actually said at the gathering of ministers, after which the court adjourned for the day.*]

The next morning

GOV. We proceeded the last night as far as we could in hearing of this cause of Mrs. Hutchinson. There were divers things laid to her charge: her ordinary meetings about religious exercises, her speeches in derogation of the ministers among us, and the weakening of the hands and hearts of the people towards them. Here was sufficient proof made of that which she was accused of in that point concerning the ministers and their ministry, as that they did preach a covenant of works when others did preach a covenant of grace, and that they were not able ministers of the New Testament, and that they had not the seal of the spirit, and this was spoken not as was pretended out of private conference, but out of conscience and warrant from scripture alleged the fear of man is a snare and seeing God had given her a calling to it she would freely speak. Some other speeches she used, as that the letter of the scripture held forth a covenant of works, and this is offered to be proved by probable grounds. If there be any thing else that the court hath to say they may speak.

[*At this point, a lengthy argument erupted when Hutchinson demanded that the ministers who testified against her be recalled as witnesses, put under oath, and repeat their accusations. One member of the court said that "the ministers are so well known unto us, that we need not take an oath of them."*]

GOV. I see no necessity of an oath in this thing seeing it is true and the substance of the matter confirmed by divers. Yet that all may be satisfied, if the elders will take an oath they shall have it given them. . . .

MRS. H. I will prove by what Mr. Wilson hath written[10] that they [the ministers] never heard me say such a thing.

MR. SIMS. We desire to have the paper and have it read.

MR. HARLAKENDEN. I am persuaded that is the truth that the elders do say and therefore I do not see it necessary now to call them to oath.

GOV. We cannot charge any thing of untruth upon them.

MR. HARLAKENDEN. Besides, Mrs. Hutchinson doth say that they are not able ministers of the New Testament.

MRS. H. They need not swear to that.

DEP. GOV. Will you confess it then?

MRS. H. I will not deny it or say it.

DEP. GOV. You must do one.

[*More on the oath followed.*]

DEP. GOV. Let her witnesses be called.

GOV. Who be they?

MRS. H. Mr. Leveret and our teacher and Mr. Coggeshall.

GOV. Mr. Coggeshall was not present.

MR. COGGESHALL. Yes, but I was. Only I desired to be silent till I should be called.

GOV. Will you, Mr. Coggeshall, say that she did not say so?

MR. COGGESHALL. Yes, I dare say that she did not say all that which they lay against her.

MR. PETERS. How dare you look into the court to say such a word?

MR. COGGESHALL. Mr. Peters takes upon him to forbid me. I shall be silent.

MR. STOUGHTON. Ey, but she intended this that they say.

GOV. Well, Mr. Leveret, what were the words? I pray, speak.

MR. LEVERET. To my best remembrance when the elders did send for her, Mr. Peters did with much vehemency and intreaty urge her to tell what difference there was between Mr. Cotton and them, and upon his urging of her she said, "The fear of man is a snare, but they that trust upon the Lord shall be safe." And being asked wherein the difference was, she answered that they did not preach a covenant of grace so clearly as Mr. Cot-

---

10. Wilson had taken notes at the meeting between Hutchinson and the ministers. Hutchinson claimed that these notes would exonerate her. They were never produced and are now lost.

ton did, and she gave this reason of it: because that as the apostles were for a time without the spirit so until they had received the witness of the spirit they could not preach a covenant of grace so clearly.

[*Here Hutchinson admitted that she might have said privately that the ministers were not able ministers of the New Testament.*]

GOV. Mr. Cotton, the court desires that you declare what you do remember of the conference which was at the time and is now in question.

MR. COTTON. I did not think I should be called to bear witness in this cause and therefore did not labour to call to remembrance what was done; but the greatest passage that took impression upon me was to this purpose. The elders spake that they had heard that she had spoken some condemning words of their ministry, and among other things they did first pray her to answer wherein she thought their ministry did differ from mine. How the comparison sprang I am ignorant, but sorry I was that any comparison should be between me and my brethren and uncomfortable it was. She told them to this purpose that they did not hold forth a covenant of grace as I did. . . . I told her I was very sorry that she put comparisons between my ministry and theirs, for she had said more than I could myself, and rather I had that she had put us in fellowship with them and not have made the discrepancy. She said she found the difference. . . . And I must say that I did not find her saying they were under a covenant of works, not that she said they did preach a covenant of works.

[*Here John Cotton tried to defend Hutchinson, mostly by saying he did not remember most of the events in question.*]

MRS. H. If you please to give me leave I shall give you the ground of what I know to be true. Being much troubled to see the falseness of the constitution of the Church of England, I had like to have turned Separatist. Whereupon I kept a day of solemn humiliation and pondering of the thing, the scripture was brought unto me—he that denies Jesus Christ to be come in the flesh is antichrist. This I considered of and in considering found that the papists[11] did not deny him to come in the flesh, nor we did not deny him. Who then was antichrist? Was the Turk antichrist only? The Lord knows that I could not open scripture; he must by his prophetical office open it unto me. So after that being unsatisfied in the thing, the Lord was pleased to bring this scripture out of the Hebrews. He that de-

---

11. *Papists* is a Protestant term for Roman Catholics, referring to the papacy.

nies the testament denies the testator, and in this did open unto me and give me to see that those which did not teach the new covenant had the spirit of antichrist, and upon this he did discover the ministry unto me, and ever since, I bless the Lord. He hath let me see which was the clear ministry and which the wrong. Since that time I confess I have been more choice and he hath left me to distinguish between the voice of my beloved and the voice of Moses, the voice of John Baptist and the voice of antichrist, for all those voices are spoken of in scripture. Now if you do condemn me for speaking what in my conscience I know to be truth I must commit myself unto the Lord.

MR. NOWEL. How do you know that that was the spirit?

MRS. H. How did Abraham know that it was God that bid him offer his son, being a breach of the sixth commandment?

DEP. GOV. By an immediate voice.

MRS. H. So to me by an immediate revelation.

DEP. GOV. How! an immediate revelation.

MRS. H. By the voice of his spirit to my soul. . . .

[*In spite of the general shock that greeted her claim that she had experienced an immediate revelation from God, Hutchinson went on to state that God had compelled her to take the course she had taken and that God had said to her, as He had to Daniel of the Old Testament, that "though I should meet with affliction, yet I am the same God that delivered Daniel out of the lion's den, I will also deliver thee."*]

MRS. H. You have power over my body but the Lord Jesus hath power over my body and soul, and assure yourselves thus much: you go on in this course you begin you will bring a curse upon you and your posterity, and the mouth of the Lord hath spoken it.

DEP. GOV. What is the scripture she brings?

MR. STOUGHTON. Behold I turn away from you.

MRS. H. But now having seen him which is invisible I fear not what man can do unto me.

GOV. Daniel was delivered by miracle. Do you think to be deliver'd so too?

MRS. H. I do here speak it before the court. I took that the Lord should deliver me by his providence.

MR. HARLAKENDEN. I may read scripture and the most glorious hypocrite may read them and yet go down to hell.

MRS. H. It may be so.

[*Hutchinson's "revelations" were discussed among the stunned court.*]

MR. BARTHOLOMEW. I speak as a member of the court. I fear that her revelations will deceive.

[*More on Hutchinson's revelations followed.*]

DEP. GOV. I desire Mr. Cotton to tell us whether you do approve of Mrs. Hutchinson's revelations as she hath laid them down.

MR. COTTON. I know not whether I do understand her, but this I say: If she doth expect a deliverance in a way of providence, then I cannot deny it.

DEP. GOV. No, sir. We did not speak of that.

MR. COTTON. If it be by way of miracle then I would suspect it.

DEP. GOV. Do you believe that her revelations are true?

MR. COTTON. That she may have some special providence of God to help her is a thing that I cannot bear witness against.

DEP. GOV. Good Sir, I do ask whether this revelation be of God or no?

MR. COTTON. I should desire to know whether the sentence of the court will bring her to any calamity, and then I would know of her whether she expects to be delivered from that calamity by a miracle or a providence of God.

MRS. H. By a providence of God I say I expect to be delivered from some calamity that shall come to me.

[*Hutchinson's revelations were further discussed.*]

DEP. GOV. These disturbances that have come among the Germans[12] have been all grounded upon revelations, and so they that have vented them have stirred up their hearers to take up arms against their prince and to cut the throats of one another, and these have been the fruits of them, and whether the devil may inspire the same into their hearts here I know not, for I am fully persuaded that Mrs. Hutchinson is deluded by the devil, because the spirit of God speaks truth in all his servants.

GOV. I am persuaded that the revelation she brings forth is delusion.

[*All the court but some two or three ministers cried out, "We all believe—we all believe it." Hutchinson was found guilty. Coddington made a lame attempt to defend Hutchinson but was silenced by Governor Winthrop.*]

GOV. The court hath already declared themselves satisfied concerning the things you hear, and concerning the troublesomeness of her spirit and the danger of her course amongst us, which is not to be suffered. There-

12. This reference is to the bloody and violent fighting that took place between orthodox Protestants and the followers of the radical Anabaptist John of Leiden in 1534 and 1535.

fore if it be the mind of the court that Mrs. Hutchinson for these things that appear before us is unfit for our society, and if it be the mind of the court that she shall be banished out of our liberties and imprisoned till she be sent away, let them hold up their hands.

[*All but three did so.*]

GOV. Those that are contrary minded hold up yours.

[*Only Mr. Coddington and Mr. Colborn did so.*]

MR. JENNISON. I cannot hold up my hand one way or the other, and I shall give my reason if the court require it.

GOV. Mrs. Hutchinson, the sentence of the court you hear is that you are banished from out of our jurisdiction as being a woman not fit for our society, and are to be imprisoned till the court shall send you away.

MRS. H. I desire to know wherefore I am banished?

GOV. Say no more. The court knows wherefore and is satisfied.

◆

Questions to Consider

Now that you have examined the evidence, at least one point is very clear: the political and religious authorities of Massachusetts Bay were determined to get rid of Anne Hutchinson, whether or not she actually had broken any law. They tried to bait her, force admissions of guilt from her, confuse her, browbeat her. Essentially, they had already decided on the verdict before the trial began. So we know that Anne Hutchinson was a threat—and a serious one—to the colony.

And yet the colony had dealt quite differently with Roger Williams, a Puritan minister banished in 1635 because of his extreme religious beliefs. Williams was given every chance to mend his ways, Governor Winthrop remained his friend throughout Williams's appearances before the General Court, and it was only with great reluctance that the court finally decided to send him out into the "wilderness."

Why, then, was Anne Hutchinson such a threat, and why was her trial such an ordeal? Obviously, she did pose a religious threat. As you look back through the evidence, try to clarify the exact points of difficulty between Hutchinson and the ministers. What was the basis of the argument over covenants of grace and works? What was Hutchinson supposed to have said? Under what circumstances had she allegedly said this? To whom? What was the role of her own minister, John Cotton, in the trial?

Remember that Hutchinson's trial took place in the midst of the divisive

Antinomian controversy. What threat did the Antinomians pose to Massachusetts Bay and Puritanism? Did Hutchinson say anything in her testimony that would indicate she was an Antinomian? How would you prove whether or not she was?

Hutchinson's place or role in the community also seems to have come into question during the trial. What do the questions about the meetings she held in her home reveal? Look beyond what the governor and members of the court are actually saying. Try to imagine what they might have been thinking. How might Hutchinson's meetings have eventually posed a threat to the larger community?

Finally, look through the transcript one more time. It provides some clues, often subtle ones, about the relationships between men and women in colonial Massachusetts. Puritan law and customs gave women approximately equal status with men, and of course women could join the church, just as men could. But in every society, there are unspoken assumptions about how men and women should behave. Can you find any evidence that Hutchinson violated these assumptions? If so, what did she do? Again, why would this be dangerous?

In conclusion, try to put together all you know from the evidence to answer the central question: Why was Anne Hutchinson such a threat to Massachusetts Bay colony?

Epilogue

Even after banishment, misfortune continued to plague the Hutchinson family. After moving to Narragansett Bay, Hutchinson once again became pregnant. By then she was more than forty-five years old and had begun menopause. The fetus did not develop naturally and was aborted and expelled with considerable pain and difficulty. Many believed that the "birth" of this "monster baby" was proof of Hutchinson's religious heresy.

In 1642, Hutchinson's husband died, and she moved with her six youngest children to the Dutch colony of New Netherland in what is now the Bronx borough of New York City. The next year, she and all but one of her children were killed by Indians.

Ten years after Hutchinson was banished from Massachusetts Bay, John Winthrop died. Winthrop believed to the end of his life that he had had no choice other than to expel Hutchinson and her family. However, even Winthrop's most sympathetic biographer, historian Edmund S. Morgan, describes the Hutchinson trial and its aftermath as "the least attractive episode" in Winthrop's long public career.

Massachusetts Bay continued to try to maintain community cohesion for years after Anne Hutchinson and her family were expelled. Quakers who tried to convert Puritans were especially persecuted, even executed. But as the colony grew and prospered, change ultimately did come. New generations seemed unable to embrace the original zeal of the colony's founders. New towns increased the colony's size and made uniformity more difficult. Growth and prosperity also seemed to bring an increased interest in individual wealth and a corresponding decline in religious fervor. Reports of sleeping during sermons, fewer conversions of young people, blasphemous language, and growing attention to physical pleasures were numerous, as were reports of election disputes, intrachurch squabbling, and community bickering.

To those who remembered the old ways of Massachusetts Bay, such straying from the true path was more than unfortunate. The Puritans believed that as the ancient Israelites had been punished by God when they broke their covenant, so they would have to pay for their indiscretions. As one Puritan minister said, "In the time of their prosperity, see how the Jews turn their backs and shake off the authority of the Lord." The comparison was lost on almost no one.

Jeremiads—stories that predicted disasters because of the decline in religious zeal and public morality—were especially popular in the 1660s. The minister and physician Michael Wigglesworth's poem "The Day of Doom" (specifically written for the general public) was "read to pieces," according to historian Perry Miller. Wigglesworth's more sophisticated but heartfelt poem "God's Controversy with New England" was equally popular among more educated readers. Hence it is not surprising that by the late 1680s (more than forty years after Anne Hutchinson's death), a wave of religious hysteria swept across Massachusetts Bay colony. Convinced that they had broken their covenant with God, many Puritans grimly awaited their punishment, spending long hours in churches listening to sermons. When in 1692 a few young girls in Salem Village began accusing some of their neighbors of being possessed by Satan, many were convinced that the day of punishment had arrived. Before that incident had run its course, twenty people had been killed, nineteen of them by hanging, and many more had been temporarily imprisoned.

The religious test for office holding was abolished in 1821, and although the Puritans' congregational church remained the official established church of Massachusetts until 1833, the original community cohesion had been altered long before that.

3

The Evolution of Colonial Chesapeake Society: A Statistical Analysis

✦

The Problem

In 1584, ship captain Arthur Barlowe was hired by Sir Walter Raleigh to make a reconnaissance voyage to Virginia to locate a site where Raleigh could plant a permanent colony in the New World. Sailing from England on April 27, 1584, in early July Barlowe and his crewmates went ashore on what later became known as Roanoke Island, in present-day North Carolina. Exploring the island and making contact with the local Native Americans (whom Barlowe described as "lustie men"), the two-ship expedition returned to England, with two Native American "savages," at which time Barlowe delivered his report to Raleigh.

As soon as he read Barlowe's report, Raleigh was eager to send colonists to Roanoke Island as quickly as possible. Essentially, Barlowe described the island as a new Eden populated by a friendly, peaceful, and deferential people. In part, Barlowe wrote:

This island has many goodly woods, and full of Deere, Conies,[1] Hares, and Fowle, even in the middest of Summer, in incredible abundance. . . . The soile is the most plentifull, sweete, fruitfull, and wholesome of all the world. . . . The earth bringeth foorth all things in aboundance, as in the first creation, without toile or labour. . . .

We found the people most gentle, loving, and faithfull, void of all guile, and treason, and such as lived after the manner of the golden age.[2]

Arthur Barlowe's account was, to say the least, misleading. Raleigh's two efforts to plant an English settlement on Roanoke Island both failed, one disastrously (the so-called "Lost Colony"). Twenty years later, approximately 100 miles north of Roanoke Island, another attempt, at Jamestown, almost collapsed several times, in part because,

1. Rabbits.
2. Arthur Barlowe, "The first voyage made to the coasts of America . . . ," in David B. Quinn, ed., *English Plans for North America. The Roanoke Voyages. New England Ventures,* Vol. 3 of *New American World: A Documentary History of North America to 1612* (New York: Arno Press, 1979), pp. 277, 279–280.

contrary to their own experiences, many of the colonists continued to believe Barlowe's fanciful report. The quality of the early colonists cannot really be determined: they died too fast for us to tell. Of the 105 original settlers of Jamestown in May 1607, only 38 were still alive by January 1608. Indeed, it took several decades before Britons could be assured that the fragile settlement would be a permanent one.

And yet, by the middle of the eighteenth century the Chesapeake society in Virginia and Maryland not only had grown, changed, and matured but also had become among the most opulent and refined of Great Britain's North American colonies and was on the brink of providing exceptionally talented leadership for the colonies as well as for the early nation.

How was the Chesapeake region able to reach such heights after such an inauspicious beginning? In other words, what factors were responsible for the evolution of the Chesapeake society by the mid-1700s? What were the key ingredients that made up that society?

The evidence you will be using in this chapter will be twenty-one sets of statistics. Analyzing statistics is one of the best ways that historians can measure and assess change over time. In this chapter, you will be doing precisely that.

◆

Background

Although the discoveries of Christopher Columbus (1446?–1506) and the forays by *conquistadores* like Hernando Cortés (1485–1547) and others proved that the so-called "New World" was a place of enormous wealth, it took nearly a century for England to turn its attention to concerted exploration and colonization. This was primarily because of internal instability as well as England's engagement in a series of wars in France, Scotland, and Ireland that kept the English home. Although Henry VII's defeat of Richard III on Bosworth Field in 1485 brought some measure of internal peace to England, it was not until the reign of Elizabeth I (queen from 1558 until her death in 1603) that the emerging nation-state could consider itself comparatively stable. Even so, bitter fighting in Ireland in 1568 (the "Northern Rebellion") and numerous plots on Elizabeth's life (prompted in part by Pope Pius V's excommunication of the English queen and call for her overthrow in 1571 and efforts to replace Elizabeth with the imprisoned Mary Queen of Scots) kept England and its government in an almost constant state of uncertainty. In addition, threats from abroad such as the Spanish Armada (1588) prompted England to keep her forces and ships at home.[3]

At the same time, however, other

3. Mary was the great-granddaughter of Henry VII and therefore the next lawful heir to the throne after Elizabeth. Roman Catholics often referred to Elizabeth as "Queen of the Heretics." Fearing that the impending attack by Spain might cause a Roman Catholic uprising in Mary's favor, Elizabeth finally had her put to death in 1587.

forces were pushing England toward the sea and colonization. Chief among them was a demographic explosion in the sixteenth century, in which England's population surged from approximately 2.3 million in 1552 to between 4.11 and 5 million by 1600. These figures are especially astounding given that England experienced a horrible influenza epidemic between 1557 and 1559 that resulted in a death toll of almost 15 percent of England's total population in 1551. To be sure, life expectancy was short (roughly 36.23 years in the period from 1551 to 1591), but crude birth rates were very high (12.72 in 1551). For its part, London's population mushroomed during the sixteenth century, from approximately 50,000 people in 1500 (2 percent of the total English population) to about 200,000 by 1600 (5 percent).[4]

England's rapid population increase was accompanied by a dramatic price revolution during the sixteenth century. A doubling of the money supply (due to increased trade and to floods of gold and silver pouring into Europe from Spanish America and elsewhere) combined with the burgeoning population and a failure of agriculture and manufacturing production to keep pace with demand caused an enormous rise in prices. Agricultural prices rose approximately 150 percent between 1510

and the 1550s, as demand for food far outstripped supply. The price of wheat tripled, and throughout the century the prices for all goods in England quadrupled. Because of population increases, wages failed to keep pace with the rise in prices, and real wages slumped from an index of 615 in 1559–1560 to 436 in 1599–1600. General famines due to crop failures in 1586 and 1598 only made a terrible situation even worse.

Seeking to increase their own incomes to keep pace with prices, landowners raised the rents they charged to peasants, driving many off the land entirely. In addition, landlords and wool merchants sought to increase wool production by dividing up the traditional open fields into individual parcels, which forced even more people off the land. Many lived in cottages and barely eked out a living on the "putting out system," whereby a merchant would deliver raw materials (wool, for instance), which would be carded, spun, and woven in the cottages and then be picked up by the merchant, who in turn brought more raw materials. Others simply abandoned their cottages and wandered as vagabonds who lived by getting odd jobs, begging, and crime.[5]

For some Englishmen, colonization was one way to remove what they considered an excessively large and increasingly dangerous population. In a extended essay on "western planting"

4. For studies of England's population, see E. A. Wrigley and R. S. Scholfield, *The Population History of England, 1541–1871* (Cambridge: Harvard University Press, 1981), esp. pp. 496–497, 528; R. A. Houston, *The Population History of Britain and Ireland, 1500–1700* (London: Macmillan, 1992); David Coleman and John Salt, *The British Population: Patterns, Trends, and Processes* (Oxford University Press, 1992), esp. pp. 20–21, 28.

5. On England's price revolution, see Barry Coward, *Social Change and Continuity in Early Modern England, 1550–1750* (London: Longman, 1988), esp. pp. 31–39, 53–55, 70. On transient labor, see Warren M. Billings, John E. Selby, and Thad W. Tate, *Colonial Virginia: A History* (White Plains, NY: KTO Press, 1986), p. 5.

(New World colonization) written by Richard Hakluyt (Hak' loot, 1152?–1616) and given to Queen Elizabeth in October 1584, the author expressed his deep concern about the "multitudes of loiterers and idle vagabonds":

> wee are growen more populous than ever . . . that they can hardly lyve one by another . . . and often fall to pilferinge and thevinge and other lewdness, whereby all the prisons of the lande are daily . . . stuffed full of them, where either they pitifully pyne awaye, or els at lengthe are miserably hanged.[6]

In Hakluyt's opinion, this was a strong argument in favor of colonization.

In addition to ridding England of its excess population, Hakluyt offered the queen other reasons why Britain should embark upon a program of colonization. He asserted that Englishmen could bring "the gospel of Christe" to other peoples, stimulate trade to "supply the wantes of all our decayed trades," establish coastal outposts for protecting and resupplying the British navy, increase revenue through custom duties, discover the immensely profitable Northwest Passage "to Cathaio and

China," and check the expansion of Spain in the New World.[7]

Yet it was easier to advocate planting colonies than actually to plant them. In 1583, Sir Humphrey Gilbert led five ships to Newfoundland, where he planted a colony; but that effort collapsed after Gilbert perished at sea (according to witnesses, his last words were: "We are as neere to heaven by the sea as by lands"). The next year, Gilbert's half-brother, Sir Walter Raleigh, convinced Queen Elizabeth to renew Gilbert's charter in his own name. Raleigh's two attempts at colonization were disastrous, however, especially the "lost colony" of 1587 in which 118 men, women, and children simply vanished into thin air. And another abortive effort, this one at Plymouth, was abandoned after two years of struggling and pain.[8]

Nor did the prospects seem more promising for the Jamestown settlement. In December 1606, the three ships *Susan Constant, Godspeed,* and *Discovery* sailed from England bound for the New World. Earlier that year, King James I had granted a charter to the Virginia Company of London (more familiarly known as the London Company, to distinguish it from the Vir-

6. Richard Hakluyt was called Richard Hakluyt the Younger to distinguish him from his cousin, also named Richard Hakluyt and also a proponent of colonization. See Hakluyt the Younger's *Discourse Concerning Western Planting* (1584) in David B. Quinn, ed., *English Plans for North America*, Vol. III of *New American World: A Documentary History of North America to 1612* (New York: Arno Press, 1979), p. 82. The words *colony* and *plantation* began to appear in English in the 1550s. See D. W. Meinig, *The Shaping of America: A Geographical Perspective on 500 Years of History* (New Haven: Yale University Press, 1986), Vol. I, p. 29.

7. Hakluyt, *Discourse Concerning Western Planting*, pp. 71–72.
8. For Gilbert's supposed last words, see William S. Powell, *Paradise Preserved* (Chapel Hill: University of North Carolina Press, 1965), p. 3. For what is probably the definitive history of the "lost colony" of Roanoke Island, see David Beers Quinn, *Set Fair for Roanoke: Voyages and Colonies, 1584–1606* (Chapel Hill: University of North Carolina Press, 1985). For a conspiratorial view of what happened to the Roanoke Island colony, see Lee Miller, *Roanoke: Solving the Mystery of the Lost Colony* (New York: Arcade Publishing, 2000).

ginia Company of Plymouth), a private corporation that hoped to imitate Spain's good fortune by finding gold, silver, and precious gems that would enrich the stockholders. On board the three vessels were 144 prospective colonists, the vast majority of them either fortune seekers or salaried company employees (such as goldsmiths, jewelers, and apothecaries[9]). None planned to be permanent settlers.

In spite of meticulous planning by the company, in Virginia things were desperate almost from the start. Only 105 would-be colonists survived the voyage, and a combination of disease, starvation, the eventual hostility of the nearby Native Americans, and conflicts between the settlement's leaders made the situation ever more dire. By the time relief ships sent by the company arrived in January 1608 with provisions and more colonists, only thirty-eight survivors remained at Jamestown.

Nor did the Virginia colony immediately improve. With few colonists skilled in agriculture and clearing land (most colonists had to be taught how to use an axe), the colony depended on food from company relief ships and trading with the Native Americans. Thus, in the winter of 1609 to 1610, Jamestown experienced its horrible "starving time," when only sixty of a fall 1609 population of five hundred survived. As one chronicler wrote:

we were constrained to eat dogs, cats, rats, snakes, toadstools, horsehides, and what not; one man out of the misery endured, killing his wife . . . to eat

her, for which he was burned. Many besides fed on the corpses of dead men.[10]

Even after the "starving time," it was by no means clear that Virginia would survive. By 1616, the colony's population hovered at only 380, and a well-coordinated Indian attack in 1622 very nearly wiped out the fledgling settlement.[11] But John Rolfe had experimented with transplanting a variety of West Indian tobacco to the "lusty soyle" of Virginia, where it thrived. In 1614, Virginia shipped four barrels of tobacco to England and by 1617 was exporting 50,000 pounds of tobacco leaves. And in spite of the facts that the London Company initially opposed the cultivation of the "noxious weed" and King James I railed against its importation and use, tobacco ultimately became the colony's salvation.[12]

In the meantime, the company had abandoned its hopes of finding gold and precious gems in Virginia and turned to long-range profits from lumber, hemp, turpentine, and finally tobacco. In order to attract settlers to the colony, in 1618 the company revised its charter to permit individuals to own land—previous to that "greate charter," all land had been owned by the company. Settlers claimed lands touching Chesa-

9. Apothecary: pharmacist, druggist.

10. Quoted in David Hawke, *The Colonial Experience* (Indianapolis: Bobbs, Merrill Co., 1966), p. 95.

11. The colonists retaliated against the Native Americans by inviting them to a peace conference at which they killed around 250 of them with poisoned wine.

12. A short excerpt from James's *A Counterblast to Tobacco* (1604) may be found in Warren M. Billings, John E. Selby, and Thad W. Tate, *Colonial Virginia: A History* (White Plains, N.Y.: KTO Press, 1986), pp. 40–41n.

peake Bay and the many rivers and streams that fed it (to use the waterways to ship their tobacco). By the time the London Company finally went bankrupt and Virginia became a royal colony (1625), landowners were building homes close to their fields and away from the settlements and stockades. Laborers were found in the form of indentured servants from England who, in exchange for their passage and a land grant after finishing their "indenture" (usually seven years), agreed to work for the landowners. Even so, it was not until around 1675 that Virginia's natural increase and not immigration replenished the colony's population.

Maryland, the other colony on Chesapeake Bay, was created by King Charles I as an immense land grant to George Calvert, a gentleman who had served King James I as secretary of state and in return had been awarded a peerage as Lord Baltimore and promised a land grant in America. James I had died in 1625, before the necessary paperwork had been completed. According to tradition, Calvert himself drew up the document, leaving a blank space where the name of the proposed colony was to go. Charles I filled in the blank with "Terra Mariae" (Mary's Land, or Maryland), named for his wife, Queen Henrietta Maria. According to the terms of the grant, the Calvert family owned all the land, could lease that land to settlers and collect rents, and totally controlled the government. The final charter was issued in 1632, two months after George Calvert's death.

Cecilius Calvert (c. 1605–1675),

George Calvert's eldest son, assumed control of the grant (6.8 million acres) and launched the first expedition on November 22, 1633. The first settlers came ashore in Maryland on March 25, 1634. Avoiding many of the errors made by the early settlers of Virginia, Maryland colonists (led by Cecilius's younger brother) purchased land from the Native Americans, planted food crops as well as tobacco, and laid claim to generous land grants on which Calvert charged low rents ("quit rents"). As was the case later in Virginia, the population was dispersed, living on or near their landholdings and thus breaking the English pattern of village life and discouraging the growth of large towns or cities.

As the proprietor, Cecilius Calvert's dream was to reproduce England's manor system in the New World, although it would be several decades before the grand plantations, plantation houses, and planters emerged. Also, since George Calvert had converted to Roman Catholicism, the Calvert family envisioned Maryland as a haven for Catholics in America. Yet the generous land grants and low quit rents attracted people of many religious persuasions, the majority of whom were Protestants. The proprietor wisely allowed religious heterogeneity. Regardless of their faiths, Marylanders worshipped land and tobacco.

By the mid-1700s, when many of those who would be the leaders of the Chesapeake society during the American Revolution were beginning to come of age, the region was dotted with large plantations, fine houses, an educated and cultured gentry class, and enough socioeconomic mobility to give at least the appearance of an open and egalitarian society. Indeed, the Chesapeake region had come a long way from the "starving time" of 1609–1610.

What were the main factors responsible for the evolution of the Chesapeake society? What were the key ingredients of that society?

The Method

How can we begin to answer such questions? Even the tiny fraction of Chesapeake colonists who left letters, diaries, sermons, or speeches (Robert Beverley, William Byrd, Charles Carroll, Thomas Jefferson, and so forth) represented only a small percentage of the Chesapeake's total population and, moreover, rarely if ever addressed these questions or issues. Indeed, it is not clear that many of those colonists who left written records were even aware of the trends and forces that were acting to shape their lives. And, of course, the vast majority of colonists left no written records at all.

Recently, however, historians have become more imaginative in using the comparatively limited material at their disposal. We know, for instance, that almost every person, even the poorest, left some record that he or she existed. That person's name may appear in any number of places, including church records of baptisms, marriages, and deaths; property-holding and tax records; civil or criminal court records; military records; ship manifests; slave auction records; and cemetery records. Thus, demographic and economic trends can be reconstructed, in some cases allowing us to understand aspects of these people's lives that they may not have perceived themselves.

How is this done? One important way is to use statistics to help reconstruct the past. Today we are bombarded almost daily with statistics—about the stock market, teenage pregnancy, illegal drug use, and the Katrina hurricane victims, for example. In order to function productively and successfully in today's world, we must use those statistics to aid us in shaping our opinions and making decisions.

Historians have learned to use these same types of statistics and statistical methods and to apply them to the past. Working carefully through those materials that still exist, historians begin to reconstruct the demographic and economic trends and forces that affected a past epoch. Were people living longer or shorter than they had been previously? Were people growing richer or poorer? Were women marrying later or earlier? Were women bearing more or fewer children? Were inheritance patterns (the methods of dividing estates among heirs) changing or not changing? To historians, each statistical summary of records (each *set* of statistics or *aggregate* picture) contains important information that increases understanding of

Table 1

Type of Record	Questions
Census	Was the population growing, shrinking, or stationary? What were the sources of population growth (natural increase, immigration)? Was the composition (age, gender, race, etc.) of the population changing or stationary?
Marriage and birth records	At what age were women marrying? Did that age change over time? Were the sizes of families increasing, decreasing, or stationary? Were the survival rates of children changing or not changing?
Wills, probate, land records	How were estates divided? Did that method change over time? Was wealth evenly distributed among the adult male population? Were various socioeconomic groups growing wealthier? poorer? Did landowners employ nonfamily labor? Did the source of that labor change over time?
Trade and custom records	Were exports increasing? decreasing? stationary? Were prices increasing? decreasing? stationary? Was the balance of trade (exports over imports) positive? negative?

a community or people being studied. Table 1 shows the types of questions historians ask with regard to several different kinds of records.

Having examined each set of statistics, the historian places the sets in some logical order, which may vary depending on the available evidence, the central questions the historian is attempting to answer, and the historian's own preferences. Some historians prefer a "birth-to-death" ordering, beginning with age-at-marriage statistics for females and moving chronologically through the collective life of the community's population. Others prefer to isolate the demographic statistical sets (birth, marriage, migration, and death) from the economic sets (such as landholding and division of estates).

Up to this point, the historian has (1) collected the statistics and arranged them into sets, (2) examined each set and measured tendencies or changes over time, and (3) arranged the sets in some logical order. Now the historian must begin asking "why" for each set. For example:

1. Why did the survival rate of children or young people change over time?
2. Why did women marry later?
3. Why did the method of dividing estates change over time?

In many cases, the answer to each question (and other "why" questions) is in one of the other statistical sets. That may cause the historian to alter his or her ordering of the sets in order to make the story clearer.

The historian is actually linking the sets to one another to form a chain. When two sets have been linked (because one set answers the "why" question of another set), the historian repeats the process until all the sets have been linked to form one chain of evidence. At that point, the historian can summarize the tendencies that have been discovered and, if desired, can connect those trends or tendencies to other events occurring in the period, such as the American Revolution.

One example of how historians link statistical sets together to answer a "why" question is sufficient. Source 4 in the Evidence section shows that British migration to the Chesapeake region (70 to 85 percent of which was by indentured servants)[13] grew rapidly from around 1650 to 1680, after which it declined precipitously. How can we account for this trend? Look at Sources 1, 2, 3, 9, 10, all of which deal with the Chesapeake's slave population. We can conclude that Chesapeake planters were changing their sources of labor from British indentured servants (who, upon serving their terms, could acquire land and begin raising tobacco to compete with their former masters) to permanent slaves from Africa.

Now ask yourself why Chesapeake planters did that. Is the answer to *that* "why" question in another statistical set? For other potential reasons, consult your instructor.

One thing you will notice almost immediately is that historians never have all the sources they need. Until the late nineteenth century, record keeping was haphazard at best; many of the statistical sets you will be examining and analyzing here have been painstakingly compiled by historians from the fragmentary data that was recorded. For example, you will see that a number of statistical sets deal with Middlesex County, Virginia, first settled by European Americans in the late 1640s and by 1700 one of the wealthiest counties in Virginia. This is because historians Darrett and Anita Rutman collected a great deal of statistical material to complete their excellent study of that county. Other counties have not been so fortunate as to have been the subject of such studies.

Also, the lack of air conditioning prior to the mid-twentieth century meant that historical records in much of the American South fell victim to a combination of heat and humidity. In some southern archives, historians could almost smell their evidence decomposing. Finally, some Chesapeake records were destroyed in the American Civil War.

Working with historical statistics is not so difficult as it may first appear. Often it is helpful to establish a small study group with a few of your classmates. As the study group talks through the problem, each individual can contribute something that possibly the other members of the group did not see, thereby broadening the group's understanding of the problem. Ana-

13. The percentages are from James Horn, "Servant Emigration to the Chesapeake in the Seventeenth Century" in Thad W. Tate and David L. Ammerman, eds., *The Chesapeake in the Seventeenth Century: Essays on Anglo-American Society* (Chapel Hill: University of North Carolina Press, 1979), p. 54. Most of the indentured servants were young, between the ages of 15 and 24. *Ibid,* p. 62.

lyzing statistics is a challenging undertaking, but the results can be immensely satisfying, as you come to "see" the *people* the statistics represent.

◆

The Evidence

Sources 1 and 2 data from the U.S. Bureau of the Census, *Historical Statistics of the United States* (Washington, D.C.: U.S. Government Printing Office, 1975), pt. 2, p. 1168; and Jim Potter, "Demographic Development and Family Structure," in Jack P. Greene and J. R. Pole, eds., *Colonial British America: Essays in the New History of the Early Modern Era* (Baltimore: The Johns Hopkins University Press, 1984), p. 138.

1. Population Growth, Virginia, 1640–1770.

Year	Whites	Increase (%)	Blacks	Increase (%)	Blacks as % of Total Pop.
1640	10.292	—	150	—	1
1650	18,326	78	405	170	—
1660	26,070	42	950	135	—
1670	33,309	28	2,000	111	6
1680	40,596	22	3,000	50	—
1690	43,701	8	9,345	212	—
1700	42,170	−4	16,390	75	28
1710	55,163	31	23,118	41	—
1720	61,198	11	26,559	15	—
1730	84,000	37	30,000	13	26
1740	120,440	43	60,000	100	—
1750	129,581	8	101,452	69	—
1760	199,156	35	140,570	39	41
1770	259,411	30	187,605	33	42

2. Population Growth, Maryland, 1640–1770.

Year	Whites	Increase (%)	Blacks	Increase (%)	Blacks as % of Total Pop.
1640	563	—	20	—	3
1650	4,204	647	300	1350	—
1660	7,668	82	758	153	—
1670	12,036	57	1,190	57	9
1680	16,293	35	1,611	35	—
1690	21,862	34	2,162	34	—
1700	26,377	21	3,227	49	11
1710	34,796	32	7,945	146	—
1720	53,634	54	12,499	57	—
1730	73,893	38	17,220	38	19
1740	92,062	25	24,031	40	—
1750	97,623	6	43,450	81	—
1760	113,263	16	49,004	13	30
1770	138,781	23	63,818	30	31

Sources 3 and 5 data from Darrett B. Rutman and Anita H. Rutman, *A Place in Time: Explicatus* (New York: W. W. Norton, 1984), pp. 28, 64.

3. Population Growth, Middlesex County, Virginia, 1668–1740.

Year	Whites	Increase (%)	Blacks	Increase (%)	Blacks as % of Total
1668	847	—	65	—	7.13
1687	1,337	58	117	80	8.05
1699	1,374	3	397	239	22.42
1704	1,436	5	553	39	27.80
1724	1,423	−1	1,293	134	47.61
1740	1,348	−5	1,596	23	54.21

Source 4 from Gloria L. Main, *Tobacco Colony: Life in Early Maryland, 1650–1720*
(Princeton: Princeton University Press, 1982), p. 10. © 1982 Princeton University Press.
Reprinted by permission of Princeton University Press.

4. Estimates of British Migration to the Americas and the Chesapeake, 1630–1700.

Years	Total Migration	To the Chesapeake	% of Total
1630–1640	41,100	9,000–10,100	21.9–24.6
1640–1650	46,100	8,100–8,900	17.6–19.3
1650–1660	58,200	16,700–18,200	28.7–31.3
1660–1670	55,200	19,500–20,900	35.3–37.9
1670–1680	53,700	21,700–23,000	40.4–42.8
1680–1690	40,200	14,600	36.3
1690–1700	44,100	15,800–16,000	35.8–36.3
Total	338,600	105,400–111,700	31.1–33.0

5. Average Age at First Marriage for White Females, Middlesex County, Virginia, 1670–1749.

Year of Marriage	Average Age at Marriage (years)
1670–1679	18.1
1680–1689	17.5
1690–1699	17.9
1700–1709	19.6
1710–1719	20.1
1720–1729	20.3
1730–1739	20.8
1740–1749	22.0

Source 6 data from Allan Kulikoff, *Tobacco and Slaves: The Development of Southern Cultures in the Chesapeake, 1680–1800,* p. 60. Copyright © 1986 by the University of North Carolina Press. Used by permission of the publisher.

6. Age at Marriage, Family Size, and Surviving Children in Tidewater, Maryland, 1650–1800.

	Years		
	1650–1700	1700–1750	1750–1800
Average white female age at first marriage	16.8	18.6	22.2
Average completed family size[14]	9.4	9.0	6.9
Average number of surviving children per couple	3.3	5.0	3.7

Source 7 data from Rutman and Rutman, *A Place in Time,* p. 55.

7. Life Expectancy of Chesapeake-born Males Who Reached the Age of 20, Middlesex County, Virginia, 1670–1729.

Birth Years	Mortality per 100, Ages 20–24[15]	Additional Years Expected to Live from Age 20
1670–1679	9.4	26.4
1680–1689	10.9	24.1
1690–1699	11.4	23.5
1700–1709	11.0	24.1
1710–1719	11.2	23.8
1720–1729	11.3	23.6

14. Completed family size: The average number of children born to women who survived married to age forty-five, hence a "completed" family.
15. The number of males twenty years old who died by the age of twenty-four, per one hundred.

Source 8 data from Philip D. Morgan, *Slave Counterpoint: Black Culture in the Eighteenth-Century Chesapeake and Low Country*, p. 41. Published for the Omohundro Institute of Early American History and Culture. Copyright © 1998 by the University of North Carolina Press. Used by permission of the publisher.

8. Plantation Size in Virginia by Number of Slaves, 1700–1779.

	Number of Slaves on Plantations			
Decade	1–5	6–10	11–20	21+
1700–1709	39%	19%	32%	10%
1710–1719	30	20	27	23
1720–1729	30	29	27	13
1730–1739	28	27	20	25
1740–1749	25	25	32	17
1750–1759	18	22	29	31
1760–1769	15	22	29	33
1770–1779	13	22	35	29

Source 9 from Richard S. Dunn, "Servants and Slaves: The Recruitment and Employment of Labor," in Greene and Pole, *Colonial British America*, p. 165, Table 6.1. © 1991 The Johns Hopkins University Press. Reprinted with permission of The Johns Hopkins University Press.

9. English Slave Imports to America, 1600–1780 (in thousands).

Years	West Indies	Southern[16] Mainland	Mid-Atlantic	New England	Total
1601–1625	—	—	—	—	—
1626–1650	21	—	—	—	21
1651–1675	69	—	—	—	69
1676–1700	174	10	—	—	184
1701–1720	160	28	2	—	190
1721–1740	199	64	4	2	269
1741–1760	267	63	1	1	332
1761–1780	335	80	2	—	417
Total	1,225	245	9	3	1,482
Black population in 1780	346	519	42	14	921

16. The Southern Mainland included Maryland, Virginia, North Carolina, South Carolina, and Georgia.

Source 10 from Main, *Tobacco Colony,* p. 26. © 1982 Princeton University Press.
Reprinted by permission of Princeton University Press.

**10. Numbers of Indentured Servants and Slaves per Estate Inventories
from Six Maryland Counties, 1662–1717.**

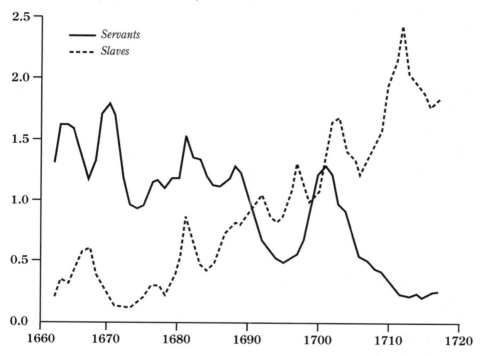

Source 11 from James Horn, *Adapting to a New World: English Society in the Seventeenth-Century Chesapeake*, p. 286. Data from St. Mary's City Commission. Published for the Omohundro Institute of Early American History and Culture. Copyright © 1994 by the University of North Carolina Press. Used by permission of the publisher.

11. Number of Servants and Slaves per Household, Lower Western Shore of Maryland, 1658–1700.

No. of Servants and Slaves per Household	No. of Households Owning	Proportion of All Households Owning	Proportion of All Households in Class Owning Mostly Slaves
1658–1674			
1–3	2	10.5%	0%
4–6	8	42.1	37.5
7–9	5	26.3	20.0
10+	4	21.1	25.0
Overall	19	100.0	26.3
1675–1684			
1–3	8	17.8%	12.5%
4–6	18	40.0	5.6
7–9	8	17.8	25.0
10+	11	24.4	36.4
Overall	45	100.0	17.8
1685–1700			
1–3	24	28.2%	33.3%
4–6	25	29.4	48.0
7–9	12	14.1	58.3
10+	24	28.2	66.7
Overall	85	99.9	50.6

Source 12 from Main, *Tobacco Colony,* p. 106. Data from probate records of six counties, Maryland, in Hall of Records, Annapolis. © 1982 Princeton University Press. Reprinted by permission of Princeton University Press.

12. Percentage of Slaves in Small and Large Bound Labor Groups,[17] 1656–1719.

Years	Number of Laborers in Group	
	2–5	6+
1656–1683	9% slave	40% slave
1684–1696	18	57
1697–1704	32	70
1705–1712	66	89½
1713–1719	68	94

Source 13 data from Social Science Research Council, *The Statistical History of the United States from Colonial Times to the Present* (Stamford, Conn.: Fairfield Publishers, 1965), pp. 765–766; Census Bureau, *Historical Statistics of the United States,* pt. 2, p. 1198.

13. Tobacco Imported by England from Virginia and Maryland (in thousands of pounds) and Maryland Tobacco Prices (in pence sterling/pound), 1620–1770.

Year	Total (in thousands of pounds)	Tobacco Prices (pence sterling/pound)
1620	119.0	12.00
1630	458.2	4.00
1640	1,257.0	2.50
1650	—	—
1663	7,371.1	1.55
1672	17,559.0	1.00
1682	21,399.0	0.80
1688	28,385.5	0.75
1700	37,166.0	1.00
1710	23,351.0	0.85
1720	34,138.0	1.19
1730	34,860.0	0.67
1740	35,372.0	0.80
1750	50,785.0	1.16
1760	51,283.0	1.60
1770	38,986.0	2.06

17. Bound labor groups included indentured servants and slaves.

Source 14 from Russell R. Menard, "Farm Prices of Maryland Tobacco, 1659–1710," in *Maryland Historical Magazine* 68 (Spring 1973): 85. Reprinted by permission.

14. Farm Prices of Maryland Tobacco, 1659–1710 (in pence sterling / pound).

Year	Mean	High	Low	Year	Mean	High	Low
1659	(1.65)			1685	1.00	1.80	0.70
1660	(1.50)			1686	1.00	1.20	0.55
1661	1.50			1687	0.85	1.00	0.60
1662	(1.60)			1688	0.75	1.00	0.50
1663	(1.55)			1689	0.70	1.00	0.50
1664	1.35			1690	(0.80)	1.00	0.50
1665	1.10			1691	(0.80)	1.00	0.60
1666	0.90			1692	(0.80)	1.00	0.60
1667	1.10			1693	0.75	1.00	0.55
1668	1.25			1694	0.75	1.25	0.35
1669	1.15			1695	0.75	1.00	0.50
1670	(1.15)			1696	0.85	1.00	0.60
1671	1.05			1697	0.90	1.50	0.60
1672	1.00			1698	1.00	1.20	0.60
1673	1.00			1699	1.05	1.50	0.60
1674	1.00			1700	1.00	1.20	0.60
1675	1.00			1701	0.95	1.20	0.60
1676	1.05			1702	1.00	1.30	0.70
1677	1.15			1703	0.85	1.00	0.30
1678	1.15			1704	0.90	1.20	0.60
1679	1.05			1705	0.80	1.20	0.35
1680	1.00			1706	0.80	1.20	0.25
1681	0.90			1707	0.90	1.20	0.60
1682	0.80			1708	0.90	1.20	0.40
1683	(0.80)	1.00	0.55	1709	0.90	1.20	0.50
1684	0.80	1.00	0.55	1710	0.85	1.00	0.30

Source 15 data from Census Bureau, *Historical Statistics of the United States*, pt. 2, pp. 1176–1177.

15. Value of Exports to and Imports from England by Virginia and Maryland, 1700–1770 (in pounds sterling).

Year	Exports (£)	Imports (£)
1700	317,302	173,481
1705	116,768	174,322
1710	188,429	127,639
1715	174,756	199,274
1720	331,482	110,717
1725	214,730	195,884
1730	346,823	150,931
1735	394,995	220,381
1740	341,997	281,428
1745	399,423	197,799
1750	508,939	349,419
1755	489,668	285,157
1760	504,451	605,882
1765	505,671	383,224
1770	435,094	717,782

Source 16 from Main, *Tobacco Colony*, p. 54. Data from probate records of six counties, Maryland, in Hall of Records, Annapolis.

16. Average Gross Personal Wealth of Ranked Strata of Maryland Probated Estates, 1656–1719 (in pounds sterling).

Strata of Estates	1656–1683	1684–1696	1697–1704	1705–1712	1713–1719	% Change 1656–83/ 1713–19
Bottom 30%	£16	£15	£14	£14	£13	−19
Lower-middle 30%	48	49	48	46	42	−12
Upper-middle 30%	142	150	169	146	146	+3
Wealthiest 10%	473	652	719	971	1009	+113

Source 17 data from Rutman and Rutman, *A Place in Time,* p. 129.

17. Wealth Distribution in Middlesex County, Virginia: Personal Property of Deceased Adult Males, 1699–1750.

Through 1699

1. The poorest 31.2% of the male population owned 3.6% of the total wealth.
2. The next poorest 28.6% of the male population owned 12.8% of the total wealth.
3. The next poorest 13.9% of the male population owned 11.1% of the total wealth.
4. The next poorest 20.8% of the male population owned 30.9% of the total wealth.
5. The wealthiest 5.6% of the male population owned 41.6% of the total wealth.

1700–1719

1. The poorest 42.5% of the male population owned 3.4% of the total wealth.
2. The next poorest 26% of the male population owned 7.9% of the total wealth.
3. The next poorest 17.8% of the male population owned 12.6% of the total wealth.
4. The next poorest 7.9% of the male population owned 14.7% of the total wealth.
5. The wealthiest 5.8% of the male population owned 61.5% of the total wealth.

1720–1750

1. The poorest 35.3% of the male population owned 3.1% of the total wealth.
2. The next poorest 30.4% of the male population owned 11.2% of the total wealth.
3. The next poorest 26% of the male population owned 31.3% of the total wealth.
4. The next poorest 5.6% of the male population owned 21.3% of the total wealth.
5. The wealthiest 2.7% of the male population owned 33.2% of the total wealth.

Source 18 data from Rutman and Rutman, *A Place in Time,* p. 238.

18. Division of Estates, Middlesex County, Virginia, 1699–1750.

Time Period	Percentage of All Sons Receiving Land
Through 1699	93
1700–1719	71
1720–1750	62

Sources 19 and 20 from Paul G. E. Clemens, *The Atlantic Economy and Colonial Maryland's Eastern Shore: From Tobacco to Grain*, pp. 194–195. Copyright © 1980 by Cornell University. Used by permission of the publisher, Cornell University Press.

19. Output of Tobacco and Wheat per Field Hand on Talbot and Kent County (Maryland) Slaveowning Plantations, 1740s and 1760s.

	1740s		1760s	
	Number of Farms	Output	Number of Farms	Output
Talbot County				
Tobacco (pounds)	59	1,520	22	880
Wheat (bushels)	12	13	18	54
Number of farms in sample	59	—	22	—
Kent County				
Tobacco (pounds)	38	1,540	16	530
Wheat (bushels)	25	40	53	93
Number of farms in sample	40	—	55	—

20. Percentage of Income Earned by Tobacco, Wheat, and Corn on Talbot and Kent County (Maryland) Slaveowning Plantations, 1740s and 1760s.

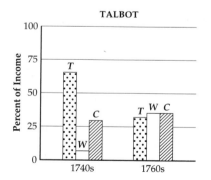
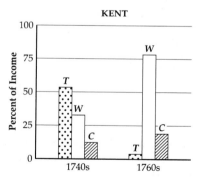

Source 21 from Robert D. Mitchell, *Commercialism and Frontier: Perspectives on the Early Shenandoah Valley* (Charlottesville, Va.: University Press of Virginia, 1977), pp. 95–100.

21. Virginia Population West of Blue Ridge Mountains, 1745–1790.

Date	Total Population	Slave Population
1745	c. 10,200	—
1750	c. 17,000	—
1755	c. 20,800	760
1782	—	6,744
1790	74,767	10,715

◆

Questions to Consider

When using statistics, first look at each set individually. For each set, ask the following questions:

1. What does this set of statistics measure?
2. How did what is being measured change over time?
3. Why did that change take place? As noted, the answer to this question can be found in another set or sets. When you connect one set to another, statisticians say that you have made a *linkage*.

Begin by examining Sources 1 through 3, dealing with population growth in Virginia, Maryland, and Middlesex County, Virginia, respectively. How did population growth change over time? What other statistical sets explain *why* the growth rates changed?

Population grows in two ways: through immigration and through natural increase. Sources 6 and 7 strongly suggest that natural increase was not the major factor in population growth until well into the eighteenth century. Why do you think this was the case? It appears that life expectancy for males who reached the age of 20 declined. Why do you think this was so? On the other hand, compare the British migration to the Chesapeake (Source 4) with the population data from Virginia and Maryland (Sources 1 and 2). What role did British migration play in the Chesapeake's population growth?

In 1699, Hugh Jones wrote, "Tobacco is our meat, drinke, cloathing and monies."[18] Unquestionably, the entire economy of the Chesapeake region revolved around the cultivation and sale of what King James I called the "noxious weed." What does Source 13 tell you about tobacco cultivation in the

18. Quoted in Lorena S. Walsh, "Slave Life, Slave Society, and Tobacco Production in the Tidewater Chesapeake, 1620–1820," in Ira Berlin and Philip D. Morgan, eds., *Cultivation and Culture: Labor and the Shaping of Slave Life in the Americas* (Charlottesville: University Press of Virginia, 1993), p. 170.

Chesapeake? What were the potential dangers of growing *too much* tobacco (see Sources 14 and 15)?

Tobacco is an extremely labor intensive crop, requiring continuous hoeing and worming as well as topping the plants (to prevent flowering and stimulate existing leaves), suckering (removal of new growth to force the plant's energy into existing leaves), cutting, hanging, curing, stripping, bundling, and packing into hogsheads (large barrels holding over 300 pounds of tobacco leaves). Therefore, a great deal of labor was needed to grow a good crop of tobacco. What were the sources of Chesapeake labor (Sources 4 and 9 through 12)? How did the source of labor change over time? How would you explain this (Source 13?)?

In addition to labor, those who would raise tobacco needed land, preferably a good amount of it because continuous cultivation of tobacco resulted in serious soil exhaustion. How did landholding patterns change over time in the Chesapeake (Sources 16, 17, and 18)? Combined with shifting labor patterns, what kind of economy was evolving in the Chesapeake region?

At this point, allow us to remind you that statistical analysis requires extreme care. For example, as you examine wealth distribution in Middlesex County, Virginia (Source 17), be very careful to note that the "wealth clusters" in the three time periods are different. For example, in the wealth distribution through 1699, the poorest group represents 31.2 percent of the male population, whereas in 1700 to 1719 the poorest group is 42.5 percent and in 1720 to 1750 it is 35.3 percent. In spite of the apparent inconsistency

of this pattern, you nevertheless will be able to see general trends of wealth distribution. What are those trends? Do you think the division of estates (Source 18) had anything to do with the trends you observed in Source 17?

Large landowners increasingly attempted to consolidate their holdings and keep them from being divided. What strategies did they employ to do this (Sources 5 and 18)?

There is little question that by the eighteenth century the evolving Chesapeake society was beginning to face increasingly severe demographic and economic troubles. What was the nature of those difficulties? Your chain of evidence should be able to give you insight into the Chesapeake residents' approaching demographic and economic crises. Can you determine any ways that the people of the Chesapeake Bay were attempting to confront their problems? It also appears that some plantation owners were beginning to practice crop diversification instead of relying almost exclusively on tobacco (Sources 19 and 20). Why do you think they did so (see sources 14 and 15)? Finally, Source 21 shows you another potential "safety valve" for Chesapeake Bay residents. What was that option?

Now sum up your work on the Chesapeake Bay colonies. What demographic and economic changes took place in those colonies between 1650 and 1750? Note especially new systems of landholding and labor. How did Chesapeake Bay colonists respond to demographic and economic changes? How might those changes have affected people living in the Chesapeake Bay colonies?

Finally, answer this chapter's central

question: What factors were responsible for the evolution of the Chesapeake society by the mid-1700s? What were the key ingredients that made up that society?

✦

Epilogue

To a person traveling through the Chesapeake Bay region in the mid-eighteenth century, all appeared well. The plantation system—complete with great planters' houses, private tutors, imported furniture, clothes, and wines, and even seasons of parties and balls—seemed to be a grander reproduction of the lives of England's country squires—except that a large percentage of the wealthiest planters had come from the "middling sort," small landowners whose hard work and good fortune had brought them to the apex of one of British North America's grandest elites.[19]

And yet, beneath the gilded surface not all was well. As the statistics clearly show, the lion's share of the Chesapeake society's benefits went to the wealthiest 10 percent of the landholders (Source 16), whereas free white smallholders' positions were eroding. Too, the shift to slave labor required an increasingly rigid and harsh system to prevent insurrections. As Thomas Jefferson later put it, such a system of bondage restricted the liberties of free and slave alike.[20]

Although only a few sensed it, the zenith of Virginia already had passed by the outbreak of the American Revolution. Overproduction of tobacco and the resulting soil exhaustion,[21] continued reliance on imported manufactured goods, the opening of new plantation lands to the south and west, the emigration of whites from eastern Virginia, and the overpopulation of slaves acted together to increase Virginia's economic troubles. By the time of Thomas Jefferson's death in 1826, the leadership of the southern states had passed from the Chesapeake to a more strident South Carolina.

Finally, one is tempted to wonder if there was any relationship between the Chesapeake's demographic and economic concerns and the region's ultimate revolution against Great Britain. Did planters' growing debts to British merchants (see Source 15) play any role in the Chesapeake's uprising against the mother country? To be

---

19. See Lois Green Carr, Russell R. Menard, and Lorena S. Walsh, *Robert Cole's World: Agriculture and Society in Early Maryland* (Chapel Hill: University of North Carolina Press, 1991), p. 15.
20. For examples of the increasing repressiveness of the Chesapeake's slave system, see Warren M. Billings, ed., *The Old Dominion in the Seventeenth Century: A Documentary History of Virginia, 1606–1689* (Chapel Hill: University of North Carolina Press, 1975), pp. 172–174.
21. See Avery Odelle Craven, *Soil Exhaustion as a Factor in the Agricultural History of Virginia and Maryland, 1606–1860* (Champaign: University of Illinois Press, 1926), esp. pp. 32–35.

sure, Patriot leaders from the Chesapeake doubtless were sincere when they avowed that they took up arms in defense of their liberties. Is it possible, however, that other, unacknowledged reasons also were pushing the colonists of the Chesapeake toward rebellion? Over a century and a half, they had laboriously constructed the Chesapeake society; but even as the revolution approached, that society was under increasing strain and tension. How to maintain the plantation system and slavery while simultaneously advocating equality and freedom became the Chesapeake—and the American—dilemma.

4

What Really Happened in the Boston Massacre? The Trial of Captain Thomas Preston

The Problem

On the chilly evening of March 5, 1770, a small group of boys began taunting a British sentry (called a *centinel* or *sentinel*) in front of the Boston Custom House. Pushed to the breaking point by this goading, the soldier struck one of his tormentors with his musket. Soon a crowd of fifty or sixty gathered around the frightened soldier, prompting him to call for help. The officer of the day, Captain Thomas Preston, and seven British soldiers hurried to the Custom House to protect the sentry.

Upon arriving at the Custom House, Captain Preston must have sensed how precarious his position was. The crowd had swelled to more than one hundred, some anxious for a fight, others simply curiosity seekers, and still others called from their homes by the town's church bells, a traditional signal that a fire had broken out. Efforts by Preston and others to calm the crowd proved useless.

And because the crowd had enveloped Preston and his men as it had the lone sentry, retreat was nearly impossible.

What happened next is a subject of considerable controversy. One of the soldiers fired his musket into the crowd, and the others followed suit, one by one. The colonists scattered, leaving five dead[1] and six wounded, some of whom were probably innocent bystanders. Preston and his men quickly returned to their barracks, where they were placed under house arrest. They were later taken to jail and charged with murder.

Preston's trial began on October 24,

---

1. Those killed were Crispus Attucks (a part African, part Native American seaman in his forties, who also went by the name of Michael Johnson), James Caldwell (a sailor), Patrick Carr (an immigrant from Ireland who worked as a leather-breeches maker), Samuel Gray (a ropemaker), and Samuel Maverick (a seventeen-year-old apprentice).

1770, delayed by the authorities in an attempt to cool the emotions of the townspeople. Soon after the March 5 event, however, a grand jury had taken sworn depositions from Preston, the soldiers, and more than ninety Bostonians. The depositions leaked out (in a pamphlet, probably published by anti-British extremists), helping keep emotions at a fever pitch.

John Adams, Josiah Quincy, and Robert Auchmuty had agreed to defend Preston,[2] even though the first two were staunch Patriots. They believed that the captain was entitled to a fair trial and did their best to defend him. After a difficult jury selection, the trial began, witnesses for the prosecution and the defense being called mostly from those who had given depositions to the grand jury. The trial lasted for four days, an unusually long trial for the times. The case went to the jury at 5:00 P.M. on October 29. Although it took the jury only three hours to reach a verdict, the decision was not announced until the following day.

In this chapter, you will be using portions of the evidence given at the murder trial of Captain Thomas Preston to reconstruct what actually happened on that March 5, 1770, evening in Boston, Massachusetts. Was Preston guilty as charged? Or was he innocent? Only by reconstructing the event that we call the Boston Massacre will you be able to answer these questions.

Background

The town of Boston[3] had been uneasy throughout the first weeks of 1770. Tension had been building since the early 1760s because the town was increasingly affected by the forces of migration, change, and maturation. The protests against the Stamp Act had been particularly bitter there, and men such as Samuel Adams were encouraging their fellow Bostonians to be even bolder in their remonstrances. In response, in 1768 the British government ordered two regiments of soldiers to Boston to restore order and enforce the laws of Parliament. "They will not *find* a rebellion," quipped Benjamin Franklin of the soldiers, "they may indeed *make* one" (italics added).

Instead of bringing calm to Boston, the presence of soldiers only increased tensions. Incidents between Bostonians and redcoats were common on the streets, in taverns, and at the places of employment of British soldiers who sought part-time jobs to supplement their meager salaries. Known

2. Adams, Quincy, and Auchmuty (pronounced Aūk′mūty) also were engaged to defend the soldiers, a practice that would not be allowed today because of the conflict of interest (defending more than one person charged with the same crime).

3. Although Boston was one of the largest urban centers in the colonies, the town was not incorporated as a city. Several attempts were made, but residents opposed them, fearing they would lose the institution of the town meeting.

✦ CHAPTER 4

What Really
Happened in the
Boston Massacre?
The Trial of
Captain Thomas
Preston

British sympathizers and informers were harassed, and Crown officials were openly insulted. Indeed, the town of Boston seemed to be a powder keg just waiting for a spark to set off an explosion.

On February 22, 1770, British sympathizer and informer Ebenezer Richardson tried to tear down an anti-British sign. He was followed to his house by an angry crowd that proceeded to taunt him and break his windows with stones. One of the stones struck Richardson's wife. Enraged, he grabbed a musket and fired almost blindly into the crowd. Eleven-year-old Christopher Seider[4] fell to the ground with eleven pellets of shot in his chest. The boy died eight hours later. The crowd, by now numbering about one thousand, dragged Richardson from his house and through the streets, finally delivering him to the Boston jail. Four days later, the town conducted a huge funeral for Christopher Seider, probably arranged and organized by Samuel Adams. Seider's casket was carried through the streets by children, and approximately two thousand mourners (one-seventh of Boston's total population) took part.

All through the next week Boston was an angry town. Gangs of men and boys roamed the streets at night looking for British soldiers foolish enough to venture out alone. Similarly, off-duty soldiers prowled the same streets looking for someone to challenge them. A fight broke out at a ropewalk between some soldiers who worked there part time and some unemployed colonists.

With large portions of both the Boston citizenry and the British soldiers inflamed, the incident on March 5 touched off an ugly confrontation in front of the Custom House, a symbol of British authority over the colonies. Both sides sought to use the event to support their respective causes. But Samuel Adams, a struggling attorney with a flair for politics and propaganda, clearly had the upper hand. The burial of the five "martyrs" was attended by almost every resident of Boston, and Adams used the event to push his demands for British troop withdrawal and to heap abuse on the mother country. Therefore, when the murder trial of Captain Thomas Preston finally opened in late October, emotions had hardly diminished.

Crowd disturbances had been an almost regular feature of life in both England and America. Historian John Bohstedt has estimated that England was the scene of at least one thousand crowd disturbances and riots between 1790 and 1810.[5] Colonial American towns were no more placid; demonstrations and riots were almost regular features of the colonists' lives. Destruction of property and burning of effigies were common in these disturbances. In August 1765 in Boston, for example, crowds protesting against the Stamp Act burned effigies and destroyed the homes of stamp distributor Andrew Oliver and Massachusetts Lieutenant Governor Thomas Hutchinson. Indeed, it was almost as if the entire community was willing to countenance dem-

---

4. Christopher Seider is sometimes referred to as Christopher Snider.

5. John Bohstedt, *Riots and Community Politics in England and Wales, 1790–1810* (Cambridge, Mass.: Harvard University Press, 1983), p. 5.

onstrations and riots as long as they were confined to parades, loud gatherings, and limited destruction of property. In almost no cases were there any deaths, and the authorities seldom fired on the crowds. Yet on March 5, 1770, both the crowd and the soldiers acted uncharacteristically. The result was the tragedy that colonists dubbed the "Boston Massacre." Why did the crowd and the soldiers behave as they did?

To repeat, your task is to reconstruct the so-called Boston Massacre so as to understand what really happened on that fateful evening. Spelling and punctuation in the evidence have been modernized only to clarify the meaning.

The Method

Many students (and some historians) like to think that facts speak for themselves. This is especially tempting when analyzing a single incident like the Boston Massacre, many eyewitnesses of which testified at the trial. However, discovering what really happened, even when there are eyewitnesses, is never quite that easy. Witnesses may be confused at the time, they may see only part of the incident, or they may unconsciously "see" only what they expect to see. Obviously, witnesses also may have some reasons to lie. Thus the testimony of witnesses must be carefully scrutinized, for both what the witnesses *mean* to tell us and other relevant information as well. Therefore, historians approach such testimony with considerable skepticism and are concerned not only with the testimony itself but also with the possible motives of the witnesses.

Neither Preston nor the soldiers testified at the captain's trial because English legal custom prohibited defendants in criminal cases from testifying in their own behalf (the expectation be-

ing that they would perjure themselves). One week after the Massacre, however, in a sworn deposition, or statement, Captain Preston gave his side of the story. Although the deposition was not introduced at the trial and therefore the jury was not aware of what Preston himself had said, we have reproduced a portion of Preston's deposition for you to examine. How does Preston's deposition agree or disagree with other eyewitnesses' accounts?

No transcript of Preston's trial survives, if indeed one was ever made. Trial testimony comes from an anonymous person's summary of what each person said, the notes of Robert Treat Paine (one of the lawyers for the prosecution), and one witness's (Richard Palmes's) reconstruction of what his testimony and the cross-examination had been. Although historians would prefer to use the original trial transcript and would do so if one were available, the anonymous summary, Paine's notes, and one witness's recollections are acceptable substitutes because probably all three people were present

◆ CHAPTER 4

What Really
Happened in the
Boston Massacre?
The Trial of
Captain Thomas
Preston

in the courtroom (Paine and Palmes certainly were) and the accounts tend to corroborate one another.

Almost all the witnesses were at the scene, yet not all their testimony is of equal merit. First, try to reconstruct the scene itself: the actual order in which the events occurred and where the various participants were standing. Whenever possible, look for corroborating testimony—that of two or more reliable witnesses who heard or saw the same things.

Be careful to use all the evidence. You should be able to develop some reasonable explanation for the conflicting testimony and those things that do not fit into your reconstruction very well.

Almost immediately you will discover that some important pieces of evidence are missing. For example, it would be useful to know the individual backgrounds and political views of the witnesses. Unfortunately, we know very little about the witnesses themselves, and we can reconstruct the political ideas of only about one-third of them. Therefore, you will have to rely on the testimonies given, deducing which witnesses were telling the truth, which were lying, and which were simply mistaken.

The fact that significant portions of the evidence are missing is not disastrous. Historians seldom have all the evidence they need when they attempt to tackle a historical problem. Instead, they must be able to do as much as they can with the evidence that is available, using it as completely and imaginatively as they can. They do so by asking questions of the available evidence.

Where were the witnesses standing? Which one seems more likely to be telling the truth? Which witnesses were probably lying? When dealing with the testimony of the witnesses, be sure to determine what is factual and what is a witness's opinion. A rough sketch of the scene has been provided. How can it help you?

Also included in the evidence is Paul Revere's famous engraving of the incident, probably plagiarized from a drawing by artist Henry Pelham. It is unlikely that either Pelham or Revere was an eyewitness to the Boston Massacre, yet Revere's engraving gained widespread distribution, and most people—in 1770 and today—tend to recall that engraving when they think of the Boston Massacre. Do not examine the engraving until you have read the trial account closely. Can Revere's engraving help you find out what really happened that night? How does the engraving fit the eyewitnesses' accounts? How do the engraving and the accounts differ? Why?

Keep the central question in mind: What really happened in the Boston Massacre? Throughout this exercise, you will be trying to determine whether an order to fire was actually given. If so, by whom? If not, how can you explain why shots were fired? As commanding officer, Thomas Preston was held responsible and charged with murder. You might want to consider the evidence available to you from the point of view of either a prosecution or defense attorney. Which side had the stronger case?

The Evidence

1. Site of the Boston Massacre, Town House Area, 1770.

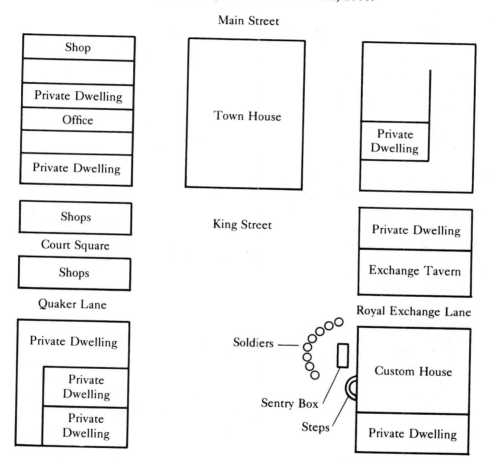

◆ CHAPTER 4

What Really
Happened in the
Boston Massacre?
The Trial of
Captain Thomas
Preston

Source 2 from *Publications of The Colonial Society of Massachusetts* (Boston: The Colonial Society of Massachusetts, 1905), Vol. VII, pp. 8–9.

2. Deposition of Captain Thomas Preston, March 12, 1770 (excerpt).

The mob still increased and were outrageous, striking their clubs or bludgeons one against another, and calling out, come on you rascals, you bloody backs, you lobster scoundrels, fire if you dare, G-d damn you, fire and be damned, we know you dare not, and much more such language was used. At this time I was between the soldiers and the mob, parleying with, and endeavoring all in my power to persuade them to retire peaceably, but to no purpose. They advanced to the points of the bayonets, struck some of them and even the muzzles of the pieces, and seemed to be endeavoring to close with the soldiers. On which some well behaved persons asked me if the guns were charged. I replied yes. They then asked me if I intended to order the men to fire. I answered no, by no means, observing to them that I was advanced before the muzzles of the men's pieces, and must fall a sacrifice if they fired; that the soldiers were upon the half cock[6] and charged bayonets, and my giving the word fire under those circumstances would prove me to be no officer. While I was thus speaking, one of the soldiers, having received a severe blow with a stick, stepped a little to one side and instantly fired. . . . On this a general attack was made on the men by a great number of heavy clubs and snowballs being thrown at them, by which all our lives were in imminent danger, some persons at the same time from behind calling out, damn your bloods—why don't you fire. Instantly three or four of the soldiers fired. . . . On my asking the soldiers why they fired without orders, they said they heard the word fire and supposed it came from me. This might be the case as many of the mob called out fire, fire, but I assured the men that I gave no such order; that my words were, don't fire, stop your firing.[7]

6. The cock of a musket had to be fully drawn back (cocked) for the musket to fire. In half cock, the cock was drawn only halfway back so that priming powder could be placed in the pan. The musket, however, would not fire at half cock. This is the origin of "Don't go off half cocked." See Source 5.
7. Depositions also were taken from the soldiers, three of whom claimed, "We did our Captain's orders and if we don't obey his commands should have been confined and shot." As with Preston's deposition, the jury was not aware of that statement. In addition, ninety-six depositions were taken from townspeople.

Source 3 from Hiller B. Zobel, ed., *The Legal Papers of John Adams* (Cambridge, Mass.: Belknap Press of Harvard University Press, 1965), Vol. III, pp. 50, 51, 52, 53, 56, 57–58, 61, 62, 65–66, 76, 77–78. Copyright © 1965 by the Massachusetts Historical Society. Reprinted by permission of the publisher.

3. The Trial of Captain Thomas Preston (*Rex v. Preston*), October 24–29 (excerpt).

Witnesses for the King (Prosecution)

Edward Gerrish (or Garrick)

I heard a noise about 8 o'clock and went down to Royal Exchange Lane. Saw some Persons with Sticks coming up Quaker Lane. I said [to the sentry] Capt. Goldsmith owed my fellow Apprentice. He said he was a Gentleman and would pay every body. I said there was none in the Regiment.[8] He asked for me. I went to him, was not ashamed of my face. . . . The Sentinel left his Post and Struck me. I cried. My fellow Apprentice and a young man came up to the Sentinel and called him Bloody back.[9] He called to the Main Guard. . . . There was not a dozen people when the Sentinel called the Guard.

Ebenezer Hinkley

Just after 9 o'clock heard the Cry of Fire. I saw the party come out of the Guard House. A Capt. cried out of the Window "fire upon 'em damn 'em." I followed 'em down before the Custom House door. Capt. Preston was out and commanded 'em. They drew up and charged their Bayonets. Montgomery[10] pushed at the people advancing. In 2 or 3 minutes a Boy threw a small stick over hand and hit Montgomery on Breast. Then I heard the word fire in ¼ minute he fired. I saw some pieces of Snow as big as Egg thrown. 3 or 4 thrown at the same time of pushing on the other End of the file, before 1st gun fired. The body of People about a Rod[11] off. People said Damn 'em they durst not fire don't be afraid. No threats . . . I was a Rod from Capt. Preston. Did not hear him give Order to fire. ½ minute from 1st Gun to 2d. same to 3d. The others quicker. I saw no people striking the Guns or Bayonets nor pelting 'em. I saw Preston between people and Soldiers. I did not see him when 1st firing.

8. To say that there was no gentleman in the regiment was an insult to the sentry's superior officer, Captain Goldsmith.
9. British soldiers' coats were red.
10. Montgomery, one of the soldiers, undoubtedly fired the first shot.
11. A rod equals 16.5 feet.

◆ CHAPTER 4

What Really
Happened in the
Boston Massacre?
The Trial of
Captain Thomas
Preston

Peter Cunningham

Upon the cry of fire and Bells ringing went into King Street, heard the Capt. say Turn out the Guard.[12] Saw the Centinel standing on the steps of the Custom house, pushing his Bayonet at the People who were about 30 or 40. Captain came and ordered the Men to prime and load.[13] He came before 'em about 4 or 5 minutes after and put up their Guns with his Arm. They then fired and were priming and loading again. I am pretty positive the Capt. bid 'em Prime and load. I stood about 4 feet off him. Heard no Order given to fire. The Person who gave Orders to Prime and load stood with his back to me, I did not see his face only when he put up their Guns. I stood about 10 or 11 feet from the Soldiers, the Captain about the midway between.

William Wyatt

I heard the bell, . . . saw People running several ways. The largest part went down to the North of the Townhouse. I went the South side, saw an officer leading out 8 or 10 Men. Somebody met the officer and said, Capt. Preston for Gods sake mind what you are about and take care of your Men. He went down to the Centinel, drew up his Men, bid them face about, Prime and load. I saw about 100 People in the Street huzzaing, crying fire, damn you fire. In about 10 minutes I heard the Officer say fire. The Soldiers took no notice. His back was to me. I heard the same voice say fire. The Soldiers did not fire. The Officer then stamped and said Damn your bloods fire be the consequences what it will. Immediately the first Gun was fired. I have no doubt the Officer was the same person the Man spoke to when coming down with the Guard. His back was to me when the last order was given. I was then about 5 or 6 yards off and within 2 yards at the first. He stood in the rear when the Guns were fired. Just before I heard a Stick, which I took to be upon a Gun. I did not see it. The Officer had to the best of my knowledge a cloth coloured Surtout[14] on. After the firing the Captain stepd forward before the Men and struck up their Guns. One was loading again and he damn'd 'em for firing and severely reprimanded 'em. I did not mean the Capt. had the Surtout but the Man who spoke to him when coming with the Guard.

12. To dress and equip so as to be ready for duty.
13. Muskets were loaded from the muzzle with powder, wadding, a ball, and more wadding. The hammer was drawn back halfway, and powder was poured into the small pan under the hammer. There was a small piece of flint attached to the cock (see Source 5) so that when the trigger was pulled, the cock would come down and the flint would spark and ignite the gunpowder in the pan. The fire would then ignite the gunpowder in the breech and fire the gun. If the powder in the pan exploded but did not ignite the powder in the breech, the result was a "flash in the pan" and a musket that did not fire.
14. A type of overcoat.

John Cole

I saw the officer after the firing and spoke to the Soldiers and told 'em it was a Cowardly action to kill men at the end of their Bayonets. They were pushing at the People who seemed to be trying to come into the Street. The Captain came up and stamped and said Damn their bloods fire again and let 'em take the consequence. I was within four feet of him. He had no surtout but a red Coat with a Rose on his shoulder.

Benjamin Burdick

When I came into King Street about 9 o'Clock I saw the Soldiers round the Centinel. I asked one if he was loaded and he said yes. I asked him if he would fire, he said yes by the Eternal God and pushd his Bayonet at me. After the firing the Captain came before the soldiers and put up their Guns with his arm and said stop firing, dont fire no more or don't fire again. I heard the word fire and took it and am certain that it came from behind the Soldiers. I saw a man passing busily behind who I took to be an Officer. The firing was a little time after. I saw some persons fall. Before the firing I saw a stick thrown at the Soldiers. The word fire I took to be a word of Command. I had in my hand a highland broad Sword which I brought from home. Upon my coming out I was told it was a wrangle[15] between the Soldiers and people, upon that I went back and got my Sword. I never used to go out with a weapon. I had not my Sword drawn till after the Soldier pushed his Bayonet at me. I should have cut his head off if he had stepd out of his Rank to attack me again. At the first firing the People were chiefly in Royal Exchange lane, there being about 50 in the Street. After the firing I went up to the Soldiers and told them I wanted to see some faces that I might swear to them another day. The Centinel in a melancholy tone said perhaps Sir you may.

Daniel Calef

I was present at the firing. I heard one of the Guns rattle. I turned about and lookd and heard the officer who stood on the right in a line with the Soldiers give the word fire twice. I lookd the Officer in the face when he gave the word and saw his mouth. He had on a red Coat, yellow Jacket and Silver laced hat, no trimming on his Coat.[16] The Prisoner is the Officer I mean. I saw his face plain, the moon shone on it. I am sure of the man though I have not seen him since before yesterday when he came into Court with others. I knew him in-

15. A quarrel.
16. The 29th Regiment, to which Preston belonged, wore uniforms that exactly matched Calef's description.

✦ CHAPTER 4

What Really
Happened in the
Boston Massacre?
The Trial of
Captain Thomas
Preston

stantly. I ran upon the word fire being given about 30 feet off. The officer had no Surtout on.

Robert Goddard

The Soldiers came up to the Centinel and the Officer told them to place themselves and they formd a half moon. The Captain told the Boys to go home least[17] there should be murder done. They were throwing Snow balls. Did not go off but threw more Snow balls. The Capt. was behind the Soldiers. The Captain told them to fire. One Gun went off. A Sailor or Townsman struck the Captain. He thereupon said damn your bloods fire think I'll be treated in this manner. This Man that struck the Captain came from among the People who were seven feet off and were round on one wing. I saw no person speak to him. I was so near I should have seen it. After the Capt. said Damn your bloods fire they all fired one after another about 7 or 8 in all, and then the officer bid Prime and load again. He stood behind all the time. Mr. Lee went up to the officer and called the officer by name Capt. Preston. I saw him coming down from the Guard behind the Party. I went to Gaol[18] the next day being sworn for the Grand Jury to see the Captain. Then said pointing to him that's the person who gave the word to fire. He said if you swear that you will ruin me everlastingly. I was so near the officer when he gave the word fire that I could touch him. His face was towards me. He stood in the middle behind the Men. I looked him in the face. He then stood within the circle. When he told 'em to fire he turned about to me. I lookd him in the face.

Isaac Pierce

The Lieut. Governor asked Capt. Preston didn't you know you had no power to fire upon the Inhabitants or any number of People collected together unless you had a Civil Officer to give order. The Captain replied I was obliged to, to save my Sentry.

Joseph Belknap

The Lieut. Governor said to Preston Don't you know you can do nothing without a Magistrate. He answered I did it to save my Men.

---

17. Lest; for fear that.
18. Jail.

Witnesses for the Prisoner (Preston)

Edward Hill

After all the firing Captain Preston put up the Gun of a Soldier who was going to fire and said fire no more you have done mischief enough.

Richard Palmes

Somebody there said there was a Rumpus in King Street. I went down. When I had got there I saw Capt. Preston at the head of 7 or 8 Soldiers at the Custom house drawn up, their Guns breast high and Bayonets fixed. Found Theodore Bliss talking with the Captain. I heard him say why don't you fire or words to that effect. The Captain answered I know not what and Bliss said God damn you why don't you fire. I was close behind Bliss. They were both in front. Then I step'd immediately between them and put my left hand in a familiar manner on the Captains right shoulder to speak to him. Mr. John Hickling then looking over my shoulder I said to Preston are your Soldiers Guns loaded. He answered with powder and ball. Sir I hope you dont intend the Soldiers shall fire on the Inhabitants. He said by no means. The instant he spoke I saw something resembling Snow or Ice strike the Grenadier[19] on the Captains right hand being the only one then at his right. He instantly stepd one foot back and fired the first Gun. I had then my hand on the Captains shoulder. After the Gun went off I heard the word fire. The Captain and I stood in front about half between the breech and muzzle of the Guns. I dont know who gave the word fire. I was then looking on the Soldier who fired. The word was given loud. The Captain might have given the word and I not distinguish it. After the word fire in about 6 or 7 seconds the Grenadier on the Captains left fired and then the others one after another. . . .

Q. Did you situate yourself before Capt. Preston, in order that you might be out of danger, in case they fired?
A. I did not apprehend myself in any danger.
Q. Did you hear Captain Preston give the word *Fire?*
A. I have told your Honors, that after the first gun was fired, I heard the word, *fire!* but who gave it, I know not.

19. A soldier in the British Grenadier Guards.

◆ CHAPTER 4

What Really
Happened in the
Boston Massacre?
The Trial of
Captain Thomas
Preston

Jane Whitehouse

A Man came behind the Soldiers walked backwards and forward, encouraging them to fire. The Captain stood on the left about three yards. The man touched one of the Soldiers upon the back and said fire, by God I'll stand by you. He was dressed in dark colored clothes. . . . He did not look like an Officer. The man fired directly on the word and clap on the Shoulder. I am positive the man was not the Captain. . . . I am sure he gave no orders. . . . I saw one man take a chunk of wood from under his Coat throw it at a Soldier and knocked him. He fell on his face. His firelock[20] was out of his hand. . . . This was before any firing.

Newton Prince, a Negro, a member of the South Church

The Capt. stood between the Soldiers and the Gutter about two yards from the Gutter. I saw two or three strike with sticks on the Guns. I was going off to the west of the Soldiers and heard the Guns fire and saw the dead carried off. Soon after the Guard Drums beat to arms.[21] The People whilst striking on the Guns cried fire, damn you fire. I have heard no Orders given to fire, only the people in general cried fire.

James Woodall

I saw one Soldier knocked down. His Gun fell from him. I saw a great many sticks and pieces of sticks and Ice thrown at the Soldiers. The Soldier who was knocked down took up his Gun and fired directly. Soon after the first Gun I saw a Gentleman behind the Soldiers in velvet of blue or black plush trimmed with gold. He put his hand toward their backs. Whether he touched them I know not and said by God I'll stand by you whilst I have a drop of blood and then said fire and two went off and the rest to 7 or 8. . . . The Captain, after, seemed shocked and looked upon the Soldiers. I am very certain he did not give the word fire.

Cross-Examination of Captain James Gifford

Q. Did you ever know an officer order men to fire with their bayonets charged?

A. No, Officers never give order to fire from charged bayonet. They would all have fired together, or most of them.

---

20. Musket.
21. A special drumbeat that signaled soldiers to arm themselves.

Source 4 from Anthony D. Darling, *Red Coat and Brown Bess,* Historical Arms Series, No. 12 (Bloomfield, Ontario). Courtesy of Museum Restoration Service, © 1970, 1981.

4. The Position of "Bayonets Charged."

Source 5 from Robert Held, *The Age of Firearms* (New York: Harper, 1957), p. 93. Drawing by Nancy Jenkins. Reprinted by permission of the author.

5. Detail of a Musket.

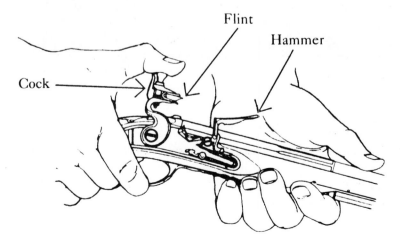

◆ CHAPTER 4

What Really
Happened in the
Boston Massacre?
The Trial of
Captain Thomas
Preston

Source 6 from the Library of Congress.

6. Paul Revere's Engraving of the Boston Massacre.

[*Notice how he dubbed the Custom House "Butcher's Hall."*]

◆

Questions to Consider

In reconstructing the event, begin by imagining the positions of the various soldiers and witnesses. Where were the soldiers standing? Where was Captain Preston standing? Which witnesses were closest to Preston (that is, in the best positions to see and hear what happened)? Where were the other witnesses? Remember that the event took place around 9:00 P.M., when Boston was totally dark.

Next, read closely Preston's deposition and the trial testimony. What major points did Preston make in his own defense? Do you find those points plausible? More important, do the witnesses who were closest to Preston agree or disagree with his recounting, or with each other's? On what points? Be as specific as possible.

Now consider the other witnesses, those who were not so near. What did they hear? What did they see? To what degree do their testimonies agree or disagree, both with each other and with Preston and those closest to him?

Lawyers for both sides spent considerable time trying to ascertain what Captain Preston was wearing on that evening. Why did they consider this important? Based on the evidence, what do you think Preston was wearing on the evening of March 5, 1770? What conclusions could you draw from that?

The attorneys also were particularly interested in the crowd's behavior *prior to* the firing of the first musket. Why did they consider that important? How would you characterize the crowd's behavior? Are you suspicious

of testimony that is at direct odds with your conclusion about this point?

Several witnesses (especially Jane Whitehouse) tell a quite different story. To what extent is her recounting of the event plausible? Is it corroborated by other witnesses?

We included Paul Revere's engraving, even though he probably was not an eyewitness, because by the time of Preston's trial, surely all the witnesses would have seen it and, more important, because later Americans have obtained their most lasting visual image of the event from that work. How does the engraving conform to what actually happened? How does it conflict with your determination of what actually took place? If there are major discrepancies, why do you think this is so? (Revere certainly knew a number of the eyewitnesses and could have ascertained the truth from them.)

After you have answered these questions and carefully weighed the eyewitnesses' evidence, answer the central question: What really happened in the Boston Massacre?

◆

Epilogue

In his closing arguments in defense of Captain Preston, John Adams noted that the crowd not only had been harassing the soldiers but also had actually threatened to attack them. Yet there was no reliable evidence to prove that Preston had ordered his men to fire into the crowd, Adams insisted. In such doubtful cases, he concluded, the jury must vote for an acquittal. The

prosecution's closing summary portrayed Preston as a murderer. The crowd's actions, the prosecution maintained, were "a few Snow-balls, thrown by a parcel of *Boys*." According to the prosecution, the rest of the people who gathered in the square were peaceful and simply curious about what was happening.

In the trial of Thomas Preston, the

◆ CHAPTER 4

What Really
Happened in the
Boston Massacre?
The Trial of
Captain Thomas
Preston

jury took only three hours to reach its verdict: not guilty. Some of the jurors were sympathetic to the British, and thus were determined to find Preston innocent no matter what evidence was presented. Also, the leaking of the grand jury depositions ultimately helped Preston's defense because defense attorneys knew in advance what the potentially most damaging witnesses would say in court. Finally, defense attorney John Adams's tactics (to create so much confusion in the minds of the jurors that they could not be certain what actually had taken place) were extremely effective. As it turned out, Preston had the advantage from the very beginning.

As for Thomas Preston himself, the British officer was quickly packed off to England, where he received a pension of £200 per year from the king "to compensate him for his suffering." He did not participate in the American Revolution and died in 1781. Of the eight soldiers (the sentry plus the seven men Preston brought to the Custom House), six were acquitted, and two were convicted of manslaughter and punished by being branded on the thumb. From there they disappeared into the mists of history.

Although they loudly asserted that the verdicts were gross miscarriages of justice, Patriot leaders Sam Adams, Joseph Warren, Josiah Quincy, and others probably were secretly delighted by Preston's and the majority of the redcoats' acquittals. Those verdicts outraged many colonists and allowed Patriot propagandists to whip up even more sentiment against British "tyranny." Speaking of Samuel Adams, one historian has claimed that "[n]o one in the colonies realized more fully than he the primary necessity of arousing public opinion, [and] no one set about it more assiduously."[22]

The so-called Boston Massacre not only was an important event that led to the American Revolution, but it also helped shape Americans' attitudes as to what their revolution was all about. Samuel Adams and others organized annual remembrances of the event. At the 1775 ceremony, held only a month before the battles of Lexington and Concord Bridge, Joseph Warren brought his audience to a near frenzy when he thundered, "[T]ake heed, ye infant babes, lest, whilst your streaming eyes are fixed on the ghastly corpse, your feet slide on the stones bespattered with your father's brains."[23]

More than one hundred years after the event, the Massachusetts legislature authorized a memorial honoring the martyrs to be placed on the site of the so-called massacre. The Bostonians' convictions were bolstered by Irish immigrants whose ancestors had known British "tyranny" firsthand, and the Bostonians remained convinced that the American Revolution had been caused by Britain's selfishness and oppression. As we can see in the Boston Massacre, the road to the Revolution was considerably more complicated than that.

Today the site of the Boston Massacre is on a traffic island beside the Old State House (formerly called the Town House and seen in the background of Paul Revere's famous engraving) in the

22. Philip Davidson, *Propaganda and the American Revolution* (Chapel Hill: University of North Carolina Press, 1941), p. 7.
23. Ibid., p. 9.

midst of Boston's financial district. With the exception of the State House (now a tasteful museum), the site is ringed by skyscrapers that house, among other institutions, the Bank of America. Thousands of Bostonians and tourists stand on the Boston Massacre site every day, waiting for the traffic to abate.

For his part, John Adams believed that the Boston Massacre was an event "which had been intentionally wrought up by designing men, who knew what they were aiming at. . . ."[24] Even so, the Patriot leader claimed that "the foundation of American independence was laid" on the evening of March 5, 1770. Although he may have overstated the case, clearly many Americans living *today* have come to see the event as a cru-

cial one in the buildup to the revolution against Great Britain.

Now that you have examined the evidence, do you think the Boston Massacre of March 5, 1770, was a justifiable reason for rebellion against the mother country? Could the crowd action on that evening secretly have been directed by the Patriot elite, or was it a spontaneous demonstration of anti-British fury? Why was Paul Revere's engraving at such variance with what actually took place?

Few Americans have stopped to ponder what actually happened on that fateful evening. Like the American Revolution itself, the answer to that question may well be more complex than we think.

24. Quoted in John C. Miller, *Sam Adams, Pioneer in Propaganda* (Stanford, Cal.: Stanford University Press, 1936), p. 187.

5

The First American Party System: The Philadelphia Congressional Election of 1794

◆

The Problem

For weeks prior to the federal congressional elections of 1794, the city of Philadelphia, the nation's temporary capital, was in a state of extreme political excitement. Not since the battle in Pennsylvania over the ratification of the United States Constitution had the city been the scene of such political tension and argument. The political factions that had appeared like small clouds over the first administration of President George Washington had grown immensely, and by 1794 in Philadelphia, they were on the verge of becoming distinct political parties.

Federalist Thomas Fitzsimons, a congressman since the beginning of the new government, was challenged by wealthy merchant and Democratic-Republican John Swanwick. Friends of the two contestants filled the air with vicious charges and countercharges in

hopes of attracting voters to their respective candidates. Fitzsimons's supporters called Swanwick an "unstable, avaricious upstart who was unknown as a public figure until he 'herded with [the people's] enemies [the Democratic-Republicans], and became their tools.'" Swanwick's friends nicknamed Fitzsimons "Billy the Fidler" and portrayed him as a mindless sycophant of Secretary of the Treasury Alexander Hamilton. Meetings were held in various parts of the city to endorse one candidate or the other, and Philadelphia's newspapers were filled with charges and countercharges. Although many people were disturbed by these eruptions in what they considered a still fragile nation, unquestionably the growing factions had broken the political calm. Would political parties shatter the new republic or strengthen it? In Philadelphia in 1794, opinion was divided.

Challenger John Swanwick won a stunning victory over incumbent Thomas Fitzsimons, carrying seven of the city's twelve wards and collecting 56 percent of the votes cast. Federalism in Philadelphia had been dealt a severe blow.

In this chapter, you will be analyzing the evidence to determine why the lesser-known Swanwick won the election. What factors do you think were responsible for his victory? You will not be relying on just one or two types of evidence, as in previous chapters. Instead, you will be examining myriad pieces of evidence to answer that question.

The election of 1794 was part of a process of political evolution from an oligarchic-based[1] society to a more democratic one. As the new nation moved into these uncharted political waters, not a few of the founding fathers grew increasingly nervous, fearing that the people might not be able to make informed electoral decisions and that they would be stampeded by demagogues.[2] If politics in America was to have any smattering of egalitarianism, these men believed it should only be at the local level, in the New England town meeting or southern county. As you will see, American politics in 1794 contained features of both oligarchy and democracy. In 1794, many citizens of the infant nation feared one or the other.

Background

The years between 1789 and 1801 were crucial ones for the young nation. To paraphrase a comment by Benjamin Franklin, Americans by 1789 (the first year of the Washington administration) had proved themselves remarkably adept at *destroying* governments: in the American Revolution, they had ended British rule of the thirteen colonies, and in the Constitutional Convention of 1787, they had ultimately destroyed the United States' first attempt at self-government, the Articles of Confederation. But they had yet to prove that they could *build* a central government that could protect their rights and preserve order and independence. For that reason, the period from 1789

to 1801 was important in terms of the survival of the new republic.

Many important questions confronted the nation's citizens during those difficult years. Could the new government create a financial system that would pay off the public debt; encourage commerce, manufacturing, and investments; and establish a workable federal tax program? Was the central government strong enough to maintain order and protect citizens on the expanding frontier? Could the na-

1. Oligarchy: government by the few; a political elite.
2. Demagogue: a person who achieves power by appealing to the emotions, prejudices, and fears of the people.

◆ CHAPTER 5

The First American
Party System:
The Philadelphia
Congressional
Election of 1794

tion's leaders conceive a foreign policy that would maintain peace, protect international trade, and honor previous treaty commitments? To what extent should national interests overrule the interests and views of the several states?

A much larger question concerned republicanism itself. A republic is a state wherein the supreme power lies with a body of citizens who are qualified to vote. These citizens directly or indirectly choose their representatives. The head of a republic is also chosen directly or indirectly by the voters, unlike hereditary monarchs or other rulers. No republican experiment of this magnitude had ever been tried before, and a number of Americans expressed considerable fears that the experiment might not survive. Some people, such as Rufus King of New York,[3] wondered whether the people possessed sufficient intelligence and virtue to be trusted to make wise decisions and choose proper leaders. Others, such as John Adams of Massachusetts, doubted that a government without titles, pomp, and ceremony would command the respect and allegiance of common men and women. Still others, such as William L. Smith of South Carolina,[4] feared that the new government was not strong enough to maintain order and enforce its will throughout the huge expanse of its domain. And finally, men such as Patrick Henry of Virginia and Samuel Adams of Massachusetts were afraid that the national government would abandon republican principles in favor of an aristocratic despotism. Hence, although most Americans were republican in sentiment, they strongly disagreed about the best ways to preserve republicanism and the dangers it faced. Some Americans openly distrusted "the people"—Alexander Hamilton of New York once called them a "headless beast." Others were wary of the government itself, even though George Washington had been chosen as its first president.

Much of the driving force of the new government came from Alexander Hamilton, the first secretary of the treasury. Hamilton used his closeness to Washington and his boldness and imagination to fashion policies that set the new nation on its initial course.

Hamilton's first task was to deal with the massive public debt. The defunct Confederation government had an unpaid debt going back to the War of Independence of more than $54 million. In addition, the various states had amassed $21.5 million of their own debts. In a bold move in 1790, the secretary of the treasury proposed that the new federal government assume the debts of both its predecessor and the states, thus binding creditors to the central government. After considerable debate and some compromising, Congress passed Hamilton's plan virtually intact. At one stroke, the "credit rating" of the new government became among the best in the world.

3. Rufus King (1755–1827) was a native of Massachusetts who moved to New York in 1786. He was a U.S. senator from 1789 to 1796 and minister to Great Britain from 1796 to 1803. He supported Alexander Hamilton's financial plans. In 1816, he was the Federalist candidate for president, losing in a landslide to James Monroe.

4. William L. Smith (1758–1812) was a Federalist congressman from South Carolina and later U.S. minister to Portugal. He was a staunch supporter of Alexander Hamilton.

To pay for this ambitious proposal, as well as to give the federal government operating capital, Hamilton recommended a system of taxation that rested primarily on taxes on foreign imports (tariffs) and an excise tax on selected products manufactured in the United States (tobacco products such as snuff and pipe tobacco, sugar products, and whiskey). The excise tax, however, raised considerable protest, especially in western Pennsylvania, where whiskey was an important commodity. In that area, farmers tried to prevent the collection of the tax, a protest that eventually grew into the Whiskey Rebellion of 1794. Prompted by Hamilton, President Washington called out fifteen thousand troops and dispatched them to western Pennsylvania, but the rebellion had fizzled out by the time the troops arrived.

Thus by 1794, when he announced that he was leaving office, Hamilton had put his "system" in place. Revenue was coming into the government coffers; the debt was being serviced; and the semipublic Bank of the United States had been created in 1791 to handle government funds, make available investment capital, and expand the nation's currency in the form of bank notes. The collapse of the Whiskey Rebellion had proved that the new federal government could enforce its laws throughout the nation. Finally, by meddling in the business of Secretary of State Thomas Jefferson, Hamilton had been able to redirect American foreign policy to a more pro-British orientation. This was because Hamilton believed the new, weak republic needed British protection of its commerce, British revenue (in the form of tariffs),

and a friendly neighbor to the north (Canada, a British possession). Using the popular Washington as a shield, Hamilton became the most powerful figure in the new government and the one most responsible for making that new government work.

It is not surprising, however, that these issues and policies provoked sharp disagreements that eventually created two rival political factions: the Federalists, led by Hamilton, and the Democratic-Republicans, led by James Madison and Thomas Jefferson. Federalists generally advocated a strong central government, a broad interpretation of the Constitution, full payment of national and state debts, the establishment of the Bank of the United States, encouragement of commerce, and a pro-British foreign policy. Democratic-Republicans generally favored a central government with limited powers, a strict interpretation of the Constitution, and a pro-French foreign policy; they opposed the bank.[5]

First appearing in Congress in the early 1790s, these two relatively stable factions gradually began taking their ideas to the voters, creating the seeds of what would become by the 1830s America's first political party system. Although unanticipated by the men who drafted the Constitution, this party system became a central feature of American political life, so much so that today it would probably be impossible to conduct the affairs of government or hold elections without it.

Yet Americans of the 1790s did not

5. These are general tendencies. Some Federalists and Democratic-Republicans did not stand with their respective factions on all these issues.

✦ CHAPTER 5

The First American
Party System:
The Philadelphia
Congressional
Election of 1794

foresee this evolution. Many feared the rise of these political factions, believing that the new government was not strong enough to withstand their increasingly vicious battles. Most people did not consider themselves members of either political faction, and there were no highly organized campaigns or platforms to bind voters to one faction or another. It was considered bad form for candidates openly to seek office (one *stood* for office but never *ran* for office), and appeals to voters were usually made by friends or political allies of the candidates. Different property qualifications for voting in each state and the exclusion of women limited the size of the electorate; in the 1790s, most states did not let the voters select presidential electors. All these factors impeded the rapid growth of the modern political party system.

Still, political battles during the 1790s grew more intense and ferocious. As Hamilton's economic plans and Federalism's pro-British foreign policy (the climax of which was the Jay Treaty of 1795) became clearer, Democratic-Republican opposition grew more bitter. Initially, the Federalists had the upper hand, perhaps because of that group's identification with President Washington. But gradually,

the Democratic-Republicans gained strength, so much so that by 1800 their titular leader, Thomas Jefferson, was able to win the presidential election and put an end to Federalist control of the national government.

How can we explain the success of the Democratic-Republicans over their Federalist opponents? To answer this question, it is necessary to study in depth several key elections of the 1790s. Although many such contests are important for understanding the eventual Democratic-Republican victory in 1800, we have selected for further examination the 1794 race for the federal congressional seat from the city of Philadelphia. Because that seat had been held by a Federalist since the formation of the new government, this election was both an important test of strength of the rival Democratic-Republicans and representative of similar important contests being held in that same year in New York, Massachusetts, Maryland, and elsewhere. Because Philadelphia was the nation's capital in 1794, political party development was more advanced there than in other towns and cities of the young republic, thus offering us a harbinger of things to come nationwide.

✦

The Method

All analyses of elections ultimately come down to an attempt to understand why voters choose one candidate for office over another. This is not as easy as it first appears because many voters do not know themselves why

they cast their ballots the way they do. As the presidential election of 2004 clearly demonstrated, many voters actually vote against one candidate rather than in favor of another. But whether citizens understand why they vote the way they do or whether they vote against one candidate rather than for her or his opponent, all studies of modern elections can be divided into four categories. These categories help political observers understand why various elections turn out as they do.

1. *Study the candidates.* How a candidate projects himself or herself may be crucial to the election's outcome. Candidates have backgrounds, voting records, personalities, and idiosyncrasies voters can assess. Candidates travel extensively, are seen by voters either in person or on television, and have several opportunities to appeal to the electorate. Postelection polls have shown that many voters respond as much to candidates as people (a strong leader, a warm person, a confident leader, and so forth) as they do to the candidates' ideas. For example, in 1952, voters responded positively to Dwight Eisenhower even though many were not sure of his positions on a number of important issues. Similarly, in 1980, Ronald Reagan proved to be an extremely attractive presidential candidate as much because of his personal style as because of his ideas and policies.

2. *Study the issues.* Elections often give citizens a chance to clarify their thinking on leading questions of the day. To make matters more complicated, certain groups (economic, ethnic, and interest groups, for example) respond to issues in different ways. The extent to which candidates can identify the issues that concern voters and can speak to these issues in an acceptable way can well mean the difference between victory and defeat. For example, in 1976, candidate Jimmy Carter was able to tap voters' post-

Watergate disgust with corruption in the federal government and defeat incumbent Gerald Ford by speaking to that issue.

3. *Study the campaigns.* Success in devising and implementing a campaign strategy in modern times has been a crucial factor in the outcome of elections. How does the candidate propose to deal with the issues? How are various interest groups to be lured under the party banner? How will money be raised, and how will it be spent? Will the candidate debate her or his opponent? Will the candidate make many personal appearances, or will she or he conduct a "front-porch" campaign? How will the candidate's family, friends, and political allies be used? Which areas (neighborhoods, regions, states, sections) will be targeted for special attention? To many political analysts, it is obvious that a number of superior candidates have been unsuccessful because of poorly run campaigns. By the same token, many less-than-superior candidates have won elections because of effectively conducted campaigns.

4. *Study the voters.* Recently, the study of elections has become more sophisticated. Polling techniques have revealed that people similar in demographic variables such as age, sex, race, income, marital status, ethnic group, and religion tend to vote in similar fashions. For example, urban blacks voted overwhelmingly for Jimmy Carter in 1976 and Al Gore in 2000.

These sophisticated polling techniques, also used for Gallup polls, Nielsen television ratings, and predicting responses to new consumer products, rest on important assumptions about human behavior. One assumption is

◆ CHAPTER 5

The First American
Party System:
The Philadelphia
Congressional
Election of 1794

that human responses tend to be strongly influenced (some say *determined*) by demographic variables; similar people tend to respond similarly to certain stimuli, such as candidates and campaigns. Another assumption is that these demographic patterns are constant and do not change rapidly. Finally, it is assumed that if we know how some of the people responded to certain stimuli, we can calculate how others possessing the same demographic variables will respond to those same stimuli.

Although there are many such patterns of voting behavior, they are easily observable. After the demographic variables that influence these patterns have been identified, a demographic sample of the population is created. Thus, fifty white, male, middle-aged, married, Protestant, middle-income voters included in a sample might represent perhaps 100,000 people who possess these same variables. The fifty in the sample would then be polled to determine how they voted, and from this information we could infer how the 100,000 voted. Each population group in the sample would be polled in a similar fashion. By doing this, one can speculate with a fair amount of precision who voted for whom, thereby understanding which groups within the voting population were attracted to which candidate. Of course, the answer to why they were attracted still must be sought with one of the other methods: studying the candidates, studying the issues, and studying the campaigns.

These four approaches are methods for analyzing modern electoral contests. In fact, most political analysts use a combination of these approaches. But can these methods be used to analyze the 1794 congressional election in Philadelphia? Neither candidate openly sought the office, and neither made appearances in his own behalf. Although there certainly were important issues, neither political faction drew up a platform to explain to voters where its candidate stood on those issues. Neither political faction conducted an organized campaign. No polls were taken to determine voter concerns. At first glance, then, it appears that most if not all of these approaches to analyzing modern elections are useless in any attempt to analyze the 1794 Fitzsimons-Swanwick congressional contest.

These approaches, however, are not as useless as they initially appear. Philadelphia in 1794 was not a large city—it contained only about 45,000 people—and many voters knew the candidates personally because both were prominent figures in the community. Their respective backgrounds were generally well known. Moreover, Fitzsimons, as the incumbent, had a voting record in Congress, and most voters would have known how Swanwick stood on the issues, either through Swanwick's friends or through the positions he took as a member of the Democratic Society. Furthermore, the Federalists and Democratic-Republicans had taken general positions on some of the important issues. In addition, we are able to establish with a fair amount of certainty which voters cast ballots for Fitzsimons and which supported Swanwick. Finally, it is possible to identify important trends and events occurring in Philadelphia. In sum, although we might not have all the evidence we would like to have (historians almost never do), intelligent use of the evidence at our disposal enables us to analyze the 1794 election employing all or most of the approaches used in analyzing modern political contests.

As you examine the various types of evidence in this chapter, divide it into four groups, one for each general approach used in analyzing elections (candidates, issues, campaigns, voters). For example, there are two excerpts from Philadelphia newspapers (one Federalist and one Democratic-Republican) dealing with the excise tax and the Whiskey Rebellion in western Pennsylvania. In what group would you put this evidence? Follow this procedure for all the evidence, noting that occasionally a piece of evidence could fit into more than one group. Such an arrangement of the evidence will give you four ways to analyze why the 1794 congressional election in Philadelphia turned out the way it did. Then, having examined and analyzed the evidence by groups, you will have to determine the principal factors that explain Swanwick's upset victory.

◆

The Evidence

1. The Candidates.

Thomas Fitzsimons (1741–1811) was born in Ireland and migrated to the colonies sometime before the Revolution, probably in 1765. He entered commerce as a clerk, worked his way up in his firm, and secured his position by marrying into the principal merchant's family. Fitzsimons served as a captain of the Pennsylvania militia during the Revolution, was a member of the Continental Congress in 1782 and 1783, and was elected to the Pennsylvania House of Representatives in 1786 and 1787. He was a delegate to the Constitutional Convention in 1787, was a signer of the Constitution, and was elected to the federal House of Representatives in 1788. He was a member of the Federalist inner circle in Philadelphia and a firm supporter of Alexander Hamilton's policies. He was a strong supporter of the excise tax (see approach 2 in the Questions to Consider section), was an instrumental figure in the compromise that brought the national capital to Philadelphia for ten years (1790–1800), and helped draft the legislation chartering the Bank of the United States in 1791. He was one of the original founders and directors of the Bank of North America, the director and president of the Insurance Company of North America, and a key figure in dispensing federal patronage in Philadelphia. He was a Roman Catholic.

◆ CHAPTER 5

The First American
Party System:
The Philadelphia
Congressional
Election of 1794

John Swanwick (1740–1798) was born in England. He and his family arrived in the colonies in the early 1770s. His father was a wagon master and minor British government official. During the Revolution, his father became a Tory and was exiled, but John Swanwick embraced the Patriot cause. In 1777, he was hired as a clerk in the merchant firm of Robert Morris. His fluency in both French and German made him invaluable to the firm, and he quickly rose to full partnership in 1783, the firm then being known as Willing, Morris & Swanwick. In 1794, he bought out Morris's share in the company. He was one of Philadelphia's leading export merchants, was a stockholder in the Bank of North America, and held a number of minor offices (under Morris) in the Confederation government. He supported the federal Constitution and Hamilton's early financial policies. Swanwick was elected to the state legislature in 1792. By 1793, he had drifted away from Federalism and had become a Democratic-Republican. In 1794, he joined the Pennsylvania Democratic Society[6] and was soon made an officer. Swanwick also was an officer in a society that aided immigrants. He opposed the excise tax but thought the Whiskey Rebellion (see approach 2 in the Questions to Consider section) in western Pennsylvania was the wrong method of protest. He wrote poetry and was never admitted to Philadelphia's social elite. He owned a two-hundred-acre country estate. He was a member of the Protestant Episcopal Church.

Source 2 from *Gazette of the United States* (a pro-Federalist Philadelphia newspaper), August 10, 1794.

2. A Pro-Federalist View of the Excise Tax and the Whiskey Rebellion.

These Societies [the Democratic Societies], strange as it may seem, have been formed in a free elective government for the sake of *preserving liberty*. And what is the liberty they are striving to introduce? It is the liberty of reviling the rulers who are chosen by the people and the government under which they live. It is the liberty of bringing the laws into contempt and persuading people to resist them [a reference to the Whiskey Rebellion]. It is the liberty of condemning every system of Taxation because they have resolved that they will not be subject to laws—that they will not pay any taxes. To suppose that

6. Democratic Societies were organizations composed principally of artisans and laborers and founded by Democratic-Republican leaders as political pressure groups against the Washington administration. Many Federalists believed that some Democratic Society members had been behind the Whiskey Rebellion. President Washington condemned the societies in 1794.

societies were formed with the purpose of opposing and with the hope of destroying government, might appear illiberal provided they had not already excited resistance to the laws and provided some of them had not publicly avowed their opinions that they *ought not to pay any taxes.*

Source 3 from *General Advertiser* (a pro–Democratic-Republican Philadelphia newspaper), August 20, 1794.

3. A Pro–Democratic-Republican View of the Excise Tax and the Whiskey Rebellion.

As violent means appear the desire of high toned government men, it is to be hoped that those who derive the most benefit from our revenue laws will be the foremost to march against the Western insurgents. Let stockholders, bank directors, speculators and revenue officers arrange themselves immediately under the banner of the treasury, and try their prowess in arms as they have done in calculation. The prompt recourse to hostilities which two certain great characters [Hamilton and Washington?] are so anxious for, will, no doubt, operate upon the knights of our country to appear in military array, and then the poor but industrious citizen will not be obliged to spill the blood of his fellow citizen before conciliatory means are tried.

Source 4 from Harold C. Syrett, ed., *The Papers of Alexander Hamilton* (New York: Columbia University Press, 1972), Vol. XVII, pp. 15–19.

4. Alexander Hamilton to President Washington, August 2, 1794.

If the Judge shall pronounce that the case described in the second section of that Act exists, it will follow that a competent force of Militia should be called forth and employed to suppress the insurrection and support the Civil Authority in effectuating Obedience to the laws and punishment of Offenders.

It appears to me that the very existence of Government demands this course and that a duty of the highest nature urges the Chief Magistrate to pursue it.[7]

7. The Militia Act ("that Act") of 1792 required that a Supreme Court justice ("the Judge," in this case Justice James Wilson) certify that the disturbance could not be controlled by civil authorities (as defined in the "second section" of the Act) before the president could order out the state militia. The "Chief Magistrate" referred to is President Washington. The majority of the United States Army was in the Northwest Territory, about to engage the Native Americans in

◆ CHAPTER 5

The First American
Party System:
The Philadelphia
Congressional
Election of 1794

Source 5 from Paul L. Ford, ed., *Writings of Thomas Jefferson* (New York: G. P. Putnam's Sons, 1895), Vol. VI, pp. 516–519.

5. Thomas Jefferson to James Madison, December 28, 1794.

And with respect to the transactions against the excise law [the Whiskey Rebellion], it appears to me that you are all swept away in the torrent of governmental opinion, or that we do not know what these transactions have been. We know of none which, according to the definitions of the law, have been anything more than riotous. . . . The excise law is an infernal one. . . . The information of our militia, returned from the Westward, is uniform, that the people there let them pass quietly; they were objects of their laughter, not of their fear.

Sources 6 through 8 from Ronald M. Baumann, "Philadelphia's Manufacturers and the Excise Tax of 1794: The Forging of the Jeffersonian Coalition," *Pennsylvania Magazine of History and Biography* 106 (January 1982): 26, 28–30.

6. Excise Tax Statistics.

There were 23 tobacconists and snuffmakers in Philadelphia in 1794 who owned real property from £26 to over £2501 and who employed over 400 workers. In addition, there were sugar refiners in the city, and Philadelphia also had 21 brewers and distillers.

7. Swanwick and the Democratic Society.

Swanwick was a member of the Democratic Society of Pennsylvania. The society passed a resolution opposing the excise tax. President Washington condemned the society in 1794, saying that he believed that it and other similar societies were responsible for the Whiskey Rebellion. The society endorsed Swanwick in 1794 and worked actively in his behalf.

---

the Battle of Fallen Timbers (August 20, 1794). Justice Wilson released his opinion that Washington could call out the troops on August 4, two days after Hamilton wrote to Washington.

8. Philadelphia Wards, 1794.

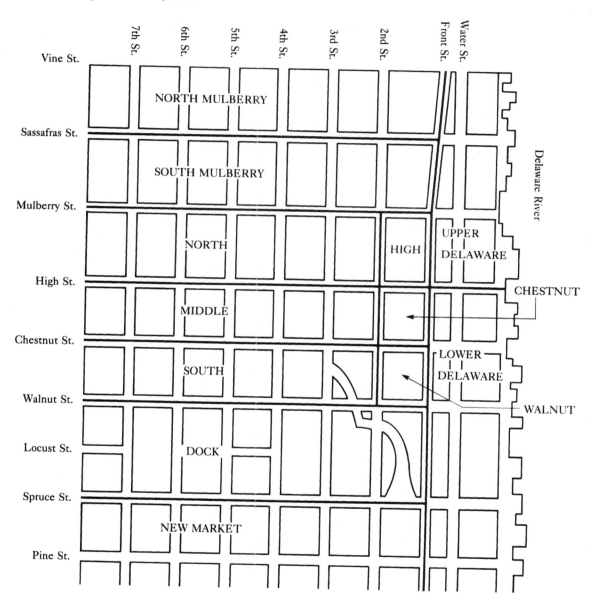

✦ CHAPTER 5

The First American
Party System:
The Philadelphia
Congressional
Election of 1794

Source 9 from James Hardie, *The Philadelphia Directory and Register* (Philadelphia, 1794).

9. A Sample of Occupations by Ward (Males Only), Philadelphia, 1794.[8]

	Upper Delaware	North Mulberry	South Mulberry	High	North	Chestnut	Middle	Walnut	South	Dock	New Market	Lower Delaware	Occupation Totals
Gentleman	3	22	31	7	21	1	15	2	8	17	25	5	157
Merchant	76	47	65	47	90	38	63	20	26	101	83	43	699
Artisan	95	353	338	333	183	46	164	48	73	131	222	71	1,757
Laborer	18	93	103	10	70	7	27	8	12	38	56	1	443
Shopkeeper	13	24	39	24	44	9	23	4	6	7	35	8	236
Inn and tavern keeper	8	17	12	3	13	5	22	3	4	12	11	6	116
Captain	6	17	14	0	3	0	1	4	1	7	37	0	90
Government employee	2	12	13	0	16	2	13	1	7	14	18	0	98
Seaman	7	15	5	1	3	1	2	2	2	9	21	2	70
Teacher	1	5	12	0	6	0	2	0	3	5	6	0	40
Doctor	1	3	10	3	5	3	2	3	6	10	9	0	55
Grocer	10	22	20	3	37	2	20	0	5	25	34	6	184
Clergy	0	5	8	0	0	0	3	0	3	4	4	0	27
Lawyer	0	3	11	2	1	0	4	1	13	12	5	1	53
Clerk	5	16	18	3	7	1	12	1	4	10	12	1	90
Broker	0	1	2	0	3	2	4	4	3	2	1	0	22
Other	1	5	0	1	3	1	0	0	1	1	2	0	15
Unknown	1	7	14	1	1	0	2	0	1	2	8	0	37
Ward totals	247	667	715	138	506	118	379	101	178	407	589	144	

8. Poor people were notoriously undercounted in city directories, as were nonpermanent residents, such as seamen.

Sources 10 and 11 from Billy G. Smith, *The "Lower Sort": Philadelphia's Laboring People, 1750–1800*, pp. 101, 110, 114, 116, 121, 232. Copyright © 1990 by Cornell University. Used by permission of the publisher, Cornell University Press. For household budgets, Smith calculated the costs of food, rent, fuel, and clothing and then established how much of these items were consumed.

10. Cost of Living Index,[9] Philadelphia (Base Year 1762 = 100).

Year	Food	Rent	Firewood	Clothing	Household Budget
1788	99		74	139	123
1789	107	165[10]	76	82	115
1790	134		79	92	131
1791	130		97	92	131
1792	131		106	110	136
1793	143		111	119	144
1794	161		130	137	158

11. Index of Real Wages,[11] Philadelphia (Base Year 1762 = 100).

Year	Laborers	Sailors	Tailors	Shoemakers
1788	95	—	68	63
1789	77	—	69	63
1790	66	59	76	44
1791	74	59	63	48
1792	88	70	80	55
1793	81	84	57	143
1794	90	161	78	77

9. An index number is a statistical measure designed to show changes in a variable (such as wages or prices) over time. A base year is selected and given the value of 100. The index for subsequent years is then expressed as a percentage of the base year.
10. No other rent index is available for 1788 through 1794. The rent index in 1798, however, was 184.
11. Real wages are wages that are actually paid, adjusted for the cost of living. To find a person's real wage, one would take the index of that person's actual wage divided by the index of household budget and multiply that figure by 100. Real wages allow us to see whether a person's wages are exceeding or falling behind the cost of living.

◆ CHAPTER 5

The First American
Party System:
The Philadelphia
Congressional
Election of 1794

Source 12 from James Hardie, *The Philadelphia Directory and Register* (Philadelphia, 1794).

12. First-Person Account of the Yellow Fever.

Having mentioned this disorder to have occasioned great devastation in the year 1793, a short account of it may be acceptable to several of our readers. . . .

This disorder made its first appearance toward the latter end of July, in a lodging house in North Water Street,[12] and for a few weeks seemed entirely confined to that vicinity. Hence it was generally supposed to have been imported and not generated in the city. This was the opinion of Doctors Currie, Cathrall and many others. It was however combated by Dr. Benjamin Rush, who asserts that the contagion was generated from the stench of a cargo of damaged coffee. . . .

But from whatever fountain we trace this poisoned stream, it has destroyed the lives of many thousands—and many of those of the most distinguished worth. . . . During the month of August the funerals amounted to upwards of three hundred. The disease had then reached the central streets of the city and began to spread on all sides with the greatest rapidity. In September its malignance increased amazingly. Fear pervaded the stoutest heart, flight became general, and terror was depicted on every countenance. In this month 1,400 more were added to the list of mortality. The contagion was still progressive and towards the end of the month 90 & 100 died daily. Until the middle of October the mighty destroyer went on with increasing havoc. From the 1st to the 17th upwards of 1,400 fell victims to the tremendous malady. From the 17th to the 30th the mortality gradually decreased. In the whole month, however, the dead amounted to upwards of 2,000—a dreadful number, if we consider that at this time near one half of the inhabitants had fled. Before the disorder became so terrible, the appearance of Philadelphia must to a stranger have seemed very extraordinary. The garlic, which chewed as a preventative[,] could be smelled at several yards distance, whilst other[s] hoped to avoid infection by a recourse to smelling bottles, handkerchiefs dipped in vinegar, camphor bags, &c. . . .

During this melancholy period the city lost ten of her most valuable physicians, and most of the others were sick at different times. The number of deaths in all amounted to 4,041.[13]

---

12. See Source 8. Working-class areas were particularly hard hit. On Fetter Lane (near North Water Street), 50 percent of the residents died. See Smith, *The "Lower Sort,"* pp. 25–26.
13. The population of Philadelphia (including its suburbs) was 42,444 in 1790.

Sources 13 and 14 from L. H. Butterfield, ed., *Letters of Benjamin Rush*[14] (Princeton, N.J.: Published for the American Philosophical Society, 1951), Vol. II, pp. 644–645, 657–658. Reprinted by permission.

13. Benjamin Rush to Mrs. Rush, August 29, 1793, on the Yellow Fever.

Be assured that I will send for you if I should be seized with the disorder, for I conceive that it would be as much your duty not to desert me in that situation as it is now mine not to desert my patients. . . .

Its symptoms are very different in different people. Sometimes it comes on with a chilly fit and a high fever, but more frequently it steals on with headache, languor, and sick stomach. These symptoms are followed by stupor, delirium, vomiting, a dry skin, cool or cold hands and feet, a feeble slow pulse, sometimes below in frequency the pulse of health. The eyes are at first suffused with blood, they afterwards become yellow, and in most cases a yellowness covers the whole skin on the 3rd or 4th day. Few survive the 5th day, but more die on the 2 and 3rd days. In some cases the patients possess their reason to the last and discover much less weakness than in the last stage of common fevers. One of my patients stood up and shaved himself on the morning of the day he died. Livid spots on the body, a bleeding at the nose, from the gums, and from the bowels, and a vomiting of black matter in some instances close the scenes of life. The common remedies for malignant fevers have all failed. Bark, wine, and blisters make no impression upon it. Baths of hot vinegar applied by means of blankets, and the cold bath have relieved and saved some. . . .

This day I have given mercury, and I think with some advantage.

14. Dr. Benjamin Rush (1745–1813) was a Pennsylvanian who was graduated from the College of New Jersey (Princeton, 1760) and studied medicine at the College of Philadelphia and the University of Edinburgh. Practicing medicine in Philadelphia, he was elected to the Continental Congress in 1776 and was a signer of the Declaration of Independence. He supported the ratification of the Constitution. By 1794, he had changed allegiances and was considered a Democratic-Republican. He participated in many reform movements, including the abolition of slavery, the end to capital punishment, temperance, an improved educational system, and prison reform. His protégé, Dr. Michael Leib, was extremely active in Democratic-Republican politics. Most physicians in Philadelphia in 1794 were Federalists. The majority fled the city when the fever broke out. Of the doctors who stayed, Rush was one of the most prominent.

✦ CHAPTER 5

The First American
Party System:
The Philadelphia
Congressional
Election of 1794

14. Benjamin Rush to Mrs. Rush, September 10, 1793, on the Yellow Fever.

My dear Julia,

Hereafter my name should be Shadrach, Meshach, or Abednego, for I am sure the preservation of those men from death by fire was not a greater miracle than my preservation from the infection of the prevailing disorder. I have lived to see the close of another day, more awful than any I have yet seen. Forty persons it is said have been buried this day, and I have visited and prescribed for more than 100 patients. Mr. Willing is better, and Jno. Barclay is out of danger. Amidst my numerous calls to the wealthy and powerful, *I do not forget the poor*, . . .[15]

Source 15 compiled from description of the committee by J. H. Powell in *Bring Out Your Dead: Plague of Yellow Fever in Philadelphia in 1793* (Philadelphia: University of Pennsylvania Press, 1949), pp. 174–180, esp. p. 179.

15. Yellow Fever Committee.

Of the eighteen people cited for contributions to the Citizens' Committee on the Fever, nine were definitely Democratic-Republicans. Of the remaining nine, only one was an avowed Federalist.

Source 16 from Powell, *Bring Out Your Dead*, p. 123.

16. Federalist Comment on Rush.

Rush "is become the darling of the common people and his humane fortitude and exertions will render him deservedly dear."

15. Italics added.

Source 17 is a sample taken from Philadelphia newspapers by the authors.

17. Sampling of Deaths from Yellow Fever, Philadelphia, 1793 Epidemic.[16]

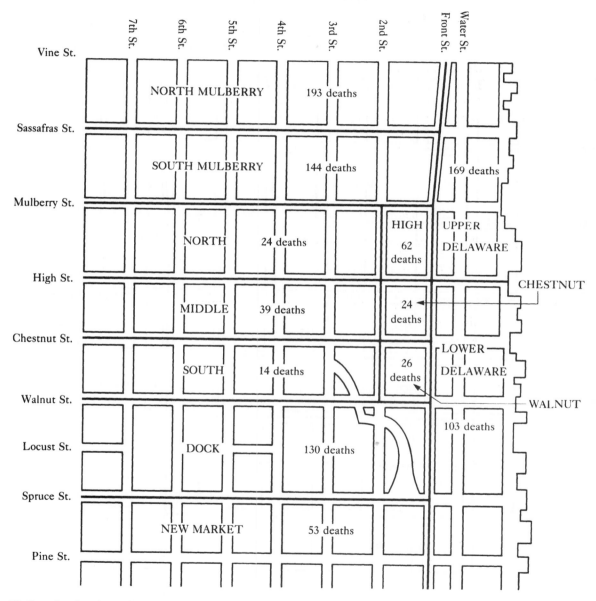

16. Sample taken from Philadelphia newspapers. After a time, officials simply stopped recording the names of those who died, except for prominent citizens. Therefore, although James Hardie reported that 4,041 people had died, one scholar has estimated the death toll at as high as 6,000, roughly one out of every seven Philadelphians.

◆ CHAPTER 5

The First American
Party System:
The Philadelphia
Congressional
Election of 1794

Source 18 from Baumann, "Philadelphia's Manufacturers and the Excise Tax of 1794,"
p. 27.

18. Congressional Election, Philadelphia, 1794.[17]

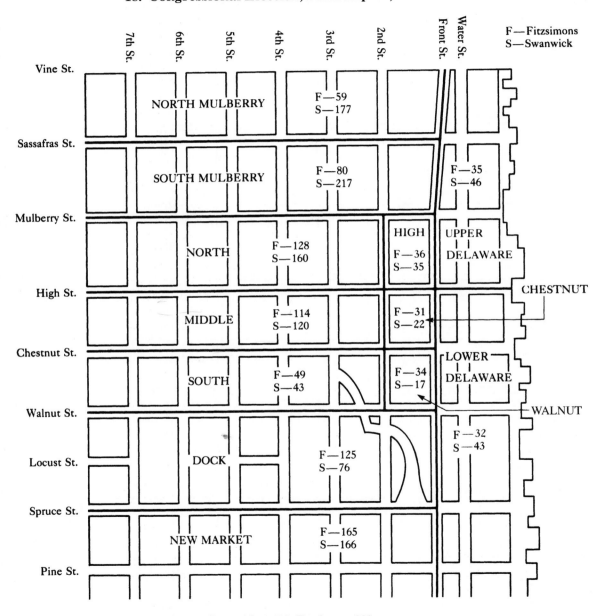

17. Total votes: Swanwick, 1,122; Fitzsimons, 888.

Questions to Consider

Philadelphia in 1794 was a prosperous, bustling city filled with small shops, market halls, inns, and merchants' warehouses. Houses ranged from imposing two-story brick and stone edifices to cramped wood-frame buildings containing one or two families and frequently boarders as well. The population was both ethnically and racially diverse; in the 1790s, one in ten residents was a free black. Laid out in a grid pattern of square blocks and straight streets along the Delaware River, Philadelphia was a "walking city" where most people lived within a six-to-ten-block area from the docks. Uncontrolled business cycles, high infant and child mortality rates, and recurring epidemics such as yellow fever made life unstable and uncertain for most residents.

No single method of analyzing elections will give you the answer to the central question of why John Swanwick was able to defeat Thomas Fitzsimons. Instead, you must use all four approaches, grouping the evidence by approach and determining what each approach tells you about why the election turned out as it did.

Before examining each group of evidence, however, try to discover who tended to vote for each candidate. Source 9 shows occupations by ward. Although there are exceptions, occupations often can be used to establish a person's wealth and status. Today many people introduce themselves by telling their name, occupation, and address. What are these people really saying? Examine carefully the occupa-

tional makeup of each ward. This can be done by matching the figures in Source 9 to the map in Source 8. For example, look at the artisan (skilled labor) population. Only a very few lived in High, Chestnut, and Walnut wards, areas that tended to be more upper-class neighborhoods. Instead, most artisans lived on the city's fringes, in North Mulberry, South Mulberry, North, Middle, Dock, and New Market wards. Follow the same procedure for merchants, laborers, shopkeepers, and so on. Although early American cities were not as residentially segregated by socioeconomic class as today's cities, you will be able to see general tendencies that will allow you to characterize each of Philadelphia's wards in 1794.

Keeping those characterizations in mind (or by using notes), turn to Source 18, the election results. How could you use these three sources (8, 9, and 18) to determine who tended to support Fitzsimons and Swanwick? Historians call this process *overlaying evidence* because one source is overlaid on another.

Pennsylvania had one of the most liberal suffrage laws in the nation. All adult white males who had lived in the state for two years preceding an election *and* had paid any state or county taxes could vote. Of the occupational groups listed in Source 9, only laborers and seamen contained large percentages of men who could not vote. Keep this in mind as you overlay the evidence.

Having established who tended to vote for Fitzsimons and who tended to

◆ CHAPTER 5

The First American
Party System:
The Philadelphia
Congressional
Election of 1794

vote for Swanwick, you are ready to answer the question of why one of the candidates was more appealing to the majority of Philadelphia voters. Here is where the four major approaches explained earlier can be brought into play.

1. *Candidates.* Source 1 supplies biographical information about the two candidates. Do not neglect to study the additional material on Swanwick (Source 7); this is material that voters not personally acquainted with the candidates still would have known. What are the significant points of comparison and contrast between the candidates?

One significant point of difference is religion. Fitzsimons was a Roman Catholic, and Swanwick belonged to the Protestant Episcopal Church. Most of Philadelphia's voters were Protestant, the two largest denominations being Lutheran and Quaker. Very few voters belonged to either the Roman Catholic or the Episcopal church. Was religion a factor in this election? How can you prove that it was or was not?

One interesting point in Swanwick's biographical sketch is that, although wealthy, he was never admitted to Philadelphia's social elite circles, a fact that some of the voters probably knew. Do you think this was an important consideration in the voters' minds? How would you prove your point?

2. *Issues.* There were a number of issues in this election, and it was fairly clear how each faction stood on those issues. Two of the most important issues were the excise tax (Sources 2, 3, 6, and 7) and the Whiskey Rebellion (Sources 4 and 5).

As noted above, to raise money, Hamilton proposed, Congress passed, and President Washington signed a bill placing an excise tax on selected domestic manufactured products, an act that eventually touched off the Whiskey Rebellion of 1794. Indeed, there is some evidence that Hamilton actually anticipated such a reaction to the excise tax when he proposed it, convinced that the crushing of such an uprising would prove that the new government had the power to enforce its laws. When examining the impact of the excise tax and the Whiskey Rebellion on the election, use the sources to answer the following questions:

a. Which groups in Philadelphia did the excise tax affect most? How? Remember to think of people as both workers and consumers.
b. How did the candidates stand on the excise tax?
c. Which groups of Philadelphians would have been likely to favor their respective positions?
d. How did each faction stand on the Whiskey Rebellion? (See Sources 2 through 5.)
e. How did the candidates stand on this issue?
f. Which groups of Philadelphians would have been likely to favor their respective positions?

3. *Campaign.* Although there were a few mass meetings and some distribution of literature, there was no real campaign in the modern sense. In the absence of an organized campaign, how did voters make up their minds?

4. *Voters.* At the time of the election, other important trends in Philadelphia might have influenced voters. For example, review the evidence on the cost

of living and on real wages compiled by Billy G. Smith (Sources 10 and 11). Regarding cost of living, if the cost of living index in 1762 was 100, were the indexes for food, firewood, and clothing rising or falling? Using household budget indexes, how much more expensive was it to live in Philadelphia in 1794 than it was in 1788 (158 minus 123 equals 35, divided by 123 equals 28.5 percent)?

Remember that real wages are actual wages adjusted for the cost of living. As you can see in Source 11, tailors and shoemakers (called *cordwainers* at this time) experienced modest gains in real wages from 1788 to 1794. Note, however, that real wages were extremely volatile and could fluctuate wildly. For example, real wages for shoemakers fell 30.2 percent between 1788 and 1790, then began a gradual recovery, due in part to a protective tariff on shoes passed by Congress in 1790. In 1793, the retail prices for shoes jumped 64.8 percent, largely because war in Europe created a great international demand for American shoes. As a result, real wages for shoemakers spiraled from 55 to 143, a gain of 160 percent. But in 1794, real wages dropped 46.2 percent. As for sailors, their wages skyrocketed from 1793 to 1794 (almost 80 percent). Keep in mind, however, that the war between Great Britain and France that broke out in 1793 made that occupation an extremely dangerous one. In sum, can the cost of living and real wage indexes give you any clues to how these occupational groups might have voted?

The pieces of evidence that appear at first glance to have nothing to do with the Fitzsimons-Swanwick contest are Sources 12 through 17, on the 1793 yellow fever epidemic that virtually paralyzed the city. After all, the fever broke out more than a year prior to the election and was over by the end of October 1793. Most of those who had fled the city had returned and were in Philadelphia during the "campaign" and voting.

Yet a closer analysis of Sources 12 through 17 offers some fascinating insights, although you will have to use some historical imagination to relate them to the election. To begin with, James Hardie (Source 12) reported that the fever initially appeared "in a lodging house in North Water Street; and for a few weeks seemed entirely confined to that vicinity." Where was North Water Street (Source 8)? Who would have lived there (Sources 8 and 9)? So long as the fever was confined to that area, Hardie does not appear to have been overly concerned. What does that tell you? Hardie further reported that almost half the total population had fled the city. Which groups would have been most likely to flee (approximately 20,000 of Philadelphia's 45,000 fled)? Who could not leave? If businessmen closed their businesses when they fled, what was the situation of workers who could not afford to leave? What impact might this have had on the election a year later?

Although perhaps a bit too graphic, Dr. Benjamin Rush's August 29, 1793, letter to his wife (Source 13) is valuable because it establishes the fact that Rush, although he could have abandoned the sick, refused to do so and stayed in Philadelphia. This was an act of remarkable courage, for no one knew what caused yellow fever and people believed that it struck its victims almost completely at random. Consider,

♦ CHAPTER 5

The First American
Party System:
The Philadelphia
Congressional
Election of 1794

however, not what Rush *says* in Source 13 but rather *who he was*. Refer again to footnote 14. Also examine Rush's letter of September 10, 1793 (Source 14), especially the last sentence. Do you think Rush might have been a factor in the Fitzsimons-Swanwick election? In what way?

Sources 15 and 16 attempt to tie the fever epidemic to party politics in Philadelphia. How might Philadelphia voters have reacted to the two parties (the Federalists and the Democratic-Republicans) after the fever? How might the voters have reacted to Dr. Rush?

Finally, examine Source 17 with some care. Where did the fever victims tend to reside? What types of people lived in those wards?

Now you are ready to answer the question of why the 1794 congressional election in Philadelphia turned out the way it did (Source 18). Make sure, however, that your opinion is solidly supported by evidence.

♦

Epilogue

As the temporary national capital in 1794, Philadelphia was probably somewhat more advanced than the rest of the nation in the growth of political factions. However, by the presidential election of 1800, most of the country had become involved in the gradual process of party building. By that time, the Democratic-Republicans were the dominant political force, aided by more aggressive campaign techniques, their espousal of a limited national government (which most Americans preferred), their less elitist attitudes, and their ability to brand their Federalist opponents as aristocrats and pro-British monocrats.[18] Although Federalism retained considerable strength in New England and the Middle States, by 1800 it no longer was a serious challenge to the Democratic-Republicans on the national level.

For his part, John Swanwick never saw the ultimate triumph of Democratic-Republicanism because he died in the 1798 yellow fever epidemic in Philadelphia. Fitzsimons never again sought political office, preferring to concentrate his energies on his already successful mercantile and banking career. Hamilton died in a duel with Aaron Burr in 1804. After he left the presidency in 1809, Jefferson retired to his estate, Monticello, to bask in the glories of being an aging founding father. He died in 1826 at the age of eighty-three.

By 1826, many of the concerns of the Federalist era had been resolved. The War of 1812 had further secured American independence, and the death of the Federalist faction had put an end to the notion of government by an entrenched (established) and favored elite. At the same time, however, new issues had arisen to test the durability of the republic and the collective wis-

18. A monocrat is a person who favors a monarchy. It was considered a disparaging term in the United States during the period.

dom of its people. After a brief political calm, party battles once again were growing fiercer as the rise of Andrew Jackson threatened to split the brittle Jeffersonian coalition. Westward expansion was carrying Americans into territories owned by other nations, and few doubted that an almost inevitable conflict lay ahead. American cities, such as Philadelphia, were growing in both population and socioeconomic problems. The twin specters of slavery and sectional conflict were claiming increasing national attention. Whether the political system fashioned in the 1790s could address these crucial issues and trends and at the same time maintain its republican principles was a question that would soon have to be addressed.

Land, Growth, and Justice: The Removal of the Cherokees

✦

The Problem

In the spring of 1838, General Winfield Scott and several units of the U.S. Army (including artillery regiments) were deployed to the Southeast to collect Native Americans known as Cherokees[1] and remove them to lands west of the Mississippi River. Employing bilingual Cherokees to serve as interpreters at $2.50 per day, Scott constructed eleven makeshift stockades and on May 23 began rounding up Native Americans and herding them into these temporary prisons. According to John G. Burnett, a soldier who participated in the removal,

> Men working in the fields were arrested and driven to the stockades. Women were dragged from their homes by soldiers whose language they could not understand. Children were often

separated from their parents and driven into the stockades with the sky for a blanket and the earth for a pillow. And often the old and infirm were prodded with bayonets to hasten them to the stockades.[2]

Just behind the soldiers came whites, eager to claim homesteads, search for gold, or pick over the belongings that the Cherokees did not have time to carry away.

On August 23, 1838, the first of thirteen parties of Cherokees began their forced march to the West, arriving in what had been designated as Indian Territory (later Oklahoma) on January 17, 1839. With some traveling by boat while others journeyed overland, a total of approximately thirteen thousand Cherokees participated in what became known as the Trail of Tears. (See Map 1.) It has been estimated that over four thousand died in the squalid stockades

1. The Cherokees referred to themselves as Ani'Yun'wiya ("principal people"). The origin of the term *Cherokee* is unknown, but the name almost certainly was given to them by Native American neighbors. See Russell Thornton, *The Cherokees: A Population History* (Lincoln: University of Nebraska Press, 1990), pp. 7–8.

2. See John G. Burnett, "The Cherokee Removal Through the Eyes of a Private Soldier," *Journal of Cherokee Studies* 3 (1978): 180–185.

or along the way.[3] But recent research has determined that the figure may have been higher than that, in part because of shoddy record keeping and in part because numerous Cherokees died in an epidemic almost immediately on reaching their destination. In addition, conflict broke out between new arrivals and those Cherokees (around six thousand) who had earlier moved. And, once in the West, those who opposed removal took out their vengeance on the leaders of the Cherokee removal faction. Cherokee advocates of removal (including leaders Major Ridge, John Ridge, Elias Boudinot, and Thomas Watie) were murdered.[4]

The forced removal of the Cherokees marked the end of a debate that was older than the United States itself. As white populations mushroomed and settlements moved ever westward, the question of how to deal with Native Americans came up again and again, especially when Native American peoples refused to sell or give their lands to whites by treaty.

In 1829, Andrew Jackson became president. In his view, Native Americans should be removed from their lands in order to make way for expanding white settlements. And although he was not known as an accomplished speaker or writer (his spelling was nearly as poor as that of George Washington), in his First Annual Message to Congress (see Source 1 in the Evidence section) Jackson almost surely was the most articulate voice in favor of removal.[5]

President Jackson did not, however, speak for all whites when it came to dealing with Native Americans. Other white people offered what they considered to be more humane alternatives to removal, and these alternatives were debated—sometimes fiercely—both in Congress and among the white population at large.

For their part, the vast majority of Cherokees opposed removal to lands west of the Mississippi River. Even so, Cherokees differed on the most effective strategies that would allow them to remain in their traditional homelands. And some Cherokees in the end supported removal, believing their chances for survival and well-being would be better far from whites, in the West.

In this chapter, you will be examining and analyzing two sets of evidence: (1) four opinions by white men (including President Andrew Jackson) on how to deal with Native Americans east of the Mississippi and (2) five opinions by Cherokees regarding how to— or whether to—resist removal. For both sets of evidence, your task is to analyze the principal arguments each person or group of people was making. What were the strengths and weaknesses of each position?

---

3. The official U.S. Army count of those removed to Indian Territory totaled 13,149, of whom 11,504 actually arrived in the West. Based on the tribal census of 1835, at least 2,000 died in the stockades.

4. See Russell Thornton, "The Demography of the Trail of Tears Period: A New Estimate of Cherokee Population Losses," in William L. Anderson, ed., *Cherokee Removal: Before and After* (Athens, Ga.: University of Georgia Press, 1991), pp. 75–95.

5. From George Washington to Woodrow Wilson, no president of the United States appeared in person before Congress. All communications between the president and Congress were conducted in writing.

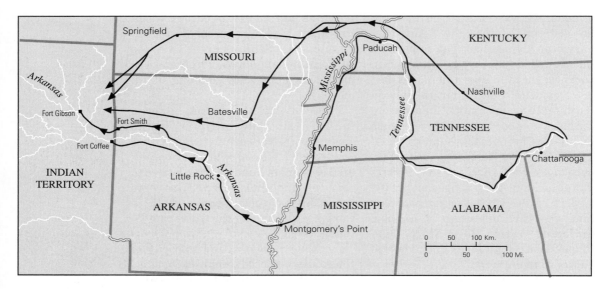

Map 1. The Trail of Tears, 1838–1839.
Adapted from Grace Steele Woodward, *The Cherokees* (Norman: University of Oklahoma Press, 1963), pp. 206–207. Copyright © 1963 by the University of Oklahoma Press, Norman, Publishing Division of the University of Oklahoma. Reprinted by permission.

◆

Background

The origins of the Cherokees are clouded in mystery. Linguistically related to the Iroquois of New England and northern New York, it is thought that the Cherokees migrated south into present-day Georgia, Tennessee (itself a derivation of the name of a Cherokee town, Tanasi), South Carolina, and North Carolina and settled the area somewhere between the years 600 and 1000, centuries before the first regular contact with white people in the late 1600s. Spread across much of the Southeast, the Cherokees were divided into three main groups: the Lower Towns, along the upper Savannah River in South Carolina; the Middle Towns, along the Little Tennessee River and its tributaries in western North Carolina; and the Overhill Towns, in eastern Tennessee and extreme western North Carolina. (See Map 2.)

Sometime before their regular contact with Europeans, the Cherokees became sedentary. Women performed most of the farm duties, raising corn and beans, whereas men hunted deer and turkey and caught fish to complete their diet. The Cherokees built towns organized around extended families. Society was *matrilineal,* meaning that property and position passed from generation to generation through the mother's side of the family. Each town theoretically was autonomous, and

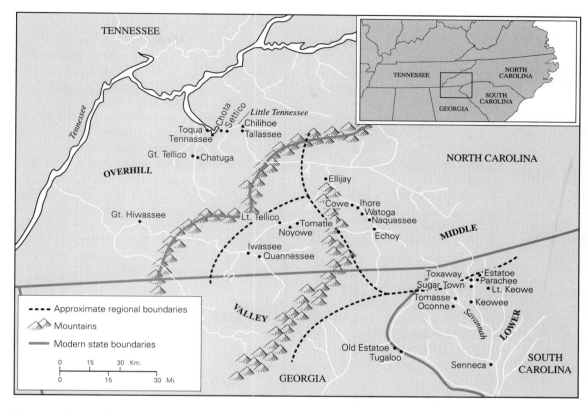

Map 2. Cherokee Settlements, 1775.
From Duane H. King, ed., *The Cherokee Nation: A Troubled History* (Knoxville: University of Tennessee Press, 1979), p. 50. Reprinted by permission.

there were no leaders (or chiefs, in European parlance) who ruled over all the towns. Local leaders led by persuasion and example, and all adults, including women, could speak in town councils. Indeed, Cherokee governing practices were considerably more democratic and consensual than the Europeans' hierarchical ways.

Initial contacts with Europeans were devastating. Europeans brought with them measles and smallpox, against which Native Americans were not immune. Also, Cherokees were attracted to European goods such as fabrics, metal hoes and hatchets, firearms, and (tragically) alcohol. In order to acquire these goods, Cherokees traded deerskins for them. By the early 1700s, Cherokees were killing an average of fifty thousand deer each year to secure their hides for barter, and estimates are that by 1735 over one million deer had been killed, almost certainly depleting the herds. Gradually, the Cherokees were losing their self-sufficiency and becoming increasingly dependent on European goods.

With European colonization and expansion in North America, the Cherokees inevitably became swept up into European peoples' wars. Initially siding with the British against the French, the Cherokees turned against the British when the colonial governor of South Carolina called thirty-two chieftains to a conference and then killed twenty-nine of them. The British retaliated against a Cherokee outburst by destroying the Lower Towns, killing over one hundred Cherokee warriors, and driving the survivors into the mountains. In the American Revolution, the Cherokees, hoping to stem white western expansion, again sided with the British. American Patriots destroyed over fifty Cherokee towns, scalping men and women indiscriminately.

After the American Revolution, the new U.S. government pursued a policy of attempting to "civilize" the Cherokees. Aided by government Indian agent Return J. Meigs (who lived with the Cherokees from 1801 to 1823) and a number of missionaries, the Cherokee Nation was able to adapt to many of the "white man's ways." Anglo-European gender roles were adopted, as men gave up hunting and took over agriculture from women. Plows, spinning wheels, and looms were introduced, and Cherokee women took up the making of cloth and clothing. As it did with white settlers, landownership and agriculture produced a class system. By 1824, the most affluent Cherokees owned 1,277 African American slaves, and most Cherokees were living in log homes similar to those of their white neighbors.

Cherokees were becoming "civilized" culturally as well. Mission boarding schools, supported by white contributions, dotted the landscape, and Cherokee children learned to read, write, and compute and also learned Anglo-European gender roles. Around 1809, the Native American Sequoyah began devising a Cherokee alphabet (he called it a syllabary) of eighty-five phonetic symbols that allowed Cherokees to become literate in their own language. In 1828, the first edition of the newspaper the *Cherokee Phoenix* appeared, edited by Cherokee Elias Boudinot.

Governmental and political forms also were modeled after Anglo-European institutions. A Native American police force was instituted in 1808, and in the following year a detailed census was taken. In 1827, a formal constitution was adopted, modeled on the United States Constitution, setting up a representative government and courts for the Cherokee Nation. Women, who were more nearly equal to men in traditional Cherokee society, saw their position deteriorate, as they were prohibited from voting or serving as representatives by the new constitution. In many ways, then, Cherokees had remade their economy, society, culture, and government. And although some people clung stubbornly to the old ways, Cherokee adaptation was generally widespread.

As it turned out, adaptation to the white people's ways would not save the Cherokees. In 1802, the U.S. government and the state of Georgia reached an agreement whereby the federal government promised to "extinguish, for the use of Georgia, as early as the same can be peaceably obtained upon reasonable terms . . . the Indian titles to all lands lying within the limits of the state."[6] The Louisiana Purchase (1804) acquired territory in the West that theoretically could be used for the relocation of the eastern Native Americans. Slowly the federal government began purchasing Cherokee lands in Tennessee, southern Kentucky, northern Alabama, South Carolina, and northeastern Georgia. In 1818, a trickle of Cherokees began to migrate to lands west of the Mississippi River.

The vast majority of Cherokees, however, refused to move. They had built farms, sawmills, tanneries, ferries, stores, and towns. The Treaty of Hopewell (1785) had promised that they would be able to hold on to their land "forever." In addition, Christian missionaries who lived among the Cherokees strengthened their resolve to resist removal, believing that the Cherokees were making great strides at becoming "civilized" where they were.

Yet one Cherokee chieftain's 1775 statement turned out to be prophetic: "Indian Nations before the Whites are like balls of snow before the sun."[7] In 1828, three events took place that would change the Cherokee Nation forever. First, gold was discovered in Cherokee lands in Georgia, setting off a rush of around four thousand whites into Cherokee territory.[8] Cherokees

fought back by attacking and burning the houses of the white prospectors, and federal troops had to be dispatched to restore order. Then, in November 1828, Tennessean Andrew Jackson was elected president. Although Cherokees had been his allies in the earlier war against the Creeks, Jackson had made no secret of the fact that he strongly favored the removal of all Native Americans to lands west of the Mississippi River. As a person who had made a great deal of money in land speculation, it is possible that Jackson recognized the potential profits that could be made by acquiring Cherokee lands and was interested in helping other land speculators.

With Jackson as president, the state of Georgia realized that it could now move with impunity. In December 1828, over three months before Jackson's inauguration, the Georgia legislature passed a bill declaring that as of June 1, 1830, all Cherokee territory would be subject to Georgia laws, and Cherokee laws (including their constitution) would be null and void. The Georgia legislature also made provisions for a lottery to distribute Cherokee lands to whites. In 1829, the Georgia legislature passed an act requiring all whites living in Cherokee territory to secure licenses, an obvious attempt to expel white missionaries who, many Georgians believed, were urging the Native Americans to resist white encroachment.

In his First Annual Message to Con-

6. Quoted in Samuel Carter III, *Cherokee Sunset, A Nation Betrayed: A Narrative of Travail and Triumph, Persecution and Exile* (Garden City, N.Y.: Doubleday, 1976), p. 28.
7. J. G. M. Ramsey, *Annals of Tennessee* (Charleston, S.C.: Walker and James, 1853), pp. 117–118.
8. Some of those who made a great deal of money from the Georgia gold rush included

the South Carolina political leader John C. Calhoun, his son-in-law Thomas G. Clemson (who used some of the profits to found Clemson College in South Carolina), and future governor of New York and Democratic presidential candidate Samuel J. Tilden.

gress of December 8, 1829 (see Source 1), President Jackson made his case for the "voluntary" removal of all Native Americans east of the Mississippi River.[9] Responding to the president's message, in February 1830 the House of Representatives took up the Indian Removal Bill. The bill, however, reignited a furious debate both in Congress and among the general public. Hundreds of petitions were sent to Congress, the majority from religious groups and benevolent societies opposed to removal. Many congressional opponents of the bill were genuinely concerned about the welfare of Native Americans, but at least an equal number were Jackson's political opponents who sought to embarrass the president. On April 23, 1830, the Senate approved the Indian Removal Bill by a vote of 28–19, the House following suit on May 24 by the close margin of 102–97. Jackson signed the bill on May 28, 1830.[10] The act empowered the president to trade land in the West for lands on which Native Americans east of the Mississippi then resided, to pay Native Americans for improvements they had made to lands they were giving up, to assist and protect Native Americans during their migration, and to superintend and care for them once they had reached their destinations.

Cherokees were divided over how to respond to the imminent loss of their lands. Believing the fight was over, about two thousand voluntarily moved west to join some Cherokees who had moved even earlier. But the majority resisted removal, appealing twice to the U.S. Supreme Court. In *Cherokee Nation v. Georgia* (1831), Chief Justice John Marshall dismissed the Cherokees' suit on technical grounds.[11] In his written opinion, however, he hinted that he might be sympathetic to the Cherokees' cause if they could bring a case to the Supreme Court in another way, and the next year, in *Worcester v. Georgia* (1832), Marshall declared that Georgia's laws did not extend to the Cherokees.[12] But President Jackson refused to enforce the Court's decision, and many Cherokees came to realize that their cause was lost.

In 1835, a minority of Cherokees signed the Treaty of New Echota whereby the Cherokees promised that, in return for $5 million and land in the West, they would give up all claims to lands they occupied in Georgia, North Carolina, Tennessee, and Alabama.[13] Outraged over actions of this minority (who were derisively labeled the "Treaty Party"), 15,665 Cherokees purportedly signed a petition to the U.S. Congress protesting their removal.

9. Approximately sixty Native American nations still resided east of the Mississippi, the largest among them being the Choctaws, Creeks, Chickasaws, and Seminoles, all in the southeastern United States.
10. For the text of the Removal Act, see Wilcomb E. Washburn, ed., *The American Indian and the United States: A Documentary History* (New York: Random House, 1973), Vol. III, pp. 2169–2171.
11. Marshall ruled that the Supreme Court could not be the court of original jurisdiction because the Cherokee Nation was not a sovereign nation such as France or Great Britain within the meaning of Article III, Section 2, of the Constitution, and therefore the case had to originate in a lower court.
12. Samuel Worcester was a white missionary who refused to secure a Georgia license to live among the Cherokees. He and a fellow missionary were thrown into jail and appealed their case to the Supreme Court.
13. The Cherokee census of 1835 reported 8,946 living in Georgia, 3,644 in North Carolina, 2,528 in Tennessee, and 1,424 in Alabama, for a total of 16,542.

The Senate, which earlier had ratified the Treaty of New Echota by a single vote, tabled the petition on April 9, 1838, and General Winfield Scott was given his orders.

About 1,100 Cherokees were permitted to remain in North Carolina, principally because a white merchant named William Holland Thomas had used money from the Treaty of New Echota to purchase thousands of acres in western North Carolina on which he encouraged Cherokees to settle (he kept the land title in his own name). In 1837, the North Carolina General Assembly acknowledged the Cherokees' right to remain in North Carolina. The fact that the land Thomas purchased for the Cherokees was land that virtually no one else wanted probably was a factor in the legislature's decision. In addition to the 1,100 Cherokees who were allowed to stay in North Carolina, an additional 300 remained scattered throughout Georgia, Alabama, and Tennessee. Some had hidden themselves from Scott's soldiers; others were related by blood and marriage to their white neighbors.

Eyewitness accounts of the Trail of Tears, by both Native Americans and U.S. Army escorts, make for grim reading. As many as 2,500 or more died in the makeshift stockades prior to the journey. And of the 13,149 (cited by army records) who began the trip, only 11,504 arrived in Indian Territory. In addition, several hundred died soon after their arrival, by either disease or violence between the new arrivals and earlier migrants or between the "accommodationists" and the last-ditch resisters.

What were the principal arguments among whites (Sources 1 through 4) both in favor of and opposed to removal? What were the strengths and weaknesses of each argument?

As for the Cherokees (Sources 5 through 9), what arguments did they use to oppose removal? Did any Cherokees support removal? What arguments did they use to support their position? What were the strengths and weaknesses of each argument?

♦

The Method

As you examine and analyze the principal arguments both in favor of and opposed to Cherokee removal, almost immediately you will see that some of the speakers and writers chose to *rephrase* the question. For example, instead of listing the reasons the Cherokees should be removed, President Jackson preferred to discuss *why the Cherokees could not remain where they were* (Source 1). By carefully reading his answers (there were several) to that question, you will be able to infer what his answers would have been to the question of *why the Cherokees ought to be removed*.

The same holds true for speakers and writers opposed to Cherokee removal. In some cases, they offered what they thought were alternatives that would have been superior to that of removal. As with Jackson's message, you will have to infer from what opponents said or wrote what they *would have* said or written regarding why the Cherokees ought *not to have been* removed.

Similarly to Jackson, many other speakers and writers offered more than one answer to the question. Therefore, as you examine and analyze the evidence, be sure to take notes carefully.

The second central question in this chapter regards the strengths and weaknesses of the principal points both in favor of and opposed to Cherokee removal. This is not nearly so easy as it may first appear. For one thing, you may not be able to uncover the real reasons a speaker or writer took a particular position. For example, almost no one in favor of removal said that Cherokees should be removed because whites wanted their lands. Indeed, Jackson himself may have come as close as any proponent of removal when he wrote that Cherokees "have neither the intelligence, the industry, the moral habits, nor the desire of improvement . . . in their condition."[14] Similarly, no opponent of removal would have been crass enough to say that the opponent's true motive was to embarrass President Jackson politically. Without considerably more information than is available here, you will have to take the speaker's or writer's comments at face value. Jackson, for example, always claimed that removal was the most humane policy for the Cherokees themselves. Is there any evidence to the contrary?

Moreover, as you assess the

strengths and weaknesses of each speaker's or writer's position, you will almost inevitably be drawn into the interesting but highly dangerous process of evaluating the alternatives to removal. Typically, historians concern themselves with what *actually did* happen rather than what *might have* happened. To be sure, some of the opponents of removal did advocate alternatives to removal, and in some cases you may have to deal with such alternatives as you determine the strengths and weaknesses of a particular position. If you plan to do this, however, use the actual facts at your disposal to assess a particular alternative. Do not *create* facts to fit your hypothesis—perhaps the worst charge that can be made against a historian. Also remember that you are dealing with people from the early 1800s, *not* the twenty-first century. Avoid putting ideas and thought processes contemporary to you into their minds.

Let us offer a final note of caution. As you examine each piece of evidence, avoid the temptation to "take sides" in the debate or to make the historical individuals into one-dimensional heroes or villains. Analyze the logic of each of the arguments, even when you find the conclusions of a speaker or writer to be reprehensible.

Exercise the same caution and attempt at objectivity when examining the Cherokee sources. Left to their own devices, virtually none of the Native Americans would have voluntarily embraced relocation to lands in the West. And yet you already know (from the Background section of this chapter) that *some* Cherokees accepted removal as preferable to their collective future

14. Fifth Annual Message to Congress, December 3, 1833, in James D. Richardson, *A Compilation of the Messages and Papers of the Presidents* (New York: Bureau of National Literature, 1897), Vol. III, p. 1252.

on their traditional lands in the East. Which individuals or groups opposed removal? What arguments did they use to support their position? What were the strengths and weaknesses of those arguments? As for those Cherokees who ultimately accepted relocation, what arguments did *they* use?

Beneath the surface of all the arguments is the *image* of Native Americans, both in the eyes of European Americans and in those of Native Americans. What underlying assumptions regarding Cherokees can you detect in both the white and Cherokee evidence?

Now proceed to the Evidence section of the chapter. Take notes as you read each selection.

The Evidence

WHITE SOURCES

Source 1 from James D. Richardson, *A Compilation of the Messages and Papers of the Presidents* (New York: Bureau of National Literature, 1897), Vol. III, pp. 1019–1022.

1. Excerpt from President Andrew Jackson's First Annual Message to Congress, December 8, 1829.

The condition and ulterior destiny of the Indian Tribes within the limits of some of our States, have become objects of much interest and importance. It has long been the policy of Government to introduce among them the arts of civilization, in the hope of gradually reclaiming them from a wandering life. This policy has, however, been coupled with another, wholly incompatible with its success. Professing a desire to civilize and settle them, we have, at the same time, lost no opportunity to purchase their lands, and thrust them further into the wilderness. By this means they have not only been kept in a wandering state, but been led to look upon us as unjust and indifferent to their fate. Thus, though lavish in its expenditures upon the subject, Government has constantly defeated its own policy; and the Indians, in general, receding further and further to the West, have retained their savage habits. A portion, however, of the Southern tribes, having mingled much with the whites, and made some progress in the arts of civilized life, have lately attempted to erect an independent government, within the limits of Georgia and Alabama. These States, claiming to be the only Sovereigns within their territories, extended their laws over the Indians; which induced the latter to call upon the United States for protection. . . .

Actuated by this view of the subject, I informed the Indians inhabiting parts of Georgia and Alabama, that their attempt to establish an independent government would not be countenanced by the Executive of the United States; and advised them to emigrate beyond the Mississippi, or submit to the laws of those States.

Our conduct towards these people is deeply interesting to our national character. Their present condition, contrasted with what they once were, makes a most powerful appeal to our sympathies. Our ancestors found them the uncontrolled possessors of these vast regions. By persuasion and force, they have been made to retire from river to river, and from mountain to mountain; until some of the tribes have become extinct, and others have left but remnants, to preserve, for a while, their once terrible names. Surrounded by the whites, with their arts of civilization, which, by destroying the resources of the savage, doom him to weakness and decay; the fate of the Mohegan, the Narragansett, and the Delaware, is fast overtaking the Choctaw, the Cherokee, and the Creek. That this fate surely awaits them, if they remain within the limits of the States, does not admit of a doubt. Humanity and national honor demand that every effort should be made to avert so great a calamity. It is too late to inquire whether it was just in the United States to include them and their territory within the bounds of new States whose limits they could control. That step cannot be retraced. A State cannot be dismembered by Congress, or restricted in the exercise of her constitutional power. But the people of those States, and of every State, actuated by feelings of justice and a regard for our national honor, submit to you the interesting question, whether something cannot be done, consistently with the rights of the States, to preserve this much injured race?

As a means of effecting this end, I suggest, for your consideration, the propriety of setting apart an ample district West of the Mississippi, and without the limits of any State or Territory, now formed, to be guarantied to the Indian tribes, as long as they shall occupy it: each tribe having a distinct control over the portion designated for its use. There they may be secured in the enjoyment of governments of their own choice, subject to no other control from the United States than such as may be necessary to preserve peace on the frontier, and between the several tribes. There the benevolent may endeavor to teach them the arts of civilization; and, by promoting union and harmony among them, to raise up an interesting commonwealth, destined to perpetuate the race, and to attest the humanity and justice of this Government.

This emigration should be voluntary: for it would be as cruel as unjust to compel the aborigines to abandon the graves of their fathers, and seek a home in a distant land.[15] But they should be distinctly informed that, if they remain within the limits of the States, they must be subject to their laws. In return for their obedience, as individuals, they will, without doubt, be protected in the enjoyment of those possessions which they have improved by their industry. But it seems to me visionary to suppose, that, in this state of things, claims can be allowed on tracts of country on which they have neither dwelt nor made improvements, merely because they have seen them from the mountain, or passed them in the chace [sic]. Submitting to the laws of the States, and receiving, like other citizens, protection in their persons and property, they will, ere long, become merged in the mass of our population.

Source 2 from Andrew A. Lipscomb and Albert Ellergy Bergh, eds., *The Writings of Thomas Jefferson* (Washington, D.C.: Thomas Jefferson Memorial Association, 1903), Vol. XVI, pp. 450–454.

2. President Thomas Jefferson to Captain Hendrick, the Delawares, Mohicans, and Munries, December 21, 1808.

The picture which you have drawn, my son, of the increase of our numbers and the decrease of yours is just, the causes are very plain, and the remedy depends on yourselves alone. You have lived by hunting the deer and buffalo—all these have been driven westward; you have sold out on the seaboard and moved westwardly in pursuit of them. As they became scarce there, your food has failed you; you have been a part of every year without food, except the roots and other unwholesome things you could find in the forest. Scanty and unwholesome food produce diseases and death among your children, and hence you have raised few and your numbers have decreased. Frequent wars, too, and the abuse of spirituous liquors, have assisted in lessening your numbers. The whites, on the other hand, are in the habit of cultivating the earth, of raising stocks of cattle, hogs, and other domestic animals, in much greater numbers than they could kill of deer and buffalo. Having always a plenty of food and clothing they raise [an] abundance of children, they double their numbers every twenty years, the new swarms are continually advancing upon the country like flocks of pigeons, and so they will continue to do. Now, my children, if we wanted to diminish our numbers, we would

15. Jackson believed, perhaps naively, that a majority of Cherokees would move to the West voluntarily. See his Third Annual Message to Congress, December 6, 1831, in Richardson, *Messages and Papers of the Presidents,* Vol. III, p. 1117.

give up the culture of the earth, pursue the deer and buffalo, and be always at war; this would soon reduce us to be as few as you are, and if you wish to increase your numbers you must give up the deer and buffalo, live in peace and cultivate the earth. You see then, my children, that it depends on yourselves alone to become a numerous and great people. Let me entreat you, therefore, on the lands now given you to begin to give every man a farm; let him enclose it, cultivate it, build a warm house on it, and when he dies, let it belong to his wife and children after him. Nothing is so easy as to learn to cultivate the earth; all your women understand it, and to make it easier, we are always ready to teach you how to make ploughs, hoes, and necessary utensils. If the men will take the labor of the earth from the women they will learn to spin and weave and to clothe their families. In this way you will also raise many children, you will double your numbers every twenty years, and soon fill the land your friends have given you, and your children will never be tempted to sell the spot on which they have been born, raised, have labored and called their own. When once you have property, you will want laws and magistrates to protect your property and persons, and to punish those among you who commit crimes. You will find that our laws are good for this purpose; you will wish to live under them, you will unite yourselves with us, join in our Great Councils and form one people with us, and we shall all be Americans; you will mix with us by marriage, your blood will run in our veins, and will spread with us over this great island. Instead, then, my children, of the gloomy prospect you have drawn of your total disappearance from the face of the earth, which is true, if you continue to hunt the deer and buffalo and go to war, you see what a brilliant aspect is offered to your future history, if you give up war and hunting. Adopt the culture of the earth and raise domestic animals; you see how from a small family you may become a great nation by adopting the course which from the small beginning you describe has made us a great nation.

Source 3 from Theda Perdue and Michael D. Green, eds., *The Cherokee Removal: A Brief History with Documents.* (Boston: Bedford Books, 1995), pp. 98–102.

3. Excerpt from William Penn (pseudonym for Jeremiah Evarts of the American Board of Commissioners for Foreign Missions), "A Brief View of the Present Relations Between the Government and People of the United States and the Indians Within Our National Limits," November 1829.

The positions here recited are deemed to be incontrovertible. It follows, therefore,

That the removal of any nation of Indians from their country by force would be an instance of gross and cruel oppression:

That all attempts to accomplish this removal of the Indians by bribery or fraud, by intimidation and threats, by withholding from them a knowledge of the strength of their cause, by practising upon their ignorance, and their fears, or by vexatious opportunities, interpreted by them to mean nearly the same thing as a command;—all such attempts are acts of oppression, and therefore entirely unjustifiable:

That the United States are firmly bound by treaty to protect the Indians from force and encroachments on the part of a State; and a refusal thus to protect them would be equally an act of bad faith as a refusal to protect them against individuals: and

That the Cherokees have therefore the guaranty of the United States, solemnly and repeatedly given, as a security against encroachments from Georgia and the neighboring States. By virtue of this guaranty the Cherokees may rightfully demand, that the United States shall keep all intruders at a distance, from whatever quarter, or in whatever character, they may come. Thus secured and defended in the possession of their country, the Cherokees have a perfect right to retain that possession as long as they please. Such a retention of their country is no just cause of complaint or offence to any State, or to any individual. It is merely an exercise of natural rights, which rights have been not only acknowledged but repeatedly and solemnly confirmed by the United States.

Although these principles are clear and incontrovertible, yet many persons feel an embarrassment from considering the Cherokees *as living in the State of Georgia.* All this embarrassment may be removed at once by bearing in mind, that the Cherokee country is not in Georgia. . . .

[Here Penn argued that the Cherokees owned their land by treaty with the U.S. government, that in 1825 the state of Georgia made a treaty with the Creek Nation to acquire their land, and hence would have to do so with the Cherokees as well.]

If the separate existence of the Indian tribes *were* an inconvenience to their neighbours, this would be but a slender reason for breaking down all the barriers of justice and good faith. Many a rich man has thought it very inconvenient, that he could not add the farm of a poor neighbour to his possessions. Many a powerful nation has felt it to be inconvenient to have a weak and dependent state in its neighbourhood, and has therefore forcibly joined the territory of such state to its own extensive domains. But this is done at the expense of honour and character, and is visited by the historian with his severest reprobation.

In the case before us the inconvenience is altogether imaginary. If the United States were examined, with a view to find a place where Indians could have a residence assigned them, so that they might be as little as possible in the way of the whites, not a single tract, capable of sustaining inhabitants, could be found more secluded than the present country of the Cherokees. It is in the mountains, among the head waters of rivers diverging in all directions; and some parts of it are almost inaccessible. The Cherokees have ceded to the United States all their best land. Not a twentieth part of what remains is of a very good quality. More than half is utterly worthless. Perhaps three tenths may produce moderate crops. The people of the United States have a free passage through the country, secured by treaty. What do they want more? If the Cherokee country were added to Georgia, the accession would be but a fraction joined to the remotest corner of that great State;—a State now scarcely inferior in size to any State in the Union except Virginia; a State having but six or seven souls to a square mile, counting whites and blacks, and with a soil and climate capable of sustaining a hundred to the square mile with the greatest of ease. There is no mighty inconvenience, therefore, in the arrangement of Providence, by which the Cherokee claim a resting place on the land which God gave to their fathers. . . .

There is one remaining topic, on which the minds of many benevolent men are hesitating; and that is, *whether the welfare of the Indians would not be promoted by a removal.* Though they have a right to remain where they are; though the whole power of the United States is pledged to defend them in their possessions; yet it is supposed by some, that they would act wisely, if they would yield to the pressure, quietly surrender their territory to the United States, and accept a new country beyond the Mississippi, with a new guaranty.

In support of this supposition, it is argued, that they can never remain quiet where they are; that they will always be infested by troublesome whites; and that the states, which lay claim to their territory, will persevere in measures to vex and annoy them.

Let us look a moment at this statement. Is it indeed true, that, in the very prime and vigour of our republican government, and with all our boasted reliance upon constitutions and laws, we cannot enforce as plain an act of Congress as is to be found in our national statute-book? Is it true, that while treaties are declared in the constitution to be the supreme law of the land, a whole volume of these supreme laws is to be at once avowedly and utterly disregarded? Is the Senate of the United States, that august body, as our newspapers have called it a thousand times, to march in solemn procession, and burn a volume of treaties? Are the archives of state to be searched, and a hundred and fifty rolls, containing treaties with the Indians, to be brought forth and consigned to the flames on Capitol Hill, in the presence of the representatives of the people, and all the dignitaries of our national government? When ambassadors from foreign nations inquire, *What is the cause of all this burning?* are we to say, "Forty years ago President Washington and the Senate made treaties with the Indians, which have been repeated and confirmed by successive administrations. The treaties are plain, and the terms reasonable. But the Indians are weak, and their white neighbors will be lawless. The way to please these white neighbours is, therefore, to burn the treaties, and then call the Indians our dear children, and deal with them precisely as if no treaties had ever been made." Is this answer to be given to the honest inquires of intelligent foreigners? Are we to declare to mankind, that in our country law is totally inadequate to answer the great end for which human laws are made, that is, the protection of the weak against the strong? And is this confession to be made without feeling and without shame? It cannot be. The people of the United States will never subject themselves to so foul a reproach.

Source 4 from *Speeches on the Passage of the Bill for the Removal of the Indians, Delivered in the Congress of the United States, April and May, 1830* (Boston: Perkins and Marvin, 1830), pp. 25–28.

4. Excerpt from Speech of Senator Theodore Frelinghuysen of New Jersey.

It is alleged, that the Indians cannot flourish in the neighborhood of a white population—that whole tribes have disappeared under the influence of this propinquity. As an abstract proposition, it implies reproach somewhere. Our virtues certainly have not such deadly and depopulating power. It must, then, be our vices that possess these destructive energies—and shall we commit injustice, and put in, as our plea for it, that our intercourse with the Indians has been so demoralizing that we must drive them from it, to save them? True, Sir, many tribes have melted away—they have sunk lower and lower—and what people could rise from a condition to which policy, selfishness, and cupidity, conspired to depress them?

Sir, had we devoted the same care to elevate their moral condition, that we have to degrade them, the removal of the Indians would not now seek for an apology in the suggestions of humanity. But I ask, as to the matter of fact, how stands the account? Wherever a fair experiment has been made, the Indians have readily yielded to the influences of moral cultivation. Yes, Sir, they flourish under this culture, and rise in the scale of being. They have shown themselves to be highly susceptible of improvement, and the ferocious feelings and habits of the savage are soothed and reformed by the mild charities of religion. They can very soon be taught to understand and appreciate the blessings of civilization and regular government. . . .

Prompted and encouraged by our counsels, they have in good earnest resolved to become men, rational, educated, Christian men; and they have succeeded beyond our most sanguine hopes. They have established a regular constitution of civil government, republican in its principles. Wise and beneficent laws are enacted. The people acknowledge their authority, and feel their obligation. A printing press, conducted by one of the nation, circulates a weekly newspaper, printed partly in English, and partly in the Cherokee language. Schools flourish in many of their settlements. Christian temples, to the God of the Bible, are frequented by respectful, devout, and many sincere worshippers. God, as we believe, has many people among them, whom he regards as the "apple of his eye." They have become better neighbors to Georgia. . . .

Let the general government come out, as it should, with decided and temperate firmness, and officially announce to Georgia, and the other States, that if the Indian tribes choose to remain, they will be protected against all interference and encroachment; and such is my confidence in the sense of justice, in the respect for law, prevailing in the great body of this portion of our fellow-citizens, that I believe they would submit to the authority of the nation. I can expect no other issue.

CHEROKEE SOURCES

Sources 5 through 7 from Theda Perdue and Michael D. Green, eds., *The Cherokee Removal: A Brief History with Documents* (Boston: Bedford Books, 1995), pp. 131–132, 43–44, 143–145.

5. Petition of Cherokee Women, May 2, 1817.

The Cherokee ladys now being present at the meeting of the chiefs and warriors in council have thought it their duty as mothers to address their beloved chiefs and warriors now assembled.

Our beloved children and head men of the Cherokee Nation, we address you warriors in council. We have raised all of you on the land which we now have, which God gave us to inhabit and raise provisions. We know that our country has once been extensive, but by repeated sales has become circumscribed to a small track [*sic*], and [we] never have thought it our duty to interfere in the disposition of it till now. If a father or mother was to sell all their lands which they had to depend on, which their children had to raise their living on, which would be indeed bad & to be removed to another country. We do not wish to go to an unknown country [to] which we have understood some of our children wish to go over the Mississippi, but this act of our children would be like destroying your mothers.

Your mothers, your sisters ask and beg of you not to part with any more of our land. We say ours. You are our descendants; take pity on our request. But keep it for our growing children, for it was the good will of our creator to place us here, and you know our father, the great president,[16] will not allow his white children to take our country away. Only keep your hands off of paper talks for its our own country. For [if] it was not, they would not ask you to put your hands to paper, for it would be impossible to remove us all. For as soon as one child is raised, we have others in our arms, for such is our situation & will consider our circumstance.

Therefore, children, don't part with any more of our lands but continue on it & enlarge your farms. Cultivate and raise corn & cotton and your mothers and sisters will make clothing for you which our father the president has recommended to us all. We don't charge any body for selling any lands, but we have heard such intentions of our children. But your talks become true at last; it was our desire to forwarn you all not to part with our lands.

---

16. President James Monroe.

6. John Ridge (a Cherokee leader) to Albert Gallatin,[17] February 27, 1826.

[*In this long letter, Ridge began by giving a geographic location of the Cherokee Nation, its population, its successful adoption of agriculture, its government, the status of women, its religious beliefs, and its educational institutions.*]

Col. Silas Dinsmore was appointed by Genl. Washington as Agent of the Nation, who from the Indian Testimony itself labored indefatigably in Teaching the Cherokees the art of agriculture by distributing hoes & ploughs & giving to the women Spinning wheels, cards & Looms. It appears when this change of Hunter life to a civilized one was proposed by the Agent to the Chiefs in Council, that he was unanimously laughed at by the Council for attempting [to] introduce white peoples' habits among the Indians, who were created to pursue the chase. Not discouraged here, the Agent turned to Individuals & succeeded to gain some to pay their attention to his plan by way of experiment, which succeeded. An anecdote is related of a Chief who was heartily opposed to the Agent's view. He came to Col. Dinsmore & said, "I don't want you to recommend these things to my people. They may suit white people, but will do [nothing] for the Indians. I am now going to hunt & shall be gone six moons & when I return, I shall expect to hear nothing of your talks made in [my] absence to induce my people to take hold of your plan." But in his absence the Agent induced his wife & daughters to Spin & weave with so much assiduity as to make more cloth in value, than the Chief's Hunt of six months amounted to. He was astonished & came to the Agent with a smile, accusing him for making his wife & daughters better hunters than he & requested to be furnished a plough & went to work on his farm. In the meantime, the Moravians opened their School for the Indians, cleared a farm, cultivated a garden & planted an orchard. The Venerable Rev. John Gambold & his amiable Lady were a standing monument of Industry, Goodness & friendship. As far as they had means, they converted the "Wilderness to blossom as the Rose." There the boys & girls were taught to read & write, & occasionally labor in the Garden & in the field. There they were first taught to sing & pray to their Creator, & here Gospel Worship was first Established. Never shall I forget father Gambold & mother Mrs. Gambold. By them the clouds of ignorance which surrounded me on all sides were dispersed. My heart received the rays of civilization & my intellect expanded & took a wider range. My superstition vanished & I began to reason correctly. . . .

17. Albert Gallatin (1761–1849) was a congressman, secretary of the treasury, and diplomat. When Ridge wrote to Gallatin, Gallatin had just been nominated as U.S. minister to Great Britain.

7. Elias Boudinot, Editorial in *Cherokee Phoenix,* November 12, 1831.

It has been customary to charge the failure of attempts heretofore made to civilize and christianize the aborigines to the Indians themselves. Whence originated the common saying, "An Indian will still be an Indian."—Do what you will, he cannot be civilized—you cannot reclaim him from his wild habits—you may as well expect to change the spots of the Leopard as to effect any substantial renovation in his character—he is as the wild Turkey, which at "night-fall seeks the tallest forest tree for his roosting place." Such assertions, although inconsistent with the general course of providence and the history of nations, have nevertheless been believed and acted upon by many well meaning persons. Such persons do not sufficiently consider that causes, altogether different from those they have been in the habit of assigning, may have operated to frustrate the benevolent efforts made to reclaim the Indian. . . .

We have on more than one occasion remarked upon the difficulties which lie in the way of civilizing the Indians. Those difficulties have been fully developed in the history of the Cherokees within the last two years. They are such as no one can now mistake—their nature is fully revealed and the source from whence they rise can no longer be a matter of doubt. They are not to be found in the "nature" of the Indians, which a man in high authority once said was as difficult to change as the Leopard his spots. It is not because they are, of all others, the most degraded and ignorant that they have not been brought to enjoy the blessings of a civilized life.—But it is because they have to contend with obstacles as numerous as they are peculiar. . . .

The Cherokees have been reclaimed from their wild habits—Instead of hunters they have become the cultivators of the soil—Instead of wild and ferocious savages, thirsting for blood, they have become the mild "citizens," the friends and brothers of the white man—Instead of the superstitious heathens, many of them have become the worshippers of the true God. Well would it have been if the cheering fruits of those labors had been fostered and encouraged by an enlightened community! But alas! no sooner was it made manifest that the Cherokees were becoming strongly attached to the ways and usages of civilized life, than was aroused the opposition of those from whom better things ought to have been expected. No sooner was it known that they had learned the proper use of the earth, and that they were now less likely to dispose of their lands for a mess of pottage, than they came in conflict with the cupidity and self-interest of those who ought to have been their benefactors—Then commenced a series of obstacles hard to overcome, and difficulties intended as a stumbling block, and unthought of before. The

"Great Father" of the "red man" has lent his influence to encourage those difficulties. The *guardian* has deprived his *wards* of their rights—The sacred obligations of treaties and laws have been disregarded—The promises of Washington and Jefferson have not been fulfilled. The policy of the United States on Indian Affairs has taken a different direction, for no other reason than that the Cherokees have so far become civilized as to appreciate a regular form of Government. . . .

That the Cherokees may be kept in ignorance, teachers who had settled among them by the approbation of the Government, for the best of all purposes, have been compelled to leave them by reason of laws unbecoming any civilized nation—Ministers of the Gospel, who might have, at this day of trial, administered to them the consolations of Religion, have been arrested, chained, dragged away before their eyes, tried as felons, and finally immured in prison with thieves and robbers.

Is not here an array of *difficulties*?—The truth is, while a portion of the community have been, in the most laudable manner, engaged in using efforts to civilize and christianize the Indian, another portion of the same community have been busy in counteracting those efforts. Cupidity and self-interest are at the bottom of all these difficulties—A desire *to posses* the Indian land is paramount to a desire to see him *established* on the soil as a *civilized* man.

Sources 8 and 9 from *Letter from John Ross, principal Chief of the Cherokee Nation of Indians: in answer to inquiries from a friend regarding the Cherokee affairs with the United States, followed by a copy of the protest of the Cherokee delegation, laid before the Senate and House of Representatives at the city of Washington, on the twenty-first day of June, eighteen hundred and thirty-six* (Washington D.C.: s.n., 1836), pp. 3, 4, 12, 13, 17, 18, 19–20, 31. From Southeastern Native American Documents, 1730–1842, accessible through the Georgia Virtual Library, Galileo, www.galileo.usg.edu.

8. Letter from John Ross, principal Chief of the Cherokee Nation of Indians, to a friend, July 2, 1836.

I wish I could acquiesce in your impression, that a Treaty has been made, by which every difficulty between the Cherokees and the United States has been set at rest; but I must candidly say, that I know of no such Treaty. I do not mean to prophesy any similar troubles to those which have, in other cases, followed the failure to adjust disputed points with Indians; the Cherokees act on a principle preventing apprehensions of that nature—their principle is, "endure and forbear;" but I must distinctly declare to you that I believe, the document signed by unauthorized individuals at Washington, will never be regarded by the Cherokee nation as a Treaty. The delegation appointed by the people to make a Treaty, have protested against that instrument "as deceptive to the world and a fraud upon the Cherokee people." You say you do *not* see my name appended to the paper in question, but that you regard the omission as a typographical mistake, because you *do* find my name among those who are mentioned in it as the future directors of Cherokee affairs.

I will answer these points separately: and, first,

My name is not, by mistake, omitted among the signers of the paper in question; and the reasons why it is not affixed to that paper, are the following:—

Neither myself nor any other member of the regular delegation to Washington, can, without violating our most sacred engagements, ever recognize that paper as a Treaty, by assenting to its terms, or the mode of its execution. They are entirely inconsistent with the views of the Cherokee people. Three times have the Cherokee people formally and openly rejected conditions substantially the same as these. We were commissioned by the people, under express injunctions, not to bind the nation to any such conditions. The delegation representing the Cherokees, have, therefore, officially rejected these conditions themselves, and have regularly protested before the Senate and House of Representatives, against their ratification. The Cherokee people, in two protests, the one signed by twelve thousand seven hundred and fourteen persons, and the other by three thousand two hundred and fifty persons, spoke for themselves against the Treaty, even previous to its rejection by those whom they had selected to speak for them. . . .

[*Ross explained here that the Treaty of Echota did not guarantee that Cherokee lands in the West would be theirs forever. Nor did that treaty assure the Cherokees that they would be able to live under their own laws. Thus the white incursions in the East might well be repeated in the West. Ross also asserted that those Cherokees who signed the Treaty of Echota were an extralegal body that had no authorization to sell tribal lands.*]

I will here take occasion to touch upon two points in reference to our negociations, which do not seem to be understood by the American people. One impression concerning us, is, that though we object to removal, as we are equally averse to becoming citizens of the United States, we ought to be forced to remove; to be tied hand and foot and conveyed to the extreme western frontier, and then turned loose among the wild beasts of the wilderness. Now, the fact is, we never have objected to become citizens of the United States and to conform to her laws; but in the event of conforming to her laws, we have required the protection and the privileges of her laws to accompany that conformity on our part. We have asked this repeatedly and repeatedly has it been denied.

The other point to which I would advert is this: a charge that the whole scope of my policy has been to get the money of the nation into my own hands. *This is a monstrous misrepresentation.* The funds of the nation never have been in my hands. They have been with the councils of the nation, as the funds of the United States are with the representatives of her people. . . .

I must bring my letter to a close. I fear it has already wearied you. But it gratifies me to find any one desirous of looking earnestly into the true state of the Cherokee questions, and I wish to afford all such enquirers every satisfaction. You have already perceived that the singular attitude into which our affairs have been thrown by the mere trickery of party, emanated entirely from the subserviency of irresponsible Cherokees to the policy, backed by the power of the administration.

9. "Memorial and Protest of the Cherokee Nation," to the Senate and House of Representatives, June 21, 1836.

To the honourable the Senate and House of Representatives of the United States of North America, in Congress assembled:

The undersigned representatives of the Cherokee nation, east of the river Mississippi, impelled by duty, would respectfully submit, for the consideration of your honourable body, the following statement: An instrument purporting to be a treaty with the Cherokee people, has recently been made public by the President of the United States, that will have such an operation, if carried into effect. This instrument, the delegation ever before the civilized world, and in the presence of Almighty God, is fraudulent, false upon its face, made by unauthorized individuals, without the sanction, and against the wishes, of the great body of the Cherokee people. Upwards of fifteen thousand of those people have protested against it, solemnly declaring they will never acquiesce. The delegation would respectfully call the attention of your honourable body to their memorial and protest, with the accompanying documents, submitted to the Senate of the United States, on the subject of the alleged treaty, which are herewith transmitted. . . .

It is the expressed wish of the Government of the United States to remove the Cherokees to a place west of the Mississippi. That wish is said to be founded in humanity to the Indians. To make their situation more comfortable, and to preserve them as a distinct people. Let facts show how this *benev-olent* design has been prosecuted, and how faithfully to the spirit and letter has the promise of the President of the United States to the Cherokees been fulfilled—that *"those who remain may be assured of our patronage; our aid, and good neighbourhood."* The delegation are not deceived by empty profes-sions, and fear their race is to be destroyed by the mercenary policy of the present day, and their lands wrested from them by physical force; as proof, they will refer to the preamble of an act of the General Assembly of Georgia, in reference to the Cherokees, passed the 2d of December, 1835, where it is said, "from a knowledge of the Indian character, and from the present feelings of these Indians, it is confidently believed, that the right of occupancy of the lands in their possession should be withdrawn, *that it would be a strong in-ducement to them to treat with the General Government, and consent to a re-moval to the west;* and whereas, the present Legislature openly avow that their primary object in the measures intended to be pursued, *are founded on real humanity to these Indians,* and with a view, in a distant region, to perpet-uate them with their old identity of character, *under the paternal care of the Government of the United States;* at the same time frankly disavowing *any selfish or sinister motives towards them in their present legislation."* This is the profession. Let us turn to the practice of *humanity,* to the Cherokees, by the State of Georgia. In violation of the treaties between the United States and the Cherokee nation, that State passed a law requiring all white men, re-siding in that part of the Cherokee country, in her limits, to take an oath of al-legiance to the State of Georgia. For a violation of this law, some of the ministers of Christ, missionaries among the Cherokees, were tried, convicted, and sentenced to hard labor in the penitentiary. Their case may be seen by reference to the records of the Supreme Court of the United States.

Valuable gold mines were discovered upon the Cherokee lands, within the chartered limits of Georgia, and the Cherokees commenced working them, and the Legislature of that State interfered by passing an act, making it penal for an Indian to dig for gold within Georgia, no doubt *"frankly disavowing any selfish or sinister motives towards them."* Under this law many Cherokees were arrested, tried, imprisoned, and otherwise abused. Some were even shot in attempting to avoid an arrest; yet the Cherokee people used no violence, but humbly petitioned the Government of the United States for a fulfilment of treaty engagements, to protect them, which was not done, and the answer given that the United States could not interfere. Georgia discovered she was not to be obstructed in carrying out her measures, *"founded on real humanity to these Indians,"* she passed an act directing the Indian country to be sur-

veyed into districts. This excited some alarm, but the Cherokees were quieted
with the assurance it would do no harm to survey the country. Another act
was shortly after passed, to lay off the country into lots. As yet there was no
authority to take possession, but it was not long before a law was made, authorizing a lottery for the lands laid off into lots. In this act the Indians were
secured in possession of all the lots touched by their improvements, and the
balance of the country allowed to be occupied by white men. This was a direct
violation of the 5th article of the treaty of the 27th of February, 1819. The
Cherokees made no resistance, still petitioned the United States for protection, and received the same answer that the President could not interpose. After the country was parcelled out by lottery, a horde of speculators made their
appearance, and purchased of the "fortunate drawers," lots touched by Indian improvements, at reduced prices, declaring it was uncertain when the
Cherokees would surrender their rights, and that the lots were encumbered
by their claims. The consequence of this speculation was that, at the next ses-
sion of the Legislature, an act was passed limiting the Indian right of occupancy to the lot upon which he resided. . . .

[*The memorial gives several examples of Cherokees who were cheated out of their lands
or who lost them to white speculators or squatters.*]

The delegation must repeat, the instrument entered into at New Echota, purporting to be a treaty, is deceptive to the world, and a fraud upon the Cherokee people. If a doubt exist as to the truth of their statement, a committee of
investigation can learn the facts, and it may also learn that if the Cherokees
are removed under that instrument, it will be by force.

✦

Questions to Consider

Remember that your task in this chapter is a dual one. First, you must examine and analyze the four sources by
white writers on how to deal with Native Americans living east of the Mississippi River, noting the strengths and
weaknesses of each argument. Then
you must repeat the process for the five
sources by Cherokee writers on how
to—or whether to—resist removal to
lands west of the Mississippi.

President Andrew Jackson gave four
principal reasons why, in his opinion,
the Cherokees should not remain
where they were as a political entity
separate from the state of Georgia
(Source 1). What were those four reasons? How important was it, in Jackson's opinion, that the Cherokees become "civilized"? In his view, what
would be the results of permitting the
Cherokees to remain in the East?

Finally, Jackson strongly maintained that any such emigration "should be voluntary," but, in his view, what would happen to the Cherokees who refused to leave? Why couldn't the president of the United States intervene to help the Cherokees remain where they were?

President Thomas Jefferson's letter of December 21, 1808 (Source 2), while not specifically referring to the Cherokees, accurately summarized his general policy with regard to Native Americans living within the boundaries of the United States. What did Jefferson believe were the causes of population decline among Native American people (note that Jackson also dealt with this problem, and in a way not terribly different from that of Jefferson)? How, in Jefferson's view, could that situation be reversed? In return for staying on their lands, what would Native Americans have had to give up? What was Jackson's opinion on this topic? In your view, which president was more eager to eliminate Native American cultures: Jackson or Jefferson? Also note that Jefferson realized that Native Americans were not simply wandering hunters, but that they already cultivated the earth ("all your women understand it"). What stereotype did Jefferson seem to believe? See Source 6 for a refutation of that stereotype. What do you make of the phrase, "you will unite yourselves with us, join in our Great Councils and form one people with us"? What was Jefferson proposing? How did Jackson treat the same subject?

Jeremiah Evarts (Source 3) also opposed removal. How did Evarts contest President Jackson's opinion that the Cherokees' position was unconstitu-

tional, according to Article IV, Section 3 of the Constitution? (Remember that even though Evarts wrote months before Jackson's message, the president's position was well known.) What was Evarts's opinion of the much-circulated notion in Georgia that Cherokees were inhabiting some of the best land in the state? What was his position on the inability of the government to protect the Cherokees where they were from intruding whites?

Senator Theodore Frelinghuysen was deeply and genuinely concerned about the fate of Native Americans. The speech excerpted here (Source 4) took approximately six hours to deliver, so it is not possible to include all of the points he made in opposition to removal. Frelinghuysen began his speech by admitting that many Native Americans living in close proximity to whites had experienced great difficulties. Yet why does he say this has happened? Why does he believe that removal will *not* work and, moreover, is *not* necessary? What alternative (by inference) might Frelinghuysen have supported? How important was it to Frelinghuysen that the Cherokees become "civilized"? Did he seem less concerned than Andrew Jackson about making the Cherokees more like their white neighbors?

The five Cherokee sources reveal deep divisions over how—or whether—to oppose their removal. What arguments did the Cherokee women make in opposition to removal (Source 5)? To whom was their petition addressed? What were the strengths and weaknesses of their position?

John Ross (Source 8) was the principal chief of the Cherokee Nation and the leading opponent of removal. What arguments did he make? What was his opinion of the Treaty of New Echota? Of those Cherokees who signed the treaty? What were the strengths and weaknesses of his position?

Ross also was one of the authors of the Memorial and Protest of the Cherokee Nation (Source 9). What was the line of reasoning used by those who wrote this document? In their view, what were the reasons that the Treaty of New Echota was invalid? What were the strengths and weaknesses of this carefully crafted protest?

You already know that both John Ridge and Elias Boudinot signed the Treaty of New Echota (both were murdered by Cherokees who believed Ridge and Boudinot had betrayed them). Can you detect in their writings (Sources 6 and 7) why they might have signed the treaty, even though initially they both had opposed removal? You will have to infer some of their motives because neither man fully explained his reasons in the sources at your disposal. What were the strengths and weaknesses of their arguments?

Having extracted from the evidence the principal arguments for and against removal, now use your text, the Background section of this chapter, and the help of your instructor to explain the strengths and weaknesses of each principal argument. In order to do so, take each argument for or against removal and use historical facts to determine its strengths and weaknesses. In some cases, another piece of evidence will assist you. For example, President Jackson claimed that the Cherokees' position was unconstitutional. Jeremiah Evarts, however, attempted (with some success) to challenge Jackson's position.

One more example will suffice. In his essay opposing removal, Evarts maintained that the Cherokees already had given up their best lands and what remained in their hands were lands that were "utterly worthless." What fact, however, did Evarts omit? In what way might that fact weaken his position?

Always keep in mind that a statement of opinion (a hypothesis) must be proved by using *facts,* and *not* by using other statements of opinion. What is the matter with the following two statements? (1) The Cherokees should be removed because they lack the industry to make their lands produce. (2) The Cherokees ought not to be removed because their lifestyle is superior to that of whites.

♦

Epilogue

The war between the older immigrants and the newer arrivals to Indian territory went on for seven years, until peace between the two factions of Cherokees finally was made in 1846. During that period, some Cherokees reversed their trek and returned to North Carolina. When the Civil War broke out in 1861, factionalism once again emerged, with some Cherokees supporting the Confederacy and others backing the Union. Fighting between these factions (a "mini–Civil War") claimed the lives of as much as 25 percent of the Cherokee population.

In 1868, Congress recognized the obvious fact that the Cherokees who remained in the East had become a distinct group, named the Eastern Band of the Cherokees (as opposed to the migrating group, which was called the Cherokee Nation). In 1875, the federal government began to acquire land in North Carolina for a reservation, named the Qualla Boundary, which ultimately contained around 56,000 acres. In 1889, the Eastern Band received a charter from North Carolina granting the Cherokees what amounted to home rule in the Qualla Boundary. Then the federal government began an intensive program to "civilize" the eastern Cherokees, an effort that was ultimately unsuccessful. Cherokees clung stubbornly to their own language and traditions, and by 1900, less than one-fourth of the population could speak English—approximately half of them young people in white-administered boarding schools. Because they consistently voted Republican, after 1900 the Democratic majority in North Carolina disfranchised the Cherokees by passing a law requiring literacy tests prior to voting.

Meanwhile the Cherokee Nation (in the West) was experiencing its own difficulties. In spite of the fact that the 1830 Indian Removal Act guaranteed that Native Americans would always hold the land onto which they were placed, land grants to railroad companies and a territorial land rush stripped a good deal of land away from the Cher-

okees. In 1891, the Cherokee Nation owned 19.5 million acres. By 1971, it owned but 146,598.

In North Carolina, the creation of the Great Smoky Mountains National Park in 1934 offered the Eastern Band a way out of its economic quagmire. In November 1934, the council appropriated $50,000 for tourist facilities, and in 1937, the first Cherokee-owned motel (Newfound Lodge) was opened for business. In 1939, an estimated 169,000 people visited the national park and purchased around $30,000 worth of Cherokee crafts.

The development of tourism undoubtedly helped alleviate a severe economic crisis for the Eastern Band. In 1932, at the low point of the Great Depression, it was estimated that 200 of the 496 Cherokee families in North Carolina needed public assistance. The New Deal did provide some jobs, through the Indian Emergency Conservation Work Program, a separate version of the Civilian Conservation Corps. But tourism also presented the Eastern Band with the problem of whether Cherokees could retain their cultural identity while at the same time catering to the desires of visitors with money.[18] In the 1990s, the Eastern Band turned to casino gambling to increase their revenues, although income from tourism and gambling is not evenly dispersed and many Cherokees still live extremely modestly.

By then, of course, the principal voices on both sides of the issue had

18. Because tourists expected to see Native Americans with ornate feathered headdresses (typical of Plains Indians but never worn by Cherokees), Cherokees accommodatingly wore them.

long been stilled. In 1837 (one year before the beginning of the Trail of
Tears), Andrew Jackson left the presidency to his hand-picked successor,
Martin Van Buren, and retired to his
plantation, the Hermitage, near Nash-
ville, Tennessee. He died in 1845, still
convinced that his advocacy of Cherokee removal was the most humane alternative for the Native Americans
themselves.

For his part, however, before his
death in 1826, Thomas Jefferson had
changed his position to one of supporting removal. Frustrated over what he
considered to be the slow progress Native Americans were making in adopting "civilization," the principal author
of the Declaration of Independence
came to believe that Native American
people and white people could not live
side by side unless the Native Americans abandoned their own culture in
favor of that of the whites.[19]

The removal of most of the Cherokees in 1838–1839 (and in a second
forced migration in 1841 to 1844) is a
chapter in the history of the United
States that is important to know. It is
also important to undertand that there
were many voices on both sides of the
removal issue, thus making the subject
of Cherokee removal not only a tragic
one but an exceedingly complex one as
well.

19. See Bernard W. Sheehan, *Seeds of Extinction: Jeffersonian Philanthropy and the American Indian* (Chapel Hill: University of North
Carolina Press, 1973).

Away from Home: The Working Girls of Lowell

The Problem

Just before the War of 1812, the successful New England merchant Francis Cabot Lowell toured Great Britain. Among other things, Lowell was very interested in the English textile industry. The invention of the power loom enabled spinning and weaving operations to be combined within one factory, but the factory system had spawned mill towns with overcrowded slums, horrible living conditions, and high death rates. The potential profits that the new technology offered were great, yet Lowell knew that Americans already feared the Old World evils that appeared to accompany the factory system.

Back in Boston once again, Lowell and his brother-in-law built a power loom, patented it, raised money, formed a company, and built a textile factory. Realizing that their best source of available labor would be young women from the surrounding New England rural areas and that farm families would have to be persuaded to let their daughters work far from home in the new factories, the company managers developed what eventually came to be known as the Lowell system.

In this chapter, you will be looking at what happened when people's ideas about women's "proper place" conflicted with the labor needs of the new factory system. What did the general public fear? How did the working girls react?

Background

By the end of the eighteenth century, the American economy began undergoing a process that historians call modernization. This process involves a number of changes, including the rapid expansion of markets, commercial specialization, improved transportation networks, the growth of credit transactions, the proliferation of towns and cities, and the rise of manufacturing and the factory system. Quite obviously, all these factors are interrelated.

Furthermore, such changes always have profound effects on people's lifestyles as well as on the pace of life itself.

While the frontier moved steadily westward, the South was primarily agrarian—tied to cash crops such as cotton and tobacco. New England's economy, however, quickly became modernized. Although agriculture was never completely abandoned in New England, by the early 1800s it was increasingly difficult to obtain land, and many small New England farms suffered from soil exhaustion. Young men, of course, could go west—in fact, so many of them left New England that soon there was a "surplus" of young women in the area. In addition, the transformation of New England agriculture and the demise of much of the "putting-out" system of the earliest local textile manufacturing left many single female workers underemployed or unemployed. What were these farmers' daughters supposed to do? What were their options?

At the same time that these economic developments were occurring, ideas about white middle-class women and their place in society also were changing. Even before the American Revolution, sharp distinctions between the "better sort" and the "poorer sort" were noticeable, especially in cities like Boston. The Revolution itself, with its emphasis on "republican virtues," drew many women away from their purely domestic duties and into patriotic work for the cause. The uncertainties of the early national period, which followed the Revolution, only intensified the concern about the new republic: How could such a daring experiment in representative government succeed? An essential part of the answer to this question was the concept of "republican motherhood": women would take on the important task of raising children to be responsible citizens who possessed the virtues (and value system) necessary for the success of the newly independent nation.

Those who study women's history disagree on the question of whether women's status improved or declined as a result of the emphasis on republican motherhood. Nevertheless, it was clear that the new focus on motherhood and child rearing would not only reduce the variety of roles women could play but also limit women's proper place to their own homes.

The study of gender roles is complex, and it is especially important to note that all women are not the same. Women differ in terms of race, ethnicity, religious beliefs, and geographical location, just to name a few variables. Yet, as historian Alice Kessler-Harris notes in her study of wage-earning women in the United States, there was a direct conflict for poorer or unmarried women between their need to earn money and the ideology that home and family should be central to *all* women's lives.[1] This emphasis on domestic ideology, Kessler-Harris concludes, sharpened class divisions and eroded any possibility of real independence for women.

Historian Christine Stansell's study of gender and class in New York City found that young, unmarried working women often dressed and behaved in

1. Alice Kessler-Harris, *Out to Work: A History of America's Wage-Earning Women* (New York: Oxford, 1982).

ways that directly challenged domestic ideology and women's place within the home. These public lifestyles, especially on the part of young, white, native-born, Protestant women, were deeply disturbing to many Americans, both male and female. On the other hand, when Nancy Grey Osterud examined the lives of rural farm women in central New York state, she found that their relationships with men were characterized by "mutuality" in both work and decision making. Because access to family farms was based on kinship and women's work was essential to the well-being of farm families, there were no sharp role divisions between men and women. Thus, she concluded, there were significant differences between gender roles for rural and urban women in this era.[2]

In periods of rapid change, such as industrialization, people often try to cling to absolute beliefs and even create stereotypes that implicitly punish those who do not conform. Such a stereotype began to emerge after the American Revolution. According to this stereotype, every "true" woman was a "lady" who behaved in certain ways because of her female nature. Historian Barbara Welter has called this phenomenon the "cult of true womanhood,"[3] and this concept provides a useful tool for analyzing the tensions created by the presence of

young, unmarried women in the industrial textile towns of New England. True women possessed four virtues: piety, purity, submissiveness, and domesticity. These characteristics, it was thought, were not so much learned as they were biologically natural, simply an inherent part of being born female. Women's magazines, etiquette books for young ladies, sermons and religious tracts, and popular short stories and novels all told women what they were like and how they should feel about themselves. Such sources are called "prescriptive literature" because they literally prescribe how people should—and should not—behave.

Of course, historians of women do not argue that there was a direct correlation between how people were *supposed* to behave and how they actually *did* behave. The doctrine of separate spheres could also be both restrictive for women and beneficial for women. At best, it was a complex metaphor for the negotiation and renegotiation of gender relations. But it is clear that in the nineteenth century, the cult of domesticity (the doctrine of separate spheres) established a very powerful and long-lasting set of gender expectations that influenced law and public policy decisions as well as interpersonal relationships.[4]

What, then, was expected of New England farmers' daughters and other respectable (white) women? They were

2. Christine Stansell, *City of Women: Sex and Class in New York, 1789–1860* (New York: Knopf, 1986); Nancy Grey Osterud, *Bonds of Community: the Lives of Farm Women in Nineteenth-Century New York* (Ithaca: Cornell University Press, 1991).
3. Barbara Welter, "The Cult of True Womanhood, 1820–1860," *American Quarterly* 18 (Summer 1966): 151–174.

4. Linda Kerber, "Separate Spheres, Female Worlds, and Women's Place: The Rhetoric of Women's History," *Journal of American History* 75 (1988): 9–39; Nancy Cott, review of *A Shared Experience: Men, Women, and the History of Gender*, edited by Laura McCall and Donald Yacovne, *American Historical Review* 105 (2000): 170–171.

supposed to be pious, more naturally religious than men (real men might occasionally swear, but real women never did). Because they were naturally logical and rational, men might pursue education, but true women should not because they might be led into error if they strayed from the Bible. As daughters, wives, or even sisters, women had the important responsibility of being the spiritual uplifters to whom men could turn when necessary.

Just as important as piety was the true woman's purity. This purity was absolute because whereas a man might "sow his wild oats" and then be saved by the love of a good woman, a "fallen woman" could never be saved. In the popular fiction of the period, a woman who had been seduced usually became insane, died, or both. If she had a baby, the child also came to a bad end. Only on her wedding night did a true woman surrender her virginity, and then out of duty rather than passion, because it was widely believed that pure women were not sexually responsive. In fact, many young women of this era knew nothing at all about their own bodies or the nature of sexual intercourse until they married.

Submission and domesticity were perhaps not as vital as piety and purity. Although women who did not submit to men's leadership were destined to be unhappy (according to the thought of the day), they could correct their mistaken behavior. Men were, after all, stronger and more intelligent, the natural protectors of women. A true woman, wrote then-popular author Grace Greenwood, should be like a "perpetual child," who is always "timid, doubtful, and clingingly de-

pendent." Such pious, pure, submissive women were particularly well suited to the important task of creating a pleasant, cheerful home—a place where men could escape from their worldly struggles and be fed, clothed, comforted, and nursed if they were ill. Even a woman who did not have very much money could create such a haven, people believed, simply by using her natural talents of sewing, cooking, cleaning, and flower arranging.

Simultaneously, then, two important trends were occurring in the early 1800s: the northern economy was modernizing, and sexual stereotypes that assigned very different roles to men and women were developing. Whereas a man should be out in the world of education, work, and politics, a woman's place was in the home, a sphere where she could be sheltered.

But what would happen if the economic need for an increased supply of labor clashed with the new ideas about women's place in society? If a young unmarried woman went to work in a factory far away from her parents' farm, would she still be respectable? Where would she live? Who would protect her? Perhaps the experience of factory work itself would destroy those special feminine characteristics all true women possessed. All these fears and more would have to be confronted in the course of the development of the New England textile industry during the 1830s and 1840s.

Although the first American textile mill using water-powered spinning machines was built in 1790, it and the countless other mills that sprang up throughout New England during the next thirty years depended heavily on the putting-out system. The mills made only the yarn, which was then distributed ("put out") to women who wove the cloth in their own homes and returned the finished products to the mills. In 1820, two-thirds of all American cloth was still being produced by women working at home. But the pace of modernization accelerated sharply with the formation by The Boston Associates of the Boston Manufacturing Company, a heavily capitalized firm that purchased a large tract of rural land in the Merrimack River valley. The Boston Associates adopted the latest technology and, more important, concentrated all aspects of cloth production inside their factories.

Because they no longer put out work, they had to attract large numbers of workers, especially young women from New England farms, to their mills. Lowell, Massachusetts (the "City of Spindles"), and the Lowell mills became a kind of model, an experiment that received a good deal of attention in both Europe and America. As historian Thomas Dublin has shown, most of the young women at the Lowell mills were fifteen to thirty years old, unmarried, and from farm families that were neither the richest nor the poorest in their area. Although some of the Lowell girls occasionally sent small amounts of money back to their families, most used their wages for new clothes, education, and dowries.[5] These wages were significantly higher than those for teaching, farm labor, or domestic services, the three other major occupations open to women.

5. A dowry is the money, goods, or property that a woman brings into her marriage.

The factory girls were required to live and eat in boardinghouses run according to company rules and supervised by respectable landladies. The company partially subsidized the cost of room and board and also encouraged the numerous lecture series, evening schools, and church-related activities in Lowell. Girls worked together in the mills, filling the unskilled and semiskilled positions, and men (about one-fourth of the work force) performed the skilled jobs and served as overseers (foremen). Work in the mills also was characterized by strict regulations and an elaborate system of bells that signaled mealtimes and work times.

During the 1840s, factory girls occasionally published their own magazines, the most famous of which was the *Lowell Offering*. This journal grew out of a working women's self-improvement society and was sponsored by a local Lowell minister. When the minister was transferred, the mill owners partially subsidized the magazine. The female editors, who were former mill workers, insisted that the magazine was for "literary" work rather than for labor reform. The Evidence section presents a description of Lowell mills and boardinghouses and several selections from the *Lowell Offering* and other sources.

The conflict between economic modernization and the cult of true womanhood was indirectly recognized by many New Englanders and directly experienced by the Lowell mill girls. What forms did this conflict take? What fears and anxieties did it reveal? How did the mill girls attempt to cope with this tension?

◆

The Method

When historians use prescriptive literature as evidence, they ask (1) what message is being conveyed, (2) who is sending the message, (3) why it is being sent, and (4) for whom it is intended. Most of the evidence you will be using in this chapter is in some ways prescriptive—that is, it tells people how women *should* behave.

An early major criticism of the effects of factory work on young women was written by Orestes Brownson, a well-known New England editor and reformer. A sharply contrasting view appears in the excerpts from a brief, popular book about Lowell written by Reverend Henry Mills in 1845. Reverend Mills was a local Protestant minister who was asked by the textile company owners to conduct surveys into the workers' habits, health, and moral character. Depending heavily on information provided by company officials, overseers, and landladies, Reverend Mills published *Lowell, As It Was, and As It Is.*

Yet the controversy continued, because only one year later, the journal owned by the Lowell Female Labor Reform Association, *Voice of Industry,* painted a much darker picture of the factory girls' "slavery." Although purchased by a militant group of women factory workers, the *Voice* had originated as a labor reform paper. Its editorial policy always addressed larger, worker-oriented issues such as a shorter workday and dedicated a special column to women workers' concerns.

The young women who worked in the textile mills also actively participated in the debate. The evidence in the selections from the *Lowell Offering* was written by factory girls during the years 1840 to 1843. Also presented is an excerpt from a book written by Lucy Larcom, one of the few children (under age fifteen) employed in the Lowell mills in the late 1830s. She was a factory girl for more than ten years, after which she went west and obtained a college education. She became a well-known teacher and author when she returned to New England. Larcom published a book about her New England girlhood when she was sixty-five years old. The final set of evidence includes two pictures of "typical" mill girls in 1860 and letters written by mill girls and their families. Although the letters were *descriptive,* the girls were also presenting an image of themselves as they wished to be seen. Thus, in that sense, the letters were also *prescriptive.*

First read through the evidence, looking for elements of the cult of true womanhood in the factory girls' writings and in the Lowell system itself. Be sure to consider all four questions: What message is being conveyed? Who is sending the message? Why is it being sent? For whom is it intended? This will tell you a great deal not only about the social standards for respectable young white women but also about the fears and anxieties aroused by a factory system that employed women away from their homes.

Reading about how people *should* behave, however, does not tell us how people actually behaved. Remember that the central question of this problem involves a clash: a conflict between ideas (the cult) and reality (the factory system). Go through the evidence again, this time trying to reconstruct what it was really like for the young women who lived and worked in Lowell. Ask yourself to what degree and in what ways they might have devi- ated from the ideal of "true" women. Also ask whether they could have achieved this ideal goal—and whether they really wanted to—while working and living in Lowell. In other words, try to clarify in your own mind the forms of the conflict and the reactions (of both society and the young women) to that conflict.

◆

The Evidence

Source 1 from Orestes A. Brownson, *Boston Quarterly Review* 3 (July 1840): 368–370.

1. Slave Labor Versus Free Labor, 1840.

In regard to labor, two systems obtain: one that of slave labor, the other that of free labor. Of the two, the first is, in our judgment, except so far as the feelings are concerned, decidedly the least oppressive. If the slave has never been a free man, we think, as a general rule, his sufferings are less than those of the free laborer at wages. As to actual freedom, one has just about as much as the other. The laborer at wages has all the disadvantages of freedom and none of its blessings, while the slave, if denied the blessings, is freed from the disadvantages. . . .

It is said there is no want in this country. There may be less in some other countries. But death by actual starvation in this country is, we apprehend, no uncommon occurrence. The sufferings of a quiet, unassuming but useful class of females in our cities, in general seamstresses, too proud to beg or to apply to the almshouse, are not easily told. They are industrious; they do all that they can find to do. But yet the little there is for them to do, and the miserable pittance they receive for it, is hardly sufficient to keep soul and body together. . . .

The average life—working life, we mean—of the girls that come to Lowell, for instance, from Maine, New Hampshire, and Vermont, we have been assured, is only about three years. What becomes of them then? Few of them ever marry;[6] fewer still ever return to their native places with reputations un-

6. According to historian Thomas Dublin in *Women at Work* (New York: Columbia University Press, 1979), the working women of Lowell tended to marry in about the same proportion as nonworking New England women, although the Lowell women married three to five years later

impaired. "She has worked in a factory" is almost enough to damn to infamy the most worthy and virtuous girl. . . .

Source 2 from Reverend Henry A. Mills, *Lowell, As It Was, and As It Is* (Lowell, Mass.: Powers, Bagley, and Dayton, 1845).

2. A Lowell Boardinghouse, 1845.

[*Reverend Mills began by describing the long blocks of boardinghouses, each three stories high, which were built in a style reminiscent of country farmhouses. Clean, well painted, and neat, these houses contained common eating rooms, parlors, and sleeping rooms for two to six boarders. The boarders, Reverend Mills observed, were sometimes a bit crowded but actually lived under better conditions than seamstresses and milliners in other towns. Men and women lived in separate houses with strict rules.*]

. . . *Regulations to be observed by persons occupying the Boarding-houses belonging to the Merrimack Manufacturing company.*

They must not board any persons not employed by the company, unless by special permission.

No disorderly or improper conduct must be allowed in the houses.

The doors must be closed at 10 o'clock in the evening; and no person admitted after that time, unless a sufficient excuse can be given.

Those who keep the houses, when required, must give an account of the number, names, and employment of their boarders; also with regard to their general conduct and whether they are in the habit of attending public worship.

The buildings, both inside and out, and the yards about them, must be kept clean and in good order. If the buildings or fences are injured, they will be repaired and charged to the occupant.

No one will be allowed to keep swine.

[*The meals might seem rushed, Mills noted, but that was common among all Americans, particularly businesspeople. Working girls could choose whichever boardinghouses they preferred, rents were very low, and their living arrangements were very respectable.*]

No tenant is admitted who has not hitherto borne a good character, and who does not continue to sustain it. In many cases the tenant has long been

---

in life and had a distinct tendency to marry men who were tradesmen or skilled workers rather than farmers.

keeper of the house, for six, eight, or twelve years, and is well known to hundreds of her girls as their adviser and friend and second mother. . . .

. . . Employing chiefly those who have no permanent residence in Lowell, but are only temporary boarders, upon any embarrassment of affairs they return to their country homes, and do not sink down here a helpless caste, clamouring for work, starving unless employed, and hence ready for a riot, for the destruction of property, and repeating here the scenes enacted in the manufacturing villages of England. . . .

To obtain this constant importation of female hands from the country, it is necessary to secure *the moral protection of their characters while they are resident in Lowell*. This, therefore, is the chief object of that moral police referred to, some details of which will now be given.

It should be stated, in the outset, that no persons are employed on the Corporations who are addicted to intemperance, or who are known to be guilty of any immoralities of conduct. As the parent of all other vices, intemperance is most carefully excluded. Absolute freedom from intoxicating liquors is understood, throughout the city, to be a prerequisite to obtaining employment in the mills, and any person known to be addicted to their use is at once dismissed. . . . In relation to other immoralities, it may be stated, that the suspicion of criminal conduct, association with suspected persons, and general and habitual light behavior and conversation, are regarded as sufficient reasons for dismissions, and for which delinquent operatives are discharged.

[*Reverend Mills also described the discharge system at the factories. For those girls whose conduct was satisfactory and who had worked at least a year, honorable discharges were issued. Discharge letters could be used as recommendations for other jobs. Those who received dishonorable discharges for infractions such as stealing, lying, leaving the job without permission, or other "improper conduct" would have difficulty finding other employment.*]

This system, which has been in operation in Lowell from the beginning, is of great and important effect in driving unworthy persons from our city, and in preserving the high character of our operatives.

[*Male overseers, or foremen, also were closely screened and had to possess good moral character. In response to Reverend Mills's questions about the male overseers, one factory owner responded as follows.*]

Lowell, May 10, 1841

Dear Sir:—

I employ in our mills, and in the various departments connected with them, thirty overseers, and as many second overseers. My overseers are married

men, with families, with a single exception, and even he has engaged a tenement, and is to be married soon. Our second overseers are younger men, but
upwards of twenty of them are married, and several others are soon to be
married. Sixteen of our overseers are members of some regular church, and
four of them are deacons. Ten of our second overseers are also members of the
church, and one of them is the Superintendent of a Sunday School. I have no
hesitation in saying that in all the sterling requisites of character, in native
intelligence, and practical good sense, in sound morality, and as active, useful,
and exemplary citizens, they may, as a class, safely challenge comparison with
any class in our community. I know not, among them all, an intemperate
man, nor, at this time, even what is called a moderate drinker.

[*Furthermore, the girls were expected to obey numerous rules.*]

Still another source of trust which a Corporation has, for the good character of its operatives, is the moral control which they have over one another. Of
course this control would be nothing among a generally corrupt and degraded
class. But among virtuous and high-minded young women, who feel that they
have the keeping of their characters, and that any stain upon their associates
brings reproach upon themselves, the power of opinion becomes an ever-
present, and ever-active restraint. A girl, *suspected* of immoralities, or serious
improprieties of conduct, at once loses caste. Her fellow-boarders will at once
leave the house, if the keeper does not dismiss the offender. In self-protection,
therefore, the matron is obliged to put the offender away. Nor will her former
companions walk with, or work with her; till at length, finding herself everywhere talked about, and pointed at, and shunned, she is obliged to relieve her
fellow-operatives of a presence which they feel brings disgrace. From this
power of opinion, there is no appeal; and as long as it is exerted in favor of propriety of behavior and purity of life, it is one of the most active and effectual
safeguards of character. . . .

[*Punctuality was required of both overseers and workers.*]

All persons are required to observe the regulations of the room in which
they are employed. They are not allowed to be absent from their work without
the consent of their overseer, except in case of sickness, and then they are required to send him word of the cause of their absence.

All persons are required to board in one of the boarding-houses belonging
to the company, and conform to the regulations of the house in which they
board.

All persons are required to be constant in attendance on public worship, at one of the regular places of worship in this place.

Persons who do not comply with the above regulations will not be employed by the company.

Persons entering the employment of the company are considered as engaging to work one year.

All persons intending to leave the employment of the company, are required to give notice of the same to their overseer, at least two weeks previous to the time of leaving.

Any one who shall take from the mills, or the yard, any yarn, cloth, or other article belonging to the company, will be considered guilty of STEALING—and prosecuted accordingly.

. . . All persons who shall have complied with [the rules], on leaving the employment of the company, shall be entitled to an honorable discharge, which will serve as a recommendation to any of the factories in Lowell. No one who shall not have complied with them will be entitled to such a discharge.

Source 3 courtesy of the American Textile History Museum.

3. Timetable of the Lowell Mills, 1853.

TIME TABLE OF THE LOWELL MILLS,

Arranged to make the working time throughout the year average 11 hours per day.

TO TAKE EFFECT SEPTEMBER 21st., 1853.

The Standard time being that of the meridian of Lowell, as shown by the Regulator Clock of AMOS SANBORN, Post Office Corner, Central Street.

From March 20th to September 19th, inclusive.

COMMENCE WORK, at 6.30 A. M.   LEAVE OFF WORK, at 6.30 P. M., except on Saturday Evenings.
BREAKFAST at 6 A. M.   DINNER, at 12 M.   Commence Work, after dinner, 12.45 P. M.

From September 20th to March 19th, inclusive.

COMMENCE WORK at 7.00 A. M.   LEAVE OFF WORK, at 7.00 P. M., except on Saturday Evenings.
BREAKFAST at 6.30 A. M.   DINNER, at 12.30 P.M.   Commence Work, after dinner, 1.15 P. M.

BELLS.

From March 20th to September 19th, inclusive.

Morning Bells.	Dinner Bells.	Evening Bells.
First bell,..........4.30 A. M.	Ring out,.............12.00 M.	Ring out,...........6.30 P. M.
Second, 5.30 A. M.; Third, 6.20.	Ring in,...........12.35 P. M.	Except on Saturday Evenings.

From September 20th to March 19th, inclusive.

Morning Bells.	Dinner Bells.	Evening Bells.
First bell,..........5.00 A. M.	Ring out,..........12.30 P. M.	Ring out at...........7.00 P. M.
Second, 6.00 A. M.; Third, 6.50.	Ring in,..............1.05 P. M.	Except on Saturday Evenings.

SATURDAY EVENING BELLS.

During APRIL, MAY, JUNE, JULY, and AUGUST, Ring Out, at 6.00 P. M.
The remaining Saturday Evenings in the year, ring out as follows :

SEPTEMBER.	NOVEMBER.	JANUARY.
First Saturday, ring out 6.00 P. M.	Third Saturday ring out 4.00 P. M.	Third Saturday, ring out 4.25 P. M.
Second " " 5.45 "	Fourth " " 3.55 "	Fourth " " 4.35 "
Third " " 5.30 "		
Fourth " " 5.20 "	**DECEMBER.**	**FEBRUARY.**
	First Saturday, ring out 3.50 P. M.	First Saturday, ring out 4.45 P. M.
OCTOBER.	Second " " 3.55 "	Second " " 4.55 "
First Saturday, ring out 5.05 P. M.	Third " " 3.55 "	Third " " 5.00 "
Second " " 4.55 "	Fourth " " 4.00 "	Fourth " " 5.10 "
Third " " 4.45 "	Fifth " " 4.00 "	
Fourth " " 4.35 "		**MARCH.**
Fifth " " 4.25 "	**JANUARY.**	First Saturday, ring out 5.25 P. M.
	First Saturday, ring out 4.10 P. M.	Second " " 5.30 "
NOVEMBER.	Second " " 4.15 "	Third " " 5.35 "
First Saturday, ring out 4.15 P. M.		Fourth " " 5.45 "
Second " · " 4.05 "		

YARD GATES will be opened at the first stroke of the bells for entering or leaving the Mills.

.   *SPEED GATES commence hoisting three minutes before commencing work.*

Penhallow, Printer, Wyman's Exchange, 28 Merrimack St.

Source 4 from *Voice of Industry,* January 2, 1846, in H. R. Warfel et al., eds., *The American Mind* (New York: American Book Company, 1937), p. 392.

4. "Slaver" Wagons, 1846.

We were not aware, until within a few days, of the *modus operandi* of the factory powers in this village of forcing poor girls from their quiet homes to become their tools and, like the Southern slaves, to give up their life and liberty to the heartless tyrants and taskmasters.

Observing a singular-looking "long, low, black" wagon passing along the street, we made inquiries respecting it, and were informed that it was what we term a "slaver." She makes regular trips to the north of the state [Massachusetts], cruising around in Vermont and New Hampshire, with a "commander" whose heart must be as black as his craft, who is paid a dollar a head for all he brings to the market, and more in proportion to the distance—if they bring them from such a distance that they cannot easily get back.

This is done by "hoisting false colors," and representing to the girls that they can tend more machinery than is possible, and that the work is so very neat, and the wages such that they can dress in silks and spend half their time in reading. Now, is this true? Let those girls who have been thus deceived, answer.

Let us say a word in regard to the manner in which they are stowed in the wagon, which may find a similarity only in the manner in which slaves are fastened in the hold of a vessel. It is long, and the seats so close that it must be very inconvenient.

Is there any humanity in this? Philanthropists may talk of Negro slavery, but it would be well first to endeavor to emancipate the slaves at home. Let us not stretch our ears to catch the sound of the lash on the flesh of the oppressed black while the oppressed in our very midst are crying out in thunder tones, and calling upon us for assistance.

Source 5 from *Lowell Offering*, Series I, Issue 1 (1840). Courtesy of the American Textile History Museum.

5. Title Page of *Lowell Offering*.

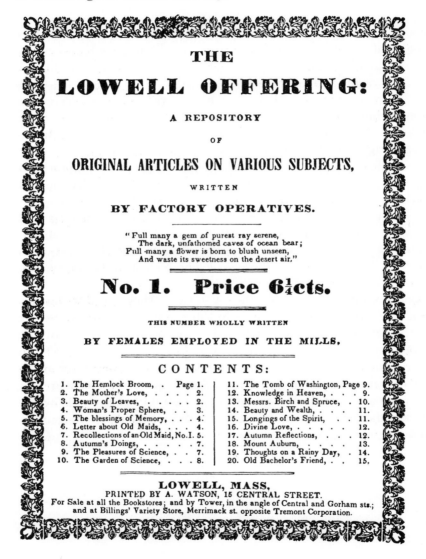

THE

LOWELL OFFERING:

A REPOSITORY

OF

ORIGINAL ARTICLES ON VARIOUS SUBJECTS,

WRITTEN

BY FACTORY OPERATIVES.

"Full many a gem of purest ray serene,
The dark, unfathomed caves of ocean bear;
Full many a flower is born to blush unseen,
And waste its sweetness on the desert air."

No. 1. Price 6¼cts.

THIS NUMBER WHOLLY WRITTEN

BY FEMALES EMPLOYED IN THE MILLS,

CONTENTS:

1. The Hemlock Broom, . Page 1.
2. The Mother's Love, ... 2.
3. Beauty of Leaves, ... 2.
4. Woman's Proper Sphere, . . 3.
5. The blessings of Memory, . . . 4.
6. Letter about Old Maids, . . . 4.
7. Recollections of an Old Maid, No. I. 5.
8. Autumn's Doings, ... 7.
9. The Pleasures of Science, . . 7.
10. The Garden of Science, . . . 8.

11. The Tomb of Washington, Page 9.
12. Knowledge in Heaven, . . . 9.
13. Messrs. Birch and Spruce, . 10.
14. Beauty and Wealth, . . . 11.
15. Longings of the Spirit, . . 11.
16. Divine Love, ... 12.
17. Autumn Reflections, . . . 12.
18. Mount Auburn, ... 13.
19. Thoughts on a Rainy Day, . 14.
20. Old Bachelor's Friend, . . 15,

LOWELL, MASS,
PRINTED BY A. WATSON, 15 CENTRAL STREET.
For Sale at all the Bookstores; and by Tower, in the angle of Central and Gorham sts.;
and at Billings' Variety Store, Merrimack st. opposite Tremont Corporation.

Source 6 from *Lowell Offering*, Series I, Issue 1 (1840), p. 16.

6. Editorial Corner.

The Lowell Offering is strictly what it purports to be, a "Repository of original articles on various subjects, written by Factory Operatives."—The objects of the publication are, to encourage the cultivation of talent; to preserve such articles as are deemed most worthy of preservation; and to correct an erroneous idea which generally prevails in relation to the intelligence of persons employed in the Mills. This number is wholly the offering of Females. . . .

We are persuaded that the citizens generally, and those engaged in the Mills particularly, will feel and manifest a lively interest in the prosperity of the Lowell Offering. That it is faultless—that the severe and captious critic will find no room for his vocation, is not to be expected. Nevertheless, while the work makes no noisy pretensions to superior excellency, it would claim no unusual indulgences. It asks only that, all the circumstances incident to its peculiar character being duly weighed, it shall be fairly and candidly judged. The Editors do not hesitate to say, that they anticipate for a favorable reception at the hands of those who have at heart the interests of that important and interesting portion of our population, whose intellectual elevation and moral welfare it aims to promote. . . .

An opinion extensively prevails, not merely beyond the limits of Massachusetts, that the Manufacturing city of Lowell is a nucleus of depravity and ignorance.

Confessedly, wherever there exists *any* depravity or ignorance, there is *too* much of it. We have this to testify however, that they who know least of the people of Lowell, including the Factory Operatives, entertain the most unworthy and unjust opinions of them. Close personal observation has satisfied us, that in respect of morality and intelligence, they will not suffer in comparison with the inhabitants of any part of moral and enlightened New England.

Sources 7 and 8 from *Lowell Offering*, Series II, Vol. II (1842), p. 192; Series II, Vol. III (1842), pp. 69–70.

7. Dignity of Labor.

From whence originated the idea, that it was derogatory to a lady's dignity, or a blot upon the female character, to labor? and who was the first to say, sneeringly, "Oh, she *works* for a living"? Surely, such ideas and expressions ought not to grow on republican soil. The time has been, when ladies of the first rank were accustomed to busy themselves in domestic employment.

Homer tells us of princesses who used to draw water from the springs, and wash with their own hands the finest of the linen of their respective families. The famous Lucretia used to spin in the midst of her attendants; and the wife of Ulysses, after the siege of Troy, employed herself in weaving, until her husband returned to Ithaca. And in later times, the wife of George the Third of England, has been represented as spending a whole evening in hemming pocket-handkerchiefs, while her daughter Mary sat in the corner, darning stockings.

Few American fortunes will support a woman who is above the calls of her family; and a man of sense, in choosing a companion to jog with him through all the up-hills and down-hills of life, would sooner choose one who *had* to work for a living, than one who thought it beneath her to soil her pretty hands with manual labor, although she possessed her thousands. To be able to earn one's own living by laboring with the hands, should be reckoned among female accomplishments; and I hope the time is not far distant when none of my countrywomen will be ashamed to have it known that they are better versed in useful, than they are in ornamental accomplishments.

C.B.

8. Editorial: Home in a Boardinghouse.

[*Factory boardinghouses were not really like homes, the editor pointed out. A place to eat and lodge, the boardinghouses often seemed crowded and impersonal.*]

But these are all trifles, compared with the perplexities to which we are subjected in other ways; and some of these things might be remedied by the girls themselves. We now allude to the importunities of evening visitors, such as peddlers, candy and newspaper boys, shoe-dealers, book-sellers, &c., &c., breaking in upon the only hours of leisure we can call our own, and proffering their articles with a pertinacity which will admit of no denial. . . . And then they often forget, if they ever knew, the rules of politeness which should regulate all transient visitors. . . .

The remedy is entirely with the girls. Treat all of these comers with a politeness truly lady-like, when they appear as gentlemen, but let your manners change to stern formality when they forget that they are in the company of respectable females. . . .

C.B.

Sources 9 through 11 from *Lowell Offering*, Series I, Issue 1 (1840), pp. 17–19, 61, 44–46.

9. Factory Girls.

"She has worked in a factory, *is sufficient to damn to infamy the most worthy and virtuous girl.*"

So says Mr. Orestes A. Brownson; and either this horrible assertion is true, or Mr. Brownson is a slanderer. I assert that it is *not* true, and Mr. B. may consider himself called upon to prove his words, if he can.

This gentleman has read of an Israelitish boy who, with nothing but a stone and sling, once entered into a contest with a Philistine giant, arrayed in brass, whose spear was like a weaver's beam; and he may now see what will probably appear to him quite as marvellous; and that is, that a *factory girl* is not afraid to oppose herself to the *Editor of the Boston Quarterly Review*. True, he has upon his side fame, learning, and great talent; but I have what is better than either of these, or all combined, and that is *truth*. Mr. Brownson has not said that this thing should be so; or that he is glad it is so; or that he deeply regrets such a state of affairs; but he has said it *is* so; and *I* affirm that it is *not*.

And whom has Mr. Brownson slandered? A class of girls who in this city alone are numbered by thousands, and who collect in many of our smaller towns by hundreds; girls who generally come from quiet country homes, where their minds and manners have been formed under the eyes of the worthy sons of the Pilgrims, and their virtuous partners, and who return again to become the wives of the free intelligent yeomanry of New England and the mothers of quite a portion of our future republicans. Think, for a moment, how many of the next generation are to spring from mothers doomed to infamy! "Ah," it may be replied, "Mr. Brownson acknowledges that you may still be worthy and virtuous." Then we must be a set of worthy and virtuous idiots, for no virtuous girl of common sense would choose for an occupation one that would consign her to infamy. . . .

That there has been prejudice against us, we know; but it is wearing away, and has never been so deep nor universal as Mr. B's statement will lead many to believe. Even now it may be that "the mushroom aristocracy" and "would-be fashionables" of Boston, turn up their eyes in horror at the sound of those vulgar words, *factory girls;* but *they* form but a small part of the community, and theirs are not the opinions which Mr. Brownson intended to represent. . . .

[*The prejudice against factory girls was connected to the degraded and exploited conditions of European workers, the angry letter writer asserted. "Yankee girls," she said, are independent, and although the work is hard, the wages are better than those in other kinds of employment. It is no wonder, she concluded, that so many intelligent, worthy, and virtuous young women have been drawn to Lowell.*]

The erroneous idea, wherever it exists, must be done away, that there is in factories but one sort of girls, and *that* the baser and degraded sort. There are among us *all* sorts of girls. I believe that there are few occupations which can exhibit so many gradations of piety and intelligence; but the majority may at least lay claim to as much of the former as females in other stations of life. . . . The Improvement Circles, the Lyceum and Institute, the social religious meetings, the Circulating and other libraries, can bear testimony that the little time they have is spent in a better manner. Our well filled churches and lecture halls and the high character of our clergymen and lecturers, will testify that the state of morals and intelligence is not low.

Mr. Brownson, I suppose, would not judge of our moral characters by our church-going tendencies; but as many do, a word on this subject may not be amiss. That there are many in Lowell who do not regularly attend any meeting, is as true as the correspondent of the Boston Times once represented it; but for this there are various reasons. . . .

And now, if Mr. Brownson is a *man,* he will endeavor to retrieve the injury he has done; he will resolve that "the dark shall be light, and the wrong made right," and the assertion he has publicly made will be as publicly retracted. If he still doubts upon the subject let him come among us: let him make himself as well acquainted with us as our pastors and superintendents are; and though he will find error, ignorance, and folly among us, (and where would he find them not?) yet he would not see worthy and virtuous girls consigned to infamy, because they work in a factory.

A FACTORY GIRL

10. A Familiar Letter.

Friends and Associates:—

With indescribable emotions of pleasure, mingled with feelings of deepest gratitude to Him who is the Author of every good and perfect gift, I have perused the second and third numbers of the Lowell Offering.

As a laborer among you, (tho' least of all) I rejoice that the time has arrived when a class of laboring females (who have long been made a reproach and byword, by those whom fortune or pride has placed above the avocation by which we have subjected ourselves to the sneers and scoffs of the idle, ignorant and envious part of community,) are bursting asunder the captive chains of prejudice. . . .

I know it has been affirmed, to the sorrow of many a would-be lady, that factory girls and ladies could not be distinguished by their apparel. What a lamentable evil! and no doubt it would be a source of much gratitude to such, if the awful name of "factory girl!" were branded on the forehead of every female who is, or ever was, employed in the Mills. Appalling as the name may sound in the delicate ears of a sensitive lady, as she contrasts the music of her piano with the rumblings of the factory machinery, we would not shrink from such a token of our calling, could the treasures of the mind be there displayed, and merit, in her own unbiased form be stamped there also. . . .

Yours, in the bonds of affection,
DOROTHEA

11. Gold Watches.

It is now nearly a year since an article appeared in the Ladies' Book, in the form of a tale, though it partakes more of the character of an essay. It was written by Mrs. Hale, and exhibits her usual judgment and talent. Her object evidently was to correct the many erroneous impressions which exist in society, with regard to the folly of extravagance in dress, and all outward show. I was much pleased with all of it, with the exception of a single sentence. Speaking of the impossibility of considering dress a mark of distinction, she observed,—(addressing herself, I presume, to the *ladies* of New England,)— "How stands the difference now? Many of the factory girls wear gold watches, and an imitation, at least, of all the ornaments which grace the daughters of our most opulent citizens."

O the times! O the manners! Alas! how very sadly the world has changed! The time was when the *lady* could be distinguished from the *no-lady* by her dress, as far as the eye could reach; but now, you might stand in the same room, and judging by their outward appearance, you could not tell "which was which." Even gold watches are now no *sure* indication—for they have been worn by the lowest, even by "many of the factory girls." No *lady* need carry one now, for any other than the simple purpose of easily ascertaining the time of day, or night, if she so please! . . .

Those who do not labor for their living, have more time for the improvement of their minds, for the cultivation of conversational powers, and graceful manners; but if, with these advantages, they still need richer dress to distinguish them from *us*, the fault must be their own, and they should at least learn to honor merit, and acknowledge talent wherever they see it. . . .

And now I will address myself to my sister operatives in the Lowell factories. Good advice should be taken, from whatever quarter it may come, whether from friend or foe; and part of the advice which Mrs. Hale has given to the readers of the Ladies' Book, may be of advantage to us. Is there not among us, as a class, too much of this striving for distinction in dress? Is it not the only aim and object of too many of us, to wear something a little better than others can obtain? Do we not sometimes see the girl who has half a dozen silk gowns, toss her head, as if she felt herself six times better than her neighbor who has none? . . .

We all have many opportunities for the exercise of the kindly affections, and more than most females. We should look upon one another something as a band of orphans should do. We are fatherless and motherless: we are alone, and surrounded by temptation. Let us caution each other; let us watch over and endeavor to improve each other; and both at our boardinghouses and in the Mill, let us strive to promote each other's comfort and happiness. Above all, let us endeavor to improve ourselves by making good use of the many advantages we here possess. I say let us at least strive to do this; and if we succeed, it will finally be acknowledged that Factory Girls shine forth in ornaments far more valuable than *Gold Watches.*

A FACTORY GIRL

Source 12 from *Lowell Offering,* Series II, Vol. II (1842), p. 380.

12. Editor's Valedictory.

It has been the object of the editor to encourage the cultivation of talent, and thus open and enlarge the sources of enjoyment in the midst of a toilsome life. . . .

We hoped ere this to have seen a spacious room, with a Library, &c., established on each Corporation, for the accommodation of the female operatives in the evenings. The example, we trust, will shortly be set by the Merrimack. And why should not bathing-rooms be fitted up in the basement of each Mill? The expense would not be felt by the Company, and the means of health and comfort thus provided, would be gratefully acknowledged. We suggest, in addition, a better ventilation of the boarding-houses. Diminution of the hours of mill-labor, and the entire abrogation of premiums to Overseers, should also be included in the list of improvements.

There is another matter, some time since presented to the operatives, and now repeated, namely, the payment of a small sum monthly, say 8 or 10 cents, to consitute a fund for the relief of the sick. The amount might be deducted by the pay-master, as agent of the Superintendent. The details of the plan could readily be agreed upon. Two cents each week would surely be well spent as insurance against the expenses of sickness, to be fixed at about three dollars weekly—to be received, not as *charity,* but as a lawful demand.

Source 13 from *Lowell Offering,* Series II, Vol. V (1845), p. 96.

13. Editorial: The Ten-Hour Movement.

[*The editor begins by reviewing the work of the Massachusetts legislature's Committee upon the Hours of Labor. Although she understands why the demand for a ten-hour workday was not accepted, she believes there were other improvements that might have been made.*]

It seems to have been generally conceded, that the time allotted to meals is very short—where the operatives have tolerable appetites: and this is usually the case with persons who *work so regularly* and indefatigably. Why not have compromised then with the petitioners, and allowed them one hour for dinner through the year, and three-quarters of an hour for breakfast? The dinner *hour* is given in some manufacturing places, therefore the plea with regard to competition is not unanswerable. We believe also that Lowell is expected to take the lead in all improvements of this nature, and, should she amend her present system, it is more probable that she would be imitated than successfully contended against. . . .

[*The editor then addresses employers' argument that there are girls waiting at the factory gate before the work bell rings, eager to get in and begin work. The author concedes that some girls compete with each other for the overseer's favors. But what of the others? she asks.*]

. . . They feel that they are unable to work all these hours, and "work upon the stretch," as they say. They are older, or weaker, or more heavily moulded, or unwilling, if not unable. Therefore they are not favorites with their overseer. They are not so "profitable servants," and the kind look and word, or obliging act, is not so often bestowed upon them. This is one instance where the testimony is liable to misconstruction, and had we space, we might find many more.

The Legislature seem to have doubted the propriety of their commencing action upon this subject. Where should it commence? How is it to be done? When, where, and by whom? All, connected with manufacturing establishments, feel confident that, "as surely as there is benevolence and justice in the heart of man," this wrong will be righted. But objections are brought against every movement. . . .

Source 14 from *Lowell Offering*, Series II, Vol. I (1841), p. 32. Courtesy of the American Textile History Museum.

14. "Song of the Spinners."

SONG OF THE SPINNERS.

1. The day is o'er, nor lon-ger we toil and spin; For ev'ning's hush withdraws from the dai-ly din. And

2. We spin all day, and then, in the time for rest, Sweet peace is found, A joyous and welcome guest. Des -

now we sing, with gladsome hearts, The theme of the spinner's song, That la-bor to lei-sure a zest imparts, Unknown to the i - - dle throng.

- pite of toil we all agree, or out of the Mills, or in, Dependent on others we ne'er will be. So long as we're a-ble to spin.

Source 15 from Lucy Larcom, *A New England Girlhood* (Boston: Houghton Mifflin, 1889).

15. Selection from *A New England Girlhood.*

[*After her husband's death, Lucy Larcom's mother moved to Lowell to run a boarding-house. Because her mother could not earn enough to support the family, Lucy, age eleven, and her older sister went to work in the mills.*]

So I went to my first day's work in the mill with a light heart. The novelty of it made it seem easy, and it really was not hard, just to change the bobbins on the spinning-frames every three quarters of an hour or so, with half a dozen other little girls who were doing the same thing. When I came back at night, the family began to pity me for my long, tiresome day's work, but I laughed, and said,—

"Why, it is nothing but fun. It is just like play."

And for a little while it was only a new amusement; I liked it better than going to school and "making believe" I was learning when I was not. And there was a great deal of play mixed with it. We were not occupied more than half the time. The intervals were spent frolicking around among the spinning-frames, teasing and talking to the older girls, or entertaining ourselves with games and stories in a corner, or exploring, with the overseer's permission, the mysteries of the carding-room, the dressing-room, and the weaving-room. . . .

There were compensations for being shut in to daily toil so early. The mill itself had its lessons for us. But it was not, and could not be, the right sort of life for a child, and we were happy in the knowledge that, at the longest, our employment was only to be temporary. . . .

[*Lucy loved elementary school and wanted to continue her studies, but her family needed her mill wages.*]

In the older times it was seldom said to little girls, as it always has been said to boys, that they ought to have some definite plan, while they were children, what to be and do when they were grown up. There was usually but one path open before them, to become good wives and housekeepers. And the ambition of most girls was to follow their mothers' footsteps in this direction; a natural and laudable ambition. But girls, as well as boys, must often have been conscious of their own peculiar capabilities,—must have desired to cultivate and make use of their individual powers. When I was growing up, they had already begun to be encouraged to do so. We were often told that it was our duty to develop any talent we might possess, or at least learn how to do some one thing which the world needed, or which would make it a pleasanter world. . . .

At this time I had learned to do a spinner's work, and I obtained permission to tend some frames that stood directly in front of the river-windows, with only them and the wall behind me, extending half the length of the mill,—and one young woman beside me, at the farther end of the row. She was a sober, mature person, who scarcely thought it worth her while to speak often to a child like me; and I was, when with strangers, rather a reserved girl; so I kept myself occupied with the river, my work, and my thoughts. . . .

The printed regulations forbade us to bring books into the mill, so I made my window-seat into a small library of poetry, pasting its side all over with newspaper clippings. In those days we had only weekly papers, and they had always a "poet's corner," where standard writers were well represented, with anonymous ones, also. I was not, of course, much of a critic. I chose my verses for their sentiment, and because I wanted to commit them to memory; sometimes it was a long poem, sometimes a hymn, sometimes only a stray verse. . . .

Some of the girls could not believe that the Bible was meant to be counted among forbidden books. We all thought that the Scriptures had a right to go wherever we went, and that if we needed them anywhere, it was at our work. I evaded the law by carrying some leaves from a torn Testament in my pocket.

[*In spite of the regulations, girls brought poetry and plants into the factory.*]

One great advantage which came to these many stranger girls through being brought together, away from their own homes, was that it taught them to go out of themselves, and enter into the lives of others. Home-life, when one always stays at home, is necessarily narrowing. That is one reason why so many women are petty and unthoughtful of any except their own family's interests. We have hardly begun to live until we can take in the idea of the whole human family as the one to which we truly belong. To me, it was an incalculable help to find myself among so many working-girls, all of us thrown upon our own resources, but thrown much more upon each others' sympathies.

Source 16 courtesy of the Mildred Tunis Tracey Memorial Library, New London, New Hampshire.

16. A "Typical" Factory Girl, Delia Page, at Age 18 or 19 (c. 1860).

Source 17 courtesy of the American Textile History Museum.

17. Two Weavers (c. 1860).

Sources 18 through 22 from Thomas Dublin, ed., *Farm to Factory: Women's Letters, 1830–1860* (New York: Columbia University Press, 1981), pp. 42, 100–104, 170–172.

18. Letter from Sarah Hodgdon.

[In 1830, Sarah Hodgdon, age sixteen, and two friends went to Lowell to work in the textile mills. After approximately ten years of working in various factories, Hodgdon married a shoemaker from her home town. This is one of her early letters to her mother.]

[June 1830]

Dear mother

I take this oppertunity to write to you to informe you that I have gone into the mill and like [it] very well. I was here one week and three days before I went into the mill to work for my board. We boord t[o]gether. I like my boording place very well. I enjoy my health very well. I do not enjoy my mind so well as it is my desire to. I cant go to any meetings except I hire a seat therefore I have to stay home on that account.[7] I desire you pay that it may not be said of me when I come home that I have sold my soul for the gay vanitys of this world. Give my love to my father and tell him not to forget me and to my dear sister and to my brothers and to my grammother tell her I do not forget her and to my Aunts and to all my enquiring friends. I want that you should write to me as soon as you can and when you write to me I want that you should write to me the particulars about sister and Aunt Betsy. Dont fail writing. I bege you not to let this scrabling be seen.

Sarah Hodgdon

Mary Hodgdon [recipient]

19. Letter from Mary Paul.

[Mary Paul left home in 1845 at age fifteen. She worked briefly and unsuccessfully as a domestic servant and then went to Lowell as a factory girl for four years. After leaving the mills, she returned home for a short while and then worked as a seamstress. Next she joined a utopian community, and finally she took a job as a housekeeper. In 1857, Paul married the son of the woman who ran the boardinghouse where she had lived in Lowell.]

7. Urban churches in this period often charged people who attended services a fee called *pew rent.*

Saturday, Sept. 13th 1845

Dear Father

I received your letter this afternoon by Wm Griffith. . . . I am very glad you sent my shoes. They fit very well indeed they [are] large enough.

I want you to consent to let me go to Lowell if you can. I think it would be much better for me than to stay about here. I could earn more to begin with than I can any where about here. I am in need of clothes which I cannot get if I stay about here and for that reason I want to go to Lowell or some other place. We all think if I could go with some steady girl that I might do well. I want you to think of it and make up your mind. Mercy Jane Griffith is going to start in four or five weeks. Aunt Miller and Aunt Sarah think it would be a good chance for me to go if you would consent—which I want you to do if possible. I want to see you and talk with you about it.

Aunt Sarah gains slowly.

Mary

Bela Paul [recipient]

20. Letter from Mary Paul.

Lowell Dec 21st 1845

Dear Father

I received your letter on Thursday the 14th with much pleasure. I am well which is one comfort. My life and health are spared while others are cut off. Last Thursday one girl fell down and broke her neck which caused instant death. She was going in or coming out of the mill and slipped down it being very icy. The same day a man was killed by the cars. Another had nearly all of his ribs broken. Another was nearly killed by falling down and having a bale of cotton fall on him. Last Tuesday we were paid. In all I had six dollars and sixty cents paid four dollars and sixty-eight cents for board. With the rest I got me a pair of rubbers and a pair of 50.cts shoes. . . . I get along very well with my work. I can doff[8] as fast as any girl in our room. I think I shall have frames before long. The usual time allowed for learning is six months but I think I shall have frames before I have been in three as I get along so fast. I think that the factory is the best place for me and if any girl wants employment I advise them to come to Lowell. Tell Harriet

8. A doffer replaced empty bobbins on the spinning frames with full ones.

that though she does not hear from me she is not forgotten. I have little time to devote to writing that I cannot write all I want to. . . .

> This from
> Mary S. Paul

Bela Paul
Henry S. Paul [recipients]

21. Letter to Delia Page.[9]

[*Delia Page lived with a foster family, the Trussells, because she did not get along well with her stepmother. In 1859, at age eighteen, she went to work at a textile mill in Manchester, New Hampshire, where she fell in love with a mill worker who had evidently deserted his wife and child in Lowell. When reports of Delia's "affair" reached home, her foster family wrote her urgent letters trying to persuade her to reconsider. Eventually, in 1866, she married an eligible, respectable single man.*]

> New London Sept. 7, 1860

Dear Delia,

I should thank you for your very good letter. I am glad to know your health is good. I trust I shall ever feel a deep interest in your welfare.

You say you are not so much in love as we imagine; if so I am very glad of it. Not that I should not be willing you should love a worthy object but the one referred to is no doubt an *unworthy* one; and should you fix you[r] affections on him, it will cause you sorrow such as you never knew; indeed we believe it would be *your ruin.* We have no reason to think, his pretensions notwithstanding, that he has any *real love for you.* Your father Trussell has told or rather written you what he has learned about him. I fear it will be hard for you to believe it, but if you will take the trouble to inquire, I think you will find it all true. He probably is incapable of even friendship, and in his apparent regard for you, is actuated by *low, base, selfish* motives.

I think you will sooner or later come to this conclusion respecting him. The sooner the better. Your reputation your happiness all you hold dear are I fear at stake. You have done well, let not your high hopes be blasted. Do the best you can, keep no company but good and you stand fair to get a good husband, one who has a real regard for you. But if you keep this man's company, the virtuous must shun you. You will not like to read this. My only excuse for writing is that I am very anxious about you. If my anxiety is unfounded so

9. Delia Page's photograph is shown in Source 16.

much the better. Unfounded it cannot be if you are keeping the company of an unprincipled libertine.

Your affectionate Mother Trussell

22. Letter to Delia Page.

[Sept. 7 1860]

My Dear Delia,

I am going to trouble you a little longer (I speak for the whole family now). In your situation you must necessarily form many new acquaintance[s] and amongst them there will be not a few who will assure you of their friendship and seek your confidence. The less worthy they are the more earnestly they will seek to convince you of their sincerity. You spoke of one girl whom you highly prised. I hope she is all that you think her to be. If so you are certainly fortunate in making her acquaintance.

But the best have failings & I should hardly expect one of her age a safe counciler in all cases. You must in fact rely upon a principal of morality within your own bosom and if you [are] at a loss you may depend upon the council of Mrs. Piper.[10] A safe way is not to allow yourself to say or do anything that you would not be willing anyone should know if necessary. You will say Humpf think I cant take care of myself. I have seen many who thought so and found their mistake when ruined. My dear girl. We fear much for those we love much, or the fear is in porportion [sic] to the Love. And although I have no reason to think that you go out nights or engage in anything that will injure your health or morrals [sic] yet the love I have for you leads me to fear lest among so much that is pleasant but evil you may be injured before you are aware of danger.

And now my Dear Girl I will finish by telling you what you must do for me.

You must take care of my little factory girl. Dont let her expose her health if you do she will be sick and loose [sic] all she has earned. Don't let her do any thing any time that she would be ashamed to have her father know. If you do she may loose her charracter [sic]. Try to have her improve some every day that she may be the wealthiest most respected & best beloved of all her sisters, brothers & kindred & so be fitted to make the best of husbands the best of wives.

[Luther M. Trussell]

---

10. The Pipers were Trussell family friends who lived in Manchester.

Questions to Consider

Why did Brownson (Source 1) believe that slaves were better off than free laborers? What did he imply about women who worked? What major advantages did Reverend Mills observe in the Lowell system (Source 2)? In what important ways did the system (the factories and the boardinghouses) regulate the girls' lives? How did it protect the morals of its female employees? Of course, not all girls lived up to these standards. What did they do? How were they punished? Do you think Reverend Mills presented a relatively unbiased view? Why or why not? In what ways did the author of the article in *Voice of Industry* (Source 4) believe factory girls were being exploited?

Look carefully at the title page (Source 5) and the first editorial (Source 6) of the *Lowell Offering*. What do they tell you about the factory girls, their interests, and their concerns? Was C.B. (Source 7) upholding the cult of true womanhood in her article about the dignity of labor? How did "home" in the boardinghouse (Source 8) differ from the girls' real homes? Based on what you read in Reverend Mills's account, in what ways might a boardinghouse have been similar to the girls' real homes?

The next three letters were written by girls who were rather angry. How did "a factory girl" (Source 9) try to disprove Brownson's view? What fears and anxieties do this letter and the one from Dorothea (Source 10) reveal? What were these two girls trying to prove? The third letter writer (Source 11) retained her sense of humor, but she also was upset. In this case, the offensive remark to which she referred appeared in *Godey's Lady's Book,* the most popular American women's magazine of the period, and was written by the highly respected Sarah Josepha Hale, the magazine's editor and author of "Mary Had a Little Lamb." What had Mrs. Hale written? What was the factory girl's response? What advice did she give her coworkers about fashion? About being a true woman? Both the editor's valedictory and the editorial about the ten-hour-day petitions (Sources 12 and 13) present wanted changes. What were they? How does the editor believe these changes can be achieved? Even "Song of the Spinners" (Source 14) contains a message. What do the lyrics tell you about the spinners' values and attitudes toward work?

What were the other realities of factory girls' lives? What does the bell schedule (Source 3) tell you? How would you describe the image that the photographs of the mill girls present (Sources 16 and 17)? The mill girls' letters make them seem very real to us, but we must not take them completely at face value. After all, they were often writing to their parents! What hopes (and fears) does the correspondence between the mill girls and their families (Sources 18 through 22) express? Why did Lucy Larcom (Source 15) have to go to work in the mills when she was so young? How did she feel about the work when she was a child? What contrast did she draw between young boys' and young girls' upbringing in the early nineteenth century? Did she and the other girls always obey the factory rules? What advantages did she discover in her factory experience? What were the disadvantages? Be careful not to overgeneralize or rely too heavily on the girls' letters or Larcom's memoir.

Now that you are thoroughly familiar with the ideas about how the working girls of Lowell were supposed to behave and the realities of the system under which they lived, you are ready to frame an answer to the central question: How did people react when the needs of a modernizing economy came into conflict with the ideas about women's place in society?

◆

Epilogue

The Lowell system was a very real attempt to prevent the spread of the evils associated with the factory system and to make work in the textile mills "respectable" for young New England women. Working conditions in Lowell were considerably better than in most other New England mill towns. Several major strikes (or "turnouts," as they were called) occurred in the Lowell mills in the mid-1830s, however, and by the mid-1840s Lowell began to experience serious labor problems. To remain competitive yet at the same time maximize profits, companies introduced the "speedup" (a much faster work pace) and the "stretch-out" (in which one worker was put in charge of more machinery—sometimes as many as four looms). The mills also cut wages, even though boardinghouse rents were rising. In Lowell, workers first tried to have the length of the workday reduced and, as did many other American workers, united in support of the Ten-Hour Movement. When women workers joined such protests, they further challenged the ideas embodied in the cult of true womanhood, especially that of submissiveness.

Even before the strikes, the Lowell system was breaking down, as more and more mills, far larger than their predecessors, were built. Construction of private housing (especially tenements) expanded, and a much smaller proportion of mill hands lived in boardinghouses. Both housing and neighborhoods became badly overcrowded. By 1850, mill owners were looking for still other ways besides the speedup and stretch-out to reduce the cost of labor. They found their answer in the waves of Irish immigrating to America to escape the economic hardships so widespread in their own country. Fewer and fewer "Yankee girls" were recruited for work in the textile mills. At one Lowell company, the number of native-born girls declined from 737 in 1836 to 324 in 1860, although the total number of female workers remained constant. Irish men, women, and increasing numbers of children filled the gap, because as wages declined, a family income became a necessity.

By 1860, what Reverend Mills had characterized as "the moral and intellectual advantages" of the Lowell system had come to an end. Indeed, many Americans could see little or no difference between their own factory towns and those of Europe.

CHAPTER

8

The "Peculiar Institution": Slaves Tell Their Own Story

The Problem

With the establishment of its new government in 1789, the United States became a virtual magnet for foreign travelers, perhaps never more so than during the three decades immediately preceding the Civil War. Middle to upper class, interested in everything from politics to prison reform to botanical specimens to the position of women in American society, these curious travelers fanned out across the United States, and almost all of them wrote about their observations in letters, pamphlets, and books widely read on both sides of the ocean. Regardless of their special interests, however, few travelers failed to notice—and comment on—the "peculiar institution" of African American slavery.

As were many nineteenth-century women writers, English author Harriet Martineau was especially interested in those aspects of American society that affected women and children. She was appalled by the slave system, believing it degraded marriage by allowing southern white men to exploit female slaves sexually, a practice that often produced mulatto children born into slavery.

The young Frenchman Alexis de Tocqueville came to study the American penitentiary system and stayed to investigate politics and society. In his book *Democracy in America* (1842), Tocqueville expressed his belief that American slaves had completely lost their African culture—their customs, languages, religions, and even the memories of their countries. An English novelist who was enormously popular in the United States, the crusty Charles Dickens, also visited in 1842. He spent very little time in the South but collected (and published) advertisements for runaway slaves that contained gruesome descriptions of their burns, brandings, scars, and iron cuffs and collars. As Dickens departed for a steamboat trip to the West, he wrote that he left "with a grateful heart that I was not doomed to live where slavery was, and had never had my senses blunted to its wrongs and horrors in a slave-rocked cradle."[1]

In the turbulent 1850s, Fredrika Bremer, a Swedish novelist, traveled throughout the United States for two years and spent considerable time in South Carolina, Georgia, and Louisiana. After her first encounters with African Americans in Charleston, Bremer wrote to her sister that "they are ugly, but appear for the most part cheerful and well-fed."[2] Her subsequent trips to the plantations of the backcountry, however, increased her sympathy for slaves and her distrust of white southerners' assertions that "slaves are the happiest people in the world."[3] In fact, by the end of her stay, Bremer was praising the slaves' morality, patience, talents, and religious practices.

These travelers—and many more—added their opinions to the growing literature about the nature of American slavery and its effects. But the overwhelming majority of this literature was written by white people. What did the slaves themselves think? How did they express their feelings about the peculiar institution of slavery?

Background

By the time of the American Revolution, what had begun in 1619 as a trickle of Africans intended to supplement the farm labor of indentured servants from England had swelled to a slave population of approximately 500,000 people, the majority concentrated on tobacco, rice, and cotton plantations in the South. Moreover, as the African American population grew, what apparently had been a fairly loose and unregimented labor system gradually evolved into an increasingly harsh, rigid, and complete system of chattel slavery that tried to control nearly every aspect of the slaves' lives. By 1775, African American slavery had become a significant (some would have said indispensable) part of southern life.

The American Revolution did not reverse those trends. Although northern states in which African American slavery was not so deeply rooted began instituting gradual emancipation, after the Revolution, the slave system—as well as its harshness—increased in the South. The invention of the cotton gin, which enabled seeds to be removed from the easily grown short staple cotton, permitted southerners to cultivate cotton on the uplands, thereby spurring the westward movement of the plantation system and slavery. As a result, slavery expanded along with settlement into nearly every area of the South: the Gulf region, Tennessee,

1. Charles Dickens, *American Notes and Pictures from Italy* (London: Oxford University Press, 1957), p. 137.
2. Fredrika Bremer, *America of the Fifties: Letters of Fredrika Bremer,* ed. Adolph B. Benson (New York: American Scandinavian Foundation, 1924), p. 96.

3. Ibid., p. 100.

Kentucky, and ultimately Texas. Simultaneously, the slave population burgeoned, roughly doubling every thirty years (from approximately 700,000 in 1790 to 1.5 million in 1820 to more than 3.2 million in 1850, for instance). Because importation of slaves from Africa was banned in 1808 (although there was some illegal slave smuggling), most further gains in the slave population were from natural increase.

But as the slave population grew, the fears and anxieties of southern whites grew correspondingly. In 1793, a slave rebellion in the Caribbean caused tremendous consternation in the white South. Rumors of uprisings plotted by slaves were numerous. And the actual rebellion of Nat Turner in Virginia in 1831 (in which fifty-five whites were killed, many of them while asleep) only increased white insecurities and dread. In response, southern states passed a series of laws that made the system of slavery even more restrictive. Toward the end of his life, Thomas Jefferson (who did not live to see Nat Turner's uprising) agonized:

> But as it is, we have the wolf by the ears, and we can neither hold him, nor safely let him go. Justice is in one scale, and self-preservation in the other.

By this time, however, Jefferson was nearly alone among white southerners. Most did not question the assertions that slavery was a necessity, that it was good for both the slave and the owner, and that it must be preserved at any cost.

It often has been pointed out that the majority of white southerners did not own slaves. In fact, the proportion of

white southern families who did own slaves was actually declining in the nineteenth century, from one-third in 1830 to roughly one-fourth by 1860. Moreover, nearly three-fourths of these slaveholders owned fewer than ten slaves. Slaveholders, then, were a distinct minority of the white southern population, and those slaveholders with large plantations and hundreds of slaves were an exceedingly small group.

How, then, did the peculiar institution of slavery, as one southerner called it, become so embedded in the Old South? First, even though only a minority of southern whites owned slaves, nearly all southern whites were somehow touched by the institution of slavery. Fear of black uprisings prompted many nonslaveholders to support an increasingly rigid slave system that included night patrols, written passes for slaves away from plantations, supervised religious services for slaves, laws prohibiting teaching slaves to read or write, and other measures to keep slaves ignorant, dependent, and always under the eyes of whites. Many nonslaveholders also were afraid that emancipation would bring them into direct economic competition with blacks, who, it was assumed, would drive down wages. Finally, although large planters represented only a fraction of the white population, they virtually controlled the economic, social, and political institutions and were not about to injure either themselves or their status by eliminating the slave system that essentially supported them.

To defend their peculiar institution, white southerners constructed a remarkably complete and diverse set of arguments. Slavery, they maintained, was actually a far more humane system than northern capitalism. After all, slaves were fed, clothed, sheltered, cared for when they were ill, and supported in their old age, whereas northern factory workers were paid pitifully low wages, used, and then discarded when they were no longer useful. Furthermore, many white southerners maintained that slavery was a positive good because it had introduced the "barbarous" Africans to civilized American ways and, more importantly, to Christianity. Other southern whites stressed what they believed was the childlike, dependent nature of African Americans, insisting that they could never cope with life outside the paternalistic and "benevolent" institution of slavery. In such an atmosphere, in which many of the white southern intellectual efforts went into the defense of slavery, dissent and freedom of thought were not welcome. Hence those white southerners who disagreed and might have challenged the South's dependence on slavery remained silent, were hushed up, or decided to leave the region. In many ways, then, the enslavement of African Americans partly rested on the limitation of rights and freedoms for southern whites as well.

But how did the slaves react to an economic and social system that meant that neither they nor their children would ever experience freedom? Most white southerners assumed that slaves were happy and content. Northern abolitionists (a minority of the white population) believed that slaves continually yearned for freedom. Both groups used oceans of ink to justify and support their claims. But evidence of how the slaves felt and thought is woefully sparse. Given the restrictive nature of the slave system (which included enforced illiteracy among slaves), this pitiful lack of evidence is hardly surprising.

How, then, can we learn how slaves felt and thought about the peculiar institution? Slave uprisings were few, but does that mean most slaves were happy with their lot? Runaways were common, and some, such as Frederick Douglass and Harriet Jacobs, actually reached the North and wrote about their experiences as slaves. Yet how typical were their experiences? Most slaves were born, lived, and died in servitude, did not participate in organized revolts, and did not run away. How did they feel about the system of slavery?

Although most slaves did not read or write, did not participate in organized revolts, and did not attempt to run away, they did leave a remarkable amount of evidence that can help us understand their thoughts and feelings. Yet we must be imaginative in how we approach and use that evidence.

In an earlier chapter, you discovered that statistical information (about births, deaths, age at marriage, farm size, inheritance, tax rolls, and so forth) can reveal a great deal about ordinary people, such as the colonists on the eve of the American Revolution. Such demographic evidence can help the historian form a picture of who these people were and the socioeconomic trends of the time, even if the people themselves were not aware of those trends. In this chapter, you will be using another kind of evidence and asking different questions. Your evidence will not come from white southerners (whose stake in maintaining slavery was enormous), foreign travelers (whose own cultural biases often influenced what they reported), or even white abolitionists in the North (whose urgent need to eradicate the "sin" of slavery sometimes led them to gross exaggerations for propaganda purposes). You will be using anecdotes, stories, and songs from the rich oral tradition of African American slaves, supplemented by the narratives of two runaway slaves, to investigate the human dimensions of the peculiar institution.

Some of the oral evidence was collected and transcribed by people soon after emancipation. However, much of the evidence did not come to light until many years later, when the former slaves who were still alive were very old men and women. In fact, not until the 1920s did concerted efforts to preserve

the reminiscences of these people begin. In the 1920s, Fisk University collected a good deal of evidence. In the 1930s, the government-financed Federal Writers' Project accumulated more than two thousand narratives from ex-slaves in every southern state except Louisiana and deposited them in the Library of Congress in Washington, D.C.

Much of the evidence, however, is in the form of songs and stories that slaves created and told to one another. Like the narratives of former slaves, these sources also must be used with imagination and care.

The central question you are to answer is this: How did the slaves themselves view the peculiar institution? How did they endure under a labor system that, at its very best, was still based on the total ownership of one human being by another?

◆

The Method

Historians must always try to be aware of the limitations of their evidence. In the Federal Writers' Project, most of the former slaves were in their eighties or nineties (quite a few were older than one hundred) at the time they were interviewed. In other words, most of the interviewees had been children or young people in 1860. It is also important to know that although some of the interviewers were black, the overwhelming majority were white. Last, although many of the former slaves had moved to another location or a different state after the Civil War, many

others were still living in the same county.

As historian Ira Berlin has pointed out in his recent edited collection of slave narratives,[4] former slaves were always patronized and sometimes intimidated by local white interviewers. Once in a while, the actual interviews were written up in a stereotypical black dialect form and occasionally the content itself was edited by the interviewers until the Federal Writers' Project

4. Ira Berlin et al., eds. *Remembering Slavery* (New York: New Press, 1998).

issued directives to stop these practices. But Berlin also notes that many, perhaps most, elderly blacks did not fear retaliation, were eager to tell their stories, and answered obliquely or indirectly when the interviewers' questions touched on sensitive racial issues. For example, former slaves might say that they themselves were treated all right but then tell about "other situations" elsewhere where slaves were badly mistreated. For an excellent example of an oblique answer, notice how a former slave responds to a question about whether slavery was "good" for the slaves by telling a story about a raccoon and a dog (Source 3).

In fact, like all historical evidence, slave narratives have both strengths and weaknesses. They are firsthand reports that, when carefully evaluated, corroborated by other testimony, and supported by additional evidence, can provide insight into the last years of slavery in the United States from the viewpoint of the slaves themselves.

These narratives reveal much about these people's thoughts and feelings about slavery. Although some of the stories or anecdotes may not actually be true, they can be taken as representative of what the former slaves wished had happened or what they really thought about an incident. Therefore, often you must pull the true meaning from a narrative, inferring what the interviewee meant as well as what he or she said.

As for slave songs and other contemporary evidence, slaves often hid their true meanings through the use of symbols, metaphors, and allegories. Here again, you must be able to read between the lines, extracting thoughts, attitudes, and feelings that were purposely hidden or concealed from all but other slaves.

Included in the evidence are two accounts of runaway slaves who escaped to the North before the Civil War. Frederick Bailey (who later changed his name to Douglass) ran away when he was about nineteen years old, but he was captured and returned. Two years later, he was able to escape, and he moved to Massachusetts, where he worked as a laborer. After joining an antislavery society and becoming a successful speaker, he published his autobiography (1845) and edited his own abolitionist newspaper, the *North Star*. Harriet Jacobs (who used the pen name Linda Brent) was twenty-seven years old when she ran away in 1845, but her narrative was not published until the beginning of the Civil War. Throughout her story, Jacobs used fictitious names and places to protect those who had helped her and to conceal the escape route she had used. Both Douglass and Jacobs were self-educated people who wrote their own books, although the abolitionist writer Lydia Maria Child made minor editorial revisions in Jacobs's manuscript.

As you examine each piece of evidence, jot down enough notes to allow you to recall that piece of evidence later. But also, perhaps in a separate column, write down the *attitude* that each piece of evidence communicates about the peculiar institution of slavery. What is the hidden message?

After you have examined each piece of evidence, look back over your notes. What attitudes about slavery stand out? What did the slaves think about the slave system?

◆

The Evidence

1. Hog-Killing Time.

I remember Mammy told me about one master who almost starved his slaves. Mighty stingy, I reckon he was.

Some of them slaves was so poorly thin they ribs would kinda rustle against each other like corn stalks a-drying in the hot winds. But they gets even one hog-killing time, and it was funny, too, Mammy said.

They was seven hogs, fat and ready for fall hog-killing time. Just the day before Old Master told off they was to be killed, something happened to all them porkers. One of the field boys found them and come a-telling the master: "The hogs is all died, now they won't be any meats for the winter."

When the master gets to where at the hogs is laying, they's a lot of Negroes standing round looking sorrow-eyed at the wasted meat. The master asks: "What's the illness with 'em?"

"Malitis," they tells him, and they acts like they don't want to touch the hogs. Master says to dress them anyway for they ain't no more meat on the place.

He says to keep all the meat for the slave families, but that's because he's afraid to eat it hisself account of the hogs' got malitis.

"Don't you all know what is malitis?" Mammy would ask the children when she was telling of the seven fat hogs and seventy lean slaves. And she would laugh, remembering how they fooled Old Master so's to get all them good meats.

"One of the strongest Negroes got up early in the morning," Mammy would explain, "long 'fore the rising horn called the slaves from their cabins. He skitted to the hog pen with a heavy mallet in his hand. When he tapped Mister Hog 'tween the eyes with the mallet, 'malitis' set in mighty quick, but it was a uncommon 'disease,' even with hungry Negroes around all the time."

2. The Old Parrot.

The mistress had an old parrot, and one day I was in the kitchen making cookies, and I decided I wanted some of them, so I tooks me out some and put them on a chair; and when I did this the mistress entered the door. I picks up a cushion and throws [it] over the pile of cookies on the chair, and Mistress came near the chair and the old parrot cries out, "Mistress burn, Mistress burn." Then the mistress looks under the cushion, and she had me whupped, but the next day I killed the parrot, and she often wondered who or what killed the bird.

3. The Coon and the Dog.

Every time I think of slavery and if it done the race any good, I think of the story of the coon and dog who met. The coon said to the dog, "Why is it you're so fat and I am so poor, and we is both animals?" The dog said: "I lay round Master's house and let him kick me and he gives me a piece of bread right on." Said the coon to the dog: "Better, then, that I stay poor." Them's my sentiment. I'm like the coon, I don't believe in 'buse.

4. The Partridge and the Fox.

A partridge and a fox 'greed to kill a beef. They kilt and skinned it. Before they divide it, the fox said, "My wife says send her some beef for soup." So he took a piece of it and carried it down the hill, then come back and said, "My wife wants more beef for soup." He kept this up till all the beef was gone 'cept the liver. The fox come back, and the partridge says, "Now let's cook this liver and both of us eat it." The partridge cooked the liver, et its parts right quick, and then fell over like it was sick. The fox got scared and said that beef is pizen, and he ran down the hill and started bringing the beef back. And when he brought it all back, he left, and the partridge had all the beef.

5. The Rabbit and the Tortoise.

I want to tell you one story 'bout the rabbit. The rabbit and the tortoise had a race. The tortoise git a lot of tortoises and put 'em 'long the way. Ever' now and then a tortoise crawl 'long the way, and the rabbit say, "How you now, Br'er Tortoise?" And he say, "Slow and sure, but my legs very short." When they git tired, the tortoise win 'cause he there, but he never run the race, 'cause he had tortoises strowed out all 'long the way. The tortoise had other tortoises help him.

6. Same Old Thing.

The niggers didn't go to the church building; the preacher came and preached to them in their quarters. He'd just say, "Serve your masters. Don't steal your master's turkey. Don't steal your master's chickens. Don't steal your master's hogs. Don't steal your master's meat. Do whatsomever your master tells you to do." Same old thing all the time.

7. Freedom.

I been preaching the gospel and farming since slavery time. I jined the church 'most 83 years ago when I was Major Gaud's slave, and they baptizes me in the spring branch close to where I finds the Lord. When I starts preaching I couldn't read or write and had to preach what Master told me, and he say tell them niggers iffen they obeys the master they goes to Heaven; but I knowed there's something better for them, but daren't tell them 'cept on the sly. That I done lots. I tells 'em iffen they keeps praying, the Lord will set 'em free.

8. Prayers.

My master used to ask us children, "Do your folks pray at night?" We said "No," 'cause our folks had told us what to say. But the Lord have mercy, there was plenty of that going on. They'd pray, "Lord, deliver us from under bondage."

9. Hoodoo Doctor.

My wife was sick, down, couldn't do nothing. Someone got to telling her about Cain Robertson. Cain Robertson was a hoodoo doctor in Georgia. They [say] there wasn't nothing Cain couldn't do. She says, "Go and see Cain and have him come up here."

I says, "There ain't no use to send for Cain. Cain ain't coming up here because they say he is a 'two-head' nigger." (They called all them hoodoo men "two-head" niggers; I don't know why they called them two-head.) "And you know he knows the white folks will put him in jail if he comes to town."

But she says, "You go and get him."

So I went.

I left him at the house, and when I came back in, he said, "I looked at your wife and she had one of them spells while I was there. I'm afraid to tackle this thing because she has been poisoned, and it's been going on a long time. And if she dies, they'll say I killed her, and they already don't like me and looking for an excuse to do something to me."

My wife overheard him and says, "You go on, you got to do something."

So he made me go to town and get a pint of corn whiskey. When I brought it back he drunk a half of it at one gulp, and I started to knock him down. I'd thought he'd get drunk with my wife lying there sick.

Then he said, "I'll have to see your wife's stomach." Then he scratched it, and put three little horns on the place he scratched. Then he took another drink of whiskey and waited about ten minutes. When he took them off her stomach, they were full of blood. He put them in the basin in some water and sprinkled some powder on them, and in about ten minutes more he made me get them and they were full of clear water and there was a lot of little things that looked like wiggle tails swimming around it.

He told me when my wife got well to walk in a certain direction a certain distance, and the woman that caused all the trouble would come to my house and start a fuss with me.

I said, "Can't you put this same thing back on her?"

He said, "Yes, but it would kill my hand." He meant that he had a curing hand and that if he made anybody sick or killed them, all his power to cure would go from him.

I showed the stuff he took out of my wife's stomach to old Doc Matthews, and he said, "You can get anything into a person by putting it in them." He asked me how I found out about it, and how it was taken out, and who did it.

I told him all about it, and he said, "I'm going to see that that nigger practices anywhere in this town he wants to and nobody bothers him." And he did.

10. Buck Brasefield.

They was pretty good to us, but old Mr. Buck Brasefield, what had a plantation 'jining us'n, was so mean to his'n that 'twa'n't nothing for 'em to run away. One nigger, Rich Parker, runned off one time, and whilst he gone he seed a hoodoo man, so when he got back Mr. Brasefield took sick and stayed sick two or three weeks. Some of the darkies told him, "Rich been to the hoodoo doctor." So Mr. Brasefield got up outen that bed and come a-yelling in the field, "You thought you had old Buck, but by God he rose again." Them niggers was so scared they squatted in the field just like partridges, and some of 'em whispered, "I wish to God he had-a died."

11. The White Lady's Quilts.

Now I'll tell you another incident. This was in slave times. My mother was a great hand for nice quilts. There was a white lady had died, and they were going to have a sale. Now this is true stuff. They had the sale, and Mother went and bought two quilts. And let me tell you, we couldn't sleep under 'em. What happened? Well, they'd pinch your toes till you couldn't stand it. I was just a boy and I was sleeping with my mother when it happened. Now that's straight stuff. What do I think was the cause? Well, I think that white lady didn't want no nigger to have them quilts. I don't know what Mother did with 'em, but that white lady just wouldn't let her have 'em.

12. Papa's Death.

My papa was strong. He never had a licking in his life. He helped the master, but one day the master says, "Si, you got to have a whopping," and my poppa says, "I never had a whopping and you can't whop me." And the master says, "But I can kill you," and he shot my papa down. My mama took him in the cabin and put him on a pallet. He died.

13. Forbidden Knowledge.

None of us was 'lowed to see a book or try to learn. They say we git smarter than they was if we learn anything, but we slips around and gits hold of that Webster's old blue-back speller and we hides it till 'way in the night and then we lights a little pine torch, and studies that spelling book. We learn it too. I can read some now and write a little too.

They wasn't no church for the slaves, but we goes to the white folks' arbor on Sunday evening, and a white man he gits up there to preach to the niggers. He say, "Now I takes my text, which is, Nigger obey your master and your mistress, 'cause what you git from them here in this world am all you ever going to git, 'cause you just like the hogs and the other animals—when you dies you ain't no more, after you been throwed in that hole." I guess we believed that for a while 'cause we didn't have no way finding out different. We didn't see no Bibles.

14. Broken Families.

I seen children sold off and the mammy not sold, and sometimes the mammy sold and a little baby kept on the place and give to another woman to raise. Them white folks didn't care nothing 'bout how the slaves grieved when they tore up a family.

15. Burning in Hell.

We was scared of Solomon and his whip, though, and he didn't like frolicking. He didn't like for us niggers to pray, either. We never heard of no church, but us have praying in the cabins. We'd set on the floor and pray with our heads down low and sing low, but if Solomon heared he'd come and beat on the wall with the stock of his whip. He'd say, "I'll come in there and tear the hide off you backs." But some the old niggers tell us we got to pray to God that He don't think different of the blacks and the whites. I know that Solomon is burning in hell today, and it pleasures me to know it.

16. Marriage.

After while I taken a notion to marry and Massa and Missy marries us same as all the niggers. They stands inside the house with a broom held crosswise of the door and we stands outside. Missy puts a little wreath on my head they kept there, and we steps over the broom into the house. Now, that's all they was to the marrying. After freedom I gits married and has it put in the book by a preacher.

Sources 17 and 18 from Gilbert Osofsky, comp., *Puttin' on Ole Massa* (New York: Harper & Row, 1969), p. 22.

17. Pompey.

Pompey, how do I look?
O, massa, mighty.
What do you mean "mighty," Pompey?
Why, massa, you look noble.
What do you mean by "noble"?
Why, sar, you just look like one *lion.*
Why, Pompey, where have you ever seen a lion?
I see one down in yonder field the other day, massa.
Pompey, you foolish fellow, that was a *jackass.*
Was it, massa? Well you look just like him.

18. A Grave for Old Master.

Two slaves were sent out to dig a grave for old master. They dug it very deep. As I passed by I asked Jess and Bob what in the world they dug it so deep for. It was down six or seven feet. I told them there would be a fuss about it, and they had better fill it up some. Jess said it suited him exactly. Bob said he would not fill it up; he wanted to get the old man as near *home* as possible. When we got a stone to put on his grave, we hauled the largest we could find, so as to fasten him down as strong as possible.

Sources 19 through 21 from Lawrence W. Levine, "Slave Songs and Slave Consciousness: An Exploration in Neglected Sources," in Tamara K. Hareven, ed., *Anonymous Americans: Explorations in Nineteenth Century Social History* (Englewood Cliffs, N.J.: Prentice Hall, 1971), pp. 112, 113, 121.

19.

We raise de wheat,
Dey gib us de corn;
We bake de bread,
Dey gib us de crust;
We sif de meal,
Dey gib us de huss;
We [peel] de meat,
Dey gib us de skin;

And dat's de way
Dey take us in;
We skim de pot,
Dey gib us de liquor,
And say dat's good enough for nigger.

20.

My old Mistiss promise me,
W'en she died, she'd set me free,
She lived so long dat 'er head got bal',
An, she give out'n de notion a dyin' at all.

21.

He delivered Daniel from the lion's den,
Jonah from de belly ob de whale,
And de Hebrew children from de fiery furnace,
And why not every man?

Sources 22 and 23 from Sterling Stuckey, "Through the Prism of Folklore: The Black Ethos in Slavery," *Massachusetts Review* 9 (1968): 421, 422. Reprinted by permission of the Editors of Massachusetts Review.

22.

When I get to heaven, gwine be at ease,
Me and my God gonna do as we please.
Gonna chatter with the Father, argue with the Son,
Tell um 'bout the world I just come from.

23.

[*A song about Samson and Delilah*]

He said, 'An' if I had-'n my way,'
He said, 'An' if I had-'n my way,'
He said, 'An' if I had-'n my way,
I'd tear the build-in' down!'

Source 24 from Frederick Douglass, *Narrative of the Life of Frederick Douglass*, pp. 1–3,
13–15, 36–37, 40–41, 44–46, 74–75. Copyright 1963 by Doubleday. Reprinted by
permission of Doubleday, a division of Bantam, Doubleday, Dell Publishing Group, Inc.

24. Excerpts from the Autobiography of Frederick Douglass.

I was born in Tuckahoe, near Hillsborough, and about twelve miles from
Easton, in Talbot county, Maryland. I have no accurate knowledge of my age,
never having seen any authentic record containing it. By far the larger part
of the slaves know as little of their ages as horses know of theirs, and it is the
wish of most masters within my knowledge to keep their slaves thus ignorant. I do not remember to have ever met a slave who could tell of his birth-
day. They seldom come nearer to it than planting-time, harvesting-time,
cherry-time, spring-time, or fall-time. . . . The nearest estimate I can give
makes me now between twenty-seven and twenty-eight years of age. I come
to this, from hearing my master say, some time during 1835, I was about sev-
enteen years old.

My mother was named Harriet Bailey. She was the daughter of Isaac and
Betsey Bailey, both colored, and quite dark. My mother was a darker complexion than either my grandmother or grandfather.

My father was a white man. He was admitted to be such by all I ever heard
speak of my parentage. The opinion was also whispered that my master was
my father; but of the correctness of this opinion, I know nothing; the means of
knowing was withheld from me. . . .

[*His mother, a field hand, lived twelve miles away and could visit him only at night.*]

. . . I do not recollect of ever seeing my mother by the light of day. She was
with me in the night. She would lie down with me, and get me to sleep, but
long before I waked she was gone. Very little communication ever took place
between us. Death soon ended what little we could have while she lived, and
with it her hardships and suffering. She died when I was about seven years
old, on one of my master's farms, near Lee's Mill. I was not allowed to be present during her illness, at her death, or burial. She was gone long before I
knew any thing about it. Never having enjoyed, to any considerable extent,
her soothing presence, her tender and watchful care, I received the tidings of
her death with much the same emotions I should have probably felt at the
death of a stranger. . . .

The slaves selected to go to the Great House Farm,[5] for the monthly allow-
ance for themselves and their fellow-slaves, were peculiarly enthusiastic.

5. Great House farm was the huge "home plantation" that belonged to Douglass's owner.

While on their way, they would make the dense old woods, for miles around, reverberate with their wild songs, revealing at once the highest joy and the deepest sadness. They would compose and sing as they went along, consulting neither time nor tune. The thought that came up, came out—if not in the word, in the sound;—and as frequently in the one as in the other. . . .

I did not, when a slave, understand the deep meaning of those rude and apparently incoherent songs. I was myself within the circle; so that I neither saw nor heard as those without might see and hear. They told a tale of woe which was then altogether beyond my feeble comprehension; they were tones loud, long, and deep; they breathed the prayer and complaint of souls boiling over with the bitterest anguish. Every tone was a testimony against slavery, and a prayer to God for deliverance from chains.

I have often been utterly astonished, since I came to the north, to find persons who could speak of the singing, among slaves, as evidence of their contentment and happiness. It is impossible to conceive of a greater mistake. Slaves sing most when they are most unhappy. The songs of the slave represent the sorrows of his heart; and he is relieved by them, only as an aching heart is relieved by its tears. At least, such is my experience. I have often sung to drown my sorrow, but seldom to express my happiness. Crying for joy, and singing for joy, were alike uncommon to me while in the jaws of slavery. . . .

[*Douglass was hired out as a young boy and went to live in Baltimore. His mistress began to teach him the alphabet, but when her husband found out, he forbade her to continue. After Douglass overheard his master's arguments against teaching slaves to read and write, he came to believe that education could help him gain his freedom.*]

The plan which I adopted, and the one by which I was most successful, was that of making friends of all the little white boys whom I met in the street. As many of these as I could, I converted into teachers. With their kindly aid, obtained at different times and in different places, I finally succeeded in learning to read. When I was sent on errands, I always took my book with me, and by doing one part of my errand quickly, I found time to get a lesson before my return. I used also to carry bread with me, enough of which was always in the house, and to which I was always welcome; for I was much better off in this regard than many of the poor white children in our neighborhood. This bread I used to bestow upon hungry little urchins, who, in return, would give me that more valuable bread of knowledge. I am strongly tempted to give the names of two or three of those little boys, as a testimonial of the gratitude and affection I bear them; but prudence forbids;—not that it would injure me, but it might embarrass them; for it is almost an unpardonable offence to teach slaves to read in this Christian country. . . .

I was now about twelve years old, and the thought of being a *slave for life* began to bear heavily upon my heart. . . . After a patient waiting, I got one of our city papers, containing an account of the number of petitions from the north, praying for the abolition of slavery in the District of Columbia, and of the slave trade between the States. From this time I understood the words *abolition* and *abolitionist,* and always drew near when that word was spoken, expecting to hear something of importance to myself and fellow-slaves. The light broke in upon me by degrees. . . .

[*After talking with two Irish laborers who advised him to run away, Douglass determined to do so.*]

. . . I looked forward to a time at which it would be safe for me to escape. I was too young to think of doing so immediately; besides, I wished to learn how to write, as I might have occasion to write my own pass.[6] I consoled myself with the hope that I should one day find a good chance. Meanwhile, I would learn to write. . . .

[*Douglass first copied the letters written on the planks of wood used in ship construction. Later, he dared small boys in the neighborhood to prove that they could spell better than he could; in that way, he began to learn how to write.*]

. . . During this time, my copy-book was the board fence, brick wall, and pavement; my pen and ink was a lump of chalk. With these, I learned mainly how to write. I then commenced and continued copying the Italics in Webster's Spelling Book, until I could make them all without looking on the book. By this time, my little Master Thomas had gone to school, and learned how to write, and had written over a number of copy-books. These had been brought home, and shown to some of our near neighbors, and then laid aside. My mistress used to go to class meeting at the Wilk Street meetinghouse every Monday afternoon, and leave me to take care of the house. When left thus, I used to spend the time in writing in the spaces left in Master Thomas's copy-book, copying what he had written. I continued to do this until I could write a hand very similar to that of Master Thomas. Thus, after a long, tedious effort for years, I finally succeeded in learning how to write. . . .

[*After the death of his owner, Douglass was recalled to the plantation and put to work as a field hand. Because of his rebellious attitude, he was then sent to work for a notorious "slave-breaker" named Covey. When Covey tried to whip Douglass, who was then about sixteen years old, Douglass fought back.*]

6. In many areas, slaves were required to carry written passes stating that they had permission from their owners to travel to a certain place.

We were at it for nearly two hours. Covey at length let me go, puffing and blowing at a great rate, saying that if I had not resisted, he would not have whipped me half so much. The truth was, that he had not whipped me at all. I considered him as getting entirely the worst end of the bargain; for he had drawn no blood from me, but I had from him. The whole six months afterwards, that I spent with Mr. Covey, he never laid the weight of his finger upon me in anger. He would occasionally say, he didn't want to get hold of me again. "No," thought I, "you need not; for you will come off worse than you did before." . . .

[*This fight was a turning point for Douglass, who felt his self-confidence increase greatly along with his desire to be free. Although he was a slave for four more years, he was never again whipped.*]

It was for a long time a matter of surprise to me why Mr. Covey did not immediately have me taken by the constable to the whipping-post, and there regularly whipped for the crime of raising my hand against a white man in defense of myself. And the only explanation I can now think of does not entirely satisfy me; but such as it is, I will give it. Mr. Covey enjoyed the most unbounded reputation for being a first-rate overseer and negro-breaker. It was of considerable importance to him. That reputation was at stake; and had he sent me—a boy about sixteen years old—to the public whipping-post, his reputation would have been lost; so, to save his reputation, he suffered me to go unpunished. . . .

[*During the Civil War, Douglass actively recruited African American soldiers for the Union, and he worked steadfastly after the war for African American civil rights. Douglass also held a series of federal jobs that culminated in his appointment as the U.S. minister to Haiti in 1888. He died in 1895 at the age of seventy-eight.*]

25. Excerpts from the Autobiography of Linda Brent (Harriet Jacobs).

I wish I were more competent to the task I have undertaken. But I trust my readers will excuse deficiencies in consideration of circumstances. I was born and reared in Slavery; and I remained in a Slave State twenty-seven years. Since I have been at the North, it has been necessary for me to work diligently for my own support, and the education of my children. This has not left me much leisure to make up for the loss of early opportunities to improve myself; and it has compelled me to write these pages at irregular intervals, whenever I could snatch an hour from household duties. . . .

[*Brent explains that she hopes her story will help northern women realize the suffering of southern slave women.*]

I was born a slave; but I never knew it till six years of happy childhood had passed away. My father was a carpenter, and considered so intelligent and skilful in his trade, that when buildings out of the common line were to be erected, he was sent for from long distances, to be head workman. On condition of paying his mistress two hundred dollars a year, and supporting himself, he was allowed to work at his trade, and manage his own affairs. His strongest wish was to purchase his children; but, though he several times offered his hard earnings for that purpose, he never succeeded. In complexion my parents were a light shade of brownish yellow, and were termed mulattoes. They lived together in a comfortable home; and, though we were all slaves, I was so fondly shielded that I never dreamed I was a piece of merchandise, trusted to them for safe keeping, and liable to be demanded of them at any moment. I had one brother, William, who was two years younger than myself—a bright, affectionate child. I had also a great treasure in my maternal grandmother, who was a remarkable woman in many respects. . . .

[*When Linda Brent was six years old, her mother died, and a few years later the kind mistress to whom Brent's family belonged also died. In the will, Brent was bequeathed to the mistress's five-year-old niece, Miss Emily Flint. At the same time, Linda Brent's brother William was purchased by Dr. Flint, Emily's father.*]

My grandmother's mistress had always promised her that, at her death, she would be free; and it was said that in her will she made good the promise. But when the estate was settled, Dr. Flint told the faithful old servant that, under existing circumstances, it was necessary she should be sold. . . .

[*Brent's grandmother, widely respected in the community, was put up for sale at a local auction.*]

. . . Without saying a word, she quietly awaited her fate. No one bid for her. At last, a feeble voice said, "Fifty dollars." It came from a maiden lady, seventy years old, the sister of my grandmother's deceased mistress. She had lived forty years under the same roof with my grandmother; she knew how faithfully she had served her owners, and how cruelly she had been defrauded of her rights; and she resolved to protect her. The auctioneer waited for a higher bid; but her wishes were respected; no one bid above her. She could neither read nor write; and when the bill of sale was made out, she signed it with a cross. But what consequence was that, when she had a big heart overflowing with human kindness? She gave the old servant her freedom. . . .

During the first years of my service in Dr. Flint's family, I was accustomed to share some indulgences with the children of my mistress. Though this seemed to me no more than right, I was grateful for it, and tried to merit the kindness by the faithful discharge of my duties. But I now entered on my fifteenth year—a sad epoch in the life of a slave girl. My master began to whisper foul words in my ear. Young as I was, I could not remain ignorant of their import. I tried to treat them with indifference or contempt. The master's age, my extreme youth, and the fear that his conduct would be reported to my grandmother, made him bear this treatment for many months. He was a crafty man, and resorted to many means to accomplish his purposes. . . . The mistress, who ought to protect the helpless victim, has no other feelings towards her but those of jealousy and rage. . . . Even the little child, who is accustomed to wait on her mistress and her children, will learn, before she is twelve years old, why it is that her mistress hates such and such a one among the slaves. . . . She listens to violent outbreaks of jealous passion, and cannot help understanding what is the cause. She will become prematurely knowing in evil things. Soon she will learn to tremble when she hears her master's footfall. She will be compelled to realize that she is no longer a child. If God has bestowed beauty upon her, it will prove her greatest curse. That which commands admiration in the white woman only hastens the degradation of the female slave. . . .

[*Afraid to tell her grandmother about Dr. Flint's advances, Brent kept silent. But Flint was enraged when he found out that Brent had fallen in love with a young, free, African American carpenter. The doctor redoubled his efforts to seduce Brent and told her terrible stories about what happened to slaves who tried to run away. For a long time, she was afraid to try to escape because of stories such as the one she recounts here.*]

In my childhood I knew a valuable slave, named Charity, and loved her, as all children did. Her young mistress married, and took her to Louisiana. Her little boy, James, was sold to a good sort of master. He became involved in debt, and James was sold again to a wealthy slaveholder, noted for his cruelty. With this man he grew up to manhood, receiving the treatment of a dog. After a severe whipping, to save himself from further infliction of the lash, with which he was threatened, he took to the woods. He was in a most miserable condition—cut by the cowskin, half naked, half starved, and without the means of procuring a crust of bread.

Some weeks after his escape, he was captured, tied, and carried back to his master's plantation. This man considered punishment in his jail, on bread

and water, after receiving hundreds of lashes, too mild for the poor slave's offence. Therefore he decided, after the overseer should have whipped him to
his satisfaction, to have him placed between the screws of the cotton gin, to
stay as long as he had been in the woods. This wretched creature was cut with
the whip from his head to his feet, then washed with strong brine, to prevent
the flesh from mortifying. . . . He was then put into the cotton gin, which was
screwed down, only allowing him room to turn on his side when he could not
lie on his back. Every morning a slave was sent with a piece of bread and bowl
of water, which were placed within reach of the poor fellow. The slave was
charged, under penalty of severe punishment, not to speak to him.

Four days passed, and the slave continued to carry the bread and water. On
the second morning, he found the bread gone, but the water untouched. When
he had been in the press four days and five nights, the slave informed his master that the water had not been used for four mornings, and that a horrible
stench came from the gin house. The overseer was sent to examine into it.
When the press was unscrewed, the dead body was found partly eaten by rats
and vermin. . . .

[*Dr. Flint's jealous wife watched his behavior very closely, so Flint decided to build a
small cabin out in the woods for Brent, who was now sixteen years old. Still afraid to
run away, she became desperate.*]

And now, reader, I come to a period in my unhappy life, which I would
gladly forget if I could. The remembrance fills me with sorrow and shame. . . .
The influences of slavery had had the same effect on me that they had on
other young girls; they had made me prematurely knowing, concerning the
evil ways of the world. I knew what I did, and I did it with deliberate calculation. . . .

I have told you that Dr. Flint's persecutions and his wife's jealousy had
given rise to some gossip in the neighborhood. Among others, it chanced that
a white unmarried gentleman had obtained some knowledge of the circumstances in which I was placed. He knew my grandmother, and often spoke to
me in the street. He became interested for me, and asked questions about my
master, which I answered in part. He expressed a great deal of sympathy, and
a wish to aid me. He constantly sought opportunities to see me, and wrote to
me frequently. I was a poor slave girl, only fifteen years old.

So much attention from a superior person was, of course, flattering; for human nature is the same in all. I also felt grateful for his sympathy, and encouraged by his kind words. It seemed to me a great thing to have such a
friend. By degrees, a more tender feeling crept into my heart. He was an educated and eloquent gentleman; too eloquent, alas, for the poor slave girl who

trusted in him. Of course I saw whither all this was tending. I knew the impassable gulf between us; but to be an object of interest to a man who is not married, and who is not her master, is agreeable to the pride and feelings of a slave, if her miserable situation has left her any pride or sentiment. It seems less degrading to give one's self, than to submit to compulsion. There is something akin to freedom in having a lover who has no control over you, except that which he gains by kindness and attachment. A master may treat you as rudely as he pleases, and you dare not speak; moreover, the wrong does not seem so great with an unmarried man, as with one who has a wife to be made unhappy. There may be sophistry in all this; but the condition of a slave confuses all principles of morality, and, in fact, renders the practice of them impossible.

[Brent had two children, Benjy and Ellen, as a result of her relationship with Mr. Sands, the white "gentleman." Sands and Brent's grandmother tried to buy Brent, but Dr. Flint rejected all their offers. However, Sands was able (through a trick) to buy his two children and Brent's brother, William. After he was elected to Congress, Sands married a white woman. William escaped to the North, and Brent spent seven years hiding in the tiny attic of a shed attached to her grandmother's house. Finally, Brent and a friend escaped via ship to Philadelphia. She then went to New York City, where she found work as a nursemaid for a kind family, the Bruces, and was reunited with her two children. However, as a fugitive slave, she was not really safe, and she used to read the newspapers every day to see whether Dr. Flint or any of his relatives were visiting New York.]

But when summer came, the old feeling of insecurity haunted me. It was necessary for me to take little Mary[7] out daily, for exercise and fresh air, and the city was swarming with Southerners, some of whom might recognize me. Hot weather brings out snakes and slaveholders, and I like one class of the venomous creatures as little as I do the other. What a comfort it is, to be free to *say* so! . . .

I kept close watch of the newspapers for arrivals; but one Saturday night, being much occupied, I forgot to examine the Evening Express as usual. I went down into the parlor for it, early in the morning, and found the boy about to kindle a fire with it. I took it from him and examined the list of arrivals. Reader, if you have never been a slave, you cannot imagine the acute sensation at my heart, when I read the names of Mr. and Mrs. Dodge,[8] at a hotel in Courtland Street. It was a third-rate hotel, and that circumstance convinced me of the truth of what I had heard, that they were short of funds and had need of my value, as *they* valued me; and that was by dollar and cents. I

7. Mary was the Bruces' baby.
8. Emily Flint and her husband.

hastened with the paper to Mrs. Bruce. Her heart and hand were always open to every one in distress, and she always warmly sympathized with mine. It was impossible to tell how near the enemy was. He might have passed and repassed the house while we were sleeping. He might at that moment be waiting to pounce upon me if I ventured out of doors. I had never seen the husband of my young mistress, and therefore I could not distinguish him from any other stranger. A carriage was hastily ordered; and, closely veiled, I followed Mrs. Bruce, taking the baby again with me into exile. After various turnings and crossings, and returnings, the carriage stopped at the house of one of Mrs. Bruce's friends, where I was kindly received. Mrs. Bruce returned immediately, to instruct the domestics what to say if any one came to inquire for me.

It was lucky for me that the evening paper was not burned up before I had a chance to examine the list of arrivals. It was not long after Mrs. Bruce's return to her house, before several people came to inquire for me. One inquired for me, another asked for my daughter Ellen, and another said he had a letter from my grandmother, which he was requested to deliver in person.

They were told, "She *has* lived here, but she has left."

"How long ago?"

"I don't know, sir."

"Do you know where she went?"

"I do not, sir." And the door was closed. . . .

[*Mrs. Bruce was finally able to buy Brent from Mr. Dodge, and she immediately gave Brent her freedom.*]

Reader, my story ends with freedom; not in the usual way, with marriage. I and my children are now free! We are as free from the power of slaveholders as are the white people of the north; and though that, according to my ideas, is not saying a great deal, it is a vast improvement in *my* condition. The dream of my life is not yet realized. I do not sit with my children in a home of my own. I still long for a hearthstone of my own, however humble. I wish it for my children's sake far more than for my own. But God so orders circumstances as to keep me with my friend Mrs. Bruce. Love, duty, gratitude, also bind me to her side. It is a privilege to serve her who pities my oppressed people, and who has bestowed the inestimable boon of freedom on me and my children. . . .

[*Harriet Jacobs's story was published in 1861, and during the Civil War she did relief work with the newly freed slaves behind Union army lines. For several years after the war ended, she worked tirelessly in Georgia to organize orphanages, schools, and nursing homes. Finally, she returned to the North, where she died in 1897 at the age of eighty-four.*]

✦

Questions to Consider

The evidence in this chapter falls into three categories: reminiscences from former slaves, culled from interviews conducted in the 1930s (Sources 1 through 18); songs transcribed soon after the Civil War, recalled by runaway slaves, or remembered years after (Sources 19 through 23); and the autobiographies of two slaves who escaped to the North: Frederick Douglass and Harriet Jacobs (Sources 24 and 25).

The evidence contains a number of subtopics, and arrangement into those subtopics may be profitable. For example:

1. How did slaves feel about their masters and/or mistresses?
2. How did slaves feel about their work? Their families? Their religion?
3. How did they feel about freedom?
4. How did slaves feel about themselves?

By regrouping the evidence into subtopics and then using each piece of evidence to answer the question for that subtopic, you should be able to answer the central question: What did slaves (or former slaves) think and feel about the peculiar institution of slavery?

As mentioned, some of the slaves and former slaves chose to be direct in their messages (see, for example, Source 19), but many more chose to communicate their thoughts and feelings more indirectly or obliquely. Several of the symbols and metaphors used are easy to figure out (see Source 23), but others will take considerably more care. The messages are there, however.

Frederick Douglass and Harriet Jacobs wrote their autobiographies for northern readers. Furthermore, both of these runaway slaves were active in abolitionist work. Do these facts mean that this evidence is worthless? Not at all, but the historian must be very careful when analyzing such sources. Which parts of Douglass's and Jacobs's stories seem to be exaggerated or unlikely to be true? What do these writers say about topics such as their work, religious beliefs, and families? Does any other evidence from the interviews, tales, or songs corroborate what Douglass and Jacobs wrote?

✦

Epilogue

Even before the Civil War formally ended, thousands of African Americans began casting off the shackles of slavery. Some ran away to meet the advancing Union armies, who often treated them no better than their former masters and mistresses. Others drifted into cities, where they hoped to find work opportunities for themselves and their families. Still others stayed on the land, perhaps hoping to become free farmers. At the end of the war, African Ameri-

[201]

cans were quick to establish their own churches and enrolled in schools established by the Freedmen's Bureau. And for the next two decades, African Americans searched for their lost kin.

As historian David Blight has shown in his study of the memories of the Civil War during the late nineteenth and very early twentieth centuries, African Americans had very mixed feelings about their slave past and the significance of the war. For some, the "peculiar institution" was a burden that saddled them with a legacy of poverty, immorality, and ignorance. For others, the Civil War was an unfinished revolution in which they had participated but that was being undermined by post-war violence and lynching in the South. A few African Americans turned toward Africa and its cultures in search of a usable past. Still others, such as Booker T. Washington, came to believe that reconciliation should be the goal, accompanied by black efforts at racial "uplift" and self-reliance.[9] By the 1890s, most former slaves seem to have wanted to look forward and not backward into the agonizing past of slavery.

Yet memories of slavery were not forgotten and often were passed down orally, from generation to generation. In 1976, Alex Haley's book *Roots* and the twelve-part television miniseries based on it stunned an American public that had assumed that blacks' memories of their origins and of slavery had been for the most part either forgotten

or obliterated.[10] Although much of Haley's work contains the author's artistic license, the skeleton of the book was the oral tradition transmitted by his family since the capture of his ancestor Kunta Kinte in West Africa in the late eighteenth century. Not only had Haley's family remembered its African origins, but stories about slavery had not been lost; they had been passed down through the generations.

While Haley was engaged in his twelve years of research and writing, historian Henry Irving Tragle was compiling a documentary history of the Nat Turner rebellion of 1831. Talking to black people in 1968 and 1969 in Southampton County, Virginia, where the rebellion occurred, Tragle discovered that in spite of numerous attempts to obliterate Turner from the area's historical memory, Turner's action had become part of the oral history of the region. As the surprised Tragle wrote, "I believe it possible to say with certainty that Nat Turner did exist as a folk-hero to several generations of black men and women who have lived and died in Southampton County since 1831."[11] Again, oral history had persisted and triumphed over time, and professional historians began looking with a new eye on what in the past many had dismissed as unworthy of their attention.

Folk music, customs, religious practices, stories, and artifacts have also received new attention since the 1960s.

9. David W. Blight, "Black Memory and the Progress of the Race," Chapter 9 in *Race and Reunion* (Cambridge: Belknap Press of Harvard University Press, 2001), pp. 300–337.

10. A condensed version of *Roots* appeared in 1974 in *Reader's Digest*.
11. Henry Irving Tragle, *The Southampton Slave Revolt of 1831: A Compilation of Source Material* (Amherst: University of Massachusetts Press, 1971), p. 12.

Increasingly, students of history have been able to reconstruct the lives, thoughts, and feelings of people once considered inarticulate. Of course, these people were not really inarticulate, but it took imagination to let their evidence speak.

Many people have argued about the impact of slavery on blacks and whites alike, and that question may never be answered fully. What we *do* know is that an enormous amount of historical evidence about slavery exists—from the perspectives of both African Americans and whites. And the memory of that institution lingers. It is part of what one southern white professional historian calls the "burden of southern history," a burden to be overcome but never completely forgotten.

The Diplomacy, Politics, and Intrigue of "Manifest Destiny": The Annexation of Texas

◆

The Problem

In his memoirs, entitled *Thirty Years' View,* powerful Senator Thomas Hart Benton of Missouri (1782–1858) recalled a letter that appeared in a Baltimore newspaper in the winter of 1842–1843 written by Virginia congressman Thomas Walker Gilmer (1802–1844) that was "a clap of thunder in a clear sky":

> Mr. Gilmer . . . [urged] the immediate annexation [of Texas], as necessary to forestall the designs of Great Britain upon that young country. These designs, it was alleged, aimed at a political and military domination on our south-western border, with a view to abolition [of slavery] and hostile movements against us.[1]

1. Thomas Hart Benton, *Thirty Years' View* (New York: Greenwood Press, photocopy of 1856 ed., 1968), p. 581. Gilmer served in the U.S. Congress from 1841 until 1844, when he was appointed secretary of the navy by President John Tyler. He was killed in a freak gun explosion on the USS Princeton on February 28, 1844. Benton, also on the ship at the time, was wounded.

Ever since the Republic of Texas achieved its independence from Mexico in 1836, there had been several efforts to make Texas part of the United States, all of which had ended in failure. Great Britain had put an end to slavery in its empire in 1833. Had Gilmer unearthed a British conspiracy to influence Texans to abolish slavery and thereby block the westward expansion of slavery in the United States? Should the United States checkmate British antislavery ambitions by immediately annexing Texas?

Or was Gilmer himself part of a *slaveholders'* conspiracy (as John Quincy Adams and other antislavery advocates claimed) to use the "abolitionist issue" to stampede Americans[2] into annexation? Indeed, rumors abounded in both the North and the

2. Although everyone living in the Western Hemisphere can be accurately referred to as an "American," we have adopted the more common, albeit inaccurate, practice of referring to Americans as residents of the United States.

South of conspiratorial plots both in favor of and against the annexation of Texas.

Your task in this chapter is to examine and analyze the evidence to the end of answering the following questions: Was there a British abolitionist conspiracy to block the United States' annexation of Texas in order to stop the westward expansion of slavery? Does the evidence point to any other conspiracies? What role, if any, did these plots—or rumors of plots—play in the ultimate annexation of Texas in 1845?

Americans in the early to mid-nineteenth century were ardent conspiracy theorists. Some men and women saw plots nearly everywhere— Roman Catholic conspiracies, Freemasons' conspiracies, abolitionists' conspiracies, slaveholders' conspiracies, and on and on. Firm believers that they had formed (as New York journalist John O'Sullivan put it) "a nation of many nations . . . *destined* to manifest to mankind the excellence of divine principles," many Americans assumed that if the divinely ordained and perfect republic stumbled, the cause must have been some conspiratorial plot of evildoers. Otherwise, "who will, what can, set limits on our onward march?"[3] In the battles over the annexation of Texas, many Americans saw conspiracies because they were *prepared* to see them. Was there in fact a British abolitionist conspiracy? Were there any other conspiracies related to the annexation of Texas?

◆

Background

Ever since the Louisiana Purchase of 1803, Americans had covetously eyed the portion of New Spain they called "Texas."[4] To acquire Florida from Spain, however, the United States (in the Adams-Onis Treaty of 1819) had relinquished any claims it might have had to the province of Texas. Even so, many Americans desired to envelop Texas into the Union.

Those hopes were reignited when Mexico's revolution against Spain broke out in 1810. Mexico declared its independence in 1821 and in 1824 a constitution was written, based in part on the United States Constitution of 1787, and the new nation declared itself a republic. An effort by Spain to retake its former colony was crushed in 1829.

The new Republic of Mexico, however, was economically destitute and politically unstable. The nation experienced revolutions in 1828, 1829, and

3. *United States Magazine and Democratic Review,* Vol. 6 (Nov. 1839), quoted in Walter A. McDougall, *Promised Land, Crusader State: The American Encounter with the World Since 1776* (Boston: Houghton Mifflin, 1997), pp. 76–77.

4. Although Americans and others referred to the area as *Texas,* technically the province's Spanish and, later, Mexican name was *Coahuila.*

◆ CHAPTER 9

The Diplomacy,
Politics, and Intrigue
of "Manifest
Destiny": The
Annexation of Texas

1832, and the government was propped up economically by foreign loans and private investments, many of them from British banks, investors, and businessmen. Beginning in 1824 (the year Great Britain recognized Mexican independence), British investment firms began selling Mexican bonds to British investors, the first two bond issues raising around $32 million. But the Mexican government could not raise enough revenue to pay back its bondholders, and in 1827 it defaulted on its loan. Faced with the total loss of all their initial investments, all British bankers and private investors could do was to loan Mexico even more money, in the hope that eventually the new republic would achieve sufficient financial stability to begin paying its obligations. By 1840, Mexico's foreign debt was over $80 million. Although Mexican bond purchases were made by private companies and individuals, the British government took a keen interest in Mexico's debt, in part because some of the larger private bondholders were powerful and influential people.[5]

In addition to supporting the Mexican government through generous loans, British investors also backed Mexican mining companies and international trade. British-supported mining companies were capitalized at around £14 million, and as early as 1809 British trade with the Spanish province already had reached £18 million, a figure that increased significantly after Mexican independence.

At the same time that Great Britain and Mexico were strengthening their economic ties, their antislavery policies drew them closer together as well. Mexico had initiated general emancipation in 1829, and Britain's abolition of slavery in its empire followed soon thereafter, in 1833. Not only did Great Britain put an end to slavery in its own empire, but the powerful British navy carried on aggressive efforts to stop the trans-Atlantic slave trade. Thus, Britain and Mexico were forming strong relations, due in no small part to their mutually beneficial economic interests and to their common stand on slavery.

And yet, even with considerable British economic aid, the Mexican government and the country's entire economy teetered on the brink of bankruptcy. Desperate for money, the Mexican government turned to its greatest asset: land. To increase land sales, Mexican leaders began to encourage immigration to Texas, largely from the United States. Land agents, known as *empresarios,*[6] received generous land grants, which they in turn divided and sold to prospective settlers. In 1821, perhaps the most successful of these *empresarios,* Stephen F. Austin, led 300 families across the Sabine River onto the fertile land of East Texas. By 1830, the number of white Americans in Texas had boomed to around 7,000. Six years later, it was 30,000.

Mexico soon realized its mistake. American colonists brazenly flouted Mexican authorities, scoffed at the requirement that settlers convert to Roman Catholicism, and openly ignored the Mexican government's 1829 prohi-

---

5. The Reform Bill of 1832 increased the political power of industrialists, bankers, and merchants in the British House of Commons.

6. Businessmen.

bition on importing more slaves into Texas. Americans, who settled mostly in East Texas, were growing cotton, an enterprise they believed required slave labor. In spite of the restriction, by 1836 there were approximately 5,000 slaves in Texas. As a last-ditch attempt to regain control of the situation in Texas, in 1830 the government tried to bar all further immigration from the United States, another edict that was openly ignored. By 1835, it was estimated that roughly 1,000 Americans were arriving in Texas each month.

In 1834, still another revolution erupted in Mexico, bringing to power one of the most charismatic and controversial figures in Mexican history: Antonio Lopez de Santa Anna, the hero of the 1829 repelling of the Spanish invasion. Attempting to establish order in the restive provinces, Santa Anna proclaimed himself a dictator and in 1835 issued a new constitution that centralized power in Mexico City and severely restricted local autonomy. Almost immediately, eight provinces rose in rebellion, one of them being Texas. Determined not to place itself under Mexican authority again, on March 2, 1836, the province of Texas declared its independence in a document that was remarkably similar to the United States' 1776 declaration.[7]

Determined to crush the Texan insurrection, Santa Anna already had led a large force into the rebellious province in the fall of 1835. At the Alamo, an abandoned mission in San Antonio, the Mexican general ordered the killing of all the defenders (he spared women and children and, according to legend, at least one native Mexican male) and then stacked their bodies like cordwood and burned them. Two weeks later, Mexicans shot all 350 Texan defenders at Goliad, even though a formal surrender had been arranged with an agreement that survivors would be spared. On April 21, 1836, however, Texans under General Sam Houston surprised Santa Anna's army at San Jacinto, killed nearly half of them in the first fifteen minutes of the battle, and took Santa Anna prisoner. In return for his release, Santa Anna promised that Mexico would recognize Texas's independence, a promise that was broken as soon as he was freed. By the end of 1836, the Republic of Texas was an independent nation, nicknamed by some the "Lone Star Republic," after its flag, which had one star.

An overwhelming majority of Texans did not want to remain an independent nation. Given their economic, cultural, and intellectual ties to the United States, most Texans wanted to be annexed to that neighboring country. As Anson Jones, a Massachusetts physician turned Texas politician who was the last president of Texas before its annexation, remarked on the ties between Texas and the United States, "So powerful has been this feeling, and so intimate has been the connection . . . that we have still thought and felt as if we were yet a part and portion of them."[8] Indeed, for many Texans an-

7. For the similarities see Oscar J. Martinez, ed., *U.S.–Mexico Borderlands: Historical and Contemporary Perspectives* (Wilmington, Del.: Scholarly Resources, 1996), pp. 13–16.

8. Anson Jones, *Memoranda and Official Correspondence Relating to the Republic of Texas, Its History and Annexation* (Chicago: Rio Grande Press, photocopy of 1859 ed., 1966), p. 116.

✦ CHAPTER 9

The Diplomacy,
Politics, and Intrigue
of "Manifest
Destiny": The
Annexation of Texas

nexation could not come too quickly. Mexico never had recognized the independence of Texas and had initiated a series of raids and forays into its former province. Moreover, rumors abounded that Mexico was preparing for a massive invasion of Texas, one that the new nation knew it might not be able to turn back. In addition, the new Texas government had almost no funds and limped along by issuing over $3.5 million of paper money, eventually worth only around 17 percent of its face value. In the eyes of many Texans, only annexation could save Texas from conquest by Mexico or financial ruin.

Yet both Presidents Andrew Jackson and Martin Van Buren rebuffed Texan efforts to be annexed by the United States, in part because both men feared that the issue would deepen a rift in the Democratic party between southern Democrats, who favored annexation, and northern and midwestern Democrats, who generally opposed it. With their principal political base in the North and Midwest, the rival Whigs also opposed annexation, fearing a diminution of their power. For its part, Mexico was in even worse financial shape than Texas, forced to continue to borrow money in order to stay afloat. In 1841, Santa Anna, who had been removed from the presidency after his humiliation at San Jacinto, returned to power, but his hold on the reins of government was shaky at best. Many Texans feared that Santa Anna would attempt to prop up his sagging political fortunes by invading Texas. Even so, many Americans, especially in the North, opposed annexation, fearing that the admission of Texas would al-

low the slave states to dominate the national government.[9]

In the midst of this melange[10] stood Great Britain, one of the most powerful nations in the world after the defeat of Napoleon Bonaparte in 1815. A major creditor of both Mexico and Texas and the United States' most important trading partner, Britain held in its hand a number of inviting possibilities. How should Great Britain deal with America's westward expansion and growing economic prowess? In what ways, if any, might Great Britain take advantage of the confusing relations between the Republic of Texas and the United States? What part, if any, would Britain's antislavery stance play in its overall foreign policy? How might Britain make use of the debts that Mexico owed to British investors? What were the benefits to Great Britain of convincing the Texans to remain independent? What were the risks?

As for the Texans themselves, should they continue to press for annexation by the United States? Or should Texas maintain its independence and seek diplomatic and commercial relations with other nations? Would Mexico ever recognize Texan independence?

Finally, President John Tyler, convinced there was a British abolitionist conspiracy, felt he could wait no longer. In April 1844, the president sent an-

9. Santa Anna had made an unsuccessful attempt to return to power in 1838, a struggle in which he had lost a leg in battle. When he assumed power in 1841, he staged a Christian burial of his severed limb. See David M. Pletcher, *The Diplomacy of Annexation: Texas, Oregon, and the Mexican War* (Columbia, Mo.: University of Missouri Press, 1973), p. 38.
10. Mixture.

other annexation treaty to the Senate,[11] hoping that the fear of a British plot would strengthen the expansionists' hand and force the Senate to approve the treaty. Tyler probably realized that his strategy was a risky one that might divide the country rather than unite it. It was, however, a gamble worth taking.

Your task in this chapter is to examine and analyze the evidence and answer the following questions: Was there a British abolitionist conspiracy designed to block the United States' annexation of Texas? Does an examination of the evidence uncover any other conspiracies having to do with the annexation of Texas by the United States? What role, if any, did conspiratorial plots—or rumors of plots—play in the ultimate annexation of Texas in 1845?

✦

The Method

How can historians hope to uncover strategies or plots that people of the past purposely meant to keep secret? How can we determine whether there really *was* a conspiracy and not just *rumors* or *threats* of a conspiracy?

Whenever we analyze a conspiracy or, indeed, just about any other form of human endeavor, we can divide our study into three parts: (1) the *goals* or objectives the person or persons seek to achieve, (2) the *options* or alternatives available to them, and (3) the *strategies* or tactics they might employ to achieve those goals. As you work through the evidence, make a chart that will allow you to recall later what goals, options, and strategies you identified in each piece of evidence. Note that not every piece of evidence explicitly contains all three, so you may have to make inferences about them.

As you examine each piece of evidence, ask yourself the following questions:

1. Did the author of the source support or oppose the goal the supposed conspiracy was meant to achieve?
2. Was the author in a position to participate in, observe at first-hand, or know about a particular secret plan?
3. In the source, did the author refer to (or hint at) a particular conspiracy?
4. Would the author's goal be achieved by a strategy other than a plot?

Also, as you analyze each piece of evidence, it would be helpful to note who the author is as well as who the recipient is. Officials of one nation (Britain, the United States, Texas) might well have been more candid with one another than they would have been when writing to an official of another nation. A good example is Lord Aberdeen's denials of a British abolitionist conspiracy. To whom were those denials ad-

11. See Source 18 in the Evidence section of this chapter.

♦ CHAPTER 9

The Diplomacy,
Politics, and Intrigue
of "Manifest
Destiny": The
Annexation of Texas

dressed? How seriously should they be taken?

Finally, as noted above, you may uncover more than one conspiracy (or rumor of a conspiracy) in the evidence. Therefore, it may be profitable to read through the evidence *three* times, once concentrating your attention on the alleged British plot, a second time focusing on American expansionists' alleged scheme to make people *believe* there was a British antislavery conspiracy in order to push the annexation treaty through the Senate, and a last time examining a possible plan on the part of Texas to bluff the United States into annexation. Each time you go through the evidence, you will have to assess whether the alleged conspiracy was real.

♦

The Evidence

Source 1 from the *Patriot* (London), July 6, 1836, quoted in Mary Lee Spence, "British Interests and Attitudes Regarding the Republic of Texas and Its Annexation by the United States" (unpub. Ph.D. dissertation, University of Minnesota, 1957), p. 5.

1. *Patriot,* July 6, 1836.

Texas belongs to a Republic which has abolished slavery; the object of the Americans is to convert it into a slave-holding State; not only to make it the field of slave-cultivation, and a market for the Maryland Slave-trade, but, by annexing it to the Federal Union, to strengthen in Congress the preponderating influence of the Southern or slave-holding States.

This atrocious project is the real origin and cause of the pretended contest for Texian independence; a war, on the part of the United States, of unprovoked aggression for the vilest of all purposes.

Source 2 from the pamphlet *Texas. An English Question* (London: Effingham Wilson, 1837), pp. 4–6, 8–10, 36–37.

2. *Texas. An English Question.*

The discerning inhabitants of the American republic well know that in it, their national prosperity—nay, the very integrity of their federal institutions, is deeply and perplexingly involved. They know, on the one hand, that if this new and, by nature, highly-favoured country, remain independent of the

Union, she will become its great and successful rival. She will drain its population, she will emulate its commerce, she will undersell its produce; she will, by reason of the vast extent of frontier, become, in spite of all precautions to the contrary, the centre of a contraband trade, most extensively injurious to its revenue; above all, she will on every occasion of state dissension or excitement, such as the anomalous combination of interests in the great northern confederacy has generated and must in time bring to a crisis, become the star of attraction, the torch of discord, and the beacon of civil war. . . .

Thus much will also serve to show, that Texas, independently of any intrinsic value of its own, must be an object of no secondary importance to ourselves. If we know any thing of our own interests, we shall know—many of us by experience,—that that which affects the general condition of the United States, affects, most materially and almost with the same vibration, our own state of prosperity—so tensely stretched is the cord wherewith commerce has already drawn the two hemispheres together! . . .

We have no longer much motive or ambition to aggrandize ourselves in the western hemisphere by further acquisitions of territory, and therefore little incentive to war. Our simple policy in this respect is, as far as possible, to oppose the inordinate growth of any other power which might be likely to endanger our colonies, or our naval supremacy; and thus avoid cause for future war. As regards the connexion of this object with Texas, England might well wait to see a result which would arrive without her interference,—a result which, though she may wish well to her alienated American children, and their institutions in general, and though she is certainly innocent of any designs against their freedom, she will perhaps still see—without any great regrets—the dismemberment of their gigantic but unwieldy confederation: that confederation which is not only dangerous to our future power from its immensely growing greatness, but immediately injurious to our commerce from the fact of its being a union, wherein the interests of those of its own members whose commercial policy corresponds with our own, that is, of those who are for a direct free trade with us, are conceded and sacrificed to the diametrically opposite interests of those interlopers whose prosperity chiefly depends upon taxing our importations, engrossing our commissions, and superseding the use of our shipping.

Without any thing invidious on the part of England, this union must, from its own nature, sooner or later dissolve,—and, it is more than probable, through the agency of Texas. England, therefore, might be content to remain an altogether passive spectator of the progress of events. . . .

Whether Texas receive our recognition or not, she will be a slave-holding state. She will import from the United States; and all that we can *directly* do to check slavery in that quarter, will be to prevent the illicit acts of individu-

◆ CHAPTER 9

The Diplomacy,
Politics, and Intrigue
of "Manifest
Destiny": The
Annexation of Texas

als, who may import from elsewhere,—a business which must be left to the vigilance of our cruisers. But if Texas become part of the Union, she will, by strengthening the slavery interest in Congress, be the essential means of retarding that sooner or later inevitable event,—total universal abolition. Slavery has reached its climax. It cannot greatly increase, for nearly all the nations have declared against it. At the same time it will not fall at once, it must spin out its natural term, it must be *prepared* for dissolution. Still, the day of its extinction may be materially accelerated or postponed. According to the means applied, it may have a comparatively rapid or a lingering decline. The union of Texas with the States would do much to procure the latter effect.

If, on the contrary, she were to remain separate, and England were to cultivate amicable relations with her, the latter (that is, England) might *indirectly*, and without offence, do much to hasten the so devoutly wished for consummation. Texas might then become the field whereon a grand experiment could be tried; an experiment, which, if it succeeded, would, by its moral example, do more, gradually to counteract slavery, than all the violent declamation, or hasty, ill-advised remedies; that overheated zeal has ever yet suggested.

Source 3 from George P. Garrison, ed., "Diplomatic Correspondence of the Republic of Texas," in *Annual Report of the American Historical Association for the Year 1907* (Washington: Government Printing Office, 1908), Vol. 2, pt. 1, p. 215.

3. Fairfax Catlett[12] to Henderson,[13] n.d. [1837]. Report of Catlett's meeting with John Forsyth, U.S. secretary of state.

I replied that I was well aware that the situation of the United States was a delicate and embarrassing one, and that it was by no means my desire to render it more so, but that the identity of interest between the two countries was so striking and apparent, and pointed so clearly to the expediency of the United States preventing Great Britain from negotiating for the purchase of Texas that I could not but encourage the hope, that some assurance would be given to my Government that if any negotiations were opened between Great Britain and Mexico, that the United States would immediately interfere. "In what way could we interfere?" "By distinctly intimating to the British Govt. that the United States could never consent to Great Britain's obtaining possession of Texas." "Great Britain in return might say the same to us." "If she did, it would be easy to reply that the United States would make no such at-

12. Secretary of the Texas legation to the United States.
13. Acting secretary of state, Republic of Texas.

tempt, that she had already acknowledged the separate existence of Texas as an Independent Republic, but that if it were the unequivocal desire of the people of Texas to be admitted into this Union, that their wishes would be properly respected and listened to." He said that the subject was certainly one of common interest, but that, for himself, he had not the least idea that Great Britain, would accede to the offer, though he doubted not that such an offer had been made:—that the Mexican debt was due not to the British Government, but to the British subjects:—that he had received no information on the subject in addition to what he had already communicated, nor did he believe that any overtures had been made to Mexico by Great Britain for the purchase of Texas. That as far as facts were concerned, he would cheerfully communicate any information in his power that would be interesting to Texas, but that it was impossible for him to express any opinion in relation to the course of policy that the Government of the United States would pursue.

Source 4 from Ephraim Douglass Adams, *British Diplomatic Correspondence Concerning the Republic of Texas, 1838–1846* (Austin: Texas State Historical Assn., n.d.), pp. 12–13.

4. Joseph Crawford[14] to Sir Richard Pakenham,[15] May 26, 1837.

I shall now state what the opinion is in that Country as to its Annexation to the United States of North America

At the time of the Election of the President last year the opinion was decidedly in favour of Annexation, and the Minister or Commissioner sent to Washington was instructed to endeavour to bring about that desideratum upon the recognition of their political Independence[.]

Since that time reflection has taught them that their interests are at varience with some portion of the North American Union, and that annexation, would be disadvantageous with a Territory extending 560,000 Square Miles under a benign climate, and a soil capable of producing, as much if not more Cotton than is grown in America and of a rich quality, what could be gained to Texas by exchanging her produce against manufactures, which She requires, if that produce was to pass thro' America and the Manufactures be received thro' the same medium. She would lose the advantage of Competition, and could reap no solid benefit by the adding her Cottons into the growth of the United States.

14. British agent or envoy in Texas.
15. British minister to Mexico, later British minister to the United States.

The opinion then has changed and they are very anxious to have a Separate, free and recognised Independent Government, to trade directly with other Nations, giving the Raw produce for the Manufactures they require, for it must be long ere there are Manufactories in Texas. I am not aware whether other Instructions are sent to the Minister in Washington but I know that annexation to that Government is not wished by the people or the Government of Texas, nor will it now be sought for. By the Constitution Slaves are permitted to be introduced over the frontier of the United States only.—No free Negro is permitted to reside in the Territory, and the introduction of Slaves, Africans or Negroes is forever prohibited and declared to be piracy, except those from the United States.

The number of Slaves as yet is by no means great and in general they are exceedingly well treated.

That notwithstanding the declaration of piracy, Slaves have been imported directly into Texas I lament to say is but too true, and whilst I make this statement it is due to the Government and especially to the President, that I should declare my conviction of their having tried every means in their power to detect the perpetrators and bring them to Justice.—I have good reason to believe that there is still one or more American Vessels employed in this most detestable traffick, landing the Slaves on the East Side of the Sabine and so evading the Laws of Texas.

Source 5 from Garrison, ed., "Diplomatic Correspondence of the Republic of Texas," (1908), Vol. 2, pt. 1, p. 317.

5. Memucan Hunt[16] to R. A. Irion,[17] March 12, 1838.

It is decidedly my opinion, and that of many distinguished gentlemen from the Southern States, that unless Texas is annexed, this Union will, at no distant period, be dissolved; say a few years. This will be the result of an interference on the part of the Northern States with the institutions of slavery in the South. Whereas, the annexation of Texas would give a preponderence in the Senate in favour of the South, and thereby, afford an ample security against the encroachments of the North, in the representative branch of the Government.

But should annexation fail, a similar security could be anticipated from no other source.

16. Texas emissary to the United States.
17. Texas secretary of state.

The ratification by Texas, of a treaty between that country and Great Britain, would indefinitely pos[t]pone the question of annexation here, as the Constitution of the United States precludes the admission of a state, whose duties and foreign policy differ from the rest.

Domestic Slavery in the United States and Texas, must, from various circumstances, stand or fall together. The failure of annexation will hazard an attack upon those institutions in civil warfare between the States holding, and those opposed; for the fanatical spirit of abolition, is unquestionably on the increase, and will so continue, in my humble judgment, unless annexation should ultimately prevail. Should this be the case, it would be so great a triumph as to check its progress, if not entirely, certainly to an extent, that would cause the slave holding States, as well as Texas, to feel a perfect security.

Sources 6 through 8 from Garrison, ed., "Diplomatic Correspondence of the Republic of Texas," (1908), Vol. 2, pt. 3, pp. 868, 887–888, 918.

6. J. Hamilton[18] to H. S. Fox,[19] May 20, 1839.

If the Minister of Texas should conclude a Treaty with Mexico, authorizing the former to pay over the amount of the indemnity to the holders of the Mexican Securities in England, nothing could be more gratifying to me, than to promote this object by every means in my power, as it would add another wreath to the glory of the descendants of the Saxon race, that after beating Mexico, despoiling her of one of the finest of her provinces, that a handfull of men should come under an obligation to pay her debts on charge in London.[20]

7. Hamilton to Lord Viscount Palmerston,[21] February 10, 1840.

My Lord:—

When I had the honor of holding an interview with you at your residence in Great Stanhope Street in September last, on which occasion I took the liberty

18. Texas envoy to Great Britain.
19. British minister plenipotentiary to the United States.
20. The British government conceived a plan whereby the Republic of Texas would pay a large sum (an "indemnity") to Mexico, in return for which Mexico would recognize the independence of Texas and use the money to pay back the holders of Mexican bonds. The plan collapsed when the Mexican government refused to go along.
21. British secretary of state for foreign affairs.

◆ CHAPTER 9

The Diplomacy,
Politics, and Intrigue
of "Manifest
Destiny": The
Annexation of Texas

of urging on you, such considerations as I thought of some value to enable you to make up your opinion, on the expediency of recognizing the Independence of Texas, I informed you that I had little doubt that, for purposes of peace and a well ascertained boundary, Texas would be willing to pay an adequate indemnity to Mexico which, under her convention with the Mexican Bondholders in London in Septr 1837 would enure to the benefit of your citizens. After this interview with your Lordship I saw several of the most respectable and influential of the Bondholders in England, and in consequence of an understanding with them, I was induced, on my recent visit to Texas, to obtain from the congress, and the Executive Government of that Republic, a distinct expression of their willingness to assent to a convention providing for such a purpose. I enclose your Lordship, confidentially, a copy of a report of the committees of foreign relations of both Houses of Congress, of which I ask your most careful and attentive perusal, together with certain Resolutions adopted by that body and approved by the President. I moreover beg leave to advise you, in equal confidence, that I have been authorized to accept the mediation of your Government, in case Mexico concurs in such a reference, and I am likewise appointed the agent to treat with the Mexican Bondholders, in the event of the Government of Mexico consenting that the indemnity should be paid over to her creditors in England. . . .

I now submit to your Lordship in the briefest possible terms, some facts with which it may be of importance for you to know, as the commercial connections between Great Britain and Mexico are certainly of no small moment to your people, to say nothing of the large public debt which Mexico owes and has long owed to your citizens.

8. Hamilton to Abner S. Lipscomb,[22] December 3, 1840.

As the Mexican Bondholders decided to have their Million Sterling commuted for Land situated between the Neayches and Rio Grande it is quite obvious that this Treaty so far from costing Texas a Farthing it will be the source of wealth population and strength to her. The Mexican Bondholders ardently desire this communication and in the event of the ratification of the Treaty by Mexico they will endeavour at once to have it effected.

They have waited on Lord Palmerston by a Deputation and signified their anxious wish not only for peace between Texas and Mexico but that commuta-

22. Texas secretary of state.

tion should be made. In the event of its being effected that they will forthwith adopt an emigration and colonization Scheme on the plan of the South Australian Colon[iz]ation system and throw a large population of our own race of valuable Emigrants into the country.

Sources 9 and 10 from Ephraim Douglas Adams, *British Interests and Activities in Texas, 1838–1846* (Baltimore: The Johns Hopkins Press, 1910), pp. 237–240.

9. Pakenham to Palmerston, August 30, 1841.

It is much to be regretted that advantage should not be taken of the arrangement some time since concluded by the Mexican Government with their creditors in Europe, to establish an English population in the magnificent Territory of Upper California.

I believe there is no part of the World offering greater natural advantages for the establishment of an English colony than the Provinces of Upper California; while its commanding position on the Pacific, its fine harbours, its forests of excellent timber for ship-building as well as for every other purpose, appear to me to render it by all means desirable, in a political point of view, that California, once ceasing to belong to Mexico, should not fall into the hands of any Power but England; and the present debilitated condition of Mexico, and the gradual increase of foreign population in California render it probable that its separation from Mexico will be effected at no distant period; in fact, there is some reason to believe that daring and adventurous speculators in the United States have already turned their thoughts in that direction.

10. Earl of Aberdeen[23] to Pakenham, December 15, 1841.

His Lordship directs me in answer, to acquaint you for the information of the Earl of Aberdeen, that he is not anxious for the formation of new and distant Colonies, all of which involve heavy direct and still heavier indirect expenditure, besides multiplying the liabilities of misunderstanding and collisions with Foreign Powers.

23. Replaced Palmerston as foreign secretary.

◆ CHAPTER 9

The Diplomacy,
Politics, and Intrigue
of "Manifest
Destiny": The
Annexation of Texas

Source 11 from Adams, *British Diplomatic Correspondence*, pp. 143–144.

11. Charles Elliot[24] to Henry Unwin Addington,[25] December 16, 1842.

The people of Texas are gasping for peace, and the best bidder. I believe that the only safe solution would be a formal offer upon the part of Her Majesty's Government to Texas, to secure the close of this contest upon the basis of It's [*sic*] consenting to place Itself in a position of *real Independence,* by an immediate and thorough organization of It's social, political and Commercial Institutions and policy upon sound, and independent principles; an[d] further offering every reasonable facility to England to negociate such a loan as would be necessary to accomplish the proposed objects. . . .

Texas would be effectually separated from the United States of the Union, and a liberal Commercial policy would as effectually detach it from the N.E. States infected by a spirit of Commercial hostility to Great Britain, and this last principle efficaciously worked out would soon relax the self injurious fiscal system of Mexico.

Source 12 from Thomas Hart Benton, *Thirty Years' View* (New York: D. Appleton and Co., 1856), Vol. 2, pp. 581, 589.

12. Thomas Hart Benton on "Bold Intrigue for the Presidency."

This letter[26] was a clap of thunder in a clear sky. There was nothing in the political horizon to announce or portend it. Great Britain had given no symptom of any disposition to war upon us, or to excite insurrection among our slaves. Texas and Mexico were at war, and to annex the country was to adopt the war. . . .

Mention has been made in the forepart of this chapter, of the necessity which was felt to obtain something from London to bolster up the accusation of that formidable abolition plot which Great Britain was hatching in Texas, and on the alleged existence of which the whole argument for immediate annexation reposed. The desired testimony had been got, and oracularly given to the public, as being derived from a *"private letter from a citizen of Maryland, then in London."* The name of this Maryland citizen was not given, but his respectability and reliability were fully vouched; and the testimony passed

24. British chargé d'affaires to Texas.
25. British permanent undersecretary for foreign affairs.
26. The letter by Gilmer, mentioned in the Problem section of this chapter.

for true. It was to the point in charging upon the British government, with names and circumstances, all that had been alleged; and adding that her abolition machinations were then in full progress. This went back to London, immediately transmitted there by the British minister at Washington, Sir Richard Pakenham; and being known to be false, and felt to be scandalous, drew from the British Secretary of State (Lord Aberdeen) an indignant, prompt, and peremptory contradiction. This contradiction was given in a despatch, dated December 26th, 1843.

Source 13 from Garrison, ed., "Diplomatic Correspondence of the Republic of Texas," (1908), Vol. 2, pt. 3, p. 1105.

13. Ashbel Smith[27] to Isaac VanZandt,[28] January 25, 1843.

There now exists another matter which has been entertained for *some months* in England; whether or not, for a longer period I am unable to say. I will develope [sic] it in a separate paragraph.

It is the purpose of some persons in England to procure the abolition of Slavery in Texas. They propose to accomplish this end by friendly negotiation and by the concession of what will be deemed equivalents. I beleive [sic] the equivalents contemplated are a guarantee by Great Britain of the Independence of Texas—discriminating duties in favor of Texian products and perhaps the negotiation of a loan, or some means by which the finances of Texas can be readjusted. They estimate the number of Slaves in Texas at 12,000 and would consider the payment for them in full, as a small sum for the advantages they anticipate from the establishment of a free State on the Southern borders of the Slave holding States of the American Union.

In July last in London, two matters were submitted to me in conversation by a person then and now having relations with the British Govt. *One* was, whether the people of Texas would listen to and consider a proposition from the English Government to abolish Slavery in consideration of concessions and equivalent advantages to be offered by that Govt. The *second* matter was, whether Texas would not be induced to divide itself into two States, one slave-holding the other nonslave holding. It was argued that but few slaves would probably be introduced into Western Texas by reason of its proximity to Mexico, and that therefore, it would be conceding but little to establish "a free state" on this frontier; and the Colorado was proposed as a dividing line. I do

27. Texas chargé d'affaires to Great Britain.
28. Texas chargé d'affaires to the United States.

◆ CHAPTER 9

The Diplomacy,
Politics, and Intrigue
of "Manifest
Destiny": The
Annexation of Texas

not know to whom is due the initiative of these matters; but I was informed that the propositions in question, had been a subject of conversation with Lord Aberdeen. And I am aware that in another conversation in which Lord Aberdeen took part, it was maintained that the population which would flock into this "free state" from Europe would be enabled to vote down the Slave holders, and thus the Texians would of themselves establish an entire non-slaveholding country.

Source 14 from Adams, *British Diplomatic Correspondence*, p. 108.

14. Sam Houston to Elliot, May 13, 1843.

The Continent of North America is regarded by the people of the U. States as their birth-right—to be secured by policy, if they can, by force if they must. Heretofore Texas has been looked upon as an appendage to the U. States. They cannot realise that we now form two Nations. Therefore every act done in reference to us by any power of which they are jealous, or for which they do not cherish kind national feelings, is regarded as an unauthorized interference and necessarily provokes their denunciation. . . .

This is the case at present in relation to England, British influence and every ridiculous humbug which their crazed imaginations can start, are conjured up and marshalled in fearful array for the purpose of alarming Texas, exciting disorder, producing disrespect towards England, and compelling us to look to the U. States as our only hope of political salvation. They are willing to see Texas tantalized by every annoyance until, in a fit of despair, she is compelled to identify herself with them, and by some act of good fortune become incorporated with them—though they cannot precisely point out the means.

Source 15 from the newspaper *Madisonian*, June 24, 1843, quoted in David M. Pletcher, *The Diplomacy of Annexation: Texas, Oregon, and the Mexican War* (Columbia: University of Missouri Press, 1973), p. 125.

15. *Madisonian*,[29] June 24, 1843.

If Great Britain, as her *philanthropists* and blustering presses intimate, entertain a design to possess Mexico or Texas, or to interfere in any manner

29. According to David Pletcher, *Madisonian* was President John Tyler's "administrative organ." See Pletcher, *The Diplomacy of Annexation*, p. 125.

with the slaves of the Southern States, but a few weeks we fancy, at any time, will suffice to rouse the whole American People to arms like one vast nest of hornets. The great Western States, at the call of "Captain Tyler," would pour their noble sons down the Mississippi Valley by MILLIONS.

Source 16 from Garrison, ed., "Diplomatic Correspondence of the Republic of Texas" (1908), Vol. 2, pt. 3, pp. 1116–1117.

16. Smith to Anson Jones,[30] July 31, 1843.

Previously to leaving London, I had a long interview on the 20th Instant with the Earl of Aberdeen Secretary for the Foreign Department, concerning the affairs of Texas. I think it proper here to state that I had reason to be pleased with the full and frank manner in which his Lordship discussed the affairs in question. As a matter of course, he treated the subject mainly and almost exclusively in reference to British policy and interests.

Some time before this interview with Lord Aberdeen, Mr J. P. Andrews whom I have mentioned in former despatches as being in London on an abolition mission requested me to present him to Mr Addington. After some reflection I consented to do so, the introduction being in no degree official, as I stated to Mr Addington, and as this course put me fairly in possession of the abolition schemes which had already been presented to the British Government. On this occasion I expressed my utter dissent from and opposition to all operations then carrying on in London, having for their object the abolition of Slavery in Texas.

In my interview with Lord Aberdeen on the 20th Instant, I stated that Mr Andrews' coming to London about abolition was his individual act wholly unauthorized by the Government or citizens of Texas; that tho' there might be some individuals in our country disposed to abolish slavery, I had no reason to believe they were numerous; but on the contrary that I had reason to think no disposition to agitate this subject existed either on the part of the Government or any respectable portion of the citizens of Texas. I also stated to Lord Aberdeen that I was informed representations would be sent out to Texas based on statements made by members of the Antislavery Convention who had called on his Lordship touching this matter, to the effect that Her Majesty's Government would afford in some way the means of reimbursing or compensating the slave owners, provided slavery were abolished in our country. I inquired what ground there was for these assertions.

30. Texas secretary of state, later president of Texas.

✦ CHAPTER 9

The Diplomacy,
Politics, and Intrigue
of "Manifest
Destiny": The
Annexation of Texas

His Lordship replied in effect, that it is the well known policy and wish of the British Government to abolish slavery every where; that its abolition in Texas is deemed very desirable and he spoke to this point at some little length, as connected with British policy and British interests and in reference to the United States. He added, there was no disposition on the part of the British Govt to interfere improperly on this subject, and that they would not give the Texian Govt any cause to complain; 'he was not prepared to say whether the British Government would consent hereafter to make such compensation to Texas as would enable the Slaveholders to abolish slavery, the object is deemed so important perhaps they might, though he could not say certainly.' I here remarked to his Lordship, that any compensation received by Texas from a foreign power for the abolition of slavery would be derogatory to our national honor and degrade and disgrace us in the eyes of the world. He observed such things can be so done as not to be offensive etc., but I believe his Lordship was of my opinion. . . .

At the close of the interview I mentioned again to Lord Aberdeen that Texas will not make any change in her institutions concerning slavery. His Lordship requested I would communicate to the Government such opinions as he had expressed, to the exclusion of such as the enthusiastic imaginations of the antislavery conventionists might attribute to him. He inquired whether he should continue to see these persons on this subject. I could not answer his Lordship, as they have no connection with the Govt of Texas.

The British Government greatly desire the abolition of slavery in Texas as a part of their general policy in reference to their colonial and commercial interests and mainly in reference to its future influence on slavery in the United States. I do not attribute to them any sinister purposes towards Texas in this matter; British policy in relation to slavery is declared to the world, and the good or ill consequences to Texas are not taken at all into consideration.

Source 17 from Garrison, ed., "Diplomatic Correspondence of the Republic of Texas," (1908), Vol. 2, pt. 2, p. 222.

17. VanZandt to Jones, October 16, 1843.

I am of opinion, that at no time since the question was first presented to this Government, have there been so many circumstances combining to secure the favorable action of the Senate of the United States. The late declarations of Lord Aberdeen in the British Parliament, in reply to the interrogatories of a certain Noble Lord, show the designs of the British Government in regard to the institutions of the United States through Texas, and make at once, the question, one of vital importance to the slave holding states. The possibility of England's (as many believe) securing an undue influence in Texas, and thereby monopolizing her growing trade, seems to have touched the secret springs of interest so fondly cherished by northern manufacturers, and presented the question in a form hitherto unheeded. The West are intent on the occupation of Oregon, in order to wrest it from the grasping power of Great Britain—it is believed that the interest of the two questions of the annexation of Texas, and the occupation of Oregon can be combined, securing for the latter the south and southeastern votes and for the former some northern and the entire western vote. Those presses which have discussed the matter place it above party grounds and unshackled with party trammels. This I think is highly advantageous for if it were made a strictly party vote, neither of the two great parties have sufficient members to carry it.

Source 18 from James D. Richardson, *A Compilation of the Messages and Papers of the Presidents, 1789–1902* (Washington: Bureau of National Literature and Art, 1903), Vol. 4, pp. 307–312.

18. President John Tyler's Message to the U.S. Senate, April 22, 1844.

To the Senate of the United States:

I transmit herewith, for your approval and ratification, a treaty which I have caused to be negotiated between the United States and Texas, whereby the latter, on the conditions therein set forth, has transferred and conveyed all its right of separate and independent sovereignty and jurisdiction to the United States.

[*The President then mentioned the commercial advantages of such an annexation and briefly reviewed the history of Texas since 1836.*]

This course has been adopted by her without the employment of any sinister measures on the part of this Government. No intrigue has been set on foot to accomplish it. Texas herself wills it, and the Executive of the United States, concurring with her, has seen no sufficient reason to avoid the consummation of an act esteemed to be so desirable by both. It can not be denied that Texas is greatly depressed in her energies by her long-protracted war with Mexico. Under these circumstances it is but natural that she should seek for safety and repose under the protection of some stronger power, and it is equally so

◆ CHAPTER 9

The Diplomacy,
Politics, and Intrigue
of "Manifest
Destiny": The
Annexation of Texas

that her people should turn to the United States, the land of their birth, in the first instance in the pursuit of such protection. She has often before made known her wishes, but her advances have to this time been repelled. The Executive of the United States sees no longer any cause for pursuing such a course. The hazard of now defeating her wishes may be of the most fatal tendency. It might lead, and most probably would, to such an entire alienation of sentiment and feeling as would inevitably induce her to look elsewhere for aid, and force her either to enter into dangerous alliances with other nations, who, looking with more wisdom to their own interests, would, it is fairly to be presumed, readily adopt such expedients; or she would hold out the proffer of discriminating duties in trade and commerce in order to secure the necessary assistance. Whatever step she might adopt looking to this object would prove disastrous in the highest degree to the interest of the whole Union. . . .

[*Tyler then warned that Texas would have to make alliances with other nations if the United States refused to admit it to the Union: ". . . if the boon now tendered to rejected Texas will seek for the friendship of others."*]

To Mexico the Executive is disposed to pursue a course conciliatory in its character and at the same time to render her the most ample justice by conventions and stipulations not inconsistent with the rights and dignity of the Government. It is actuated by no spirit of unjust aggrandizement, but looks only to its own security. It has made known to Mexico at several periods its extreme anxiety to witness the termination of hostilities between that country and Texas. Its wishes, however, have been entirely disregarded. It has ever been ready to urge an adjustment of the dispute upon terms mutually advantageous to both. It will be ready at all times to hear and discuss any claims Mexico may think she has on the justice of the United States and to adjust any that may be deemed to be so on the most liberal terms. There is no desire on the part of the Executive to wound her pride or affect injuriously her interest, but at the same time it can not compromit by any delay in its action the essential interests of the United States. Mexico has no right to ask or expect this of us; we deal rightfully with Texas as an independent power. The war which has been waged for eight years has resulted only in the conviction with all others than herself that Texas can not be reconquered. I can not but repeat the opinion expressed in my message at the opening of Congress that it is time it had ceased. The Executive, while it could not look upon its longer continuance without the greatest uneasiness, has, nevertheless, for all past time preserved a course of strict neutrality. It could not be ignorant of the fact of the exhaustion which a war of so long a duration had produced. Least of all was it ignorant of the anxiety of other powers to induce Mexico to enter into terms of reconciliation with Texas, which, affecting the domestic institutions of Texas, would operate most injuriously upon the United States and might most seriously threaten the existence of this happy Union. Nor could it be unacquainted with the fact that although foreign governments might disavow all design to disturb the relations which exist under the Constitution between these States, yet that one, the most powerful amongst them, had not failed to declare its marked and decided hostility to the chief feature in those relations and its purpose on all suitable occasions to urge upon Mexico the adoption of such a course in negotiating with Texas as to produce the obliteration of that feature from her domestic policy as one of the conditions of her recognition by Mexico as an independent state. The Executive was also aware of the fact that formidable associations of persons, the subjects of foreign powers, existed, who were directing their utmost efforts to the accomplishment of this object. To these conclusions it was inevitably brought by the documents now submitted to the Senate. I repeat, the Executive saw Texas in a state of almost hopeless exhaustion, and the question was narrowed down to the simple proposition whether the United States should accept the boon of annexation upon fair and even liberal terms, or, by refusing to do so, force Texas to seek refuge in the arms of some other power, either through a treaty of alliance, offensive and defensive, or the adoption of some other expedient which might virtually make her tributary to such power and dependent upon it for all future time. The Executive has full reason to believe that such would have been the result without its interposition, and that such will be the result in the event either of unnecessary delay in the ratification or of the rejection of the proposed treaty.

Source 19 from Anson Jones, *Memoranda and Official Correspondence Relating to the Republic of Texas, Its History and Annexation* (Chicago: Rio Grande Press, photocopy of 1859 ed., 1966), pp. 335–336.

19. Jones's note in his diary, no date [1844].

The United States are recovering a little from their alarm. I will have to give them another *scare*. One or two doses of *English* calomel and *French* quinine will have to be administered, and the case will be pretty well out of danger.

✦ CHAPTER 9

The Diplomacy,
Politics, and Intrigue
of "Manifest
Destiny": The
Annexation of Texas

Source 20 from Clyde Wilson, ed., *The Papers of John C. Calhoun*, (Columbia: University of South Carolina Press, 1988), Vol. 18, pp. 274–278.

20. John C. Calhoun[31] to Pakenham, April 18, 1844.

So long as Great Britain confined her policy to the abolition of slavery in her own possessions and colonies, no other country had a right to complain. It belonged to her, exclusively, to determine according to her own views of policy whether it should be done or not. But when she goes beyond, and avows it as her settled policy, and the object of her constant exertions, to abolish it throughout the world, she makes it the duty of all other countries, whose safety or prosperity may be endangered by her policy, to adopt such measures as they may deem necessary for their protection.

It is with still deeper concern the President regards the avowal of Lord Aberdeen of the desire of Great Britain to see slavery abolished in Texas; and, as he infers, is endeavoring, through her diplomacy, to accomplish it, by making the abolition of slavery one of the conditions on which Mexico should acknowledge her independence. It has confirmed his previous impressions as to the policy of Great Britain in reference to Texas, and made it his duty to examine with much care and solicitude, what would be its effects on the prosperity and safety of the United States should she succeed in her endeavors. The investigation has resulted in the settled conviction that it would be difficult for Texas, in her actual condition, to resist what she desires, without supposing the influence and exertions of Great Britain would be extended beyond the limits assigned by Lord Aberdeen; and that, if Texas could not resist, the consummation of the object of her desire would endanger both the safety and prosperity of the Union. Under this conviction, it is felt to be the imperious duty of the Federal Government, the common representative and protector of the States of this Union, to adopt, in self-defence, the most effectual measures to defeat it. . . .

It is well known that Texas has long desired to be annexed to this Union; that her People, at the time of the adoption of her constitution, expressed by an almost unanimous vote, her desire to that effect; and that she has never ceased to desire it, as the most certain means of promoting her safety and prosperity. The United States have heretofore declined to meet her wishes; but the time has now arrived when they can no longer refuse consistent with their own security and peace, and the sacred obligation imposed by their constitutional compact, for mutual defence and protection. . . .[32]

31. A major figure in American politics from the War of 1812 to his death in 1850. In 1844–1845, he was U.S. secretary of state. The April 18, 1844 letter to Pakenham was made public and caused a firestorm of controversy.
32. The annexation treaty was still before the Senate. It was defeated on June 8, 1844.

It belongs not to this Government to question whether the former have decided wisely or not; and if it did, the Undersigned would not regard this as the proper occasion to discuss the subject. He does not, however, deem it irrelevant to state, that, if the experience of more than half a century is to decide, it would be neither humane nor wise in them to change their policy. The census and other authentic documents show that, in all instances in which the States have changed the former relation between the two races, the condition of the African, instead of being improved, has become worse. They have invariably sunk into vice and pauperism, accompanied by the bodily and mental inflictions incident thereto—deafness, blindness, insanity and idiocy, to a degree without example; while, in all other States which have retained the ancient relation between them, they have improved greatly in every respect—in number, comfort, intelligence, and morals, as the following facts, taken from such sources will serve to illustrate. . . .

[*Here Calhoun singled out the free states of Maine and Massachusetts, claiming that in both states African Americans had declined both physically and socially since being freed.*]

It may, in truth, be assumed as a maxim, that two races differing so greatly, and in so many respects, cannot possibly exist together in the same country, where their numbers are nearly equal, without the one being subjected to the other. Experience has proved, that the existing relation in which the one is subjected to the other in the slave-holding States, is consistent with the peace and safety of both, with great improvement to the inferior; while the same experience proves, that the relation which it is the desire and object of Great Britain to substitute in its stead, in this and all other countries, under the plausible name of the abolition of slavery, would, (if it did not destroy the inferior by conflicts to which it would lead,) reduce it to the extremes of vice and wretchedness. In this view of the subject, it may be asserted that what is called Slavery, is, in reality, a political institution, essential to the peace, safety, and prosperity of those States of the Union in which it exists. Without, then, controverting the wisdom and humanity of the policy of Great Britain, so far as her own possessions are concerned, it may be safely affirmed, without reference to the means by which it would be effected, that, could she succeed in accomplishing in the United States, what she avows it to be her desire, and the object of her constant exertions to effect throughout the world, so far from being wise or humane, she would involve in the greatest calamity the whole country, and especially the race which it is the avowed object of her exertions to benefit.

✦ CHAPTER 9

The Diplomacy,
Politics, and Intrigue
of "Manifest
Destiny": The
Annexation of Texas

Source 21 from Jones, *Memoranda and Official Correspondence*, p. 343.

21. Charles H. Raymond to Jones, April 24, 1844.

I have just been informed that Mr. Calhoun has, in his letter to the Senate, placed the question almost solely on the ground of British interference with the institution of slavery, and presents this as the grand argument for the measure. Such a position may answer with the South, but it will only create and strengthen opposition North and West. Indeed I heard this morning that the views of Mr. Calhoun had brought the Ohio Senators into the opposition. They say if this Government rest the policy of the measure upon the alone fact, as Calhoun's letter does, of the question of slavery, they cannot, in justice to the State they represent, and the interests of even the whole confederacy, vote for the treaty. I cannot suppose, however, that the Senate will be restricted in their views, when deciding upon this treaty, to the arguments of Mr. Calhoun or the President, yet they may be influenced adversely by them.

Source 22 from Benton, *Thirty Years' View*, p. 589.

22. Benton on a "British Abolitionist Conspiracy."

[*Benton returns to his recollections, begun in Source 12, of a private citizen from Maryland who alleged that there was an abolitionist plot on the part of the British government and the denial of such a conspiracy by Sir Richard Pakenham, British minister in Washington, and Lord Aberdeen, British secretary of state.*]

Then it was taken up, and, on the 18th day of April, was elaborately answered by Mr. Calhoun in a despatch to the British minister—not to argue the point of the truth of the Maryland citizen's private letter—but to argue quite off upon a new text. It so happened that Lord Aberdeen—after the fullest contradiction of the imputed design, and the strongest assurances of non-interference with any slavery policy either of the United States or of Texas—did not stop there; but, like many able men who are not fully aware of the virtue of stopping when they are done, went on to add something more, of no necessary connection or practical application to the subject—a mere general abstract declaration on the subject of slavery; on which Mr. Calhoun took position, and erected a superstructure of alarm which did more to embarrass the opponents of the treaty and to inflame the country, than all other matters put together. This cause for this new alarm was found in the superfluous declaration, "*That Great Britain desires, and is constantly exerting herself to pro-*

cure the general abolition of slavery throughout the world." This general declaration, although preceded and followed by reiterated assurances of non-interference with slavery in the United States, and no desire for any dominant influence in Texas, were seized upon as an open avowal of a design to abolish slavery every where. These assurances were all disregarded. Our secretary established himself upon the naked declaration, stripped of all qualifications and denials. . . . So, making the declaration of Lord Aberdeen the text of a most elaborate reply, he took up the opposite ground (support and propagation of slavery), arguing it generally in relation to the world, and specially in relation to the United States and Texas; and placing the annexation so fully upon that ground, that all its supporters must be committed to it.

Source 23 from Garrison, ed., "Diplomatic Correspondence of the Republic of Texas" (1908), Vol. 2, pt. 1, p. 282.

23. Houston to VanZandt and Henderson,[33] May 17, 1844.

Gentlemen,

Intelligence which your last communications brought to me, seems adverse to the calculations which were made when Genl. Henderson was accredited to the U.S. If truly that Govt. is not disposed to consummate the plan of annexation, it would seem useless for him longer to remain at the Court of Washington. Whatever the desires of this Govt. or the people are, or might have been in relation to annexation, I am satisfied that they are not ambitious at this time, nor will ever be again to be seen in the attitude of a bone of contention, to be worried or gnawed by the influence of conflicting politicians. The views of the Executive of this country, as well as its citizens, were fairly presented in a willingness to become annexed to the U.S. And though the advantages presented to the U.S. were incalculably greater than those resulting to Texas, she was willing to stand the hazard of the adventure.

The statesmen of that country appear to be united in opinions adverse to our admission into the Union of the North. We must therefore regard ourselves as a nation to *remain forever separate.* It would be unpleasant for us to enter into a community as a member where we should be regarded ungraciously by either of the political parties. Texas alone can well be sustained, and no matter what sincere desire we may have entertained for a connection

33. By 1844, Henderson had been appointed as the Texas agent to Britain and France.

◆ CHAPTER 9

The Diplomacy,
Politics, and Intrigue
of "Manifest
Destiny": The
Annexation of Texas

with that Govt., and the affectionate enthusiasm that has existed in this towards it, we will be compelled to reconcile ourselves to our present condition, or to assume such attitude towards other countries, as will certainly look to our Independence. This can be accomplished if the U.S. will carry out the pledges which they have already given. The compromittal of our national honor I cannot apprehend, nor would I entertain any proposition which could be adverse to our character as an Independent Nation; but Texas can now command interests which will require no such sacrifice. We must act!!

Source 24 from Adams, *British Diplomatic Correspondence*, pp. 405–406.

24. Aberdeen to Elliot, December 31, 1844.

These Papers will put you in possession of the line of conduct which Her Majesty's Government have pursued and intend to pursue both with regard to Mexico and to the United States, with reference to Texas. That line of conduct may be summed up in a few words. It is to urge Mexico by every available argument, and in every practicable Manner, to recognize without delay the Independence of Texas, as the only rational course to be taken for securing the real interests of Mexico, to which Country, the Annexation of Texas to the United States would be ruinous, while, an [sic] the other hand, we have carefully abstained from any ostensible Act which could influence the wild and dangerous spirit which, partly from National, but more from party purposes, has been roused and sustained by demagogues in the United States, in favour of the Annexation of Texas, and which wanted but the evidence of active interference on the part of Great Britain to be kindled at once into a flame.

This policy we propose still to pursue, because, under present Circumstances, and until we can see our way more clearly with reference to the intentions of Mexico, as well as to those of the United States, under the altered circumstances which the Election of a new President may exhibit, we think a passive course, or rather a course of observation, the most prudent, and the least likely to involve us in difficulties with Mexico, or with the United States. . . .

Her Majesty's Government desire, therefore, that you should observe the greatest Caution in all your dealings and Conversations with the Authorities of Texas, and that you should in no way Commit your Government to any line of active policy with regard to that Country.

We have undoubtedly every reason to hope and believe that the present ruling Authorities in Texas will be found favourable to the Independence of their

Country. Mr. Anson Jones has the reputation of a Man of worth, judgment, and high minded feelings; and Mr. Ashbel Smith, who seems to be designated for the post of Secretary of State, is, to our personal knowledge, a man of excellent capacity, calm reflection, and holding sound opinions respecting the position and interests of his Country. In these two Gentlemen, therefore we could place entire confidence. But we must always remember that the tide of public opinion may be too strong for them to withstand, especially if the pressure from without be, as it is not unlikely to be, applied with great force and craft.

Source 25 from Pletcher, *The Diplomacy of Annexation*, p. 177.

25. John Tod[34] to Robert Walker,[35] on Houston's position on the annexation of Texas by the United States, December 23, 1844.

When *sober,* he was for annexation; but when *drunk,* or in liquor, he would express himself strongly against the measure.

Source 26 from Wilson, ed., *The Papers of John C. Calhoun,* Vol. 20, p. 544.

26. Calhoun to William R. King,[36] December 13, 1844.

If England ["should" *interlined*] consummate her grand scheme of commercial monopoly, disguised under the guarb [*sic*] of abolition, it would not only subject the commerce of the world to her control, but would, on all that portion of this continent lying south of Mason & Dixon line, end in a war between races of the most deadly & desolating character; to be terminated in a large portion in the ascendency of the lowest & most ["savage" *interlined*] of the races [*one word or partial word interlined and then canceled*] & a return to barbarism. England from her position, would necessarily become the patron of the coulered races ["of all hues" *interlined*], negroes, indians & mixed, ag[ai]nst the white, which unless France and the contin[ent]al powers, generally, ["but" *interlined*] especially her should become the supporter of the ["latter" *canceled and then interlined*], would give them the superiority.

34. U.S. Army captain and often a diplomatic courier.
35. U.S. senator from Mississippi; a pro-annexation Democrat.
36. U.S. minister to France.

✦ CHAPTER 9

The Diplomacy,
Politics, and Intrigue
of "Manifest
Destiny": The
Annexation of Texas

Source 27 from Adams, *British Diplomatic Correspondence*, pp. 509–510.

27. Aberdeen to Elliot, July 3, 1845.

The policy which Her Majesty's Government have pursued with respect to Texas and Mexico has been perfectly clear and open. It has never required any concealment. We naturally desired to preserve the independence of Texas, with which State we had entered into engagements, and concluded Treaties, but we also considered that the welfare of Mexico required that She should, if possible, be preserved from immediate contact with the United States.

We thought it probable that upon such separation the peace of the North American Continent, and therefore of the World, might materially depend. We accordingly employed our efforts, but openly and fairly, to accomplish this object. We looked upon it's [*sic*] furtherance as no less desirable for the United States than for Mexico, since we do not believe that the aggrandizement of the United States will in any way contribute to their strength, or to the advancement of the material interests of their people. On the contrary, we believe that such aggrandizement will be found to have a precisely opposite effect, and that it will eventually excite discord in the bosom of that great Country. But such dissention could scarcely fail to act injuriously upon British interests, considering the vast amount of British Capital which is engaged in Commerce with the United States. Our well understood national interests require that the United States should remain peaceful and united amongst themselves; but the system of extention of their territory which they are now pursuing seems to us to place their internal peace and union, as well as the peace of the whole Continent in jeopardy. For that reason therefore, as well as for those above pointed out, we have constantly sought to uphold the independence of Texas. But in pursuing this policy we have no specified British interests in view, apart from general interests, for we do not conceive that any material or direct British interest is involved in the independence of Texas. Had it been so, it would undoubtedly have been the duty of Her Majesty's Government to promote such interests by every fair means in their power; but we should still have pursued that object as a clear and obvious publick obligation, without the smallest concealment.

Questions to Consider

Years ago, distinguished historian Claude Van Tyne remarked that what *actually* was true was less important than what people *thought was true*. It would be well to keep Van Tyne's observation in mind in this chapter, for whether there *actually was* a British conspiracy to block the expansion of slavery may have been less important than whether Americans *believed* there was such a conspiracy.

How would you go about determining whether such a conspiratorial plot actually existed? To begin with, separate the British sources (1, 2, 4, 9–11, 24, and 27) from the other evidence in the Evidence section of this chapter. Is there any evidence of British abolitionist intrigue? How much weight should you give to Britain's denials of such a plot? to Americans who claimed there was no such plan? to American accusations that there was such a secret plan? Finally, does the evidence suggest *any other reasons besides abolition* that Britain would oppose and try to block the unification of the United States and Texas? What role, if any, did the Texas and Mexican debt to British investors play in that nation's foreign policy? After examining and analyzing all the evidence, how would you answer the questions above? How would you prove your opinions?

Almost immediately, you will recognize that there were at least two other possible conspiracies: (1) a possible plan by President John Tyler, Secretary of State John C. Calhoun, Virginia congressman Thomas Walker Gilmer, and others to push annexation through the U.S. Senate by frightening senators into believing that Great Britain was engaging in an abolitionist plot, and (2) a plan by some Texas leaders to scare the U.S. Senate into approving annexation by warning that an independent Texas might be forced to ally with some other nations for support and commerce.

What evidence suggests that there was a conspiracy hatched by Tyler, Calhoun, Gilmer, and others? Or did these men sincerely believe that there was such a British plot? Is there any evidence to suggest they knew there was no such scheme?

As to the possible Texas intrigue, if it did in fact exist, what was its purpose? What roles did Sam Houston, Anson Jones, and other Texans play? To what extent do you think their warnings to the United States were sincere? How would you use the evidence to support your points?

Now return to the central questions in this chapter. How would you answer *them*? How would you use the available evidence to support your answers?

◆ CHAPTER 9

The Diplomacy,
Politics, and Intrigue
of "Manifest
Destiny": The
Annexation of Texas

◆

Epilogue

On June 8, 1844, President John Tyler's gamble backfired. In a strictly party and sectional vote, the United States Senate voted 16–35 to reject the annexation treaty.[37] Almost immediately the president announced his intention of submitting to both houses of Congress a joint resolution approving annexation, a move which, Tyler claimed, would have the same authority as a treaty.

Yet Congress waited, in large part because the nation was beginning to focus its attention on the upcoming 1844 presidential election. Many legislators hoped that the election would serve as a mandate either in favor of or opposed to westward expansion, especially given that the Democratic Party's nominee turned out to be pro-expansionist James Knox Polk of Tennessee and the Whigs' nominee was lukewarm expansionist Henry Clay of Kentucky.[38]

The contest turned out to be one of the closest presidential elections in American history. With over 2.6 million votes cast for either Polk or Clay, Polk's popular vote total was a bare 38,000 votes more than Clay's. Indeed, the popular vote was so close in New York, Ohio, Michigan, and Maryland that the Liberty Party's James G. Birney held the balance in those states. Polk's margin in New York (with 36 electoral votes) was only 6,000 votes. A shift in just over half of those 6,000 votes would have given the election to Clay.

Although the presidential election was far from an unqualified mandate in favor of westward expansion, many congressmen fully understood that the new president would push hard for the annexation of Texas. Thus both houses of Congress surrendered to the inevitable and approved the joint resolution, albeit by very close margins: the House of Representatives passed the resolution 120–98 on January 25, 1845, and the Senate followed suit on February 27, 1845 by the razor-thin vote of 27–25. President Tyler signed the joint resolution on March 1, three days before he was to leave office. Mexico, which had never recognized Texan independence, immediately broke relations with the United States.[39]

What roles any conspiratorial plots or rumors of such played in the Senate's June 1844 rejection of the treaty or the early 1845 passage of the joint resolution is impossible to know. It appears that the British government was engaged in no such abolitionist plot, although it would have preferred that Texas remain independent. Also, some British agents and officials in the field, such as Charles Elliot, might have

---

37. For the partisan nature of the Senate's vote, see VanZandt and Henderson to Jones, June 10, 1844, in "Diplomatic Correspondence of the Republic of Texas," (1907), Vol. 2, pt. 1, p. 285.

38. Early in the election campaign Clay had written a letter opposing annexation. His later attempts to backtrack on that letter were only partially successful.

39. For the joint resolution, see *The Public Statutes at Large of the United States of America* (Boston: Little and Brown, 1850), Vol. 5, pp. 797–798.

participated in some schemes unbeknownst to their government in London. As for Tyler, Gilmer, Calhoun, and others who tried to alarm Americans with dark warnings of a British abolitionist conspiracy, we will never know for certain whether they were sincere in their fears or merely manufacturing a bogus British plot to force Texas's annexation. When it came to Texas officials, however, it appears evident that they were willing to frighten Americans into approving annexation by threatening to seek an alliance with Great Britain. What are your opinions regarding these plots or rumors of plots? How would you prove your hypotheses?

In a last-ditch effort to block annexation, the Republic of Mexico, possibly encouraged by Britain, announced that it would acknowledge the independence of Texas on the condition that Texas remain independent of the United States. That desperate ploy was to no avail: on July 4, 1845, the Texas Congress voted unanimously to accept the United States' offer of annexation.[40]

Even before his inauguration, Polk confided to a friend and future member of his Cabinet that one of the goals of his administration would be the acquisition of California, at the time another province of Mexico. Great Britain earlier had shown some interest in California, and as Lord Aberdeen stated in a December 31, 1844, communication, Britain considered it "a matter of serious importance . . . that California, if it shake off the rule of Mexico, should not place itself under the protection of any other Power whose supremacy might prove injurious to British Interests," a thinly-veiled reference to the United States. But Polk was rebuffed by Mexico when he offered to purchase California (referred to at the time as "Upper California"). Frustrated by Mexico's refusal, the president in effect manipulated Mexico into firing on United States troops in the disputed area, along the south Texas border between the Nueces and Rio Grande rivers. The president then announced to Congress (on May 11, 1846) that war had broken out when Mexican troops "have at last invaded our territory and shed the blood of our fellow-citizens on our own soil.[41]" The war lasted approximately a year and a half, and the United States' "manifest destiny" in North America was fulfilled. Yet the sectional tensions that had delayed the annexation of Texas grew even stronger, as proslavery and antislavery advocates argued over whether slavery would be permitted to follow the flag westward. Only a horrific war settled that question.

For many years, the British had rec-

40. For the last-ditch effort, see G. W. Terrell to Ashbel Smith, May 9, 1845, in "Diplomatic Correspondence of the Republic of Texas," (1908), Vol. 2, pt. 3, p. 1190.

41. For early British interest in California, see Source 9. On California, see Aberdeen to Barron, December 31, 1844, in Adams, *British Interests and Activities in Texas,* p. 249. One diplomat in the Tyler administration claimed that "it will be worth a war of twenty years to prevent England from acquiring [California]," a risk that Lord Aberdeen was unwilling to take. See Andrew F. Rolle, *California: A History* (New York: Thomas Y. Crowell Co., 2nd Ed., 1969), p. 195. For Polk's war message, see Richardson, *Messages and Papers of the Presidents,* Vol. 4, pp. 437–442.

◆ CHAPTER 9

The Diplomacy,
Politics, and Intrigue
of "Manifest
Destiny": The
Annexation of Texas

ognized the potential value of conducting business in Mexico and, after the Texas Revolution of 1836, in the new Republic of Texas as well.[42] Not only did private investors seek profits by purchasing Mexican government bonds and investing in Mexican commerce and extractive industries, but the British government knew full well that the United States soon would be a major commercial and industrial rival. An independent Texas would block United States expansion, thereby cutting off American access to Pacific ports and the commerce of Asia.

And yet, Great Britain had a huge empire to oversee, one that within a few decades would expand into Africa. An anticolonial rebellion had broken out in Canada in 1837, and some of India's native potentates were growing increasingly restive (the Sepoy Mutiny would erupt in 1857). Therefore, a war with the expansion-minded United States was to be avoided (did the *threat* of such a conflict offer the United States still another diplomatic card to play?). Thus, in spite of the hopes of British investors and some British diplomats, Great Britain decided to remain on the sidelines and concentrate its efforts and power elsewhere.

As for the British bondholders, most of them came to realize that they had made poor investments. Between 1837 and 1846, they received only about one-third of what Mexico had promised to repay, and as late as 1883, the Mexican government still owed British bondholders approximately £15 million. Several schemes were hatched, but by 1920, the heirs of the original bondholders still were owed over 76 million pesos.[43]

Texas formally became the twenty-eighth state on December 29, 1845. Throughout the state's history, however, oftentimes Texans have thought of themselves as unique, different from other states in some indefinable ways. So pronounced has this impulse become at times that one author referred to Texans as "Super Americans."

For his part, Anson Jones, the former Massachusetts physician who became the last president of the Republic of Texas before its annexation, became embittered over his loss of power. In an effort at a political comeback, Jones wrote his memoirs, sometimes stretching the truth (was he *really* for annexation or against it?). Disappointed and disconsolate, he took his own life in 1858.

42. See an early parliamentary debate in *Hansard's Parliamentary Debates*, Third Series (London: T. C. Hansard, 1836), Vol. 35, esp. pp. 931–934.

43. Margaret L. Bennett, "British Interests in Mexico, 1830–1845" (unpublished M.A. thesis, University of California, 1930), pp. 15, 52, 56; Edgar Turlington, *Mexico and her Foreign Creditors* (New York: Columbia University Press, 1930), esp. pp. 197, 207–208, 335.

10

"No More Pint o' Salt for Me":[1] The Port Royal Experiment, 1861–1865

The Problem

On November 7, 1861, a United States naval squadron under the command of Commodore S. F. DuPont sailed into Port Royal Sound, South Carolina, and reduced the two Confederate batteries to rubble. Nervous white planters and their families gathered to watch the bombardment and, when it became clear that the Confederate forts would fall, made ready to abandon the islands along the South Carolina coast.

For their part, the slaves on the Sea Island plantations were fully aware of what was taking place. When one black child mistook the ships' guns for thunder, his mother comforted him, saying, "Son, dat ain't no t'under, dat Yankee come to gib you freedom."[2]

The original objective of the United States Navy was to capture and occupy the Sea Islands for use as a base of operations for the Union blockade of the Confederacy. But when Commodore DuPont's squadron leveled the rebel forts and when Union soldiers the next day began to occupy the major Sea Islands, all but four of the approximately two thousand whites fled to the mainland, leaving around ten thousand slaves to shift for themselves. In addition, once slaves on the South Carolina mainland learned of the "Yankee" occupation, many of them also began to melt away from the plantations and head for the Union lines.

This situation in the Sea Islands raised a number of important ques-

1. The "pint o' salt" refers to a slave's rations. See the slave song "Many Thousand Go," in William Francis Allen, Charles Pickard Ware, and Lucy McKim Garrison, *Slave Songs of the United States* (Gretna, La.: Pelican Publishing Co., 1998 [orig. pub. 1867]), p. 48.
2. *The War of the Rebellion: Official Records* (Washington: Government Printing Office, 1885), series 1, Vol. 6, p. 6. For the slave

mother, see Willie Lee Rose, *Rehearsal for Reconstruction: The Port Royal Experiment* (Indianapolis: Bobbs-Merrill, 1964), p. 12. For a report on the Federal bombardment, see Frank Moore, ed., *The Rebellion Record* (New York: G. P. Putnam, 1864), supplement to Vol. 1, pp. 192–197.

✦ CHAPTER 10

"No More Pint o'
Salt for Me":
The Port Royal
Experiment,
1861–1865

tions for the United States government. To begin with, what should be done with the roughly two hundred cotton plantations, many of which were sizable land holdings? If the planters themselves were considered traitors to the United States, should their lands be confiscated (as was the property of Tories during the American Revolution)? And if the lands *were* to be confiscated, who should own them?

Questions regarding the slaves were even thornier. What was their status after Union occupation? Should they be freed, or should they be held as slaves in the hope that the Sea Island planters would abandon the Confederacy to reclaim their property? Or was there some middle path between freedom and slavery? And with the planters gone, should the blacks continue to work the cotton crop, and if so, under whose supervision or guidance? Finally, in the northern states African Americans had volunteered for service in the Union Army, although those offers had been rejected.[3] Should Sea Island blacks be used in the capacity of soldiers?

Thus, from the occupation of the Sea Islands late in 1861 until the end of the war and even beyond, the debate over the institution of slavery that had played such an important role in bringing on the Civil War reached a new dimension. There on the coastal islands of South Carolina was the opportunity for many people to conduct an experiment to test their theories about slavery, emancipation, and African Americans. If African Americans were granted their freedom, were they capable of maintaining it? Would they be productive workers outside the slave system? Could they be educated to become good and law-abiding citizens? Could they be responsible landowners, voters, soldiers? As you can see from these questions, notions of black inferiority were not confined to the southern states. Indeed, even some abolitionists possessed them.

Your task in this chapter is to examine and analyze the evidence concerning the "Port Royal Experiment" so as to answer the following central questions:

1. Would the Sea Island blacks be able to use the educational, economic, and military opportunities made available to them to become knowledgeable, responsible, and productive citizens of the United States?
2. Would they be able to dispel the widespread prejudices and perceptions that whites, North and South alike, had of slaves?

The late historian of the American South C. Vann Woodward called the Port Royal Experiment a "dress rehearsal for Reconstruction acted out on the stage neatly defined by the Sea Islands of South Carolina."[4] Thus, according to Woodward and his former student Willie Lee Rose, what would take place in the South after the Civil War was thought about, discussed, and argued over *during* that momentous conflict. In what ways was the Port Royal Experiment a "rehearsal for Reconstruction"?

3. For African American volunteers, see James M. McPherson, *The Negro's Civil War: How American Negroes Felt and Acted During the War for the Union* (New York: Pantheon Books, 1965), pp. 33, 162.

4. Rose, *Rehearsal for Reconstruction*, p. xv.

Background

The Sea Islands is a string of over seventy-five islands that runs approximately 175 miles along the coastline from present-day Georgetown, South Carolina, to Golden Isles, Georgia, separated from the mainland by a series of bays, rivers, and marshes. By the mid-1500s, both Spain and France showed considerable interest in the islands, the Spanish looking for protective havens for their treasure fleets and the French hoping to establish a trading post on the shore of the deep-water Port Royal Sound. Efforts by both Spain and France to found permanent settlements in the area proved unsuccessful, however.

About a century later, England also began to show some interest in the Sea Islands. In 1663, English sea captain William Hilton sailed into Port Royal Sound and claimed the island that later bore his name (Hilton Head) and the surrounding mainland for England. The first permanent settlement, near present-day Charleston, South Carolina, was established in 1670.

Earlier, in the 1620s, the English had begun seizing islands in the West Indies. At first settlers attempted to imitate Virginia's success by growing tobacco and using indentured servants from England for labor. The collapse of tobacco prices,[5] however, prompted the planters to shift from raising tobacco to growing sugar cane, a transformation that resulted in an economic and social revolution in the British West Indies. Because sugar production required significant capital investment, small farmers were gradually forced out and the islands increasingly belonged to large-scale planters, not a few of them absentee owners (by 1680, 175 men, a bare 7 percent of all the property owners on Barbados, owned over half the land). At the same time, West Indian planters stopped recruiting white indentured servants and began importing slaves from Africa (by 1680, Barbados was roughly 75 percent black). Profits were staggering, with Barbados alone in 1670 producing approximately 65 percent of all the sugar consumed in England. Later, in his famous *Wealth of Nations,* Adam Smith wrote that the "profits of a sugar plantation in any of our West Indian colonies are generally much greater than those of any other cultivation that is known either in Europe or America."

Thus, it is understandable that early South Carolina planters, many of them immigrants from Barbados, attempted to duplicate West Indian planters' fabulous wealth by raising sugar on large plantations with African slave labor. Results proved disappointing, however, for sugar cane did not grow well in South Carolina soil. But rice did. By 1710, planters were exporting around 400,000 pounds of rice. A decade later, they had quadrupled production and by 1720 had quadrupled it again. Plantations were large and the labor was provided by slaves, 80 percent of whom came directly from Africa. By 1720, 67 percent of South Carolina's population consisted of slaves, a proportion that, in the eyes of whites, required an especially rigid and severe slave system not

5. See Chapter 3.

◆ CHAPTER 10
"No More Pint o'
Salt for Me":
The Port Royal
Experiment,
1861–1865

unlike that practiced by the British in the West Indies.[6]

The continual importation of slaves from Africa (two-thirds of whom were male) and the physical separation from the mainland were responsible for the emergence of a distinct culture among the slaves of the Sea Islands, a culture that was a mixture of strains from Africa and Europe. For example, whereas slaves on the mainland generally accepted Christianity, African Americans on the Sea Islands resisted conversion during the colonial period, and when they finally did become Christians after 1740, their religion was a melding of Western Christianity and traditional African religious forms, music, and beliefs. Whites who attended slaves' religious services often found the experience extremely disturbing.

Even more dramatic was the evolution of the slaves' language, known as Gullah, a language that combined English vocabulary with West African grammar and pronunciation. To white visitors, Sea Island slaves' speech was virtually indecipherable.[7]

The Revolutionary War took a heavy

toll on the Sea Islands after 1778, when the British altered their strategy and concentrated their attention on the southern colonies. After forcing Charleston to surrender and incarcerating Patriot leaders on prison ships, British troops laid waste to many Sea Island and mainland plantations and Tories wreaked vengeance on Patriots who had persecuted them. Indeed, it took years for the Sea Islands and Low Country South Carolina to recover from the War of Independence.

Once independence had been achieved, Sea Island planters encountered serious economic problems. Much of the rice cultivation was intended to feed the slaves in the British West Indies. Now outside the protective arms of the British Empire, American rice no longer could be shipped to British colonies in the West Indies. Similarly, the indigo crop that Sea Island planters also raised was no longer profitable, because British government bounties to indigo planters ceased to be available and the British were turning to other plants to produce the dye for which indigo was famous. Thus, Sea Island planters once again had a plantation system and large numbers of slaves but were without a profitable crop to raise.

In 1786, cotton was first introduced to the Sea Islands, brought from the Bahama Islands. The climate and soil of the Sea Islands were ideal for growing long-staple cotton, a variety from which the cotton seeds could easily be separated by feeding it through rollers. William Elliott, a planter on Hilton Head, grew the first successful cotton crop on the Sea Islands. By the Civil War, approximately 5,500 acres in the

---

6. Robert M. Weir, *Colonial South Carolina* (Millwood, N.Y.: KTO Press, 1983), pp. 145–146.
7. On slaves' resistance to conversion, see *ibid.,* p. 185. For Gullah, see William S. Pollitzer, *The Gullah People and Their African Heritage* (Athens, Ga.: University of Georgia Press, 1999); Betty M. Kuyk, *African Voices in the African American Heritage* (Bloomington, Ind.: Indiana University Press, 2003). On slaves' religion, see Rupert Sargent Holland, ed., *Letters and Diary of Laura M. Towne* (New York: Negro Universities Press, 1969 [orig. pub. 1912]), pp. 20–21; Brenda Stevenson, ed., *The Journals of Charlotte Forten Grimke* (New York: Oxford University Press, 1988), pp. 393, 422; Charles Nordhoff, "The Freemen of South Carolina," *New York Evening Post,* March 26 and April 15, 1863.

Sea Islands were devoted to cotton production, raising roughly 730,000 pounds of long-staple cotton. The British textile industry's almost insatiable demand for cotton accelerated the shift to cotton cultivation and kept cotton prices high.[8]

Because cotton was such a labor-intensive crop, more slaves were required. Sea Island cotton planters petitioned the South Carolina state legislature to reopen the African slave trade, and when that body agreed to do so, the importation of slaves shot up dramatically. On St. Helena Island alone, between 1800 and 1810 the slave population increased 86 percent, and by 1860 slaves outnumbered whites on that island by approximately six to one. In 1862, special U.S. Treasury agent Edward L. Pierce estimated that the average Sea Island plantation had around 40 slaves, with the largest plantation having 260 slaves. According to Pierce, only seven other counties in the United States exceeded Beaufort County (in which the Sea Islands were located) in the proportion of the population that were slaves.[9]

By the nineteenth century, Sea Island cotton planters were among the most opulent of the South's slaveholder elite. One northern newspaper referred to the Sea Islands as "the exclusive home of the most exclusive few of that most exclusive aristocracy." The St. Helena Episcopal Church (founded in 1724) was reputed to have "as high a concentration of aristocracy per pew as gathered anywhere along the South Atlantic." Indeed, if cotton was king, these men and women were its princes and princesses.[10]

As noted earlier, the rapid capture of the Sea Islands presented several problems for the United States government. According to General Thomas W. Sherman, "hordes of . . . disaffected blacks" were pillaging the "beautiful estates of the planters." Food and winter clothing for the slaves were in especially short supply, and Sherman appealed to northern charitable organizations to send both as quickly as possible. And as slaves from plantations on the mainland learned of the United States' capture of the Sea Islands, an increasing number of slaves from the mainland slipped away from their plantations and headed for the Sea Islands in search of freedom and opportunity.

In command of the Sea Islands was General Sherman, a native of Rhode Island, a member of the 1836 class of the United States Military Academy, and a moderate abolitionist. Almost immediately, Sherman set to work attempting to improve the desperate situation in

8. Guion Girffis Johnson, *A Social History of the Sea Islands* (New York: Negro Universities Press, 1969 [orig. pub. 1930]), p. 23. Statistics are from Edward L. Pierce to U.S. Sec. of the Treasury Salmon P. Chase, Feb. 3, 1862 and June 2, 1862 in Moore, *Rebellion Record,* supplement to Vol. 1, pp. 309, 318. Short-staple cotton, grown on mainland and upland South Carolina, was not profitable until Eli Whitney invented the "cotton engine," or "gin."
9. Edward L. Pierce, "The Negroes at Port Royal, S.C., Report of the Government Agent, Feb. 3, 1862," in Moore, *Rebellion Record,* supplement to Vol. 1, pp. 302–315, esp. 303, 309; Pierce, "Second Report, June 2, 1862," in *ibid.,* pp. 315–323, esp. 316; Johnson, *Sea Islands,* pp. 37–38, 44, 106. Of the seven counties exceeding Beaufort in percentage of slave popu-

lation, one was in South Carolina, three were in Mississippi, and three were in Louisiana.
10. Quoted in Rose, *Rehearsal for Reconstruction,* pp. xvi–xvii, 7.

◆ CHAPTER 10

"No More Pint o'
Salt for Me":
The Port Royal
Experiment,
1861–1865

which the islands' blacks found themselves. Appealing to northern antislavery societies for assistance, within a year 35,829 books and pamphlets, 91,834 pieces of clothing, 5,895 yards of cloth, and $3,000 worth of farm implements and seed had arrived in the Sea Islands.[11]

Sherman also recognized that if blacks ever would be able to gain their freedom, they would need education to retain it. South Carolina slave codes prohibited teaching slaves to read and write, so the African Americans of the Sea Islands, though not unintelligent, were almost universally illiterate. Sherman therefore appealed to abolitionists in Boston, New York, and Philadelphia to recruit teachers to establish schools throughout the Sea Islands for black adults and children alike. Soon thereafter, 53 volunteers arrived, 35 of them from Boston. Most were young, well educated, from wealthy families, and fiercely idealistic. As Laura Towne, one of the teachers explained, "We have come to do antislavery work. . . . [N]ever did a vessel bear a colony on a nobler mission, not even the Mayflower." By mid-1862, approximately 2,500 children and many times that number of adults were enrolled in the 30 schools established in the Sea Islands throughout the war.[12]

Sherman faced two other questions: the status of African Americans on the Sea Islands and how they would be organized to work the cotton crop that some federal government officials thought should be sold to help finance the war as well as operations in the Sea Islands. For a number of reasons, early in the war President Abraham Lincoln resisted the abolition of slavery, going so far as to countermand emancipation proclamations by two of his own generals (in Missouri and South Carolina). And yet, when the Union Army began to push into the South, the question arose as to the legal status of African Americans in the areas controlled by U.S. troops. In late May 1861, Major General Benjamin Butler ruled that some slaves within the Union lines near Fortress Monroe in Virginia were "contraband"—that is, material used by a belligerent to make war that therefore may be legally confiscated by the opposing force. Generally meant to refer to armaments, ammunition, and so on, Butler expanded the definition of "contraband" to include human beings who were working for the Confederacy (or for someone loyal to the Confederacy). Sherman borrowed the concept from Butler, thus placing African Americans on the Sea Islands in a legal status of neither slave nor free.[13]

11. Benjamin Quarles, *The Negro in the Civil War* (New York: Russell & Russell, 1953), p. 125; *First Annual Report of the National Freedman's Relief Association, New York, February 19, 1863*, copy in the American Antiquarian Society, Worcester, Mass., p. 2.
12. On slave codes, see Rose, *Rehearsal for Reconstruction*, p. 86. For teachers, see *ibid.,* p. 43; Quarles, *Negro in the Civil War,* p. 124. On the slaves' intelligence, one teacher remarked that 10 of his 135 pupils would have been considered bright in any school in the United States. Rose, *Rehearsal for Reconstruc-* *tion,* p. 88. For Laura Towne's remarks, see Quarles, *Negro in the Civil War,* p. 120; [Laura Towne], "The Freedmen at Port Royal," *Atlantic Monthly,* Vol. 12 (September 1863), p. 298. For more on schools, see Elizabeth Hyde Botume, *First Days Amongst the Contrabands* (Boston: Lee and Shepard, 1892), pp. 19–108; [E. E. Hale], "Education of the Freedmen," in *North American Review,* Vol. 101 (October 1865), p. 531.
13. [Edward L. Pierce], "The Contrabands of Fortress Monroe," in *Atlantic Monthly,* Vol. 8 (November 1861), pp. 626–680, esp. p. 627.

The second question had to do with organizing the "contrabands" into a labor force to produce a profitable cotton crop. To Salmon P. Chase, secretary of the treasury and the person ultimately responsible for deciding how the laborers would be organized, two alternatives presented themselves: (1) lease the plantations to cotton agents who would organize the "contrabands" into a labor force, produce a cotton crop, and receive a portion of the profits and (2) hire superintendents who would work directly for the Treasury Department, receive a salary, and bring in the crop. For aid in making the decision, Chase sought the services of Edward L. Pierce, a Boston attorney who had studied law in Chase's law office and who had written an article on the "contrabands" of Fortress Monroe in Virginia. In two reports to Chase (February 3 and June 2, 1862), Pierce argued persuasively that leasing to cotton agents would give control of the "contrabands" to people primarily interested in their own profits and not in the welfare of the laborers. Chase was convinced, and Pierce was put in charge of recruiting superintendents at salaries of $1,000 per year. Many of them came from the same groups that provided the teachers, men (and a few women) filled with the spirit of abolition and eager to help slaves make the transition from bondage to freedom. In Pierce's opinion, the African Americans of the Sea Islands would not be returned to slavery, but at the same time they would have to prove that they could work with energy and diligence as free men and women. Many whites, in the North as well as in the South, believed they could not. Thus, perhaps this was the most important aspect of

the Port Royal Experiment, as it came to be called.[14]

The need for a decision became even more pressing because of an act passed by Congress on June 7, 1862. Not long after the start of the war, Congress had levied an annual tax on all states and territories to finance the war. Naturally, none of the Confederate states had paid the tax. Therefore, on June 7, 1862, Congress mandated that the property of disloyal citizens in states that had not paid their taxes would be confiscated and sold to pay the tax bill. The first sale of Sea Island property was scheduled to take place on February 11, 1863.[15]

Would the "contrabands" be permitted to purchase the properties of their former masters? If not, what would their status be? Free laborers? Slaves? If they were to be allowed to purchase property, where would the money come from? Was Congress merely exchanging one set of masters for another? And once the war was over, would the whites who originally had fled their plantations be allowed to return and reclaim them? Decisions needed to be made—and quickly.

The last major issue to be dealt with was whether the "contrabands" would be allowed to volunteer for service in the United States Army to fight against their former masters. President Lincoln opposed such a policy, even after

14. Edward L. Pierce, "The Negroes at Port Royal, S.C.," February 3 and June 2, 1862, in Moore, ed., *The Rebellion Record*, supplement to Vol. 1, pp. 302–323, esp. pp. 310–312; Quarles, *The Negro in the Civil War*, pp. 160–167.
15. On the congressional act of June 7, 1862, see Johnson, *A Social History of the Sea Islands*, p. 183; Rose, *Rehearsal for Reconstruction*, p. 201.

◆ CHAPTER 10

"No More Pint o'
Salt for Me":
The Port Royal
Experiment,
1861–1865

Congress specifically granted him the power "to employ as many persons of African descent as he may deem necessary and proper for the suppression of this rebellion." The President feared that white northerners would not fight alongside blacks, that African Americans would panic and desert at the first sound of gunfire, and that the Confederacy would fight even more fiercely.

When Major General David Hunter replaced Sherman in March 1862, however, he specifically defied Lincoln's wishes. An ardent abolitionist, Hunter touched off a furious debate in Congress and throughout both the United States and the Confederacy when, on April 19, he began issuing "deeds of emancipation" to individuals who had "heretofore [been] held in involuntary servitude." Then, on May 6, enlisting the help of an African American clergyman who was popular with the "contrabands," Hunter issued a call for volunteers to form an all-black regiment in the Union Army. Disappointed with the turnout, three days later he ordered his troops to round up and send to Hilton Head all able-bodied black men capable of bearing arms and, at the same time, issued a general emancipation proclamation covering all slaves living in Georgia, Florida, and South Carolina. Furious, on May 19, Lincoln overruled Hunter's proclamations and ordered that the First South Carolina Volunteer Regiment not be equipped or paid. Morale among the new recruits collapsed, and Hunter was forced to disband the regiment, which he did on August 10, 1862.[16]

And yet, just two weeks after Hunter had disbanded his regiment, General Rufus Saxton (Hunter's replacement) was authorized "to arm, uniform, equip, and receive into the service of the United States such number of volunteers of African descent as you may deem expedient." The reversal of policy had come about because Confederate General Robert E. Lee's Army of Northern Virginia had routed Union General George McClellan's Army of the Potomac, and additional troops were desperately needed to protect Washington. Of the 17,000 Union troops in the Sea Islands, 10,000 were sent to save the nation's capital. Only a reinstatement of the First South Carolina Volunteers could hold the Sea Islands and guard the valuable cotton crop from Rebel destruction. But would they fight? Many, including Lincoln, had serious doubts.[17]

Thus, what came to be called the "Port Royal Experiment" was indeed a

16. On Hunter, see Hondon B. Hargrove, *Black Union Soldiers in the Civil War* (Jeffer-son, N.C.: McFarland & Co., 1988), pp. 36–37. For Hunter's April 19 proclamation, see William Wells Brown, *The Negro in the American Rebellion, His Heroism and His Fidelity* (Boston: Lee & Shepard, 1867), pp. 72–73. For Hunter's May 9 proclamation and Lincoln's overruling, see Roy P. Basler, ed., *The Collected Works of Abraham Lincoln* (New Brunswick: Rutgers University Press, 1953), Vol. 5, pp. 222–223. See also George Washington Williams, *A History of the Negro Troops in the War of the Rebellion, 1861–1865* (New York: Bergman Publishers, [orig. pub. 1888]), pp. 91–93; Noah Andre Trudeau, *Like Men of War: Black Troops in the Civil War, 1862–1865* (Boston: Little, Brown, 1998), pp. 15–16.

17. Edwin Stanton (Secretary of War) to Brigadier-General Rufus Saxton, Aug. 25, 1862, in *Official Records of the War of the Rebellion*, series 1, Vol. 14, pp. 377–378; *ibid.*, series 3, Vol. 2, pp. 152–153. For the danger to the nation's capital, see Rose, *Rehearsal for Reconstruction*, pp. 182–190.

"dress rehearsal for Reconstruction," confronting as it did issues concerning education of the "contrabands," the extent to which they would work as free people and not slaves, their ability to acquire and retain land, and their fitness for military service. Hovering over all these questions were the racial stereotypes of African Americans held by whites in the North and in the South. To what extent could the Port Royal Experiment be used to challenge and even to overturn these stereotypes? To what extent would the blacks of the Sea Islands have the opportunity to do so?

The Method

On Sunday, October 12, 1862, at the dedication of the "negro church" on Hilton Head, General Ormsby Mitchel addressed the "contrabands" who had gathered for the ceremony:

> Good colored friends, you have a great work to do, and you are in a position of responsibility. The whole North, all the people in the free States, are looking at you and the experiment now tried in your behalf with the deepest interest. . . . Upon you depends whether this mighty result shall be worked out, and the day of Jubilee come to God's ransomed people.[18]

In the eyes of many, General Mitchel did not overstate the importance of the "Port Royal Experiment." Would Sea Island blacks be able to take advantage of the educational opportunities offered them? Would they work as free laborers outside the slave system, and would they be able to function as landowners in addition to working on land owned by others? Would the "contrabands" make good soldiers? Finally, would the transition from slavery to citizenship be accelerated or retarded by white attitudes regarding African Americans? As General Mitchel stated, the answers to the above questions could well determine the collective fate of the approximately four million African American men, women, and children in slavery.

Due to the notoriety of the "Port Royal Experiment," historians face a real problem: instead of having *not enough* evidence to examine and analyze, in this case there is a virtual *tidal wave* of primary sources. Almost everyone who visited or passed through the Sea Islands wrote accounts of their experiences and opinions. Also, the U.S. Treasury Department, the army, and other governmental bodies kept voluminous records. Finally, northern newspaper and magazine coverage was extensive, suggesting that large numbers of readers in the free states were interested in and regularly followed the "Port Royal Experiment."

18. *Liberator,* October 31, 1862. Before volunteering for service in the Union army, Ormsby Mitchel (1810–1862) was a nationally known astronomer. He died while on duty in the Sea Islands, of either malaria or yellow fever. The freedmen's village Mitchelville was named in his honor.

♦ CHAPTER 10

"No More Pint o'
Salt for Me":
The Port Royal
Experiment,
1861–1865

We have attempted to offer a representative sample of the literally thousands of pieces of available evidence. The 28 pieces of evidence in this chapter are divided into four general categories: (a) education, (b) work and land, (c) military service, and (d) attitudes regarding African Americans. As you examine and analyze the evidence in each category, keep in mind the central questions you ultimately must answer. Take notes as you go along, recording how the author(s) of each piece of evidence would answer the particular category's central question. In some cases, the piece of evidence does not attempt to answer the question directly, and you will have to *infer* from the selection what such an answer would have been.

Finally, we offer one comment. In the fourth category, that of attitudes concerning African Americans, there are only seven pieces of evidence. As you examine evidence from the other three categories, however, you will quickly see that several of those pieces of evidence may also be used to answer the question in the fourth category. Indeed, not a few pieces of evidence may be helpful in more than one category.

Keep in mind that many ideas we have today regarding what some contemporaries might refer to as the "human family" were not universally accepted in the mid-nineteenth century. Even some white abolitionists harbored racial attitudes that many in the early twenty-first century would label as "prejudiced" or even "racist." As you read each selection, do not condemn at the outset the author without trying to delve more deeply into that person's ideas, hopes, and fears.

Once you have used the evidence to answer questions a, b, c, and d (as presented in the first paragraph of this section), then return to the Problem section at the beginning of the chapter to answer the two central questions.

♦

The Evidence

EDUCATION

Source 1 from Charlotte Forten,[19] "Life on the Sea Islands, "*Atlantic Monthly,* Vol. 13 (May 1864), pp. 591–592.

1. One Teacher's Account.

The first day at school was rather trying. Most of my children were very small, and consequently restless. Some were too young to learn the alphabet. These little ones were brought to school because the older children—in whose

19. Charlotte Forten (1837–1914) came from a prominent and well-to-do African American family in Philadelphia, Pa. She is said to have been the first African American to teach white students in Massachusetts.

care their parents leave them while at work—could not come without them. We were therefore willing to have them come, although they seemed to have discovered the secret of perpetual motion, and tried one's patience sadly. But after some days of positive, though not severe treatment, order was brought out of chaos, and I found but little difficulty in managing and quieting the tiniest and most restless spirits. I never before saw children so eager to learn, although I had had several years' experience in New-England schools. Coming to school is a constant delight and recreation to them. They come here as other children go to play. The older ones, during the summer, work in the fields from early morning until eleven or twelve o'clock, and then come into school, after their hard toil in the hot sun, as bright and as anxious to learn as ever.

Of course there are some stupid ones, but these are the minority. The majority learn with wonderful rapidity. Many of the grown people are desirous of learning to read. It is wonderful how a people who have been so long crushed to the earth, so imbruted as these have been,—and they are said to be among the most degraded negroes of the South,—can have so great a desire for knowledge, and such a capability for attaining it. One cannot believe that the haughty Anglo-Saxon race, after centuries of such an experience as these people have had, would be very much superior to them. And one's indignation increases against those who, North as well as South, taunt the colored race with inferiority while they themselves use every means in their power to crush and degrade them, denying them every right and privilege, closing against them every avenue of elevation and improvement. Were they, under such circumstances, intellectual and refined, they would certainly be vastly superior to any other race that ever existed.

After the lessons, we used to talk freely to the children, often giving them slight sketches of some of the great and good men. Before teaching them the "John Brown" song, which they learned to sing with great spirit, Miss T.[20] told them the story of the brave old man who had died for them. I told them about Toussaint,[21] thinking it well they should know what one of their own color had done for his race. They listened attentively, and seemed to understand. We found it rather hard to keep their attention in school. It is not strange, as they have been so entirely unused to intellectual concentration.

20. Miss T: Laura Towne (1825–1901), one of the principal teachers. She remained in the Sea Islands as a teacher until her death in 1901.
21. Toussaint Louverture (1743?–1803) was the leader of a slave rebellion in Saint Domingue (present-day Haiti).

◆ CHAPTER 10

"No More Pint o'
Salt for Me":
The Port Royal
Experiment,
1861–1865

Source 2 from Elizabeth Hyde Botume, *First Days Amongst the Contrabands* (Boston: Lee and Shepard, 1892), pp. 42–43, 68, 107–109.

2. Another Teacher's Account.

I sketch the picture of this, my first schoolroom, with tenderness. Rude and uncouth as it was, there are others besides myself who hold this place as sacred. I believe this was the first building ever erected exclusively for a colored school. It was built for the colored refugees with a fund sent to General Saxton for this purpose by a ladies' freedman's aid society in England. All the "contraband schools" were at that time kept in churches, or cotton-barns, or old kitchens. Some teachers had their classes in tents.

Inspection over, I vigorously rang a little cracked hand-bell which I found on the desk. Then I saw several pairs of bright eyes peering in at the open door. But going towards them, there was a general scampering, and I could only see a head or a foot disappearing under the house. Again I rang the bell, with the same result, until I began to despair of getting my scholars together. When I turned my back they all came out. When I faced about they darted off. In time, however, I succeeded in capturing one small urchin, who howled vociferously, "O Lord! O Lord!" This brought out the others, who seemed a little scared and much amused. I soon reassured my captive, so the rest came in. Then I tried to "seat" them, which was about as easy as keeping so many marbles in place on a smooth floor. Going towards half a dozen little fellows huddled together on one bench, they simultaneously darted down under the seat, and scampered off on their hands and feet to a corner of the room, looking very much like a family of frightened kittens. Hearing a noise and suppressed titters back of me, I looked around, and saw four or five larger boys rolling over and over under the benches towards the door. Whether for fun or freedom I could not tell; but as the first boy sprang to his feet and out of the door, I concluded they all planned escape. But I "halted" the rest, and got them on to their feet and into their seats. Then I looked them over. They saw I was not angry, but in earnest, so they quieted down. The runaway peeped in at the door, then crept along and sat down by his companions. . . .

Whilst the zeal of these people for learning never flagged, they had no possible conception of time, or the fitness of things. Men, women, and children hurried to the schoolhouse at all hours and at most unseasonable times, expecting "to catch a lesson." Reproof was unheeded, or not understood; "Us had something *particular* to do," was the invariable excuse. Finally I told the children to start for school as soon as they had eaten their breakfast. This had no effect. I learned in time that breakfast, as we understand it, was to them an unknown term. They ate when they were hungry. Then I said, "Come as soon as you are up." The next morning by daylight I heard a low chattering and suppressed laughter, and looking out of my window I saw the piazza was filled with black heads. An eager crowd was waiting for me. Every morning after that the whole "gang" came to escort me to school. Usually one bolder than the rest would come to the door and announce, "Us waiting on you, ma'am." I soon began to feel that it was I who was under supervision and kept up to my duty, and not my poor neighbors. In order to establish regularity and to push things on, we had sewing-school every Saturday. . . .

There was no day without Northern visitors to the school. Most of these were interested, but all were full of curiosity.

I must confess, the ignorance of some of these visitors in regard to the condition of the contrabands was positively astounding. The questions asked of teachers and scholars were amusing and exasperating.

In this connection I wish to ask why so many well-intentioned people treat those who are poor and destitute and helpless as if they were bereft of all their five senses. This has been my experience. Visitors would talk before the contrabands as if they could neither see nor hear nor feel. If they could have seen those children at recess, when their visit was over, repeating their words, mimicking their tones and gestures, they would have been undeceived. This was, however, but one class, of which there was a great variety. Many of our visitors left us encouraged and strengthened by their kind words and appreciation.

Before my school was well organized some strangers called. One gentleman asked, "How do these children progress in arithmetic?" I looked surprised. "I mean how far along have they got? Are any of them able to take up book-keeping, for instance?"

At first I thought he could not be in earnest, but he looked so grave, I replied only a few were able to count to one hundred without making mistakes, and I had not yet succeeded in teaching them their right hand from their left. . . .

Imagine my surprise, when they had sung and answered a few general questions, to have one of the visitors get up and ask, "Children, who is Jesus Christ?" For a moment the whole school seemed paralyzed. Then one small boy shouted out, "General Saxby, sar." Upon this an older boy sprang up, and, giving him a vigorous thrust in the back, exclaimed, "Not so, boy! Him's Massa Linkum."

◆ CHAPTER 10

"No More Pint o'
Salt for Me":
The Port Royal
Experiment,
1861–1865

Source 3 from [W. C. Gannett], "The Freedmen at Port Royal," *North American Review*, Vol. 101 (July 1865), pp. 2–4.

3. Education at Port Royal—Another View.

The first inquiry in regard to them naturally concerns their intellect. Of the mental faculties, those in close connection with the outward senses are alone developed. That they observe well, is proved by their quickness in imitation; and their memory often surprises persons used to note-books and memoranda. But while they apprehend and hold detached facts easily, they are slow to comprehend them in connection,—are deficient in the more ideal operations, which require reflection and reasoning. Hence arises an appalling mental inaccuracy. Nothing reveals more strikingly this mental degradation than the confusion of ideas that blurs their common statements. It even accounts for much of their apparent dishonesty, and most curiously distorts the structure of their language. An intercourse of several months is needed thoroughly to understand their jumbled speech. Their minds are by no means inactive, however, though the range of thought is so limited; nor does their ignorance appear dulness. The impression made by a short acquaintance with the Sea Island negroes, and confirmed by a longer one, is that they have capacity, but lack ability,—the term properly applicable to the mind which by discipline has control of its powers. That the faculty exists dormantly and awaits its training is indicated by the fact that in many individuals it is already partially developed. The slight education obtained by familiarity with white people has, for instance, lifted the class of house servants to a decidedly higher grade of intelligence, and rough talent is not unfrequently met with that compels genuine respect.

Of course the instruction which the children principally have received during the last three years cannot have visibly affected this condition. It is to these children alone, and not at once to them, that we may fairly look for evidence of greater mental ability than that exhibited by their parents. Many friends of the Port Royal movement have a very exaggerated notion of the extent of the education already accomplished there. We have even been asked, how many negroes were yet qualified to take the place of teachers. Perhaps the teachers, for want of material to form definite reports, were obliged to make general statements at first, and may have colored them too warmly. Attention has been given chiefly to reading, spelling, and writing. The higher classes have gone through the multiplication table, and in many schools the cardinal operations of arithmetic, with a little geography and history, have been introduced. None can read with perfect confidence, few without frequent hesitation. The majority of the scholars are young children still in their First or Second Primer. In writing and spelling, for the length of time spent, the relative advancement has been greater than in reading.

WORK AND LAND

Sources 4 through 6 from Ira Berlin, et. al., eds. *Freedom: A Documentary History of Emancipation*, series 1, Vol. 3, *The Wartime Genesis of Free Labor* (Cambridge: Cambridge University Press, 1990), pp. 121–122, 153–154, 185.

4. Wm. H. Reynolds, Treasury Department Cotton Agent, to the Secretary of the Treasury, January 1, 1862.

The Negroes seem very well disposed, & quite well pleased with the new order of things here, most of them preferring to remain on the Plantation where they were raised, if they can receive something for their labor— I would respectfully suggest whether it would not be well to consider the plan of leasing the Plantations in our possession to loyal citazens at a fair rate, under proper restrictions, the Negroes to be paid a fair compensation for their services— In this way another Crop of Cotton might be secured, the negroes properly supported, & profitably employed— The present seems to be a fitting time to try the experiment of producing cotton in one of the oldest slaveholding states with paid labor—

5. Order by the Commander of the South Carolina Expeditionary Corps (General T. W. Sherman), February 6, 1862.

HILTON HEAD, S.C.   February 6, 1862, GENERAL ORDERS, No. 9.   The helpless condition of the Blacks inhabiting the vast area in the occupation of the forces of this command calls for immediate action on the part of a highly favored and philanthropic people. . . .

Blacks have been abandoned by their constitutional guardians, not only to all the future chances of anarchy and of starvation; but in such a state of abject ignorance and mental stolidity as to preclude all possibility of self-government and self-maintenance in their present condition.

Adequate provision for the pressing necessities of this unfortunate and now interesting class of people being therefore imperatively demanded, even by the dictates of humanity alone, an additional duty, next only in importance to

◆ CHAPTER 10

"No More Pint o'
Salt for Me":
The Port Royal
Experiment,
1861–1865

that of the preservation of a world revered Constitution and Union, is now forced upon us by an unnatural and wicked rebellion.

To relieve the Government of a burden that may hereafter become insupportable, and to enable the Blacks to support and govern themselves in the absence and abandonment of their disloyal guardians, a suitable system of culture and instruction must be combined with one providing for their physical wants.

Therefore, until proper legislation on the subject, or until orders from higher authority, the country in occupation of the forces of this command will be divided off into districts of convenient size for proper superintendence. For each of these districts a suitable Agent will be appointed to superintend the management of the plantations by the Blacks, to enroll and organize the willing blacks into working parties, to see that they are well fed, clad and paid a proper remuneration for their labor, to take charge of all property on the plantations, whether found there, provided by the Government, or raised from the soil, and to perform all other administrative duties connected with the plantations, that may be required by the Government. A code of regulations on this subject, as well as a proper division of districts will be furnished in due time.

In the meanwhile, and until the Blacks become capable of themselves, of thinking and acting judiciously, the services of competent instructors will be received—one or more for each district—whose duties will consist in teaching them, both young and old, the rudiments of civilization and Christianity—their amenability to the laws of both God and man—their relations to each other as social beings, and all that is necessary to render them competent to sustain themselves in social and business pursuits.

6. Plantation Superintendent on St. Helena Island to a Massachusetts Businessman, April 12, 1862.

I go to the Fripp's Point plantation in P.M. Find the people had quit work in middle of forenoon, tasks only half done. Men were all here helping load Cotton & women left to work alone—so (of course) got quarelling, felt discouraged about pay, & declared they wouldn't work on Cotton without the usual supply of clothes. I called them all up and had a grand pow-wow. I first heard their complaints, & then told them the usual facts about the difficulty of getting clothing &c. during the war, told how much they had at stake in their own welfare and that of millions of other negroes, and that if they failed to show now that they could work as hard without the whip as they used to work with it, that the Gov^t would be disgusted with them & believe all the stories their masters told us about their laziness &c. &c. hinting that if they didn't raise Cotton enough to pay for all the comforts they wanted the people of the north would say "these islands are not worth keeping, let's take our soldier's away & let the Secesh come back." I told them I had just bought some salt at Beaufort with my own money, meaning to give them a quart all round, but that if they behaved lazy I shouldn't try to do much more for them. They all broke out at this with "Thank you massa" thank you a thousand times! "We *will* work. You shan't call us lazy. We will never work again for old massa & his whip. We only wanted to know if we were sure of our pay, it is so hard living without clothes a whole year, & we get sick putting sea water in our hominy, & haven't had our salt for so many months." A good many promised to make up the unfinished tasks, of the morning, & I called the children together for school, leaving all in good humor.

Sources 7 through 9 from Elizabeth Ware Pearson, ed., *Letters from Port Royal Written at the Time of the Civil War* (Boston: W. B. Clarke Co., 1906), pp. 92, 108–109, 177–178.

7. E. S. P., October 7, 1862.

October 7.   I received on Sunday a copy of President Lincoln's proclamation.[22] I now feel more than ever the importance of our mission here, not so much for the sake of the few hundreds under my own eyes as for the sake of the success of the experiment we are now trying. It is, you know, a question even with our good President whether negroes can be made available as free laborers on this soil. I, for one, believe they can, and I am more than ever in earnest to show it, for the importance of this question is greater than ever, now that we are so near a general crash of the whole social fabric in the Southern States. I don't think the old masters will ever be successful in employing the blacks, but I do believe that Yankees can be.

Our people are picking the cotton very industriously, and though they have only about one third of last year's crop to gather, they are determined to make the most of it, and allow none to waste.

22. The Preliminary Emancipation Proclamation, issued on September 22, 1862. See Basler, ed., *The Collected Works of Abraham Lincoln,* Vol. 5, pp. 433–436.

◆ CHAPTER 10
"No More Pint o'
Salt for Me":
The Port Royal
Experiment,
1861–1865

8. E. S. P., November 16, 1862.

We had a very interesting discussion on Wednesday about the future management of the plantations. I advocated the subdivision of the land, allotting to each family what it could cultivate and measuring their crops separately. Mr. Bryant, who came from Edisto last June, preferred working the people in a gang with a foreman, and paying them by the month. His people had worked very well in that way, but it would be impossible to work the people on this island in that way. They are too independent and too ignorant to see the advantages of it, and too deceitful to enable any foreman to discriminate between the lazy and industrious. Such a system, with the insufficient force of white foremen we could supply, would be only a premium on deceit and laziness, and would fail to call out the individual exertions of the people.

9. W. C. G., March 14, 1863.

March 14. On March 9th the estates were at last offered for sale. On our island two thirds were bidden in by the Government and I presume they will remain under the system of superintendence. The other third was bought by Mr. Philbrick and two or three sutlers.[23] No agents of Southern owners and no dangerous speculators made their appearance, to my knowledge. Where any person evinced a desire to buy, the commissioners, by their bids, forced an offer of one dollar per acre and let the place go for that price. Several plantations, perhaps one in five or six, were bidden in for the special purpose of negro reservations; but in what way they will be offered to the people is undecided. Indeed, nothing is certain except that the sales have been made and titles given. . . .

Every one says that these island negroes are more ignorant and degraded than the great majority of the slaves, and I feel no doubt that, under conditions of peace, three years would find these people, with but very few exceptions, a self-respecting, self-supporting population. Almost everything about them, even to their distrust and occasional turbulence, has that in it which suggests to me the idea of capacity and power of development. Their principal vices,—dishonesty, indolence, unchastity, their dislike of responsibility, and unmanly willingness to be dependent on others for what their own effort might bring,—their want of forethought and inability to organize and combine operations for mutual benefit,—nearly all their mental and moral weak-

23. A person who followed the army and sold provisions to the soldiers.

nesses can be traced naturally and directly to slavery,—while on the other hand, the fact that at my close view I cannot make them out to be characteristic traits confirms that opinion as to their origin. Industry is very certainly the *rule;* there is much idleness, but apply the spurs of which you think a white man worthy, and you are sure to obtain earnest and persistent exertion. Manliness and self-respect are sufficiently strong and common to excite an expectation of finding them. Instances of plan, contrivance, forethought are very numerous; you are constantly meeting "smart" fellows. Their eagerness and aptitude in learning to read surprises every one. . . .

The discussion whether they will ever be equal to the white race in anything seems to me to be entirely irrelevant to everything. The only question of importance is whether they can become a moral, self-supporting, and useful part of our population, and of this I cannot feel the slightest doubt.

Source 10 from *Boston Commonwealth,* March 20, 1863.

10. Extract from the Report of the Tax Commissioners . . . to Secretary Chase.

It must be obvious to even slight observation, that the system of *free* labor on the part of those who were so recently enslaved, has not had even the semblance of a fair trial. . . .

The great impediment in the way of immediate progress appears to be the uncertainty which overhangs the future of the colored population. It is a very great mistake to suppose that they are unmindful of their present condition, or of their future destiny. Destitute of all means of present livelihood, powerless to grasp or to use such means as their rebel masters have abandoned, without a foot of soil or an implement of husbandry to which they could lay claim, they painfully appreciate the fact that, though free and capable of earning under present circumstances a daily support, they are, nevertheless, but tenants at will upon the grace of the government, and subject to all the incidents of military caprice or necessity.

Another prominent feature of their character is their strong desire to obtain permanent and free homes in the region of the country where they were born and reared. Although to obtain or retain their deliverance from the crushing weight of slavery, they would sacrifice all the delights of local and home attachments, they nevertheless feel most keenly the longings of that inhabitative instinct which is so marked in their social and individual character and habits.

With scarcely an exception this class of people have been found willing and

✦ CHAPTER 10

"No More Pint o'
Salt for Me":
The Port Royal
Experiment,
1861–1865

even anxious to work; but owing to the peculiar system of labor incident to slavery, most of them have been trained their life-long to one kind of labor and no other, and hence wanting that versatility and adaptation to occasion which free labor necessitates, it is not remarkable that now and then the hand is suspected to be tardy, when in fact the will is merely uninformed or improperly directed.

They seem to feel the necessity of some guiding minds to direct them into a new state of existence, the immense magnitude of which they seem to appreciate, but the details of which they are unable to comprehend. The transition from abject slavery, from the condition of a chattel to that of a man, might seem perilous in regard to a less docile people; but in the present case it requires only intelligent but firm administration to make it a perfect success. . . .

[*Here the commissioners referred to the government sales of Sea Island plantations.*]

One great object will certainly have been gained—treason supplanted, rebel soil abandoned and owned and reoccupied by loyal citizens, and fertilized by the cheerful sweat of free laborers.

As soon as the government shall have acquired title to the lands it is suggested that early steps be taken to have them subdivided and offered for sale in small parcels with the privilege of pre-emption, so that the freedman may secure himself and family a home at an early day, and from his own earnings, that he may feel its value. The anxiety of these people to obtain a home in their own right and feel safe in its possession is intense.

Sources 11 and 12 from Berlin, et al., eds., *The Wartime Genesis of Free Labor,* series 1, Vol. 3, pp. 253, 276.

11. Testimony by a South Carolina Freedman before the American Freedman's Inquiry Commission, June 1863.

Q. What would the colored people like the government to do for them here?

A. They would like to have land—4 or 5 acres to a family.

Q. How many here could manage and take care of land?

A. A good many. I could take care of 15 acres and would not ask them to do any more for me.

Q. Suppose the government were to give you land, how long would you take to pay for it—five years?

A. I would not take five years; in two years I would pay every cent. The people here would rather have the land than work for wages. I think it would be better to sort out the men and give land to those who have the faculty of supporting their families.

12. Direct Tax Commissioner for the State of South Carolina to the Commissioner of Internal Revenue, December 12, 1863.

I think it proper to inform you that I have heard from different persons who have been present that speeches have been made to the negroes at their gatherings on the Sabbath, urging them to adopt the squatter sovereignty plan and prevent white men if possible bidding against them at the public sales. Mr French, Chaplain on General Saxton's staff advocates this plan; and to me he tried to underrate the President's Instructions. Judge Smith goes out with Mr French on these appointments. I was told by the best authority that they got the negroes on St Helena Island, at their church, to adopt some very violent resolutions. The negroes consequently in some instances have been placing stakes for themselves on lands not selected for them, and I fear, instructed as they are, they will be either greatly disappointed or may give us some trouble. The true friend of the negro, it seems to me, ought to encourage white men to purchase plantations among them as protectors, teachers and employers; and their own homesteads, so generously allowed them by the Government, will thereby be greatly increased in value intrinsically.

Source 13 from Edward S. Philbrick to Albert G. Browne, March 25, 1864, in *Abraham Lincoln Papers*, Series 1, General Correspondence, Library of Congress.

13. Philbrick to Browne, March 25, 1864.

I was at the Church on St. Helena Island S.C. on Sunday, Feb. 14th last when the news was published that the instructions concerning the preemption of public lands issued at Washington Dec 30th 1863, authorizing preemption of the lands in the Sea Islands were *suspended* by more recent orders.

Rev. Mansfield French was there and spoke on the subject for some time. I heard him use the following language on this occasion, sympathizing with the disappointment of the negroes in not being allowed to take possession of the land. Viz. "If the time comes when you *have to give up* what God has just given

◆ CHAPTER 10

"No More Pint o'
Salt for Me":
The Port Royal
Experiment,
1861–1865

you, let it cost the Government *a struggle* to turn you off: *Cling to your land!*
Hang on! Don't give it up until you are driven off! Go on planting and sowing
your patches. If you are finally driven off I shall weep with you. God is on your
side. Changes may come but God can change it back."

I took these words out of his own mouth & wrote them down on the spot.
The effect upon the negroes, several hundred of whom were present, was to
render them reluctant to work for any one buying the land. I heard negroes
say shortly after that the land was theirs & they would shoot the first man
coming on to it to dispossess them.

Source 14 from [Towne], "The Freedmen at Port Royal," pp. 308–310.

14. "The Freedmen at Port Royal."

The laborers, during the first year under the new system, have acquired the
idea of ownership, and of the security of wages, and have come to see that labor and slavery are not the same thing. . . . A superintendent on St. Helena
Island said, that, if he were going to carry on any work, he should not want
better laborers. . . .

Next as to the development of manhood. This has been shown in the first
place, in the prevalent disposition to acquire land. It did not appear upon our
first introduction to these people, and they did not seem to understand us
when we used to tell them that we wanted them to own land. But it is now an
active desire. At the recent tax sales, six out of the forty-seven plantations
sold were bought by them, comprising two thousand five hundred and ninety-
five acres, sold for twenty-one hundred and forty-five dollars. [The purchases]
were made by the negroes on the plantations combining the funds they had
saved from the sale of their pigs, chickens, and eggs, and from the payments
made to them for work,—they then dividing off the tract peaceably among
themselves.

Sources 15 and 16 from Berlin, et al., eds., *The Wartime Genesis of Free Labor,* series 1, Vol. 3, pp. 291, 297–298.

15. Northern Minister to the Commissioner of Internal Revenue, February 23, 1864.

Dear Sir. I promised to advise you from time to time about affairs in this Department. I regret not having done so, especially, as matters have gone so badly. We seem to be retrograding rapidly. The sale of public lands, which, under the late instructions, were all to be preempted, has wrought immense mischief. The surveys have been now turned, mostly, to the account of speculators. and the public lands (or those designated for auction sales) are going off rapidly & at too high prices for the freedmen, while, as yet, very few lots have been sold to the freedmen, from even the lands specially set apart for them. On the reception of the late instructions, only 19 deeds had been given, & up to this date only 43 deeds are given, and those for tracts of ten, & five acres. More land was sold yesterday to speculators, than all that has been deeded to the freedmen. Supposing the late instructions would remain in full force, the people scattered all over the islands laid their claims, commenced listing & preparing the lands for planting. Some had commenced building, many had moved several miles to get a good home, & on the old homestead, where they had been born, & had laborered & suffered. Now *all* such, as were so unfortunate as to locate on lands originally selected for sale, are being sold out. The disappointment to them is almost unbearable. They see neither justice nor wisdom in such treatment. The white man loves power & money, and is sharp enough to grasp both, when he can.

16. South Carolina Freedmen to the President, March 1, 1864.

Sir. Wee the undersigned. beleaveing wee are unfarely delt with, Are led to lay before you, these, our greaveiences first; then our petetion. And wee here beeg, though it may be long, You will beare kindly with; Reade & answere uss, And as now so, henceforth, our prayrs shall asscende to the Throan of God, for your future success on Earth & Tryumph in Heaven.

For what wee have receaved from God, through you, wee will attempt to thank you, wee can only bow our selves, and with silent lips feel our utter inability to say one word, the semblence of thanks. Trusting this our Petetion in the hands of Allmighty God, and your kindness, wee now say, Let there be what success may in stor for you and your Armies, Wither our freedom is for

◆ CHAPTER 10

"No More Pint o'
Salt for Me":
The Port Royal
Experiment,
1861–1865

ever or a day, wither as Slaves or Freemen, wee shall ever, carry you & your kindness to us in our hearts, may Heaven bless you.

Our greaveincess

Mr Edward Philbrick. (A Northern Man) has bought up All our former Masters Lands under falls pretences;

To wit

He promis'd to buey in, at public sale, with our consent all the Lands on the following Plantations,

Mr Coffin's Place, Mr. Coffin's Cherrie Hill, Maulbuery Hill place. Big House place. Corner place. Dr Fuller's place, Pollawanney place, Mary Jinkins'es place. Hamelton Frip place, Morgan Island, & John Johntson's place, of Ladies Island.

Before bueying he promised to sell to us again any ammount of the Land at $1.00 one Dollar pr Acre wee wish'd to purchas, Said sail was to be made when ever the Government sold the balance of its Land to the People resideing thereon. . . .

On the 18th day of last month sailes of Publick Lands began in Beaufort, & what doo wee see to day, on all the Plantations our Breathern are bueying thr Land. getting redy to plant ther cropps and build ther Houses, which they will owne for ever

Wee hav gon to Mr Philbrick & Ask'd him to sell us our Land, and get for an answere he will not sell us one foot, & if he does sell to any one he will charge $10.00 Ten Dollars pr Acre. Wee have work'd for Mr Philbrick the whole year faithfully, and hav received nothing comparatively, not enough to sustaine life if wee depended entirely uppon our wages, he has Stors here chargeing feerefull prices for every nessary of life, and at last the People have become discouraged, all most heart broken.

He will not sell us our Land neither pay us to work for him; And if wee wish to work for others where wee might make something, he turns us out of our Houses, he says wee shall not live-on his plantation unless wee work for him, If wee go to Gen¹ Saxton he tells us if Mr Phlbrick sees fit he will sell us the Land according to agreement If not then wee must go on Government Land where wee can buey as much as wee please, But, the Tax Commissioners say they cannot sell to us unless wee are living on the Plantations now selling, Wee go to the Supᵗ Gen¹ of the Island; Mr Tomlinson, he says work For Mr Phibrick for what ever wages he sees fit to pay. if wee do not Mr Philbrick may drive us off the Land and wee shall not taks our Houes with us, He says, 'Mr Philbrick bought everything Houses Lands & all.'

Why did Government sell all our Masters Land's to Mr Philbrick for so trifling a sume; we are all redy & willing of truth anxious to buey all our Masters Land, & every thing upon them; and pay far more than he did for them. . . .

If possible wee Pray for either one of theese two things.

Petetion

1st Either let Mr Philbrick be compeeld to live up to his promises with us, and sell us as much Land as wee want for our owne Homes at a reasonabele price, giving us cleare deeds for the same.

2nd Otherwise wee pray Government to repurchas the Land of Mr Philbrick and then let us farm it giveing one half of all that is rais'd to the Goverment. wee would much rather this and will furnish everything ourselves and will warrent there will be but few feet of Ground Idle. As Mr Philbrick has broken his part of the contract is Government bound to keep thers?

Source 17 from Don Carlos Rutter and Laura Towne to Abraham Lincoln, May 29, 1864, in *Abraham Lincoln Papers*, Library of Congress.

17. Rutter and Towne to Lincoln, May 29, 1864. Rutter dictated his thoughts to Towne, who transcribed them.

My name is Don Carlos, and I hope my letter will find you and your family in perfect health. Will you please to be so kind Sir, as to tell me about my little bit of land. I am afraid to put on it a stable, or cornhouse, and such like, for fear it will be taken away from me again. Will you please to be so kind as to tell me whether the land will be sold from under us or no, or whether it will be sold to us at all. I should like to buy the very spot where I live. It aint but six acres, and I have got cotton planted on it, and very fine cotton too; and potatoes and corn coming on very pretty. If we colored people have land I know we shall do very well—there is no fear of that. Some of us have as much as three acres of corn, besides ground-nuts, potatoes, peas, and I don't know what else myself. If the land can only be sold, we can buy it all, for every house has its cotton planted, and doing well, and planted only for ourselves— We should like to know how much we shall have to pay for it—if it is sold—

I am pretty well struck in age Sir, for I waited upon Mrs. Alston that was Theodosia Burr,[24] daughter of Aaron Burr, and I remember well when she was taken by pirates,—but I can maintain myself and my family well on this land.

24. Theodosia Burr (1783–1812), the only child of Aaron Burr. In 1812, the ship *Patriot,* on which she was a passenger, vanished off the Outer Banks of North Carolina. It was commonly believed that it had been captured by pirates.

✦ CHAPTER 10

"No More Pint o'
Salt for Me":
The Port Royal
Experiment,
1861–1865

My son got sick on the Wabash (Flagship at Hilton Head) and he will never get well, for he has a cough that will kill him at last. He cannot do much work, but I can maintain him. I had rather work for myself and raise my own cotton than work for a gentleman for wages, for if I could sell my cotton for only .20 cts a pound it would pay me.

What ever you say I am willing to do, and I will attend to whatever you tell me.

Your most obedient servant.

MILITARY SERVICE

Sources 18 and 19 from Pearson, ed., *Letters from Port Royal*, pp. 43, 102.

18. W. C. G., May 27, 1862.

May 27. Negroes—plantation negroes, at least—will never make soldiers in one generation. Five white men could put a regiment to flight; but they may be very useful in preventing sickness and death among our troops by relieving them of part of their work, and they may acquire a certain self-respect and independence which more than anything else they need to feel, if they are soon to stand by their own strength.

19. E. S. P., October 27, 1862.

The last time I saw General Saxton he seemed to think our whole destiny depended on the success of this negro recruitment. It *is* certainly a very important matter, but I think as before that it is doomed to fail here at present, from the imbecile character of the people.

Sources 20 and 21 from Berlin, et. al., eds., *Freedom: A Documentary History of Emancipation*, series 2, *The Black Military Experience* (Cambridge: Cambridge University Press, 1982), pp. 54–55, 526–527.

20. Superintendent of Contrabands in the Department of the South to the Secretary of War, January 25, 1863.

Dear Sir.   I have the honor to report that the organization of the 1st Regt. of South Carolina Volunteers is now completed. The regiment is light infantry composed of ten companies of about eighty six men (each) armed with muskets, and officered by white men. In organization, drill, discipline, and morale, for the length of time it has been in service, this regiment is not surpassed by any white regiment in this Department. Should it ever be its good fortune to get into action I have no fears but it will win its own way to the confidence of those who are willing to recognize courage, and manhood, and vindicate the wise policy of the administration in putting these men into the field and giving them a chance to strike a blow for the country and their own liberty. In no regiment have I ever seen duty performed with so much cheerfulness, and alacrity, and as sentinels they are peculiarly vigilant. I have never seen in any body of men such enthusiasm and deep seated devotion to their officers as exists in this. They will surely go wherever they are led. Every man is a volunteer and seems fully persuaded of the importance of his service to his race. In the organization of this regiment I have labored under difficulties which might have discouraged one who had less faith in the wisdom of the measure, but I am glad to report that the experiment is a complete success. My belief is that when we get a footing on the main land regiments may be raised which will do more than any now in service to put an end to this rebellion[.] I have sent the regiment upon an expedition to the coast of Georgia the result of which I shall report for your information as soon as it returns. I have the honor also to report that I have commenced the organization of the 2nd Regt which is to be commanded by Col Montgomery. I am Sir with great respect Your Obedent Servant[.]

21. Colonel Thomas Wentworth Higginson to General Rufus Saxton, February 1, 1863.

No officer in this regiment now doubts that the key to the successful prosecution of this war lies in the unlimited employment of black troops. Their superiority lies simply in the fact that they know the country, while white troops

◆ CHAPTER 10

"No More Pint o'
Salt for Me":
The Port Royal
Experiment,
1861–1865

do not; and moreover that they have peculiarities of temperment, position, and motive, which belong to them alone. Instead of leaving their homes and families to fight, they are fighting for their homes and families; and they show the resolution and the sagacity which a personal purpose gives. It would have been madness to attempt, with the bravest white troops, what I have successfully accomplished with black ones. Everything, even to the piloting of the vessel, and the selection of the proper points for cannonading, was done by my own soldiers; indeed the real conductor of the whole expedition up the St. Mary's was Corporal Robert Sutton of Company G. formerly a slave upon the St. Mary's River, a man of extraordinary qualities, who needs nothing but a knowledge of the alphabet to entitle him to the most signal promotion. In every instance when I followed his advice, the predicted result followed, and I never departed from it, however slightly, without finding reason for subsequent regret. I have the honor to be, General, Very respectfully, Your obedient Servant[.]

Sources 22 through 25 from Berlin, *The Black Military Experience,* series 2, pp. 388, 391–395.

22. Officers of a South Carolina Black Regiment to the Adjutant General of the Army, November 21, 1863.

General. We the undersigned Officers of the Third Regiment of South Carolina Infantry do most respectfully beg leave to call the attention of the President of the United States regarding the circumstances attending the payment of Colored Troops in the Department of the South. The Paymasters make a distinction based on their color and refuse to pay the Soldiers of African desent the stipulated wages of United States Volunteer Troops.

The colored Troops raised in this Department under Genl R Saxton were enlisted with the promise of the same pay clothing and rations as is accorded to other soldiers in the United States Service.

In the first organization of the regiments they received this amount, subsequently it was reduced and it has again been reduced this present month[.]

Whatever may be the policy of the Government in regard to colored Troops raised in other insurectionary States we rely on the plighted honor of the Government that no discrimination be made in this Department of any class of Soldiers on account of their color or Nationality.

The cause of the present reduction of pay now offered to the colored Troops has been based on an Act of Congress of July 1862 but which at that time bore no reference to colored enlisted men but only to those otherwise employed by the Government.

We respectfully request therefore an explanation of the interest and purpose of this Act to be forwarded to the Paymaster of this Department in order that the colored Troops may be paid their just dues.

23. Court-Martial Testimony by the Commander of a South Carolina Black Regiment, January 11, 1864.

QUESTION BY JUDGE ADVOCATE: On that day did you see the accused [*Sergeant William Walker*]?

ANSWER: I did.

QUESTION BY JUDGE ADVOCATE: State his conduct as far as it came under your observation on that day, and what occurred in relation thereto?

ANSWER: On the morning of Nov. 19, 1863, when a portion of the command was in a state of mutiny, I noticed the accused, with others of his company and regiment stack his arms, take off his accoutrements and hang them on the stack. I inquired what all this meant, and received no reply, and again repeated the question, when the accused answered by saying, that they "would not do duty any longer for seven dollars per month." I then told the men the consequences of a mutiny, and what they might expect. I told them if they did not take their arms and return to duty, I should report the case to the Post Commander and they would be shot down. While saying this, I heard the accused tell the men not to retake their arms, but leave them and go to their street, which command of his they obeyed. Again, later in the day, in the evening, I ordered the accused in arrest, and told him not to leave his tent without my permission, if he did, I should confine him to the Provost Guard. The next morning, Nov. 20th 1863, I received information he had broken his arrest, by leaving his tent and going into anther tent & company street. I then ordered him to the Provost Guard House.

24. Court-Martial Statement by Sergeant William Walker, January 12, 1864.

I was exempted from conscription— . . . on the promise solemnly made by some who are now officers in my regiment, that I should receive the same pay

♦ CHAPTER 10

"No More Pint o'
Salt for Me":
The Port Royal
Experiment,
1861–1865

and allowances as were given to all soldiers in the U.S. Army,—voluntarily entered the ranks. For an account of the treatment that has been given to the men of the 3d Reg't S.C. Vols. by a large majority of their officers, nine-tenths of those now in service there will be my witness that it has been tyrannical in the extreme, and totally beneath that standard of gentlemanly conduct which we were taught to believe as pertaining to officers wearing the uniform of a government that had declared a "freedom to all" as one of the cardinal points of its policy. This treatment, prepared the way for the events that occurred when it was announced to us that we could receive but $7 per month pay.

As to my conduct on the 19th day of November last, when the Regiment stacked arms and refused farther duty, I believe that I have proved conclusively by the testimony of the non-commissioned officers and men of my company that I did not then exercise any command over them—that I gave no word of counsel or advice to them in opposition to the request made by our commanding officer—and that, for one, I carried my arms and equipments back with me to my company street. I respectfully suggest that these men are less apt to be mistaken, than officers who feared that they were facing a general mutiny, and were ignorant of the next movement that might be made by the excited crowd before them—but an assemblage who only contemplated a peaceful demand for the rights and benefits that had been guaranteed them.

25. Superintendent of Black Recruitment M. S. Littlefield to the Provost Marshal General of the Department of the South, June 3, 1864.

Colonel. I have the honor to acknowledge the receipt of a communication from you, dated June 2d, in which you ask me to state what I know of the mutiny, in the late 3d S.C. Vol. now the 21th U.S.C.T. which accured last fall, at Hilton Head, S.C. that you can report upon the guilt or innocence of those now in confinement at the Provost Guard House.

The conversation I had with Lt. Col. Bennett, in command of the Regiment, is all I know of the facts in the case: as I understand it is this: The 3d S.C. Vol was organized by Gen. Hunter, in the spring of '63. as Fatigue men, with a promis that they should have $13.d per. month, The men immediately placed in camp, with inferior clothing, having no care, worked hard and with little or no instruction; they were commanded by inferior officers, a portion [of] whom have been dismissed from service: When the paymaster came to pay them they were offered but $7.00 & not knowing what they were doing, supposing they could stop doing duty, as they had done when at work, if they pay did not suit them; they stacked arms, & refused to *longer* be *soldiers:* as soon however, as the worthless officers left & good officers took charge, & explained to the men, thir obligation *all at once entered willingly to their duties:* The Regiment is one of the best now, we have, & it under Lt. Col. Bennett, The points I make are these:

1ˢᵗ   The men were guilty of no crime, as they did not know they were doing wrong, consequently no wrong was committed.

2ᵈ   The partial manner with which these men were tried and the irregularities of the records, has rendered it impossible for these men to have Justice: Humanity calls that they should be released from their long confinement; & the best interest of the service will be promoted by having these men in the ranks with muskets in hands, rather than being kept on public expence where they are.

3ᵈ   Maj Gen. Gillmore ordered these men all be returned to duty, in January last, when the men were consolidated with my own Regiment, hence they augh not to suffer from these long & vexatious delays, & their pay should at least commence January 1, 1864, but I urge as the colonel of the Regiment, that they all be returned to duty with *no* stopage of pay.

ATTITUDES CONCERNING AFRICAN AMERICANS

Source 26 from Esther Hill Hawks, *A Woman Doctor's Civil War Diary,* Gerald Schwartz, ed., (Columbia: University of South Carolina Press, 1984), pp. 37, 48–49.

26. Dr. Esther Hill Hawks's Attitudes About African Americans.

They have certain notions in regard to religion which is quite detrimental to their moral character—and the system of religious instruction adopted by the Freedmen's Ass. tends rather to encourage this state of things rather than to eradicate it by teaching a truer code of morality. They have little or no idea of *practical religion.* The "Golden rule" has never entered very largely into their every day life. For instance, one of their people, having no special claim upon their sympathy may die for want of a little care and nursing or a few of the commonest necessaries of life and no one think of supplying them—then they would get together in large numbers and spend a half day in funeral exercises lamenting and singing in a manner to convinse one that their community had met with a very calamitous bereavement. So in the hospitals where they are employed as nurses. They do what you tell them providing you keep an eye on them—but if you ask or expect them to help each other they will probably tell you that they came to Hospital to get well and not to work—and

✦ CHAPTER 10

"No More Pint o'
Salt for Me":
The Port Royal
Experiment,
1861–1865

no amount of *talk* will induce them to admit that they ought to do anything for the comfort of each other—unless they are *hired* as *nurses;* many times indeed *always* they would do a thing to oblige me because they liked *me*—but not because they felt any moral obligation to do it. Their perception of duty towards each other is very obtuse! . . .

From my first connexion with these people, I have felt quite at home among them, and there is nothing repelant to my feelings about them any more than there is to all dirty people—but here in Hospital we could keep them as clean as we chose, so I circulated among them with the greatest freedom—prescribing for them, ministering to their wants, teaching them, and making myself as thoroughly conversant with their inner lives as I could. I do not think, at this time, without a degree of inhumanity, a hospital for colored, could be conducted on the same rigid principles, as for white troops. These negroes are like ignorant unformed children, and the difficulty of reasoning them out of an opinion or ideas when it once takes possesion of them, can never be known 'till tried. You talk to willing listeners—they assent heartily to what you say but—they are of the same opinion still.

They are not thoughtful for each others comfort, and I never cease wondering at their indifferance to the death of their comrads and even of near friends. There is seldom any display of feelings and in but few instances have I seen sufficient emotion visable to look upon it as grief at the loss of a son or brother. No doubt their religious belief has much to do with this as one of the strongest articles in their creed is, that "no one dies before his time." To return to the Hospital from which I seldom allow myself to be absent so long, I do not think this Hospital was admited to the brotherhood of hospitals on quite an even footing. Favors were a little grudingly bestowed. White soldiers near us were hardly respectful to our patients and little annoyances, such as throwing bits of old iron at them, got for the purpose at a blacksmith's shop, calling names and other impertenances were of frequent occurance. These troubles came mostly from a Co. of regulars whose camp was quite near, and as the buildings were not very well suited for hospital purposes, it was thought best to change the location, and so run away from many sources of anoyance.

Source 27 from Nordhoff, "The Freedmen of South Carolina," *New York Evening Post,* April 15, 1863.

27. Charles Nordhoff's Attitudes.

The planters have always persuaded us that their four millions of slaves were a dangerous class; and the precautions they took and their evident apprehensions in regard to this population prove that they were in earnest. As slaves then, they were dangerous to the community, so every slaveholder told you: as free men they have proved themselves peaceable, law-abiding and useful. As slaves, special laws, cruel punishments and disgraceful guards were required—in the opinion of the slaveholders—to keep them from murder and rapine; but our experience in these Sea Islands shows that as freemen these same people are so harmless, so kind, so ready to submit to all laws and to all proper guidance, so averse from violence, that in all parts of the island ladies are stationed as teachers, and move about among them unguarded, unarmed and unharmed. . . .

I had occasion to see here, one day, how far the bitter and mean prejudices of a pro-slavery man will carry him. Smalls, of the Planter, was ordered to go to the Wabash to see the Admiral. He went alongside in a boat in which it happened that Brig.-General Seymour also was. The General called to the officer of the deck and said to him: "Officer, this *boy* wants to see the Admiral; will you please let him know that the boy is waiting?" Then turning to Smalls, he cried out, in a sharp voice: "Here, *boy,* you can go aboard, and the officer will tell you when the Admiral is ready to see you."

Now Smalls is *not* a boy; he is a man of, I should think, thirty years, and wears a beard sufficient to show it. I blushed for Gen. Seymour when I heard him use the old cant of the slave-master toward this man, who performed one of the bravest and most brilliant acts of the war. General Seymour is himself a brave man, and if a white man had done what Smalls did, he would no doubt have honored him for it. But because this gallant fellow happens to have a black skin, he speaks to him in a way that seemed to me, unwillingly listening to him, contemptibly mean.

Smalls was engaged to be one of the pilots to take in the fleet to attack Charleston. He is thoroughly familiar, I am told, with the creeks and intricate channels along this coast; and his knowledge has been of great value to our army and navy. He seems a very quiet man, without the slightest swagger. How he looked or felt when he was called "boy" in this way, I can not tell you—for I dared not look in the poor fellow's face.

◆ CHAPTER 10

"No More Pint o'
Salt for Me":
The Port Royal
Experiment,
1861–1865

Source 28 from [Gannett], "The Freedmen at Port Royal," pp. 1–2, 7–8, 13.

28. "The Freedmen at Port Royal."

The slaveholder's institution is a nursery for perpetuating infancy; and the more enlightened the nurse, the more successful his efforts. The world has waited for the nineteenth century and republican institutions to develop slavery in its hugest and most direful proportions; and now that the man-owner's reckless pride has made its fatal mistake, the most shameful spectacle that ever saddened earth is opened for the nations to behold,—the spectacle of a race of stunted, misshapen children, writhing from the grasp of that people which, in so many respects, is the foremost of the age.

It is this immaturity that occasions the chief difficulty in analyzing the negro's nature, as we see it in the South. In each separate faculty of his mental and moral constitution we miss the effect of training. No tendency has had scope to display its direction and vigor. Careful study is required, therefore, of the specific effects of slavery, both to distinguish what is innate from what really belongs to this condition, and to estimate the qualities of those who have been slaves at their true worth under natural laws of development. It is because this is often neglected, that the negro's friends and his enemies differ so widely in describing his character. . . .

It accords with what has been said to add that the negro temperament is one which dismisses responsibility and knows little of care. It is his armor; it receives oppression as sand receives the cannon-ball, neither casting it off nor being shattered by it. It is also the secret of his weakness,—inviting attack, and rendering conquest easy. They certainly seem to be a light-hearted, laughing race, finding far more joys than sorrows in life. To the Anglo-Saxon of this century the burden of slavery would sadden every thought and moment. With the negro, it has crushed and dwarfed his nature,—an effect which he but little realizes,—and added a certain amount of physical suffering to his lot. But unless it be very constant, it is not physical suffering which sobers a man's life. The harder masters have indeed left their private mark upon their people for the Yankees now to read. . . .

[I]t is upon the ground of their existence that the Northerner points his sneer or excuses his indifference, and that the Southerner justifies his institution,—nay, seriously calls it God's appointed means of civilization. Ignorance and vice necessitate servitude, he argues, but he omits the other half of the circle,—slavery produces vice and maintains ignorance. In fairness, the severest inference from these facts is the admission already made, that the negro's will is weak and his nature plastic,—weak and plastic to that degree that pressure has forced these vices into peculiar prominence. Till we know him under natural conditions of growth, it is illogical as well as unjust to call the vice itself inherent. And it becomes hard to repress our indignation when we try to *lift* our thoughts to the purity and disinterestedness of those men, North and South, who are most apt to abuse this race of slaves for their original sin. Under the most favorable circumstances, it will be very long before the negro enjoys the same conditions of success as those which determine the character and prosperity of the white man; yet it is always with ourselves, at our present height, that we involuntarily compare him.

Questions to Consider

As you examine and analyze each piece of evidence, keep in mind that virtually everyone connected with the enterprise and the vast majority of northern observers thought of the "Port Royal Experiment" as an important test of African Americans' capabilities to be free, productive, and contributing citizens of the United States. Could they take advantage of educational opportunities offered them? Would they work as free men and women? Should they be sold or given land to farm? Were they capable of bearing arms in their own interests and those of the country? Finally, perhaps the most important test was whether they could dispel the racial prejudice against them and the widespread notions that they were incapable of living as free and equal members of American society. Thus, General Mitchel was not exaggerating when he said that the fate of millions was on the shoulders of the black men, women, and children of the Sea Islands.

Charlotte Forten and Elizabeth Botume (Sources 1 and 2) were teachers in the schools that General Sherman had established for "contraband" children and adults. What general impression did they want their readers to have of African Americans' capacity for education? What examples do they offer to support their points? What was Elizabeth Botume's opinion of northern visitors? In what ways did W. C. Gannett (Source 3) support or contradict Forten's and Botume's impressions?

Sources 4 through 7 deal with the former slaves' capacities to work as free men and women, a major subject of debate in the North. What is the opinion of each person on this question? Can you detect any underlying prejudice in these accounts? Given the federal government's overall plan for the Sea Islands (see the Background section of this chapter, especially with regard to the Treasury Department), what problems were created by the African Americans' refusal to raise cotton? How would they be persuaded—or made—to do so?

The flight of the Sea Island planters together with the federal laws permitting the confiscation of Confederates' property raised the interesting question of what should be done with those Sea Island plantations. If those lands

◆ CHAPTER 10

"No More Pint o'
Salt for Me":
The Port Royal
Experiment,
1861–1865

were to be divided among the "contrabands," would they have the talent and industry to become free subsistence farmers? What were the various opinions regarding what should be done with the land (Sources 8 through 17)? Which of the sources were wholeheartedly in favor of distribution to African Americans? Which sources expressed reservations? What were those reservations?

Sources 12 and 13 deal with incidents involving the Rev. Mansfield French, an army chaplain, that took place in late 1863 and early 1864. What was French afraid of? What did he counsel freedmen to do? According to the sources, how did blacks respond? What do the sources reveal about the issue of selling or giving land to freedmen?

One of the people reporting the Rev. French's activities was Edward S. Philbrick. Who was he (see Source 16)? What do Sources 15 and 16 tell you about the government land sales? How do those sources in part contradict the account of Laura Towne (Source 14)?

In sum, which authors were optimistic about the economic future for Sea Island blacks? Which expressed reservations?

The issue of whether blacks would make good soldiers (Sources 18 through 25) had been debated for some time prior to President Lincoln's reversal of policy that permitted recruitment of African Americans into the armed services. Where do each of the sources stand on this issue? According to the sources, how did the behavior of the First Regiment of South Carolina Volunteers, in spite of the way the regi-

ment initially was raised, affect the opinions of whites regarding blacks as fighting men (Sources 20 and 21)?

One of the major issues among blacks and many of their white supporters was that of equal pay for African Americans in military service (Sources 22 through 25). What role did that issue play in the court-martial trial of Sergeant William Walker (Sources 23 through 25)? What was the ultimate outcome of those proceedings (Source 25)?

On August 16, 1862, the *New York Tribune* published a letter to the editor which said in part:

> I am quite sure there is not one man in ten but would feel himself degraded as a volunteer if negro equality is to be the order in the field of battle. . . . I take the liberty of warning the abettors of fraternizing with the blacks, that one negro regiment, in the present temper of things, put on equality with those who have the past year fought and suffered, will withdraw an amount of life and energy in our army equal to disbanding ten of the best regiments we can now raise.[25]

Is there any evidence in Sources 18 through 25 to confirm or contradict the author of the letter?

Underlying all of the questions above were the attitudes that northern whites held regarding African Americans. Sources 26 through 28, however, deal directly with those attitudes and perceptions—or misperceptions. How does each source display an attitude

---

25. McPherson, *The Negro's Civil War*, pp. 163–164.

about the Port Royal African Americans that might affect how the author would approach the issues discussed above?

Now reexamine your notes to make sure you have answered all of the questions in this chapter. Have you dealt with every piece of evidence?

◆

Epilogue

On September 1, 1864, General William Tecumseh Sherman and his army of 60,000 Union troops captured Atlanta. Roughly two months later, he began his devastating march to the sea, cutting a swath sixty miles wide through the heart of Georgia. On December 21, Savannah fell, and Sherman cabled President Lincoln, "I beg to present to you, as a Christmas gift, the city of Savannah." Responding to an appeal of twenty African American clergymen, on January 12, 1865, Sherman issued Special Field Order Number 15, which set aside over 400,000 acres of land in the Sea Islands and along the South Carolina coast, to be distributed to the former slaves. Each family was to receive 40 acres.[26]

Thus, armed with the rudiments of education, proof of loyalty to the United States through military service, and now land on which to make a living, it appeared that the former slaves of the Sea Islands would be able to make a smooth transition from slavery to freedom. To many whites, therefore, the "Port Royal Experiment" had been an unqualified success, a model that

could be employed throughout the former Confederacy.

But that was not to be. Soon after Lee's surrender at Appomattox Court House, planters began to return to the Sea Islands to claim their former holdings. Anxious to restore the Union as quickly as possible, in late 1865 President Andrew Johnson ordered the ceasing of land sales, and in January 1866 he removed General Saxton from his post, pardoned many of the Sea Island planters, and ordered that the 400,000 acres confiscated by Sherman's Special Field Order Number 15 be returned to their former owners. Freedmen and women were urged to go to work for their former masters as paid laborers. Thus, in the end most of the former slaves lost nearly everything they had gained: educational opportunities, the right to vote, land ownership, and even their dignity. The "Port Royal Experiment" had proved a great deal, but few seemed to want to listen.[27]

In 1902, Susie King Taylor, a former slave who became a laundress with the First South Carolina Volunteers and traveled with that regiment, looked

---

26. Rose, *Rehearsal for Reconstruction,* p. 328. Lands confiscated from Confederate planters and sold at government land sales in 1863 and 1864 remained in the hands of those who had purchased them.

27. See "Direct-Tax Commissioners for the State of South Carolina to the Secretary of the Treasury," December 11, 1865, in Berlin, ed., *The Wartime Genesis of Free Labor,* series 1, Vol. 3, pp. 342–344.

✦ CHAPTER 10

"No More Pint o'
Salt for Me":
The Port Royal
Experiment,
1861–1865

back across her eventful life. At the same time, she criticized the young African Americans of Boston, her adopted home:

> I look around now and see the comforts that our younger generation enjoy, and . . . see how little some of them appreciate the old soldiers. My heart burns within me, at this want of Appreciation. There are only a few of them left now. . .[28]

In some ways Taylor was incorrect. Many people, white and black, know of the "Port Royal Experiment," a "dress rehearsal for Reconstruction" that was never put into practice beyond the extraordinarily lovely Sea Islands, islands that today boast beautiful upscale permanent and vacation homes of the republic's well-off men and women, wonderful golf courses, and haunting memories of what might have been.

28. Susie King Taylor, *Reminiscences of My Life in Camp with the 33rd U.S. Colored Troops, Late 1st South Carolina Volunteers*, ed. Patricia W. Romero (Princeton, N.J.: Markus Weiner Publishing, 1988), p. 120.

The Reconstruction Era: Farmers and Workers in the West and North, 1866–1877

◆

The Problem

The Civil War tore the nation apart, sometimes even splitting individual families, and pitted Union soldiers against Confederate soldiers for four long years. In the period between the firing on Fort Sumter in 1861 and Lee's surrender at Appomattox Court House in 1865, over 630,000 people were killed and many thousands more were wounded. Deaths during the Civil War, both in numbers and in proportion to total population, far exceeded deaths during any other war in our nation's history.

Those who survived were faced with uncertainties about their roles in a rapidly changing world. Daniel Sawtelle was the Republican son of a Democratic New England farmer. After enlisting in the 8th Maine Infantry at age 23, he served in Florida and South Carolina, later reenlisting as a sharpshooter and a member of the occupation army in Virginia. Ill and exhausted when he finally returned home in 1866, he wrote in his memoirs: "Only think of a big boy, man grown, almost

twenty-eight, wanting mother more than anything else on earth. Sick and worn with my long journey, I was too glad to cry and too sick to laugh."[1] Restless after a few months at home, he decided that there were more opportunities for farmers out West and moved first to Wisconsin, then Minnesota, then South Dakota, and finally Oregon.

Elisha Hunt Rhodes was the son of a Rhode Island sea captain who had drowned on a voyage. At the age of 16, Rhodes was supporting his family by working as a clerk. Nineteen years old when he enlisted as a private in the 2nd Rhode Island Volunteers, he was discharged as a colonel in 1865. Writing in his diary on the day he said good-bye to his regiment, he reflected:

It was sad, yet joyful, for the war is over and we are at home. No more suf-

1. Peter H. Buckingham, ed., *All's for the Best: The Civil War Reminiscences and Letters of Daniel W. Sawtelle* (Knoxville: University of Tennessee Press, 2001), p. 200.

◆ CHAPTER 11

The Reconstruction
Era: Farmers and
Workers in the West
and North,
1866–1877

fering, no more scenes of carnage and death. Thank God it is over and that the Union is restored. And so at last I am a simple citizen.[2]

Rhodes returned to his home state, married, and later traveled throughout the South and West as a representative for woolen and cotton mills. Active in veterans' affairs, he often took his grandsons to visit Civil War battlefields. "I don't think that Grandpa owned a house," wrote one of Rhodes's grandsons years later. "He and Grandma used to board on Benefit Street and out at Fruit Hill, and sometimes they stayed with Aunt Alice. . . ."[3]

These two Union soldiers' experiences were similar to those of thousands of young men during the Reconstruction era immediately following the Civil War. Popular literature of the times exhorted young men to strive to be successful. Some, like Sawtelle, went West to try their luck at farming on the plains. Others, like Rhodes, went to the newly expanding cities, lured by the opportunities offered by business and industry. What characteristics were thought to be essential for "success?" What difficulties did farmers and workers face in the decade following the War? What actions did they take to try to overcome these problems?

◆

Background

Historians generally treat Reconstruction as the story of the South, defeated by the Union and occupied by as many as 200,000 federal troops immediately after the Civil War. Economically devastated, with their crops, homes, transportation, and monetary system destroyed, the former Confederate states also faced a political crisis with the disenfranchisement of their former leaders. Overshadowing the economic and political problems, however, were questions related to the newly freed slaves. No one knew what the place of the free African Americans would be in Southern society nor the nature of the future relationships between blacks and whites.

During Reconstruction, white Southerners began to restrict the rights of African Americans through coercive labor contracts, labor "gangs" that resembled work patterns under slavery, black codes limiting mobility, and vagrancy laws. Vigilante violence occurred and organizations such as the Ku Klux Klan were formed to intimidate African Americans, while sharecropping, tenant farming, and the crop lien system increased among blacks and poor whites, trapping them in a permanent cycle of indebtedness.

In the North, President Ulysses Grant's administration, as well as state and city governments, were marked by scandals, corruption, and bribery. The presidential election of 1876 was between two very similar men, both former reform governors: Republican

2. Robert Hunt Rhodes, ed., *All for the Union* (Lincoln: Andrew Mowbray Inc., 1985), p. 248.
3. Ibid., p. 249.

Rutherford Hayes of Ohio and Democrat Samuel Tilden of New York. Both sides claimed fraud, and a special electoral commission, voting along strict party lines, gave the election to Hayes. As part of the subsequent political compromise in 1877, the activities of federal troops in the South were curtailed and the rights of freed blacks in the former Confederate states were left without any federal protection.

There is no question that the story of the South, along with the political situation in the North, is central to our understanding of the Reconstruction era, 1866–1877. However, in many ways Reconstruction was truly a *national* phenomenon, involving the incorporation of far-reaching economic and social changes that had begun long before the Civil War but were accelerated by the War. Three of the most significant trends of the postwar era were industrialization, urbanization, and the westward expansion of farming into the Great Plains. By focusing only on the struggles of black and white Southerners and the political battles and corruption in the North during the Reconstruction era, we sometimes overlook the important experiences of the millions of other Americans who went West hoping to become prosperous farmers or who left their rural and small town homes to go to nearby cities in search of new economic opportunities in manufacturing, business, and the professions.

The westward movement, of course, had been a constant element of the nineteenth century. With the rapid expansion of railroads and favorable legislation from both the U.S. Congress and state legislatures, railroad compa-

nies acquired enormous power to set their own rates and schedules. Railroads also possessed large land grants along their routes, which they sold at a profit to land companies and farmers.

Although the Homestead Act of 1862 had granted 160-acre farms to settlers who would live on the land and improve it, this farm size was too small to be profitable for farmers on the plains. Most settlers had to buy more land and often borrowed money to purchase their farmsteads. Extremes of temperature and precipitation; the lack of trees to provide wood for houses, fences, and fuel; the need for oxen or horses to plow the ground and reap the crop; and the unsuitability of eastern seeds and crops for plains agriculture— all made the work of establishing successful, productive farms in states such as Kansas and Nebraska very difficult. Family farms depended on the work of women and children, who had to perform heavy physical labor cleaning, cooking, and washing, as well as helping with outdoor chores. Often geographically isolated, farm women depended upon distant women neighbors for help in childbirth, sickness, and other emergencies. In spite of these challenges, the census reveals the striking fact that in 1870 there were 2.7 million farms on the plains and prairies, and ten years later there were 4 million farms.

Struggling western farmers resented the roles played by eastern bankers and capitalists, the middlemen who operated grain-storage elevators, and the railroad owners whose monopoly on regional transportation systems enabled them to set arbitrary rate and time schedules. As early as 1867, a social

✦ CHAPTER 11

The Reconstruction
Era: Farmers and
Workers in the West
and North,
1866–1877

and educational organization for farmers had been founded, the National Grange of the Patrons of Husbandry. As a result of the depression of 1873 and the increasing competition from overseas farmers, agricultural prices began to fall. By the mid-1870s, with over 1.5 million members, the Grange had become an important political and economic force in midwestern states such as Wisconsin, Minnesota, Illinois, and Iowa. In the late 1870s, after some political successes on the state level, the Grange gradually reverted to its original functions as an educational and social organization for farm families.

As successive waves of miners, cattle and sheep ranchers, and farm families moved West, they came into increasing conflict with the Native American inhabitants. In response to Eastern demands for fairer treatment of Indians, President Grant had announced a "peace policy" that called for the establishment of reservations where Native Americans could live and be instructed in Christianity and agriculture. Little was done to implement any sort of government aid, however, and Indian affairs fell victim to the same corruption that characterized the rest of the Grant administration. The same railroads that made it easier for settlers to emigrate to the West also encouraged commercial and "sport" hunting of buffalo. During the 1870s, such hunting resulted in the slaughter of over *5 million* buffalo. The big herds, upon which the Indians depended, had been exterminated by the end of the decade. Native Americans raided wagon trains travelling across the plains and defeated Custer and his troops at Little Big Horn, but eventually they succumbed to the Army's determined efforts to contain Indians on reservations and punish those who resisted.

Like the westward movement, the emigration of Americans from rural areas and villages into towns and cities had begun earlier, continued during the war, and increased dramatically in the last quarter of the nineteenth century. The real population gains in the late 1860s and 1870s were to be found in medium-sized cities and large towns. The number of towns with populations between 10,000 and 25,000 doubled between 1860 and 1870, and increased by another 26 percent by 1880. The number of cities with populations between 50,000 and 100,000 doubled between 1860 and 1870, and increased by 27 percent more by 1880.

Along with the increase in urbanization came the expansion of business and industry. Many of the emerging, wealthy business elite, such as John D. Rockefeller, had avoided military service and laid the foundation of their later industrial fortunes during the Civil War. Below the business elite were the new, salaried managers, whose well-being depended on the degree to which they contributed to the profitability of the business through adopting new technologies and increasing workers' productivity. Generally speaking, both the government and the courts were favorable to business interests during the Reconstruction era. Social Darwinism, as popularized in the United States through self-help literature, seemed to give legitimacy to ideas about the "survival of the fittest."

The power and influence of big business did not go unchallenged, however.

From the founding of the short-lived National Labor Union in 1866 to that of the broad, all-encompassing Noble Order of the Knights of Labor in 1869, workers and reformers tried to gain more equality for labor. The prolonged depression that began in 1873 affected workers as well as farmers. Historians estimate that in the years between 1873 and 1877, only two out of ten people in the labor force had full-time, steady employment. Another two out of ten were unemployed, and about four out of ten worked only six or seven months of each year. Violent demonstrations and strikes occurred throughout the 1870s, for example when mounted police charged into a crowd of unemployed workers in New York City in 1874, beating them with billy clubs.

Labor activism in the mining industry, which the mine operators blamed on the secret labor society the Molly Maguires, also ended in violence, characterized by the use of spies, private police, and Italian strikebreakers. By the summer of 1877, labor unrest was widespread. Pennsylvania railroad workers, who worked shifts as long as 15 to 18 hours and whose wages had already been cut by more than one-third, were informed that there would be another wage cut. Spontaneous strikes occurred in cities throughout Pennsylvania and spread to West Virginia, Illinois, and Ohio. Many of these strikes included workers not connected with the railroads, and ended in riots during which federal troops fired on crowds of people. In total, the railroad strikes of 1877 destroyed more than $10 million worth of railroad property.

In this problem, you will be examining some self-help literature to see the characteristics that were considered essential for young men who wished to "succeed" in the post–Civil War era. You will also look at some experiences of farmers and workers in the West and North. What challenges and difficulties did they face? How did they try to solve these problems through organizations such as the Grange and the Knights of Labor?

The Method

For many years, historians who studied major events such as the American Revolution, urbanization, or industrialization focused mainly on the events themselves. This meant that the majority of people who lived during the times being studied became somewhat secondary to the understanding of the times. In other words, they were *acted upon,* rather than being *actors* in historical events or periods of important changes. To the degree that any people were important historical figures, it was because they were generals or presidents or business leaders who were in positions of power and influence.

During the 1960s and 1970s, some European historians continued to see history this way, especially those who studied large geographical areas such as the Mediterranean region over very long periods of time. Historians who believe that certain theories can ex-

♦ CHAPTER 11

The Reconstruction
Era: Farmers and
Workers in the West
and North,
1866–1877

plain historical change and events also tend to conclude that people are acted upon by major forces over which they have no control. In the United States, however, historians' new interest in ordinary people's lives and experiences led them in a different direction. Although no one would deny that people are influenced by major geographical, economic, social, and political forces, historians began to study the ways in which people chose from among alternatives and took action.

In this problem, you will be looking at farmers and workers who lived in a period of economic and social change, and who were affected by these changes. Yet they were not merely *acted upon,* but rather they had choices and took action to solve what they perceived as their problems. In examining the evidence, it is very important for you to place farmers and workers firmly into their historical setting and then to determine why and how they acted to change their situations.

♦

The Evidence

EXCERPTS FROM INSPIRATIONAL LITERATURE

Source 1 from Horatio Alger, Jr., *Ragged Dick and Mark, the Match Boy* (New York: Collier/Macmillan, 1962), pp. 43–44, 75, 110–111.

1. *Ragged Dick* (1867).

[*When we are first introduced to Ragged Dick, he is a boy about twelve years old, dirty, and wearing torn and tattered clothing. He sleeps on the street in doorways, carts, or old boxes. He also has some bad habits: he smokes cigarettes, gambles, goes to the theater, and occasionally eats in taverns. He is a "bootblack" who shines shoes for a living.*]

I have mentioned Dick's faults and defects, because I want it understood, to begin with, that I don't consider him a model boy. But there were some good points about him nevertheless. He was above doing anything mean or dishonorable. He would not steal, or cheat, or impose upon younger boys, but was frank and straight-forward, manly and self-reliant. His nature was a noble one, and had saved him from all mean faults. I hope my young readers will like him as I do, without being blind to his faults. Perhaps, although he was only a bootblack, they may find something in him to imitate. . . .

[*When Ragged Dick encounters a young boy, Frank, who is visiting his uncle on his way to boarding school, Dick offers to show Frank around New York City. None of Dick's friends recognize him, as he is wearing clothes that Frank gives him. Frank tells Dick that he could make a better life for himself.*]

"A good many distinguished men have once been poor boys. There's hope for you, Dick, if you'll try."

"Nobody ever talked to me so before," said Dick. "They just called me Ragged Dick, and told me I'd grow up to be a vagabone (boys who are better educated need not be surprised at Dick's blunders) and come to the gallows."

"Telling you so won't make it turn out so, Dick. If you'll try to be somebody, and grow up into a respectable member of society, you will. You may not become rich,—it isn't everybody that becomes rich, you know,—but you can obtain a good position, and be respected."

"I'll try," said Dick, earnestly. "I needn't have been Ragged Dick so long if I hadn't spent my money in goin' to the theatre, and treatin' boys to oyster-stews, and bettin' money on cards, and such like." . . .

[*By the end of the day, Ragged Dick and Frank have become friends, and they promise to write to each other.*]

"Uncle, Dick's ready to go," said Frank.

"Good-by, my lad," said Mr. Whitney. "I hope to hear good accounts of you sometime. Don't forget what I have told you. Remember that your future position depends mainly upon yourself, and that it will be high or low as you choose to make it."

He held out his hand, in which was a five-dollar bill. Dick shrunk back.

"I don't like to take it," he said. "I haven't earned it."

"Perhaps not," said Mr. Whitney; "but I give it to you because I remember my own friendless youth. I hope it may be of service to you. Sometime when you are a prosperous man, you can repay it in the form of aid to some poor boy, who is struggling upward as you are now."

"I will, sir," said Dick, manfully.

He no longer refused the money, but took it gratefully, and, bidding Frank and his uncle good-by, went out into the street.

[*Ragged Dick changes his ways and gives up his bad habits after Frank leaves. He rents a room, saves his money, and studies on his own. After diving off a ferry to save the life of a young boy, Dick is rewarded by the boy's father, who gives him a job as a clerk in his bank. Ragged Dick now calls himself Richard Hunter, Esquire.*]

✦ CHAPTER 11

The Reconstruction
Era: Farmers and
Workers in the West
and North,
1866–1877

Source 2 from Russell Conwell, *Acres of Diamonds* (Westwood, N.J.: Fleming H. Revell Company, 1960), pp. 24–27.

2. "Acres of Diamonds" Lecture (1870).

[*Conwell begins his lecture by telling the story of an ancient Persian, Ali Hafed, a wealthy farmer who owned a large, prosperous farm. One day, a visitor tells Ali Hafed about diamonds and the immense wealth that they bring to their owners. Hafed becomes restless and discontented, sells his farm, leaves his family, and goes in search of diamonds. In all his travels, he never finds any diamonds, and he dies poor and unhappy. In the meantime, the man who bought Ali Hafed's farm finds a fabulous lode of diamonds in his own garden. Opportunity for success, Conwell insisted in his lecture, can be found in your own "backyard."*]

I say that you ought to get rich, and it is your duty to get rich. How many of my pious brethren say to me, "Do you, a Christian minister, spend your time going up and down the country advising young people to get rich, to get money?" "Yes, of course I do." They say, "Isn't that awful! Why don't you preach the gospel instead of preaching about man's making money?" "Because to make money honestly is to preach the gospel." That is the reason. The men who get rich may be the most honest men you find in the community.

"Oh," but says some young man here tonight, "I have been told all my life that if a person has money he is very dishonest and dishonorable and mean and contemptible." My friend, that is the reason why you have none, because you have that idea of people. The foundation of your faith is altogether false. Let me say here clearly, and say it briefly, though subject to discussion which I have not time for here, ninety-eight out of one hundred of the rich men of America are honest. That is why they are rich. That is why they are trusted with money. That is why they carry on great enterprises and find plenty of people to work with them. It is because they are honest men.

Says another young man, "I hear sometimes of men that get millions of dollars dishonestly." Yes, of course you do, and so do I. But they are so rare a thing in fact that the newspapers talk about them all the time as a matter of news until you get the idea that all the other rich men got rich dishonestly.

My friend, you take and drive me—if you furnish the auto—out into the suburbs of Philadelphia, and introduce me to the people who own their homes around this great city, those beautiful homes with gardens and flowers, those magnificent homes so lovely in their art, and I will introduce you to the very best people in character as well as in enterprise in our city, and you know I will. A man is not really a true man until he owns his own home, and they that own their homes are made more honorable and honest and pure, and true and economical and careful, by owning the home. . . .

Money is power, and you ought to be reasonably ambitious to have it. You ought because you can do more good with it than you could without it. . . . The man who gets the largest salary can do the most good with the power that is furnished to him. Of course he can if his spirit be right to use it for what it is given to him.

I say, then, you ought to have money. If you can honestly attain unto riches in Philadelphia, it is your Christian and godly duty to do so. It is an awful mistake of these pious people to think you must be awfully poor in order to be pious.

Some men say, "Don't you sympathize with the poor people?" Of course I do, or else I would not have been lecturing these years. I won't give in but what I sympathize with the poor, but the number of poor who are to be sympathized with is very small. To sympathize with a man whom God has punished for his sins, thus to help him when God would still continue a just punishment, is to do wrong, no doubt about it, and we do that more than we help those who are deserving. While we should sympathize with God's poor— that is, those who cannot help themselves—let us remember there is not a poor person in the United States who was not made poor by his own shortcomings, or by the shortcomings of someone else. It is all wrong to be poor, anyhow.

Source 3 from Samuel Smiles, *Character* (New York: Harper & Bros, 1877 [?]), pp. 13, 48–49, 165–166.

3. *Character* (1871).

Character is one of the greatest motive powers in the world. In its noblest embodiments, it exemplifies human nature in its highest forms, for it exhibits man at his best. . . .

Although genius always commands admiration, character most secures respect. The former is more the time, afterwards springing up in acts and thoughts and habits. Thus the mother lives again in her children. They unconsciously mould themselves after her manner, her speech, her conduct, and her method of life. Her habits become theirs; and her character is visibly repeated in them.

This maternal love is the visible providence of our race. . . . It begins with the education of the human being at the outstart of life, and is prolonged by virtue of the powerful influence which every good mother exercises over her children through life. When launched into the world, each to take part in its

✦ CHAPTER 11

The Reconstruction
Era: Farmers and
Workers in the West
and North,
1866–1877

labors, anxieties, and trials, they still turn to their mother for consolation, if not for counsel, in their time of trouble and difficulty. The pure and good thoughts she has implanted in their minds when children continue to grow up into good acts long after she is dead. . . .

Man is the brain, but woman is the heart of humanity; he its judgment, she its feeling; he its strength, she its grace, ornament, and solace. Even the understanding of the best woman seems to work mainly through her affections. And thus, though man may direct the intellect, woman cultivates the feelings, which mainly determine the character. While he fills the memory, she occupies the heart. She makes us love what he can only make us believe, and it is chiefly through her that we are enabled to arrive at virtue. . . .

Work is one of the best educators of practical character. It evokes and disciplines obedience, self-control, attention, application, and perseverance; giving a man deftness and skill in his special calling, and aptitude and dexterity in dealing with the affairs of ordinary life.

It is idleness that is the curse of man—not labor. . . . it is this power which constitutes the real distinction between a physical and a moral life, and that forms the primary basis of individual character.

WESTERN FARMERS

Source 4 photos from Long Collection, Kansas Collection; Wisconsin Historical Society.

4. Sod House Pictures.

A. An early, simple sod house in Kansas.

B. A nineteenth-century sod house on the prairie.

Sources 5 and 6 from Cass G. Barns, *The Sod House* (Lincoln: University of Nebraska Press, 1970), pp. 90, 217.

5. Grasshoppers (1875).

This year we had another very dry season resulting in light crops on which the grasshoppers came down by multiplied millions. Great destitution and suffering followed. . . . The grasshoppers came in such swarms that they looked in the distance like fast-gathering rain clouds flying through the air. In some places on the fields of grain they were so numerous that the grain was completely hid from sight. If they had kept still, a man with a scoop shovel could have filled a common wagon bed with them in a few minutes. For a number of years it seemed to be our lot to meet with the grasshoppers, which would take meat, bread and other things from our table.

6. Bugs (1876).

In moving into all kinds of houses we find all kinds of insects that prey upon human blood. One house we found as nearly alive with bugs as a house could be, and not walk off. Soon after going to bed the first night, the bugs sallied out upon us by the hundreds, as if we were sent there on purpose to feed them. . . . After killing the first squad that came out of ambush, we began to count as fast as we destroyed them, and by actual count we killed more than two hundred besides the many we had deprived of life before beginning to count.

Source 7 from Howard Ruede, *Sod-House Days: Letters from a Kansas Homesteader, 1877–78* (New York: Columbia University Press, 1937), pp. 28–29, 50, 52–53.

7. A Homesteader's Experience in Kansas (1877).

[*Howard Ruede traveled from Pennsylvania to Kansas by train, a trip that took three days and three nights. Writing home to his family, Ruede explained how sod houses were built and described the dugout that he and his friends were building. Many of his letters and diary entries were also about food.*]

The sod wall is about 2 feet thick at the ground, and slopes off on the outside to about 14 inches at the top. The roof is composed of a ridge pole and rafters

✦ CHAPTER 11

The Reconstruction
Era: Farmers and
Workers in the West
and North,
1866–1877

of rough split logs, on which is laid corn stalks, and on top of those are two layers of sod. The roof has a very slight pitch, for if it had more, the sod would wash off when there is a heavy rain. . . .

Occasionally a new comer has a "bee," and the neighbors for miles around gather at his claim and put up his house in a day. Of course there is no charge for labor in such cases. The women come too, and while the men lay up the sod walls, they prepare dinner for the crowd, and have a very sociable hour at noon. A house put up in this way is very likely to settle and get out of shape, but it is seldom deserted for that reason.

At first these sod houses are unplastered, and this is thought perfectly all right, but such a house is somewhat cold in the winter, as the crevices between the sods admit some cold air; so some of the houses are plastered with a kind of "native lime," made of sand and a very sticky native clay. . . . I will have to be contented with a very modest affair for a while, but perhaps I can improve it later. . . .

AT THE DUGOUT, KILL CREEK, KANSAS

Turned out about 6 and made fire. Forgot to put the beans to soak last evening, so it took a little longer to boil. Wind n.w., and the fire smokes a good deal, but that kills the meat flies, so I can stand it. While the breakfast was cooking I went out and cut wood so it will be drying out. Rather cloudy this morning. Levin took his ink with him, so I'll have to get a bottle when I go to town again. About 9 o'clock went to chopping again. Guess I'll have to quit, because it makes me short-breathed. Quit about 11, and got as far as Hoot's, on the way back. He was at work on a breaking plow and I stopped to help him a bit. It was raining right smart, and we had showers all day. We tinkered away at the plow till noon, and then I would have left, but they asked me to stop, so I went in and had a square meal. The meat he told me to guess at. I guessed veal, but it was coon. Learned a little about setting the rolling cutter on a breaking plow by watching him and Snyder. When I left for the ranch I bought a loaf of bread from Mrs. Snyder, and I felt as good as if I had drawn a prize in the lottery. Tried a new dodge with the cornmeal. Mixed it with a little water and salt, and baked it over the fire, and it went down a heap better than mush. My supper will be a slice of ham boiled with beans, and a slice of bread. How is that for high toned? The wind is n.e. and the room is full of smoke. . . .

AT THE DUGOUT, KILL CREEK, KANSAS

Turned out about 6, and after breakfast went over to Snyder's. John was shelling corn, and I turned in and helped him. He soon left, to go and herd the cattle, but I kept on till near noon; and I stayed to dinner to pay for my work. . . . As I have no oil, I go to bed with the sun, and try to get up with it, though as yet I have not done so. . . . The start we have made goes very slow, but I think we will get ahead so that next spring we can go to farming and not have to work round. I have a hard time with the meat flies and have taken thousands of eggs off of the ham. I have no dark or smoky place to keep it in, and they get inside of the paper in which it is wrapped. Hardly know what to do with it. It weighs 20 lb. and was twice as big as I wanted, but I could not get a smaller one. The provisions I bought on the 16th cost $2.80. I'll see how long they last. Pickled or smoked hog meat costs 10¢ per lb., corn meal $1.25 per cwt. Hope I'll get papers or a letter with this evening's mail.

Source 8 from John Stands-in-Timber and Margot Liberty, *Cheyenne Memories*, 2nd ed. (New Haven: Yale University Press, 1998), pp. 276–278.

8. Native Americans and Western Farming (1877).

Farming and Gardening

The government started the Indians raising gardens as soon as they surrendered. Some had gardens of corn and other crops at Fort Keogh. They had forgotten how, though they all used to garden in the old days before they hunted buffalo. Now they were learning about new crops as well, things they had never seen before. The Dull Knife people got to Oklahoma in 1877 about the time the watermelons ripened, and when the Southern Cheyennes gave them some they cut them up and boiled them like squash. They did not know you could eat them raw. But later when they planted their own they put sugar with the seeds. They said it would make them sweeter when they grew.

When they reached Tongue River every man was supposed to have a garden of his own. A government farmer went around to teach them. And many of them worked hard, even carrying buckets of water from the river by hand. . . .

Another time when they practiced plowing down there, one man plowed up a bull snake and the next man plowed up a rattlesnake, and after that they were all afraid to go.

In Montana they began to help each other. The government issued plows to quite a few men, and in Birney the Fox Military Society used to plow together as soon as the frost was out. They would all gather at the farthest place up the river and work together until that was done, and then move to the next. They had seven or eight plows and it went faster that way. Besides, it was more fun.

✦ CHAPTER 11

The Reconstruction
Era: Farmers and
Workers in the West
and North,
1866–1877

One year they decided to finish every garden in ten days, and any member who did not show up would be punished. Everything was fine for several days, until they got to Black Eagle's place. And Looks Behind never came. The rest of them finished plowing for Black Eagle and Medicine Top and Broken Jaw. Then they all got on their horses, and us kids followed them to the Medicine Bull place on Tie Creek and there was Looks Behind, fixing his fence.

They all yelled and fired their guns, and galloped by and hit him with their quirts. There were twenty or thirty of them. Looks Behind had a shovel and at first he was going to fight, but he took it. Afterwards he could hardly talk. They made him get on his horse and go back and start plowing right away.

Source 9 from John L. Commons, et al., *A Documentary History of American Industrial Society,* Vol. X, (Cleveland: Arthur H. Clark Company, 1911). pp. 76–79, 132–136.

9. The Grange.

A. Circular announcing the formation of the Grange (1868).

National Grange, Washington, D.C., September, 1868.

In response to numerous inquiries in regard to the organization and objects of our Order, this circular is issued. . . . It is founded upon the axioms that the products of the soil comprise the basis of all wealth; that individual happiness depends upon general prosperity, and that the wealth of a country depends upon the general intelligence and mental culture of the producing classes. . . .

Women are admitted into our Order, as well as young persons of both sexes over the age of sixteen and eighteen respectively. In its proceedings a love for rural life will be encouraged, the desire for excitement and amusement, so prevalent in youth, will be gratified, instead of being repressed; not, however, in frivolities, as useless for the future as they are for the present, but by directing attention to the wonder-workings of nature, and leading the mind to enjoy and appreciate that never-ending delight which follows useful studies, relating to the animal, vegetable, and mineral kingdoms. . . .

Its objects, as already indicated, are to advance education, to elevate and dignify the occupation of the farmer, and to protect its members against the numerous combinations by which their interests are injuriously affected.

There is no association that secures so many advantages to its members as this.

The Order of the Patrons of Husbandry will accomplish a thorough and systematic organization among farmers and horticulturists throughout the

United States, and will secure among them intimate social relations and acquaintance with each other, for the advancement and elevation of its pursuits, with an appreciation and protection of their true interests. By such means may be accomplished that which exists throughout the country in all other avocations, and among all other classes—combined co-operative association for individual improvement and common benefit. . . .

Among other advantages which may be derived from the Order, can be mentioned, systematic arrangements for procuring and disseminating, in the most expeditious manner, information relative to crops, demand and supply, prices, markets, and transportation throughout the country, and for the establishment of depots for the sale of special or general products in the cities; also for the purchase and exchange of stock, seeds, and desired varieties of plants and trees, and for the purpose of procuring help at home or from abroad, and situations for persons seeking employment; also for ascertaining and testing the merits of newly invented farming implements, and those not in general use, and for detecting and exposing those that are unworthy, and for protecting by all available means, the farming interests from fraud and deception of every kind.

In conclusion, we desire that agricultural societies shall keep step with the music of the age, and keep pace with improvements in the reaping machine and steam engine. In this Order we expect to accomplish these results.

B. Excerpts from the 13th National Meeting of the Grange (1879).

Thirteen years' experience and association in the Grange has satisfied the American farmers, whom we represent, that their grievances will never be removed until farmers are elected as representatives to the law-making bodies of our states, and to the national legislatures, in such numbers as will constitute those bodies with a fair share of our people. . . . To this end we recommend farmers to make such alliance, whenever representatives to the state legislatures or to the national legislature are to be chosen, as will enable them by their votes to elect from their own number an even handed, fair share of representatives. . . . The assumption of this constitutional right is but the assertion of our manhood, and we cannot longer be dominated by party associations which deny us our equality, or support a partizan press that ignores the association of American farmers.

American farming is growing less profitable and less encouraging. In a country possessing so many facilities of cheap production this discouraging aspect of agriculture must be and is the result of other than natural causes. The annual additions of wealth under the enlightened system of agriculture

◆ CHAPTER 11

The Reconstruction
Era: Farmers and
Workers in the West
and North,
1866–1877

are enormous, but from the unequal divisions of the profits of labor and the unjust discriminations made against it, the enlistments of property show that the farmers of the United States are not prospering. . . .

The farmers of America have on all occasions shown themselves to be a patient and enduring people, and further submission to wrong and injustice will be a sacrifice of manhood and exhibition of cowardice. Stirred with a just sense of right and supported by the integrity of our purpose, the National Grange of the Patrons of Husbandry, in the name and interests of the farmers of the United States, sternly demand—

1st. That the Department of Agriculture shall be made an Executive Department, and the Commissioner a Cabinet officer.

2d. That the Agricultural Department shall be sustained and supported by annual appropriations commensurate with the importance of the great and permanent industry it represents.

3d. That commercial treaties shall be made with all foreign countries, giving to American products equal and unrestricted intercourse with the markets of the world.

4th. That governments be administered in a cheaper and simpler manner, consonant with the conditions of the people.

5th. That a more rigid economy in the expenditures of public moneys be reestablished.

6th. That the laws shall be plain and simple, to the end that justice shall be speedy, crime punished, and good government maintained.

7th. That the creation or allowing of monopolies to exist is in violation of the spirit and genius of free republican government.

8th. That the tariffs of freight and fare over railroads and all transportation companies shall be regulated, and all unjust discriminations inhibited by law.

9th. That taxation shall be equal and uniform, and all values made to contribute their just proportion to the support of the government.

10th. That the revenue laws of the United States shall be so adjusted as to bear equally upon all classes of property, to the end that agriculture shall be relieved of the disproportion of burdens it bears.

11th. That the patent laws of the United States be so revised that innocent purchasers of patent rights shall be protected, and fraudulent venders alone held responsible for infringements of rights and violations of law.

12th. That a system of elementary agricultural education shall be adopted in the common schools of the country.

13th. That we are entitled to and should have a fair representation in the legislative halls of the country, chosen from the ranks of the farmers. . . .

With manly dignity we boldly declare our rights and interests, and with unwavering devotion will maintain and defend them on all occasions, and this warning is defiantly thrown to the world.

NORTHERN WORKERS

Source 10 from James C. Sylvis, *The Life, Speeches, Labors & Essays of William H. Sylvis* (New York: Augustus M. Kelley, 1968), pp. 296, 316–318.

10. National Labor Union, Letter to the *Evening Advocate* from William Sylvis (1868).

WHAT WE WANT.

We now want:

1. A new department at Washington, to be called THE DEPARTMENT OF LABOR, the head of said department to be called the Secretary of Labor, and to be chosen directly from the ranks of workingmen. To this department should be referred all questions of wages and the hours of labor in the navy-yards and all other government workshops, the registry and regulation of trades-unions and co-operative associations, the disposition of public lands, and all other questions directly connected with and affecting labor.

2. The unconditional repeal of all laws bearing upon the disposition of the public domain.

3. The adoption of a plain, unvarnished law for the giving away of the public lands to actual settlers in parcels of not less than forty nor more than one hundred acres, no man being allowed to hold in his own name, the name of his wife, nor any other name, more than one tract.

4. Every man taking up land to be required to proceed to live upon, improve, and cultivate it within one year, or forfeit his claim.

5. Appropriations to be made from the United States Treasury to assist workingmen who desire to locate upon the public domain, but who are destitute of the means to do so.

6. No grants of public land to be made to railroad companies or to other corporations, nor to individuals, except actual settlers, under any circumstances, nor for any purpose.

7. All lands granted to railroad companies or other corporations, or individuals, remaining unoccupied and uncultivated at the end of five years from the date of said grant, to revert back to the government, and be sold at government price ($1.25 per acre), the proceeds to go to the person or persons to whom the grant was made. This provision should apply to *all* grants that have been made.

✦ CHAPTER 11

The Reconstruction
Era: Farmers and
Workers in the West
and North,
1866–1877

8. All uncultivated lands held by grant of Congress, by any person or persons, shall pay a tax of *ten cents per acre* into the treasury of the United States until said lands are cultivated, or have reverted to the government.

9. All uncultivated lands now held by grant of Congress, by any person or persons, shall be immediately placed in the market at one dollar and twenty-five cents per acre.

Anticipating the opposition that will be made to the proposition to give the public lands away, and pay the expenses of the poor workingmen who desire to move upon and cultivate these lands, upon the ground that they cost the government something, I will answer, that whatever these lands did cost for surveys, etc., came out of the public treasury; and all the money that is or ever was in said treasury was put there by *the labor of the country*. The lands belong to the people, were paid for by the people, and the people have a right to enjoy them without paying for them a second time. And, all things considered, the proposition to assist the very poor in getting to these lands is a very modest one. We only ask that a very little of the taxes paid by labor be returned to those who paid it, while hundreds of millions are being appropriated for other purposes.

Source 11 from Terence V. Powderly, *Thirty Years of Labor, 1859–1889* (New York: Augustus M. Kelley, 1967), pp. 64–65.

11. Excerpts from the Preamble of the Knights of Labor (1870).

"The recent alarming development and aggression of aggregated wealth, which, unless checked, will inevitably lead to the pauperization and hopeless degradation of the toiling masses, render it imperative, if we desire to enjoy the blessings of the government bequeathed to us by the founders of the Republic, that a check should be placed upon its power and unjust accumulation, and a system adopted which will secure to the laborer the fruits of his toil; and as this much-desired object can only be accomplished by the thorough unification of labor, and the united efforts of those who obey the divine injunction, 'In the sweat of thy face shalt thou eat bread,' we have formed the INDUSTRIAL BROTHERHOOD, with a view of securing the organization and direction, by co-operative effort, of the power of the industrial classes; and we submit to the people of the United States the objects sought to be accomplished by our organization, calling upon all who believe in securing 'the greatest good to the greatest number' to aid and assist us:

"I. To bring within the folds of organization every department of productive industry, making knowledge a standpoint for action, and industrial, moral and social worth—not wealth—the true standard of individual and national greatness.

"II. To secure to the toilers a proper share of the wealth that they create; more of the leisure that rightly belongs to them; more societary advantages; more of the benefits, privileges and emoluments of the world; in a word, all those rights and privileges necessary to make them capable of enjoying, appreciating, defending and perpetuating the blessings of republican institutions.

"III. To arrive at the true condition of the producing masses in their educational, moral and financial condition, we demand from the several States and from the national government the establishment of bureaus of labor statistics.

"IV. The establishment of co-operative institutions, productive and distributive.

"V. The reserving of the public lands, the heritage of the people, for the actual settler—not another acre for railroads or speculators.

"VI. The abrogation of all laws that do not bear equally upon capital and labor, the removal of unjust technicalities, delays and discriminations in the administration of justice, and the adoption of measures providing for the health and safety of those engaged in mining, manufacturing or building pursuits.

"VII. The enactment of a law to compel chartered corporations to pay their employes at least once in every month in full for labor performed during the preceding month in the lawful money of the country.

"VIII. The enactment of a law giving mechanics and other laborers a first lien on their work.

"IX. The abolishment of the contract system on national, State and municipal work.

"X. To inaugurate a system of public markets, to facilitate the exchange of the productions of farmers and mechanics, tending to do away with middlemen and speculators.

"XI. To inaugurate systems of cheap transportation to facilitate the exchange of commodities.

"XII. The substitution of arbitration for strikes, whenever and wherever employers and employes are willing to meet on equitable grounds.

"XIII. The prohibition of the importation of all servile races, the discontinuance of all subsidies granted to national vessels bringing them to our shores, and the abrogation of the Burlingame Treaty.

"XIV. To advance the standard of American mechanics by the enactment and enforcement of equitable apprentice laws.

✦ CHAPTER 11

The Reconstruction
Era: Farmers and
Workers in the West
and North,
1866–1877

"XV. To abolish the system of contracting the labor of convicts in our prisons and reformatory institutions.

"XVI. To secure for both sexes equal pay for equal work.

"XVII. The reduction of the hours of labor to eight per day, so that laborers may have more time for social enjoyment and intellectual improvement, and be enabled to reap the advantages conferred by labor-saving machinery, which their brains have created.

"XVIII. To prevail upon the government to establish a just standard of distribution between capital and labor by providing a purely national circulating medium based upon the faith and resources of the nation, issued directly to the people, without the intervention of any system of banking corporations, which money shall be a legal tender in the payment of all debts, public or private, and interchangeable at the option of the holder for government bonds, bearing a rate of interest not to exceed three and sixty-five hundredths per cent., subject to future legislation of Congress."

Source 12 from John Garraty, ed., *The Transformation of American Society, 1870–1890* (Columbia: University of South Carolina Press, 1969), pp. 88–96.

12. Massachusetts Bureau of Statistics of Labor Report (1878).

From a Carpet-Mill Operative.—I am satisfied with sixty hours a week: it is plenty time for any man, although there are some employed in the same place over that time, and get nothing extra for it. . . .

From a Shoemaker.—I think there ought to be an eight-hour law all over the country. There is not enough work to last the year round, and work over eight hours a day, or forty-eight hours a week. There can be only about so much work to do any way: and, when that is done, business has got to stop, or keep dragging the year round, so that a man has to work for almost any price offered. . . .

From a Carpenter.—I think that eight hours a day is enough for a man to work at his trade. Then I think there would be more work; and he would have time to make his house and garden look more tidy, if he has one, or to study and improve the mind. I think that a man would do more work at home when he is at work than he would when unemployed; for he is down-hearted, and does not feel like working at home. I find too, that, the lower wages are, the more work they expect a man to do. . . .

From a Carpenter.—In regard to the number of hours a day's work should consist of, I think ten hours is a fair day's work, and do not think an eight-hour law would be any help to the laboring class. There are some who would make good use of their spare time; and there are others who would not. This same class would want pay for ten hours, and would strike if they could not get it. I for one never could see where the laboring class gains any lasting good by a strike. I think a man should make the best terms possible with his boss; and, if he cannot get as much as he wants, he should try other places. He cannot expect to have every thing as he did in good times. If he gets enough to eat, and plain clothes to wear, he should be content for the present. Better times will come soon. . . .

From a Harness-Maker.—In answer to the question, "Do you consider yourself overworked?" I answered, "Yes"; and it is my honest and firm conviction that I am, by at least two hours a day. With the great increase in machinery within the last fifteen or twenty years, I think, in justice, there ought to be some reduction in the hours of labor. Unless the hours of labor are shortened in proportion to the increase of machinery, I consider machinery an injury rather than a benefit to humanity. I tell you that ten hours a day, hard, steady work, is more than any man can stand for any length of time without injuring his health, and therefore shortening his life. For my own part, although my work is not very laborious, when I stop work in the evening, I feel completely played out. I would like to study some; but I am too fatigued. In fact it is as much as I can do to look over the evening paper; and I am almost certain that this is the condition of a majority of workingmen. . . .

From a Shoe-Finisher.—Some piece hands work more than ten hours. Under these circumstances, I consider that, in boot and shoe towns, the laboring classes are overworked, having no time for social enjoyment or self-culture, or for acquiring information. If they get the time, they are unfit for it after ten hours' hard labor. . . .

From a Machinist.—In reply to your question concerning overwork, I wish to say, that, in employment requiring close application of mind or body, to be successful, the diligent and conscientious workman often, I might say always, finds his energy exhausted long before his ten hours are up. . . . I do not think I should be able to follow up work in this way until the age of sixty-five. Hope to find some way to avoid some of the long hours and some of the heavy work before then. I do not mean to complain; but it does seem as if the burdens and the pleasures of this world were very unequally divided. . . .

From a Boot and Shoe Cutter.—Tax machinery. Bring it in common with hand labor, so a man can have twelve months' work in a year, instead of six or eight months. Protect hand labor, same as we protect trade from Europe, by tax or tariff.

From a Machinist.—Machinery and the swarms of cheap foreign labor are

◆ CHAPTER 11

The Reconstruction
Era: Farmers and
Workers in the West
and North,
1866–1877

fast rendering trades useless, and compelling the better class of mechanics to change their occupation, or go to farming. . . .

From a Clerk in a Country Store.—I do believe that, if a person enjoys good health, and is willing to work, he may earn an honest living, and perhaps lay aside a few dollars for future wants. A large portion of our poor people have poor ways: they will sit around the corner groceries and saloons, chew and smoke tobacco, swear and curse those who seem to be prospering, complain of the hard times and their hard luck. . . .

From a Machinist.—The great need now of the laboring man is honesty and contentment. I mean, being willing to do an honest day's work, and contented with the wages his labor will bring in the market. The idea that a man can get rich, without hard work of some kind, must be given up. Thirty-three years of hard work, and yet far from being rich, is my condition.

From a Shoe-Cutter.—There is no way I think I could be paid more fairly than I now am. I do not consider that my employers profit unfairly by my labor. My labor is in the market for sale. My employers buy it just as they buy a side of leather, and expect, and I think are willing to pay, a fair market price for it. . . . All trades-unions and combinations I also consider as injurious to the mass of working-people. A few profit by these associations, and the many pay the bills. If working-people would drop the use of beer, tobacco, and every thing else that is not of real benefit, and let such men as_____and a host of others earn their own living, they would have far more money for the general expenses of a family than they now have. I live in a village of about two thousand inhabitants; and I do not know of a family in destitute circumstances which has let alone vicious expenditures, and been industrious. It is the idle, unthrifty, beer-drinking, don't-care sort of people, who are out at the elbows, and waiting for some sort of legislation to help them. The sooner working-people get rid of the idea that somebody or something is going to help them, the better it will be for them. In this country, as a general thing, every man has an equal chance to rise. In our village there are a number of successful business men, and all began in the world without any thing but their hands and a will to succeed. The best way for working-people to get help is to help themselves. . . .

From a Steam and Gas Fitter.—The war created a class of money aristocrats. . . . Fifteen years ago a man could start a successful business with from one hundred to three hundred dollars; while it now requires one to three or more thousand, thereby making a poor man's chances poorer every year. In fifteen years this country will be worse off than the old countries of Europe and Asia. The rich will be very rich, the poor very poor, and the government will be controlled by the moneyed class. . . .

From a Custom Shoemaker.—The best thing the government (national) can do for workingmen is to let them alone. The wise and the prudent need no help; for the unwise and imprudent nothing effectual can be done. Forethought and economy, carefully practised in early life as well as age, would banish poverty; and nothing else ever will.

From a Comb-Maker.—I do not know of any legislation that will help the workingman, and not affect the successful employer. He has the capital; and, if he cannot employ it so as to make it pay more than in other investments, he would not be likely to employ many workingmen at very high prices.

Source 13 from Samuel Gompers, *Seventy Years of Life and Labour: An Autobiography*, Vol. I, (New York: Augustus M. Kelley, 1967), pp. 155–157.

13. Samuel Gompers's "Strike Baby" (1878).

The Cigar Manufacturers' Association had declared that under no circumstances would any leaders of the strike be employed for at least six months. As a consequence, for nearly four months I was out of employment. I had parted with everything of any value in the house, and my wife and I were every day expecting a newcomer in addition to the five children we already had.

My family helped in every way possible. Part of the time they were hungry and without the necessaries of life. Never once did my wife falter. Blacklisted, I desperately sought employment, going home at night where my brave wife prepared soup out of water, salt, pepper, and flour. . . .

Once I was ready to commit murder. All the children were ill, probably because of winter cold and under-nourishment; they were subject to illness and fever. I walked around looking for work and could not find it, and as I left my wife in the morning again to look for work there were indications that the newcomer was about due, but by previous experience I thought that that condition would last a couple of days. But when I came home, my sister-in-law, who was living with us and sharing whatever little we had, told me that the child was born. There had been nobody to help the mother or the child. I stood by, dazed, and then rushed to the man who had acted as our physician. He was the physician paid by the Hand-in-Hand Society. But he was not in and like a madman I rushed back, but the situation was the same as it was before.

It dawned on me that there was a physician on the next block and I went to him and told him of the condition and that I wanted him to come down and attend to my wife. He asked me if I had money. When I told him I did not, he re-

◆ CHAPTER 11

The Reconstruction
Era: Farmers and
Workers in the West
and North,
1866–1877

plied that he was not our regular physician. I said I knew that but my wife was in such a serious condition and the child there and I wanted him to come to attend her right away. He said, "Well, I do not feel like it and I won't do it."

I walked up to him, looked him square in the eye and said, "Yes you will, you will come and see my wife now." He said, "Well, I will not." I put my hand on his coat collar and said, "You will come now with me or you will never make another move." He said he wanted me to pay him and I said: "I have got no money. I have been out of work, but I will promise to pay you everything I can gather tonight, but you will come with me without another minute's hesitation or I will not be responsible for what I will do to you. Come along." He put on his hat and coat and he went with me. While he was attending the mother and child, I went around among the members of my family and gathered up two dollars and gave it to him. He prescribed some medicine and I did not have the money to get the prescription filled and finally prevailed upon the druggist with whom I was acquainted through living in the neighborhood to trust me for it and we pulled her through. The baby was my Al. He was our strike baby, born in the forenoon of February 28, 1878.

◆

Questions to Consider

In this problem, you are examining western farmers' and northern workers' experiences in the immediate post–Civil War era. As you saw in the Method section, your focus is on the ways in which people were *actors* in their own lives rather than merely *acted upon* by forces beyond their control. However, it is very important to situate these farmers and workers firmly in their own historical time period first, before examining the choices they made. The first three pieces of evidence (Sources 1 through 3) should help you understand how people thought about "success" and what characteristics they believed were necessary to achieve it.

Horatio Alger was a Harvard graduate who became a Unitarian minister under pressure from his father, even though his real love was literature and writing. Prevented from enlisting in the Civil War by a series of physical mishaps, he began writing short stories, novels, and, later in his career, biographies of self-made men. *Ragged Dick* (Source 1), an enormously popular bestseller, was followed by more than 130 other books, mostly fiction about poor newsboys, shoeshine boys, messengers, and street musicians who overcame all obstacles to become successful. Russell Conwell was a Civil War veteran and lawyer who became a Baptist minister in 1879 and later founded Temple University in Philadelphia. He was famous for his inspirational lecture, "Acres of Diamonds" (Source 2), which he claimed to have delivered—with variations—over 6,000 times. Samuel Smiles, one of eleven children, grew up in Scotland and was a self-made man who became a doctor and a writer. Source 3 is an excerpt from his book, *Character,* the sequel to his very popular book, *Self-Help* (1860). These two advice books, along with Smiles's *Thrift* (1875) and *Duty* (1880), sold over a million copies in the United States.

What do these three authors believe constitutes "success" for young men? What qualities would a successful young man possess? Smiles also writes about women's roles, although Alger and Conwell do not. In what ways does "success" for women differ from "success" for men?

The second group of evidence (Sources 4 through 9) examines western farmers' lives and activities. Source 4 consists of two pictures of the sod houses in which farmers lived. How would you describe these houses and their surroundings to a student who could not see the pictures? Sources 5 and 6 reveal the conditions faced by a young Methodist minister and his family in Kansas. What happened to them? Howard Ruede (Source 7) was a twenty-three year old Pennsylvanian who emigrated to Kansas to file a homestead claim in 1877. His father, two younger brothers, mother, and sister eventually joined him. Like many settlers, Ruede first built a dugout (a partially underground shelter), and he worked for the town printer or on other people's farms. Sometimes he earned wages; sometimes he worked in return for food or the use of farm equipment. What were some of the hardships he faced?

During the same period, the federal government insisted that Native Americans who were living on reservations take up plains farming. John Stands-in-Timber, a Cheyenne, discusses these efforts (Source 8). How and why did the Indians' farming experiences differ from those of the white settlers? As farming expanded westward and became more dependent on the transportation of farm products to distant markets, farmers sought relief from some of their problems. What were the general purposes of the Patrons of Husbandry, commonly known as the Grange (Source 9)? What grievances did the farmers voice at the 13th meeting of the Grange?

Workers' attempts to organize had begun well before the Civil War and continued during the war itself. What economic changes did William Sylvis, head of the National Labor Union, ask for in his letter (Source 10)? In the 1870s, the Knights of Labor, a broad-based labor union that included both skilled and unskilled workers, superseded the National Labor Union. Which of the Knights' demands, outlined in Source 11, were similar to those of the National Labor Union? Which were different?

Source 12 is a sample of some workers' responses to a Massachusetts labor survey taken in 1878. What were their major complaints? Do any of these workers' statements reflect the ideas found in the self-help literature written by Alger, Conwell, and Smiles? Influenced by the Great Railroad Strike of 1877, many other workers also struck for better wages in 1877–1878. In New York City, Cigarmakers' Union president Samuel Gompers tried

◆ CHAPTER 11
The Reconstruction
Era: Farmers and
Workers in the West
and North,
1866–1877

to help striking cigar makers who worked in tenement houses. What working-class family dilemmas does his story about the "strike baby" (Source 13) illustrate?

Finally, return to the central questions of this chapter. How would you sum up the popular attitudes of the 1870s toward success? What was the impact of these ideas? What problems did the farmers and workers face? What actions did they take to try to solve these problems?

◆

Epilogue

In the summer of 1877, California newspaperman Henry George began writing a book entitled *Progress and Poverty*. In it, he argued that the extremes of wealth and poverty in the United States were caused by rich Americans' monopolistic control of the land and the rents they charged. George advocated a "single tax" on the increasing value of land, which would enable the government to abolish all other forms of taxation. As a result, George believed, the gap between the rich and the poor would narrow. The evils that resulted from the unequal and unfair distribution of wealth, George wrote, "are not incidents of progress, but tendencies which must bring progress to a halt; that they will not cure themselves, but, on the contrary, must, unless their cause is removed, grow greater and greater. . . ."[4] When *Progress and Poverty* was published in 1879, it sold more than two million copies in the United States and was also widely read and admired abroad.

During the decade of the 1880s, farm prices continued to fall. Wheat, which had sold for $1.20 a bushel in 1881, was 70 cents a bushel in 1889; during the same years, the price of cotton fell from 11 cents a pound to less than a penny a pound. Farmers' Alliances gained membership rapidly in the South and West, including a Colored Alliance that had nearly a quarter of a million African American members. After demonstrating their power in the elections of 1890, farmers formed the Populist party. Their candidates ran on a platform of far-reaching political and economic reforms, and the party enjoyed considerable success on the state level. In fact, many of the Populist party reforms were implemented in the first quarter of the twentieth century.

Under the Dawes Act of 1887, Native Americans were granted 160-acre farms on their reservations, and the "extra" land was sold to white settlers. The opening in 1889 of Oklahoma, a territory reserved for Indians since the 1820s, reduced the Indian landholdings to just one-third of their previous total. Finally, fearing a Sioux uprising during the Ghost Dance movement of 1891, the army, using machine guns, killed 146 Native Americans at Wounded

4. Henry George, *Progress and Poverty* (New York: Modern Library, 1929 [1879]), p. 544.

Knee Creek on a reservation in South Dakota.

Workers also suffered serious setbacks in the 1880s and 1890s, as police, private security forces, and federal troops were regularly called out to quell labor disturbances. In the Haymarket Affair of 1886, a bomb exploded during an outdoor labor meeting in Chicago, resulting in the arrests of eight people and the execution of four of them. The 1892 Homestead Strike against Carnegie Steel Works outside Pittsburgh involved a gun battle between the strikers and private security guards; federal troops were called in to break the 1894 Pullman strike near Chicago. The Knights of Labor declined after a series of unsuccessful strikes in the 1880s and was replaced by the more conservative American Federation of Labor. Organized in 1888, the AF of L included only unions of skilled, white workers and confined its demands to the "bread-and-butter" issues of wages and hours. The use of child labor peaked during the late nineteenth century, thousands of workers were killed or injured each year on the job, and another depression in 1894 had severe, long-lasting effects on working-class families.